Aesthetics of Sorrow

Aesthetics of Sorrow

The Wailing Culture of Yemenite Jewish Women

Tova Gamliel

Translated by Naftali Greenwood

WAYNE STATE UNIVERSITY PRESS
Detroit

18 17 16 15 14 5 4 3 2 1

ISBN 978-0-8143-3476-8 (cloth) / ISBN 978-0-8143-3975-6 (e-book)

Library of Congress Control Number: 2013948977

Designed and typeset by Charlie Sharp, Sharp Des!gns, Lansing, Michigan
Composed in Adobe Caslon

shed sorrow,
no tears.

published with the support of
Jewish Federation of Greater Hartford

To my mother

Contents

Acknowledgments

IT IS MY PLEASANT DUTY TO THANK THE MANY PEOPLE WHO PARTICIPATED in the effort that brought this book to reality.

I begin by expressing my profound gratitude to those who, by awarding me postdoctorate scholarships, helped to fund the five years of research that made this book possible: the Planning and Grants Committee of the Israel Council for Higher Education, the Research Authority and Department of Psychology at the University of Haifa, and the Lady Davis Foundation and the Department of Sociology and Anthropology at the Hebrew University of Jerusalem.

The original Hebrew version of this book would have remained inaccessible to the Anglophone world were it not for Dror Gabbai, Nimrod Vered, and Vicky Agam, whose generosity allowed me to have the work translated, and for Naftali Greenwood, who provided a superb translation. I am infinitely thankful to them.

Finally, I extend my boundless gratitude and appreciation to Professor

Dan Ben-Amos, editor for the Raphael Patai Series in Jewish Folklore and Anthropology; to Kathryn Wildfong, editor-in-chief for Jewish studies, regional studies, and citizenship studies at Wayne State University Press; and to the staff of Wayne State University Press, for their professional guidance and devoted attention to all stages in the process of publishing this book.

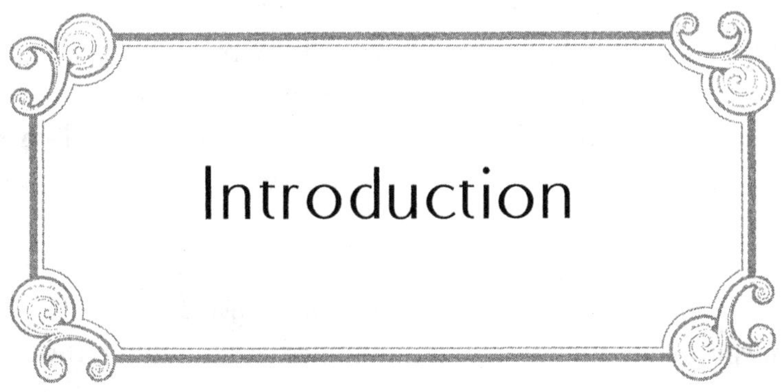

Introduction

THE EVENT THAT EVOLVED INTO A CULTURAL ENIGMA TOOK PLACE ONE village afternoon. We were at a house of mourners. The house, so-titled for seven days, was packed with adults and surrounded by children who scampered across its verdant lawn. I was one of them, and as we played hide-and-seek, the thing that I culled from that little girl's memory happened. The house was full of mourners; we children satiated ourselves with the game and its mystery and revelations as the tree at the edge of the yard awaited the touch of our competing hands. The sun stood overhead, soft in its spring light; the azure of the sky blanketed the house and the village with calm assurance. In our scurrying, the colors and odors jumbled, and our lungs filled with crisp air. We were happy, exultant, over the opportunity to play together, all together, and feeling free from our parents' watchful eyes. After all, they had long since vanished into the interior of the house, and who knew when they would pop out? Occasional passersby entered and exited the house grim-faced, but that neither interested us nor augured anything for us. Those adult faces belonged to a different world and a different era. To and fro we ran, heedless of the demand to lower our voices and "respect the place." So it went until a very unexpected moment that ruined the game and threw its moves out of whack, at least for me. A woman's lachrymose voice blurted, erupted, from the room inside where the women were sitting. It began quietly but then crescendoed until it filled the yard and the street, roaring, groaning, and warbling with incomprehensible words in Arabic. Everything, even the jumble of voices inside the house, stopped in sorrow at that moment. The voice crowded out the game. The sidewalk heaved before my eyes, blocking my path to the tree. Gripped by a sense of weakness, I paused at the doorway and listened, holding my breath, not knowing whether the other children had also stopped playing. The woman's voice took me by storm. Her woeful melody blotted out the sun and filled everything—the yard, the tree, the children, the grass—with gloom and guilt. It became a sin to play. I maintained an anxious silence; I did not know what had suddenly happened and how to decode the shock. Lengthy minutes passed until I consciously sought to leave the yard. I wanted to sprint away, escape, flee for my life from this great terror. But where to? I do not remember how long I stood there, rooted to my spot, as the people's moaning cascaded all around. I only remember that the moment this woman's voice fell silent—this woman whom I had never seen—everyone there, including me, was released from a painful grip and was allowed to sigh, stretch, and speak. She was "the wailer," they told me.

What happened behind the wall of humanity that blocked the doorway whence the voice had emanated? Since that day, I seized various opportunities to find out. I learned to imagine and re-create what had happened back then in my childhood, as if instead of playing outside I had been seated in the inner room with the rest of the women who had come to console the bereaved. I "saw" her seated on a chair, wearing a long dress that covered embroidered trousers that descended to her feet, a colorful snood on her head. In one hand she clutched a small cloth kerchief that she pulled tight over her eyes. Her body, all of it, rocked right and left on the chair. Her other hand made circular motions that illustrated lyrics, which she enunciated in a sad warbling melody, about the deceased and his family. He had been kindhearted and pious, she sang, and above all he had been pure, as everyone knew. Those around her—the women seated close by—burst into weeping at the very sound of her voice, pressing toward her in a cozy, disciplined circle until the moment she stopped, pausing to lift her sad eyes and observe the audience's tears.

The picture of the wailer at work demands this dramatization. Any other wording would fail to usher us through the portal of the melancholy ambiance that wailing generates, the code with which it all began. Still, my account of the event leaves many questions unanswered. Who is this woman whom everyone calls "the wailer"? What does she want? Why does she choose to perform this way? How does she captivate people with tears? What does she feel? And above all, the paragon question of concern in this book: What is wailing?

The *Yalqut Teiman* dictionary defines wailing as a genre of songs associated mainly with the oral art of women who knew the deceased and could improvise rich poetry that was "set" to wailing. Performed at the bedside of the deceased or during the days of mourning, it described the deceased's virtues and the disaster that befell his relatives. Generally, audible wailing is an improvised narrative of sorts that addresses the meaning of death and the loss associated with the dead—a special genre in oral traditions (Finnegan 2001), a lyric poem that creates an evocative integration of speech and weeping. Because it sets to words the sorrow that accompanies a person's death, some regard wailing as the expression of a transition from tears to ideas (Holst-Warhaft 1995)—a transition typical of women's song.

Anyone who has attended a wailing performance would probably agree that these definitions are a far cry—a conspicuously unique cry—from the experience that they represent. The wailing performance, consisting of text, sound, motion, and visual drama, is a singular thing, separate unto itself. Thus, the foregoing definition does not convey the slightest hint of the picturesque experience that envelops the wailer and the audience alike, even though the shades of melancholy involved do not lie outside the range between black and white.

"I hear her voice and feel that it carries all the sadness in the world." Thus a friend of mine expressed his impression some thirty years after my childhood epiphany, as the mourners' house had transmogrified into my parents' house, and I was grieving over my father's death. Someone from town who was unschooled in his friend's cultural origins—so unschooled that even though the woman's wailing made a deep impression on him, it had not driven him to tears—even offered me a whispered hypothesis about the primeval characteristic of wailing. Nevertheless, the word chosen by this noncognoscento in reference to the terror, the ignorance, and also the difficulty in getting to the root of the experience is valuable, because "primeval" signifies something that is first, ancient, Genesis-like. Even though he had not meant it that way, primevalness is consistent with references to Jewish wailing in biblical sources, from the eras of the prophets and the kings. David bewailed the death of Saul and Jonathan (II Samuel 9), the prophet of rage urged the "wise" wailing women to sadden the sinners' hearts (Jeremiah 9), and Lamentations, retelling the buildup to the exile to Babylon, is couched in wailing language. The narrative performance of wailing in these sources places wailing in the ancient cradle of civilization and enhances the validity of considering wailing and the wailer an epistemological enigma.

Like other ethnographies that trace their research to special motives, the one that follows places the enigma in the setting where I first became aware of it. I returned to my origin group, Yemenite Jews in Israel, and transformed them—including those who were closest and most familiar to me—into respondents. The memory of that game of hide-and-seek accompanied me as I visited their houses of mourning, participated in funeral and burial rituals, and held encounters with them. As my probings became systematic, the ramified secrets of the enigma emerged bit by bit. They included actors who played roles, symbols pregnant with meaning, a discourse of women and men, and patterns of customs and beliefs that jelled to form a culture or, to be exact, a subculture within the broader framework of the Yemenite Jewish culture. Such a culture comprises everything that an individual should know or believe in order to behave in a manner accepted to its members (Goodenough 1957); its subjects inhabit a world of their own creation (Geertz 1983). As time passed, I phrased the enigma in ethnographic language and privileged it with a name—"the wailing culture of Yemenite Jewish women"—that captures the topic of my study.

The gender bias intrinsic to this name—after all, the culture is shared by men *and* women—signals the centrality of wailing women in the segment of it that belongs to death rituals and the management of men that these women perform. Women's wailing creates a ripple effect that is not only vocal but also symbolic and is endowed with rules of custom and action. This statement is in no way exceptional; after all, in many ethnic groups around the world, it is women who are associated with wailing and are known as wailers. The term "wailing culture" also corresponds to women's mourning patterns in many diverse societies, such as rural Greece (Holst-Warhaft 1995; Danforth 1982), Bedouin in Saudi Arabia (Abu-Lughod 1986), and Macronesians (Lutz 1988). Beyond the need to determine whether wailing is natural for women or is the outcome of social structuring processes, the ethnographic literature considers wailing to be a fundamentally female practice that reflects a style of emotion unique to women and a discourse of vulnerability that is typical of women (Abu-Lughod 1986). Wailing is associated with women's life-cycle experiences via the caregiving connection that birth and death events maintain (Holst-Warhaft 1995). Wailing may be an informal institution for the articulation of women's mourning, a protective enclave from whence women can express their attitude toward a given sociopolitical order (Seremetakis 1991) and confirm their supremacy in emotional expression (Briggs 1993). Various ethnographies of my acquaintance elucidate the nexus of power and death that wailing women, in contrast to men, establish—a nexus that corresponds to beliefs among members of the culture about the elements of naturalness, ambivalence, and danger that populate so-called female emotionality in the death arena.

I once asked, determined but failing to crack this self-evident nut, "Why do women wail and not men?" One of my octogenarian women interviewees sighed, "What can I tell you? I don't know. That's how it is. Women know how to cry." Then, perhaps to say that the gender difference is not something from days of yore, the interviewee borrowed an expression from a well-known Israeli song and concluded, offering no explanation whatsoever, "Men don't cry in the day. They cry at night." In my extensive conversations with elderly women about women's wailing, I found that from their perspective, wailing is a cultural form that accommodates their natural emotionality in a way that distinguishes them from men. They consider this style of lamenting the departure of the deceased to be material in defining their femininity. They connect the sorrow and suffering that wailing expresses with additional roles that they play in the life cycle—being a daughter, someone's wife, a mother of children, and a grandmother of grandchildren. They almost want to liken the tears they sing to a fluid fetus in a woman's body, which should be awaited within the framework of the ritual and welcomed with understanding. While feminist theories wrestle with the question of woman's material characteristics and their intrinsic legitimacy in the definition of her nature (Millet 1970; Scott 1988; De Beauvoir 2001), my women subjects had no doubt that the public display, the externalization of tears, is one of the definitive domains of femininity, of womanhood.

That Yemenite Jewish women's wailing operates on a different plane than similar or proximate art forms is evidenced in three additional ways that abet its eclipsing in the literature and the emphasis of its inferior status in gender and cultural terms. First, if wailing is mentioned at all, it is put forward as a theme that does not stand on its own. Being Jewish, it is attributed to broad categories, such as "song" and "melody," that are typical of both sexes (Tzadok 1967; Dahoah Halevi 1995); being Yemenite, it is parked behind the camouflage of the Muslim practice, the characteristics of which are shared by other wailing cultures (Holst-Warhaft 1995; Abu-Lughod 1986, 1993). Also important, the validity of this conclusion is diminished only by one eye-opening study that stationed it at the focus of its investigation of Yemenite Jewish women's wailing. Madar's analysis of various aspects of women's wailing provides a painstaking transcription and translation of lamentations (wailing texts), establishes Jewish women's wailing as a specific genre, and subjects it to a style of scholarship involving documents and academic sources that is typical of folklore research (Madar 2002, 2005a, 2005b, 2005c, 2006).[1]

The second way to discern the inferior status of women's wailing is to notice that women's singing—in contrast to women's wailing—has been privileged with relatively respectable documentation and presence in several sources. Binyamin-Gamliel's book *Ahavat Teiman* (Love of Yemen, 1975) and Serri's *Bat Teiman* (Daughter of Yemen, 1994) are two such sources. A third example is Sulami's article "Protest Motives in Yemenite Women's Song" (2005), which reduces Yemenite women's singing to motives, depicts it as having an educational and emotional function of the highest order, and above all shows it to be a meaningful pattern of communication among Jews and Arabs in Yemen. However, the reader can only assume that the insights presented include wailing as a significant case of the lyric element that the author attributes to women's song (Sulami 1995).

The third way to probe the matter is by contemplating songs that men and women sing. The singing of Yemenite Jewish men is described as different from non-Jewish singing because it is typically in Hebrew and replete with melancholy and yearnings for the advent of the messiah and redemption from lives of suffering, poverty, and enslavement in a fanatical Muslim country. The singing of Jewish women, in contrast, is defined as being rooted in Arabic and replete with the agonies of daily life: hard work, betrayal by a husband who has taken on a second wife, women's nostalgia for their parents' home, and the like. Viewed from these confines, which doom Jewish and Muslim women to equal and inferior status, women's wailing is not described in its full significance; instead, it remains a singing or melodic form that reflects the outpouring of the soul at its highest. The literature discriminates against the wailing form of singing so blatantly that one wonders about its cultural status as well. Does the literature deem women's singing to be more cultural than women's wailing? Or is it the unique configuration of a dialogue with death in wailing that undermines it?

The more general research literature does not propose a different dialogue about Jewish wailing and instead gives Jewish wailing only slightly more ink than the amount that a traditional phenomenon should leave behind. Rubin's book *Qets ha-hayyim* (The End of Life, 1997), which discusses burial and mourning customs in Jewish society, represents women's wailing as sourcebooks of rabbinical law would. Rubin describes wailing and proximate customs—nurturing and praise—rather tersely and solely from the perspective of the way they are mirrored in Mishnaic/Talmudic sources. His definition of wailing as "talking—evidently in the form of song—that expresses pain and sadness" (194) reflects strict adherence to the intentions of the Mishna and the Talmud more than anything else.

Another representation of Jewish wailing, a faint one, is found in Pollock's "On Mourning and Anniversaries" (1972), which does an amazing job of examining the psychological stages of grief in view of the Jewish stages of grief. As stated, this work mentions women's wailing but does so en passant and in accordance with its general scheme as one of a number of practices that characterize the shivah stage (Pollock 1972). The traditional forms of mourning among Jewish communities are also represented in Palgi's anthropological study (1974) and again in a work that, although recent, adds nothing (Witztum 2004). Both sources tersely present women's wailing and mourning patterns in various communities one after the other. The descriptions emphasize major characteristics not only from a researcher's point of view but also from the unsympathetic perspective of an outsider. Here is an example:

> In eastern or Islamic cultures, the intensity of mourning is gauged by the extent of screaming and shouting or the intensity of the lamentations that are wailed at the funeral. . . . Tolerance of the various customs is needed because sometimes it seems to us that others behave strangely and shockingly relative to the manner that we accept, and this may even evoke negative responses. (Witztum 2004, 21–23)

Even when we broaden the canvas to include knowledge about mourning in Israeli society, we find a similar picture. Much of this literature focuses on the grieving of families who lost offspring in wars and the Israeli ethos surrounding the heroism of the fallen (Weiss 1997). Amid the occupation with these themes, the very existence of traditional death rituals among various groups and their connection with Jewish cultural symbols is ignored. This literature generally excludes religious models, beliefs, and folklore (Hasan-Rokem, Madar, and Sherira 2006), as though families of Moroccan, Ashkenazic, Caucasian, and Yemenite origin all gather in one mourners' tent. To explain this phenomenon, one may argue that research literature reflects a social reality or at least dominant tendencies in it. The heroism ethos and the establishment of the bereaved family are examples of far-reaching reality projects in Israeli society. They are almost synonymous, I would say, with the melting pot; unlike the pot, however, their role is to satisfy the needs of a society well versed in crises. They signify the preference of a collective identity based on Jewish nationhood and a clear tendency to marginalize the Jewish tradition, with its ethnic diversity (Rubin, Malkinson, and Witztum 1999). In this state of affairs, the likelihood of including an Oriental woman's wailing for a dead soldier in an analysis of the components of bereavement is nil. Wailing is unrepresented in this literature because it is perceived as based on other cultural values that are totally excluded from the national discourse.

The wailer's voice erupts from the core of the private domain, the home. The expression "Yemenite Jewish home" carries various meanings, including the original location of the female voice. If the voice erupts and cascades into the street, one doubts whether passersby in Israel would know how to call it by its name or treat it with anything more than a stereotyped and uninformed raising of an eyebrow. This special voice is a hidden and unfamiliar one; it speaks neither in synagogues nor in halls of religious study but instead largely in the homes of mourners. Against the backdrop of the innerness and uniqueness—or, should we say, the mysteriousness—of this voice, the wall of people that buffered between me and the wailer back then has metamorphosed into a wall that separates the ethnic inside from everything outside. The experience that I found unfathomable at first is expected to assume the form of an exotic culture—a Jewish parallel, so to speak—to a religious ritual of a faraway tribe. Jewish wailing is unfamiliar to ordinary people or is familiar in its unfamiliarity.

The cultural enigma that I mentioned above almost certainly would have remained unsolved had it not been possible to convert the aforementioned sources into partners of the culture—women and men who had studied this culture from up close—or had the research been put off for a few years. The research began in February 2001 and continued until the end of 2005, with some further development of the findings as the book was being written. The main findings were furnished by elderly research subjects (aged 60–80+), most of whom came to Israel in Operation MAGIC CARPET, the mass immigration of 1948–53.[2] Many of the people whom I observed were women; apart from a group interview in which some forty men participated, fifty-three people were interviewed, two-thirds women and one-third men. Twelve of the women interviewed were wailers. The respondents fit the profile of the wailing culture and considered themselves members of it. Notably, members of this immigration wave and their offspring served as research subjects in two ambitious ethnographies written in the late 1980s about their traditions and customs in the intercultural encounter in Israel: L. Gilad's *Ginger and Salt* (1989) and H. S. Lewis's *After the Eagles Landed* (1989). These ethnographies shed light on this ethnic cohort, although their accounts exclude the culture of women's wailing. As for other respondents in my research, some findings were provided by Yemenite Jews (one man and six women) who had immigrated to Israel in the early 1990s. These women conduct their wailing performances in the homes of relatives who live in the same neighborhood; they hardly go anywhere else. Finally, twenty younger men and women, second- and third-generation immigrants in Israel, participated in the study. As members of a new generation that takes its image seriously, they speak differently about the wailing culture, and their voice is reported in the epilogue of this book. As a second-generation immigrant myself, I belong to this group in various ways. For one, I am a Hebrew speaker who, while understanding the Yemenite Arabic dialect in which the elders of my childhood spoke, finds the wailers' metaphorical Arabic difficult to comprehend.

I met with my respondents in towns and villages in central Israel, some ethnically mixed and others relatively homogeneous and populated largely by families of Yemenite origin. My visits to these locations did not always pay off, at least relative to my expectations. I attribute this to the existential nature of wailing: even though it took place in mourners' homes and cemeteries, it was doled out in random snippets. Thus, the timing of my research forays was a decisive factor in eliciting the findings. It was in this manner that the enigma, some three decades old by now, was revealed to me in its last moments—moments that served me as a frame for contemplation. Therefore, I must repeat in regard to Yemenite Jewish wailing a known fact about Jewish wailing in ethnic groups in Israel and elsewhere: it is dying out and is already so far into its home stretch (Holst-Warhaft 1995) that the understanding I attained in my research could no longer be attained practically as this book was being written (and, a fortiori, as it is being read). The population of wailers—elderly women all—is steadily dwindling. It would be hard to find them again. Once they are gone, they say, their likes will no longer exist, and their glorious tradition will have died.

The next two sections relate to Yemenite Jewish women's wailing in terms of its meanings as a tradition and the way this tradition relates to modern and postmodern outlooks in the academic discussion and in life in Israel. Jim Wilce, in his book *Crying Shame* (2009), pioneered the occupation with this topic from a comprehensive perspective, analyzing a broad array of connections between wailing and these outlooks and their implications for important areas of life such as religion, ethnicity, nationality, and Western emotion values. As an ethnographer who gained other experiences than mine in his research field in Finland, Wilce describes the sociocultural fate not only of declining wailing cultures but also of those that are enjoying a revival. His comprehensive and reflective work yields an analytical and insightful metaperspective based on reviews of many ethnographies. In his writings about the anthropologists' lament about the recently expired culture of wailing, Wilce positions himself as the last of the ethnographers to deal with the matter. For this reason, the following sections should be read as a particularistic derivative of the broader discussion that Wilce proposes, and the ethnography that follows should be seen as a case study.

All Alone: Tradition and the Snapping of the Chain

Women's wailing belongs to the domain of traditions that no longer enjoy intergenerational transmission even though its voice is still heard and some picture of the wailer's performance remains possible. In this process, the focus in wailing is gradually receding into the past and will soon be reclaimable from memory only. This snapping of the chain is inseparable from one of the additional meanings of wailing, that of being a tradition. It is this cessation of transmission that abets the perception of a tradition as being rooted in circumstances of a historical period, a captive of its past, and distinct unto itself. In this obvious sense, a tradition resembles childhood: a field of meaning that has lost almost all its validity. Affixed in a set of symbols and beliefs preceding the continuum of development, it is deemed marginal in the appreciation of human achievements. However, time also invests it with charm, color, experience, longing, and nostalgia. These characteristics are represented by the radical thesis (Heelas 1996).

Women's wailing is a blend of two traditions that nourished each other during the Jewish exile in Yemen (Tzadok 1976; Muchawsky-Schnapper 2000). On the one hand, women's wailing is enunciated in Yemenite Arabic and abounds with Arab folk motives; on the other hand, it is part and parcel of the mourning customs of a canon Jewish religion. Because wailing is verbal, unwritten, performed by uneducated women as folk art, and appreciated and usually transmitted collectively and unwittingly from the generation of mothers to that of the daughters, it can be considered an oral tradition (Finnegan 2001). When wailers were young, they sat in an audience of adult wailers—mothers—and absorbed the lyrics, the rhyme and meter, the contents, and the metaphors through movements and from the air. This intergenerational transmission took place in Yemenite Arabic, a vernacular that took several steps up the ladder when used for wailing, becoming liturgical, lyrical, aesthetic, and existentially charged. Everyone in the mourners' house understood this singing in its Yemenite language, a tongue that carved out segments of its own within the language of Jerusalem, that is, the holy tongue, Hebrew, in which men performed their worship and religious study.

Wailing in Arabic was woven inseparably into a broader tradition, the Jewish religion. In this sense, even though women were exempt from most devotional duties that were incumbent on men, wailing could not be considered nonreligious or the concern of women only. For centuries, Yemenite Jews maintained a strictly religious way of life; unlike other isolated Jewish communities in the Middle East, they were known for adherence to their teachings and separatism even as subjects of an Islamic regime (Muchawsky-Schnapper 2000; Eraqi-Klorman 1993). Their religiosity dominated all aspects of their lives. Furthermore, Yemen was so inured to foreign influences as to exclude any identifiable form of secularism.

Therefore, the significance of a ritual, a text, or a traditional custom of the Jews of Yemen—including women's wailing—cannot be gauged outside the context of their Jewish identity and heritage. This is true for research into this ethnic group in Palestine/Israel as well insofar as their tradition endures and perseveres.

THE RELIGIOUS ENVELOPE THAT CONTAINS WOMEN'S WAILING IS THE so-called seven days—the shivah—within which time and space are allocated to the practice. According to Jewish religious law, the close relatives of the dead sit shivah. This means that for seven days following the death of their loved one, they adopt a set of restrictions that apply to people who assume the social role of mourners. During this time, it is the custom among Yemenite Jews for mourners to sit on the floor and avoid all purposeful labor and even some activities in service of their own needs. They spend most of their time seated on mattresses, men and women separately. At prayer time, male mourners pray with guests who have come to comfort them; women mourners listen to the prayers and acknowledge them by saying "amen" in unison with the men. All mourners are expected to listen to religious teachings or sermons delivered by rabbis or religious scholars. Relatives who are not among the mourners serve the mourners their meals and meet all their immediate needs. Mourners avoid bathing and all other aesthetic care, including shaving the beard and trimming fingernails. It is their duty to receive consolation throughout the seven-day period, that is, to respond to every gesture of consolation shown them. In the main, they nod as they say "amen" in response to trite expressions of consolation such as "May God console you," as are stated to them scores of times each day by the many members of the community who visit the home and participate in the prayers and meals.

These mourning practices and those of the Arabs of Yemen are similar in part. The similarity pertains to the apportionment of the mourning period (the intervals of three and thirty days are meaningful for both groups, for example), compulsory consolation by acquaintances of the grieving family, the community's responsibility for keeping the mourners and the consolers fed, restrictions on mourners in terms of hygiene and embellishments of dress, compulsory seating on mattresses and avoidance of entertainment (e.g., watching television), and the importance of men's prayer and devotional study for the transmigration of the soul. As for expressing grief, mourners are allowed to weep in public only for two days after the death, during the first formal gathering known as the *thalith*. Meleney's (1996, 133) ethnography also highlights a product of the limits imposed on the weeping: "Some women seem harshly unsympathetic, hissing, 'forbidden!' [*Haram, haram!*] or 'God forgive this blasphemy!' [*Istaghfar Allah!*]."

In contrast to the stifling role played by Arab women, Jewish women encourage weeping within the permissible boundaries. The first three days of Jewish mourning are days of tears, as the rabbinical sages taught: "Three days are for tears, seven are for eulogies, and thirty are for [the eschewing of] ironing and cutting the hair."[3] This time limitation of the display of emotions is especially pertinent in regard to women's wailing customs. This is because from the moment of death to the seventh day, the deceased is mentioned in men's prayers in segments of eulogy and requiem, but these texts are read out almost like any other prayer service. The role of men is one of learners. They read from sacred texts for a special purpose: raising the soul of the dead. The vocalization of the melody by the group of men and the special order of the sentences determine the proper form of delivery—an uninterrupted enunciation of verses. In view of this, the phrase "three days of tears" actually denotes affective authorization of *the public mourning function of women.*

Unlike men's rituals, it is the practice in many cultures that modernity's sieve refuses to let through, dooming it to be left behind. Examining cultural coping with death in modern societies, we find that death has not surrendered its primacy as the trigger of the most threatening disorder in human experience. Death remains an event that demands emotional and cognitive working-through and affects the future comportment of social communities and networks (Rubin 1990; Palgi and Avramovitch 1984). However, insofar as wailing may serve as an effective coping pattern, it is important to note that the canon death rituals are the ones that persist or, at least, avoid the intensity of resistance that women's wailing evokes. The Yemenite Jewish culture is no different: its funeral, burial, and shivah practices have retained their religious complexion and are still performed in accordance with rabbinical law.[4] The death rituals of this group have proved less susceptible to secularization and reform than those among other groups in Israeli society (Deshen 1970; Rubin 1986). Thus, given the sunset of wailing, we observe a hierarchy that isolates ritual from performance or the masculine from the feminine. Furthermore, the religious sanction captured by the expression "three days are for tears" makes a statement of sorts about the inferior status of women's wailing relative to men's prayer traditions and the observance of canon religious rituals. From the internal standpoint of the boundaries of the traditional community, wailing is assumed to be a practice, that is, something of lesser importance; this initial query may abet its relative vulnerability to external factors such as places, fashion, states of mind, and period.

My interviewees, while referring in detail to the customs of their tradition, also gave thought to broader circles of context that enveloped their wailing culture and invested it with relative meaning. When they did this, their obvious tendency was to mention two broad categories that protrude in Israel's Jewish ethnic landscape. These categories are Ashkenazim and Mizrahim. My respondents attributed the wailing culture to only one side, and this attribution showed me that they excluded wailing from the domains of values and thinking that are charged to modernity. To them as to Israelis at large, Ashkenazi-ism represents the Western world and its modern characteristics, including its emotional ones, whereas Mizrahi-ism has the deficiency of opposite stereotypes rooted in the perception that the countries of origin are Muslim and not modern (Ben-Rafael and Sharot 1991).

The respondents depicted wailing, as a tradition of emotion and religious mourning, much as the findings in the literature do: a phenomenon that lacks the levels of conceptualization and continuity and has no theoretical uncertainties. I mean this in the sense that this cultural phenomenon distinguishes, simply and absolutely, between those who originate in northern Africa and Asia, of whom it is typical, and those of European and American extraction, to whom it is alien and unfamiliar. As a case in point, the respondents presented themselves this way relative to the group of Others. One woman in a group interview stated that when someone dies, "The Ashkenazim don't care. Everyone mourns on his own." "The wailing profession is dignified," another wailer in the group said, "very dignified. But the Ashkenazim have nothing." One of my interviewees offered a description that mirrored a finding in *After the Eagles Landed* (Lewis 1989, 137), an ethnography about Yemenite Jewish immigrants in Israel: "The Ashkenazim are amazed about how lots of people come to the Yemenites' house of mourning when there's been a tragedy. They say, 'What's this, a wedding?!'" A male interviewee explained that "With progress, wailing's going to stop; it's as if the population [of Yemenite Jews] has become more modern," that is, acculturating (or assimilating) into the dominant Ashkenazic group (Shokeid 1985; Bar-Yosef 1968). By clinging to the wailing tradition, the respondents were making a statement, so to speak, about their Mizrahiness and their religiosity. By affiliating themselves with this collective, they banished what they considered Ashkenazi or secular, thereby expressing the perception of a binary relationship between the wailing culture as a tradition and the modern.

Wailing traditions have been encountered among the Sephardim in Jerusalem and the Jews of Morocco, Kurdistan, Calcutta, the Caucasus, Iran, and Iraq. Notably, even though their form, as documented in the literature, attests to similarity in approach, such cultures among Israeli ethnic groups are not identical. They differ in interesting ways, probably tracing to the culture of the country of origin and not to any religion, be it Muslim or Jewish.[5] Some descriptions of these wailing cultures convey something of the atmosphere of the Jewish Diaspora. Wailing among the Jews of Bukhara, for example, was called *abaz anaz*. The wailers in this group "invited themselves to mourners' homes and brought their friends along. It was their practice to clap their hands and tap their knees and faces." In addition to being paid for their wailing, they are described as having received items of the deceased woman's clothing, "sewn or not, new or old." In the Caucasus, "Women sat in a circle and mourned, beat their breasts and heads, appealed to the deceased, and cried. They spent the entire seven-days mourning period sitting [there] from morning to evening, crying, beseeching, and wailing"

(Moshavi 1974, 255–59). Iranian wailers are said to have torn their hair and pinched themselves, and "Persian women's wailing is terrifying in its howling and weeping" (Mizrahi 1959, 94). The women of Kurdistan "gather in a room around the deceased and begin to wail. They strike and scratch their faces; they place mortar in their hair and smear it on their faces and shoulders. . . . There are also professional wailers who are especially well versed in dirges and heartbreaking song" (Brauer 1947, 161). "How is a death announced?" asks a text that concerns itself with Iraqi Jewish women. It answers in a similar vein: "The women in the home of the deceased mussed their hair and launched into screaming and heartrending keening, tapping their cheeks or their breasts" (Aslan and Nissim 1982, 64). On rare occasions, such accounts include lamentation lyrics. The following quotation belongs to Moroccan Jewish wailers: "The blades of grass grow and give their color, and this heart of mine lives with its pain" (Weich-Shahak 1987, 117). To broaden the landscape of wailing traditions that were transported to Israel, I should expand on this brusque and incomplete account and note that as I participated in funerals and asked questions, I found that Ethiopian Jewish women also wail for the dead, making special motions and uttering anguish-inducing words at the grave. I also discovered that wailing is typical of Bedouin and Arab women in Israel. The wailing culture of Arab women, in its various aspects, is explicated in Granqvist's (1965) ethnographies about the inhabitants of Artas village south of Bethlehem.

When I read Abu-Lughod's (1986) ethnography, I was impressed by the strong psychological and cultural similarity between Yemenite Jewish singing women and the women of the Avalad 'Ali Bedouin tribe in Egypt. Among several levels of interpretation that Abu-Lughod offers for these women's singing and wailing, description plays a major role in creating this impression. One special root of the similarity is the fact that both groups of women use similar words to denote "song" (*shira, ghinnawas*) and "wailing" or "weeping" (*bakha, bka*) and attribute similar meanings to both activities. This linguistic similarity, although important in itself, does not capture the entire matter. To expand on it, we should add several additional examples. First, wailing in both cultures is partly improvised and structurally and technically similar to singing. Second, even though Yemenite Jewish wailing leaves very little room for the expression of anger and rage, it resembles Bedouin women's wailing in its articulation of sorrow and, in its recounting of the departure of a beloved man, affects the personal state of the wailer and the deceased's relatives. Third, in both groups, women consolers join the wailing circle to honor the deceased and his relatives, but when they wail, they mention their own departed relatives. In another example of the cultural similarity, both groups of women define a beautiful song as one that induces weeping and can change listeners' thinking. Finally, both performance communities strongly appreciate the interplay of verbal forms and the quality of the woman's voice.

Abu-Lukhod is an exception in her extensive reference to Muslim women's poetry. In regard to this part of the world, Caton's work *"Peaks of Yemen I Summon"* (1990) is central and very important in a review of ethnographies on Muslim poetry in Yemen; however, it excludes women's poetry (23–24).[6] The singing of the *muzayyināt,* Arab women in Yemen who are expert crooners for weddings, is merely hinted at in Dorsky (1986), as is a well developed domain of women's poetry. The topic is buried in descriptions of wedding and marriage practices; poetic texts are not documented. If so, what can we learn about an intercultural women's connection in Yemen? Like Yemenite Jewish women singers, the *muzayyināt* sing and pound drums as they escort the bride and are responsible for ritual arrangements at wedding and mourning events. Mundy's (1995) and Meneley's (1996) ethnographies suggest a limited similarity between the *muzayyināt* and Jewish women wailers. Both groups of women are responsible for preparing bodies for burial and encouraging the community to support the aggrieved. In verbal coping with grief, however, their roles differ. The *muzayyināt,* like other elderly Arab women, supervise women's weeping (as distinct from wailing) to ensure that it does not get out of control or transgress the boundaries of modesty as modeled by the men; the *muzayyināt* prefer to listen to the paid specialist, the *nashshādah,* who is expected to recite religious verses. The *nashshādah* is the closest of all to the Jewish wailer, but she operates within the bounds of the Muslim faith, which forbids the expression of grief emotions largely due to a fear of challenging God's will (Halevi 2004). This injunction is reinforced in three ways: the discouraging parallel that the women draw among grief, anger, and illness; the women's belief that weeping afflicts the deceased's soul; and the sharing of moving personal narratives about loved ones outside the formal mourning sessions. I justify the centrality of Abu-Lughod's work in my case study due to the hypothesis that surfaces from the aforementioned sources as well as from my respondents that women's wailing in Yemen was well developed only among the Jews.

As I gathered these cultural tableaux, which are not exclusively Jewish, I discovered that wailing is a configuration of demonstrative coping with death. Wailers are those who have the talent to express emotions. They shriek, abrade their skin, and gesticulate dramatically. In the least elaborate form of the wailing performance, they content themselves with a song of pain and loss; that is, they make sounds and produce words accompanied by measured movements of the body. Accordingly, it would be correct to say that the difference between traditional wailing and modern emotional values is captured in the very act of articulating or demonstrating. I support this argument by citing the view that in terms of emotional expression and symbolic design, tradition and modernity represent two clashing cultural points of view—the former representing wealth and the latter representing the attenuation of wealth. Tradition is a synonym for a rituality that is rich in language, symbols, and color. In contrast, modernity is tainted with a rationalism that purges religion and erstwhile traditions of their symbols until loss of meaning occurs (Jung 1959). When theoreticians such as Bauman (1992), Aries (1981), and Irion (1993) describe the cultural difference, they do so from the perspective of tradition as a modality that is both positive and valuable in human coping.

According to them, modern people lack the religious symbolization that would connect them with forms of life that transcend them. Furthermore, they are estranged from the transcendental and affective forms of the tradition, which integrate death and the human experience in multiple levels of meaning.

A similar dichotomy of cultural values emerges when scholars pause to consider the context of wailing, that is, the mourning situation. They describe mourning as modern societies construe it and assert that the language, as a corpus of symbols, is steadily thinning. Mourners and consolers are expected to be differentiated in minute details that pertain to mundane practices and emotional expression. Even though the sharing of emotional pain and the demonstration of commiseration are complementary needs, the consoler and the bereaved tumble into a situation in which they cannot find words that meet their mutual expectations. Bauman expresses the resulting embarrassment mordantly: sneaked glances, inconsistent murmurings that camouflage the lack of words, the ease with which the consolers leave the venue—these are plain symbols of an inability that is mired in an ongoing conspiracy of silence. People do not learn ways to respond to others' bereavement, and the individual does not find an outlet for his or her grief (Bauman 1992, 135). Similarly, in Aries's estimation, people ignore the existence of a scandalous situation that they cannot prevent. By behaving as though the situation does not exist, they mercilessly force the bereaved to say nothing (Aries 1981, 624).

My Yemenite Jewish respondents made the same point in a different way. One of them explained that "The intention in wailing is really to help [the bereaved] and give the feeling that you've lost someone and that everyone there cares. We share it with you. Not by shaking hands and kissing and saying 'we commiserate' in a lip-service way. Instead, you have to go in [be emotionally involved]." To distinguish quiet mourning from traditional wailing, which conveys honor, women interviewees often used expressions such as "like they're burying a cat" and "dead, dead, a dog died today; the people in that house [the mourners] cried a little." Tradition relates to death intimately and confronts it in a manner that is rich in symbols and demonstration of emotions. In these senses, women's wailing obviously belongs to the realm of tradition. In fact, wailing may be the most significant configuration of symbolization and expression upon a death event that tradition can invent.

Dialogue: The Ambit of Tradition

Thus far, the cessation of transmission of the wailing tradition has been remembered solely as an event that signifies nothing but a watershed in the history of a culture, meaning that the present and the future are not examples of the past. The interpretative narrative that has been presented is consistent with the absolute meanings of the discontinuity and the lack of paths of transmission. Since wailers are merely aging or aged women who have been losing their communities' sympathy, this reality is alluded to and judged with a tendency toward gravity and belief in the immutability of tradition, that is, traditionalism (Delanty 2000). The question to ask now is whether the theme of this book can be viewed in some other way or whether wailing belongs entirely to the past. In other words, is bewailing the disappearance of the wailing tradition our only remaining option? In this section, I wish to alleviate the agonizing impression that the word "cessation" conveys and argue that another narrative for the wailing tradition may exist. Such a narrative derives its meaning from a recent theoretical approach known as the coexistence thesis (Heelas 1996), which is elaborated in Jim Wilce's book *Crying Shame* (2009).

According to this approach, tradition does not and cannot die in the modern era; consequently, there are no justifiable reasons to bewail it (Luke 1996). This proves to be the case if we contemplate the waning of a tradition from a process perspective—something that happens over time—and not in view of the finality of its outcome. This reading of the matter construes Yemenite Jewish wailing as a tradition that has a long-term expectancy of decline. Yes, Jewish women from Yemen have been wailing less and less since they immigrated to Israel, but only in recent years has the practice been ceasing. Whether or not I state that the era of this tradition will end after a fifty-six-year period of decline, the possibility that the decline per se has a life and form of its own, which should be contemplated as something of interest and importance, should not be belittled.

The ethnography that I present in this book is unique due to the dialogue between tradition and modernity that takes place amid the investigation of the Yemenite Jewish wailing culture. Wilce (2009) offers one of the few ethnographies about wailing cultures that expands the mediating role of women's wailing to this level. Wailing ethnographies usually present this role in its metaphysical senses, that is, mediation between life and death or among people. The invasion of the cultural domain by researchers may explain the epistemological difference: it is an impressive invasion because it represents the transition from one world, that of the researcher, to another. This invasion preserves the exotic halo of the phenomenon or at least leaves the halo free of visible injury. Today, such invasions are rare in anthropological research, the sort that, as it were, closes an imaginary door of time behind the researcher's back and absolves him or her of concern about issues of intercultural diffusion or cultural authenticity. This study is different—it is neither a travelogue of a trip to Yemen, a collection of stories per se, nor the product of archival and historical documents. Furthermore, it should not be categorized among the so-called salvage studies in the conventional folkloristic sense of the word (Stillman 2002), even though it does document the tradition and trace its components and origins. The idea is the dialogue between Yemenite Jewish wailing and values and outlooks external to it. This dialogue should be regarded as a motive that is intertwined in the ethnographic narrative, is material to it, and even defines it insofar as the context of modern Israeli society and theoretical interpretation are concerned. This study is neither the first nor the only ethnography about Yemenite Jews in Israel that adopts the approach of a dialogue between tradition and modernity. The aforementioned study *Ginger and Salt,* for example, highlights a similar dialogue, but the dialogue in that study is between immigrant mothers and their Israel-born daughters (Gilad 1989). What remains necessary is to track the various aspects of the encounter between origin and reality in the life of an immigrant ethnic group.

Since this dialogue is a focal interest of ours, we now turn our attention to the meanings of the wailing tradition—a narrated past, a way to understand the world and cement the sense of belonging, and a practice that has descended from the public domain to the microlevel of relations. These aspects of the structuring of tradition tie into additional questions: Does a collective, a public, exist? Who are the narrators of the traditional past? How does their narrative help us to understand the reality that they inhabit? And how does the story of the tradition connect with social belonging? These are worthy questions in view of the disintegration of the Yemenite Jewish community since it immigrated to Israel and the relative erosion of its unifying values.

In its translocation from Yemen, this community changed its patterns of communication, shed some of its institutions, and lost some of its cultural distinctiveness. However, the now-erstwhile Jews of Yemen—having settled in a more rural locality than in an urban neighborhood—still maintain some extent of intimacy in relations among each other via family ties and participation in religious activities and informal support systems. Indeed, among all of Israel's Mizrahic communities, the Yemenite community stands out for its relative dearth of cultural assimilation (Loeb 1985). The first-generation immigrants, their children who maintain a religious way of life, and those who embrace religiosity in midlife belong to a community whose borders are drawn by the encounter with the urban and the modern. To my way of thinking, this encounter stresses above all the meaning of a community in its sense as a "structure of emotion" (Appadurai 1996, 199).

The wailing culture is an element of this "structure of emotion," which is steadily crumbling. This is the state of the core configuration that has remained of the ramified traditional community structure that had existed in Yemen. Respondents spoke about the wailing tradition in the awareness of its decline and from a position of convergence into their community consciousness. From this diminished location, they could not only recount their participation in the culture but could also resemble observers elsewhere. As stated, from an observer's position they located their tradition and their contemporaries via the relativity that an intercultural encounter welcomes. They used the wailing tradition as a theme for a dialogue between the familiar and the Other in the abstract and in its personified form—between Us and Them. As witnesses to a languid process in which the new drives out the old, they had enough time to reflect on the tradition as it had existed in its salad days and on the loss associated with it and its aftermath. The following remarks of a woman interviewee, expressing the tradition in its hermeneutic, interpretive, or explanatory sense, were offered from the position of a reflective observer:

> The customs of Yemen and Yemenite Jewry are deep inside me and I love them: the modesty, the Jewishness, keeping kosher, the discipline. A boy listened to his father, a girl to her mother. It was just wonderful

> in Yemen. There was peace of mind. . . . In Israel there's so much pain, so many problems, that this wailing is redundant. Besides, there's so much killing, so much murder, that people don't cry anymore. The tears have dried up. . . . In Yemen, when someone died, people were stunned and cried all year long.

This dialogue with otherness was possible became the interviewee contemplated the topic from one vantage point, the traditional world of values. This is not to say that she sought to justify these values only due to her familiarity with and respect for them; instead, each of the three additional aspects of tradition (belonging/identity, normative, and legitimate) continues to play some role in her life and is valid at some level. She is a religious woman, as the kerchief on her head, her long dress, her spicy Arabic-Hebrew, and her quoting of Scripture attest. Some of her weekday and festival customs involve spiritual and emotional cooperation with others, and these others belong to her ethnic group, in the midst of which she lives. Via the wailing tradition, this woman belongs to the local community of emotion and the nonlocal community of her generation of Yemenite Jewish immigrants. She knows how to tell anecdotes about wailing because she witnessed and heard them; thus, she also knows how to delve into the minutiae of what is accepted and not accepted in this tradition. However, a tone of nostalgia accompanies her words almost from the very start; the pictures that she draws have already begun to fade under the pounding of reality. What is the nature of this reality? The interviewee concludes her remarks by limiting women's wailing to the cultural-historical context that Yemen represents for her. She chooses this method—among others that she could have chosen—to speak about a tradition that has strayed so far from its place that it is lost. Frequent death events and ongoing terror in Israel are obviously tragic, but tragedy also has a socioaffective meaning. In this interviewee's eyes, the new characteristics of death in Israel make wailing and its community trappings altogether unnecessary.[7]

A comprehensive examination of the dialogue between the traditional world of the elderly women who had emigrated from Yemen and the patterns of life that they discovered in modern Israel shows that wailing is one of the community customs that saddens them in particular by having gone into decline. This is consistent with the lengthy persistence of wailing before its ultimate disappearance, the adamancy of some of the interviewees to continue performing at the time of my research and even to maintain the custom stubbornly despite attempts to silence them, and the fact that elderly women in Israel, like counterparts in other Western countries, suffer from low social status (Arber and Ginn 1995). Yemenite Jewish women immigrants tend to be rather selective in the preservation of gender roles, in accordance with their need for improved status in the family and the community and the importance of religion in their lives. For these women, Yemen is a place that strongly represents confinement to the home. They have strong memories of having no control over the wages they brought home, no political rights, and no formal schooling. Their immigration to Israel allowed them to consolidate their status as working women, largely free of their husbands' authority, and as valued contributors to community activity. They experienced this relative liberation as something that was correct and adequate, without embracing the "Ashkenazi package deal" and its secular values (Gilad 1989, 229; Katzir 1976). Hence, it is clear why these women's ambition to shake off their past, with its baggage of inferiority, discrimination, and servitude, does not clash with the preservation of the wailing culture; in fact, the one is consistent with the other. For these women, wailing and the religious legitimacy that it commands are a special arena of control in the community sphere.

As in a tragic play, wailers today are delivering a lengthy aria before they totally fall silent. They believe in the value of their practice. The Yemenite Jewish wailers, like their Greek counterparts, recognize the status that wailing may grant them, and they protect their craft jealously (Seremetakis 1990; Caraveli-Chaves 1980). They take vocal offense when they are ignored; they negotiate for permission to utter fragments of lamentations at houses of mourning or, at least, at the burial; and some of them remind us that wailing is a form of honoring the dead and that they themselves should be honored on this account. They operate amid two sets of clashing images that are known in various cultures and are intuitively familiar to them, too. One image is the wailer as a deranged, dangerous witch; the other image, dominant in the wailing tradition in Yemen but now threatened, considers the wailer a dignified, authoritarian, and wise individual—a crone woman (Holst-Warhaft 1995; Sered 1994; Bolen 2002). Outside the community sphere, an agenda of alienation exists that rules out the possibility of dialogue between an aged Yemenite Jewish wailer and an audience of Israelis, the former close to the grave and the latter far from it.

Champions of Mizrahi ("Eastern" from the Israeli social perspective, that is, of immigrants from Islamic countries) feminism will argue that despite the implicit power of the wailer's voice, these women represent voicelessness in the Israeli domain of identities. Those of this persuasion would liken the social fate of an elderly Yemenite Jewish wailer to that of an elderly Jewish wailer of Iraqi, Tunisian, Moroccan, or other provenance. These women are deemed to be voiceless not only because they are women and elderly but also due to something that Israel has given them; that is, the label of being Mizrahi women. Indeed, in a society still dominated by the Western patriarchal order, the last of the wailing women are susceptible to this kind of triple marginalization. If one may apply to them a common metaphor in the field of critical gerontology, one may say that they are "transparent," like most elderly women in modern societies and women who belong to groups that come into contact with values that glorify bodily aesthetics, beauty, youth, and efficiency (Arber and Ginn 1991). Furthermore, one may detect their absence in the feminist discourse, which until recently excluded aged women from the collective of women whose status merits discussion (Bernard, Chambers, and Granville 2000) and, oddly, their absence in the Israeli feminist discourse, which, in addition to excluding aged women, has focused almost entirely on Ashkenazic women (Motzafi-Haller 2001; Dahan-Kalev 2002, 2005). These findings about the wailers' absence from both the social eye and the social discourse, not to mention the outright gagging that they endure at cemeteries, might sustain a trenchant dialogue that derives its tone of voice from the domain of identity politics (Taylor 1994; Fraser 2000).

Against the background of such a dialogue, one might argue that the following testimony of a wailer can be understood only in terms of a struggle that she is waging and her awareness that her performance is typically subversive: "It's very, very important for me to wail. Until I die and fade away I'll carry on in my way. I'm not giving up!" The crucial question for me is what this woman is actually trying to say within the community to which she has limited herself. Hearkening to the political-identity discourse, one is tempted to attach to her remark the hope that her voice, literally her voice, will vault the hurdles of the images that relate not only to gender, anxiety, and crisis at death events but also to ethnicity. I am also tempted to take up the role of a researcher who defends women who express their protest. This, however, is not the kind of dialogue that this book presents, mainly because there is no visible evidence of a special dialogue concerning the Mizrahiness of wailers or elderly Yemenite Jewish women in Israeli society, and I see no justification for inventing a voice for my respondents in which they themselves did not speak. Whenever my women respondents addressed themselves to Mizrahiness, they, like my male respondents, wished only to glorify and praise their traditional mourning patterns and affirm their uniqueness relative to those of the Ashkenazim. The women respondents claimed that in the intercultural comparison—an agenderic enterprise—their ways would prevail. Admittedly, they occasionally spoke jealously about wailing but only within the boundaries of their ethnic community, thereby expressing their realization that this is the appropriate arena for their traditional performance. Their conversation about the decline of wailing in Israel did not elicit remarks of opposition, protest, or a wish to adapt their performance to the new reality or turn the clock back; the conversation only expressed some degree of a sadness that already was wrapped in nostalgia and acquiescence. Accordingly, my impression is that the Mizrahic feminist dialogue may be foreign and forced in this context; it may cloud the nature of the field and the information gleaned from it; and, above all, it may distract attention from the purpose of the study: to decode the cultural enigma.

The ethnography that follows presents the respondents' practical and verbal interpretation of their tradition and my own interpretation, based partly on theirs, and also satisfies an additional hermeneutic idea, which treats tradition as a concept *by* which, not *about* which, one may think (Ben-Amos 1984, 97). I believe that insofar as ethnography is a creation of modernity, one may include it not only in forms that express ways in which the meanings of the tradition are understood but also in forms that interpret the tradition creatively. Furthermore, the ethnography reflects my dual point of view as a researcher and as an object of research, that is, as an Israeli woman who shares the respondents' origin and participates with them randomly and regularly in areas other than research or study. Thus, the ethnography includes the musings of an additional respondent—the author—about the tradition. The difference between me and other respondents is that since I am an ethnographer, my interpretative structuring of the tradition is not limited to musing or responding in ways that include the tendering of an opinion but instead is geared to deciphering the implicit cultural codes of the tradition and translating them into familiar systems of meaning. The ethnography is a finish line toward which the ambit of the tradition is extended.

The Aesthetics of Sorrow

This book amplifies the light that dangles over the stage where the focal event in what I choose to call a wailing culture is performed. In other words, this book presents wailing from the additional perspective of its meaning as folklore and verbal art (Finnegan 2001). In accordance with Ben-Amos's approach, wailing may be viewed as "a mutual social activity that takes place via the artistic medium," a communication that is "materially different from all other forms of speech and gesture" (Ben-Amos 1973, 421). In this manner, the book reveals something of the multifaceted beauty of wailing and the wailer and demonstrates the centrality of aesthetics as a value in the wailing culture. The description of the intrinsic wisdom in this cultural performance, which includes verbal virtuosity, melody, voice, metaphors of love, feminine religion, and an additional range of symbolic assets, returns time and again to the picture of the masked woman, the grace of her movements, and her heartrending lyrics. The ethnography illuminates the act of bewailing the dead in its diverse meanings but cannot separate the poetical side of the loss, the pleasure of the emotional unburdening, and the delicacy of the performer's hand and head gestures from them. Furthermore, wailing is likened to a canvas of beauty on which the performer paints the persona of the deceased, his ways, his body, and his limbs. By so doing, wailing provides an interpretation from the realm of female aesthetics of the religious value of honoring the dead, akin to the gesture of scattering multicolored flower petals over the grave. As we follow link by link the chain of the value of honoring, we find that the links lead to a pinnacle: the deceased's honor and that of the mourners depend on the honor of the wailer, and the wailer's honor depends on the audience's aesthetic judgment. When the audience has its say, wailing is judged mainly in terms of the beauty or lack of beauty that it embodies as a complete performance with lyrics, melody, voice, and movement. Those present assess each of these elements in accordance with the tastefulness that their culture embeds in it.

The title of this book, *Aesthetics of Sorrow,* was chosen not only as part of the conceptualization of wailing as folklore but also in a reflection of the respondents' words and the importance that they attributed to this aspect of wailing. My conversations with them often led to expressions of nostalgia for something that had once been, that still remains a little, and that will soon be totally lost. Sometimes they even shook their heads sadly over the loss of cultural assets that their immigration to and acculturation in Israel had caused them. That they were still witnesses to the existence of wailing and participants in the community of emotion had no effect on many of their descriptions, which were already wreathed in reminiscences. It made me wonder: Does the realization that their tradition is disintegrating affect their assessments? Does nostalgia—an act of remembrance that itself can induce wailing—make something beautiful into something very beautiful, the ordinary into the sublimely graceful, and the familiar into a calculated craft? The question seems unanswerable; it is an additional and different aspect of the perspective of this ethnography on the intercultural encounter. It is impossible to separate the contours of a past reality from the way it is remembered. However, the question raises a possibility, one that should be treated with importance, about the respondents' contribution to the images of their culture. Glorification of wailing culture and dismay over its decline are common in ethnographic accounts and interpretative choices. This squares with the dominant approach in ethnography, the emic approach, which tells the story from the respondent's point of view even though it allows other if not contrasting voices to express themselves.

While I was in conversations in people's living rooms, on terraces that face city streets, at a golden-age club that was established with the help of the state lottery, and in a Mitsubishi automobile en route to the mourners' tent, wailing came across as the opposite of mundaneness, something far from daily reality. Talking about wailing amid Israeli secularity magnified the poetic message of wailing and charged it with meaning. Talking forced the respondents to confront not only a gap of values relating to time and place but also a vanishing aesthetic reality. This confrontation became a background factor in their remarks about wailing. The remarks were typified by a sentimentality that had a powerful effect on the creation of the exotics of wailing as a cultural practice.

The exotification of wailing has more than one aspect. The respondents' attitudes, taken collectively, revealed two clashing approaches: yearning and revulsion. Even though both emotions signified the same thing—circumscription of the influence of the culture and emphasis on its aesthetic singularity—the elderly immigrant generation typically adopted the positive approach, whereas those of the second and third generations, especially those who were averse to religion, characteristically embraced a derogatory and dismissive attitude toward wailing and what it represents. If we may capture the gist of the attitude toward wailing as an object of yearning, we should put the aesthetic element first and define wailing as a configuration of self-exaltation. According to this approach, feelings of sorrow, melancholy, and distress are raw materials that the wailer puts to amazing use in her art by distancing herself from the pain and its attendant shock. Her wailing has the ability to refine the crude and spontaneous form of emotion that sweeps through the body upon the loss of someone close. The wailer gathers up rather bestial vocalizations—heaves of weeping and gasping—and turns them into rhymed verses delivered in a pleasing vocal tune. Even the mourners' bewildered, confused, and jumbled words of sorrow, repeated time and again, are privileged with organization and metaphorical beautification. Wailing in its positive sense is an art that creates a desired distance from sorrow and, in turn, induces a flow of tears. As stated, however, wailing also has a negative connotation: the younger generation considers it a performance that molds a subjective emotion in order to fit it into a cultural agenda. Wailing applies the coercive power of art at a time of crisis. For some, wailing and wailers are off-putting from the value standpoint, and they wonder: how can there be a stylized articulation of sadness, and how can performance intersect with spontaneity and sincerity? In their eyes, wailing, among all traditional death rituals, is a conspicuous form of deception (Wouters 2002) that breaches the boundaries of emotional autonomy and impairs the authenticity of the self.

Performed Weeping

The essence of wailing as performed weeping leaves ethnographers sorely puzzled. What does this pairing of words signify? Should wailers' weeping be considered make-believe or a device that women use to powerfully vent their sadness? What is the meaning of the weeping that the audience emits in response to the wailer's performance? In what sense is this weeping performed? The impression of ostensibly spontaneous weeping may prove simplistic in view of the performative characteristics of this weeping and its rules of expression. Briggs (1992) investigated wailing rituals among the Waraos in Venezuela, and in his book about the development of his research he speaks to this point by alluding to the misleading potential of wailing. By taking part in a funeral in another community, Briggs became acquainted with its musical characteristics and powerful emotional effect. Consequently, he was able to see the Warao wailing ritual as a highly potent form of social action. Until then, he had considered wailing a manifestation of intensive sadness and anger as the mourners experienced them (Briggs 1992, 338).

The common underlying assumption in many ethnographies is that personal emotion in a mourning situation creates a dissonance between self and society (Seremetakis 1990). In other words, a person's death creates a social crisis that entails emotional expression by the community at large, but this expression is hard to translate into a subjective experience and channel into the individual's innerness. Thus, the individual, although part of the mourning community, finds him/herself uninvolved. Wailing is considered a way of resolving this dissonance. As performed weeping, it is an in-between configuration that may bridge between the internal (subjective) and the external (social) worlds, between the spontaneous and the structured, and between grief (the affective response to a loss) and mourning (actions that express grief) (Stroebe and Stroebe 1987). This vagueness in the characterization of wailing explains why wailing is perceived as a cultural enigma that presents an interpretive challenge and also explains the diversity of ways in which ethnography copes with wailing. Ethnographers have portrayed wailing as "wept thoughts" (Feld 1995; Kaeppler 1993), "thoughtful crying" (Feld 1995), or a shift from tears to ideas (Holst-Warhaft 1995). The lament, a composite of integrated qualities, is termed by Feld (1995, 96) "melodic-text-sung weeping" and is perceived as expressing a "mélange of affect and cognition."

This mélange in wailing, if we may call it one, is amply represented in many ethnographers' interpretative efforts. Their various interpretations establish a basis for the ambivalent meaning of wailing, that is, its being on the one hand and on the other, a practice that concurrently directs personal emotion and satisfies a social need. In the opinion of Urban (1988), who researched Brazilian wailing, the wailing ritual accommodates a secret about the social order that relates to the question of how a culture controls emotional processes. The secret, in his judgment, lies in an alchemy that transforms emotion into a metaeffect, that is, that turns emotion into a catalyst of social cohesion. However, Urban was undecided about the emotional state that wailing creates, as another argument of his implies. The wailing ritual, he says, may prompt people to act under one of two stimuli: the awakening of an inner sense of grief or the awakening of their wish to impress others and prove that they share the socially correct emotion (392).

Remarks on the Dramaturgical Dimension

The ethnographic commentary reflects a cultural belief about the ideal emotionality in death rituals: all members of the community should commiserate with the bereaved. The question now is how wailing helps people to act out this belief. How does it invest an external social rule with internal validation? This question leads us to the performance. Wailing as performed probably eases the tension that exists between the emotional and the social—or, to be more exact, the tension between the authentic and the socially proper. Ethnographies note various qualities of wailing as a complex performance, including text, vocalization, and motions. Each component separately, and the ways in which the components are integrated, solo and in chorus, are presented in the context of emotional arousal that is generated among the audience. Scholars, however, tend to assess the emotional power of wailing not per se but as a vehicle for the shaping of social relations around the circumference of the performance circle.[8] Within this framework, they relate to a great many things: the poetics and contents of the text as a story of suffering (Benedicte 1994; Kaeppler 1993); a collective vocalization that creates polyphony and intertextuality (Briggs 1993; Feld 1995; Seremetakis 1991); types of icons of crying; the level of tone of the wailing (Urban 1988); bodily movements that attest to suffering, panic, and identification with the deceased; and even the distance between wailing women and the body (Seremetakis 1990; Abu-Lughod 1993). The ethnographies show that wailing women are adept at creating the impression of sincerity in their emotions; it is this that excites the audience. This dramaturgical element, however, is rarely discussed on its own. In fact, sometimes its importance is belittled in comparison with the social outcome of the emotional performance.

Researchers of wailing cultures are strongly captivated by the dual nature of wailing and by the interpretive possibilities that may bridge between grief emotions and social and political relations. This sense of captivation that wailing produces may explain the tendency of many researchers to adopt an epistemological approach that treats the decoding of wailing as a dramatic presentation built along the lines of performance and impression management. This approach also ignores how the audience relates to the wailer, who realizes that her wailing has a dramaturgical dimension and asks herself how sincere her performance really is. Lutz and White (1986) represent this stance by arguing that the dichotomy of "genuine" versus "conventional" emotional expression in death rituals may stem from "local concerns with 'sincerity' and the conjunction between inner and outer lives." These local concerns, they claim, "may be too simple to do justice to the variety of ways in which cultural thought and ritual act together to construct emotional experience" (413). Both scholars almost ask a rhetorical question that "What theoretical harvest may we reap by studying the affective intentions of the wailer or of the participants in the wailing as a group?!"

The intercultural-encounter perspective presented in this book clashes with this approach and even demands an investigation of the audience's interest in the sincerity of the wailer's emotion. Below I show that the participants in the Yemenite Jewish wailing culture are not a homogeneous or distinct local collective that is prone to the emotional stress implied by the convention of "I *should* commiserate" and to the commitment to the wailer's authority that this convention creates. Jewish immigrants from Yemen are susceptible to a much more substantive and visible stress in that their wailing culture is already being encircled by the clashing emotional values that their offspring have assimilated. For them, the term "aesthetics of sorrow" denotes not only words that once clashed but have been reconciled by wailing but also, and rather, a reality that underlies an intercultural collision. The significance of this difference between audiences of performances in other ethnographies and my respondents is that the latter, being aware of the protracted decline of their culture and testing one value against another—individual versus community, spontaneity and sincerity versus conformity—strip the performance of its erstwhile artistic integrity and help to discover the dramaturgical assets of wailing. In this sense, the ethnography that follows tends to de-romanticize traditional wailing, presenting the respondents' subversive attitudes in a way that may rip the mask off the wailer's performance and expose what underlies the human and magic enchantment of her wailing.

Chapters in a Dialogue with the Authentic

Why one should expect respondents to co-opt researchers into a dialogue that they are conducting with their tradition, a dialogue that would not exist had they not noticed the decline of an authentic element in their lives? In this kind of research, the authentic seems to shrink into a tiny kernel surrounded by a halo so broad that it exchanges one value for another: the authentic for a dialogue.

Are we dealing with two contradictory concepts? I propose that we are not. Taylor (1991) rescues authenticity from the archaeological dustbin by showing that it is a relative open-ended concept that cannot be understood except via negotiations over symbols and ideas. To Taylor, authenticity is not an enemy of demands originating outside the self, the individual, or the collective; instead, authenticity assumes the existence of such demands. Authenticity is always defined in a relation of self vis-à-vis Other; that is, authenticity is dialogic in essence. Thus, Taylor gave back to my respondents their authenticity and made it a reward for the fact of their having occupied themselves with the matter, for having tried to circumscribe their wailing and its reality in response to research questions, and for having responded to the distances between real and ideal, yesterday and today, that the encounter with Israeli society has opened up.

The wailer performs an amazing act of existential mediation: speaking with the dead and representing their point of view. This ethnography not only describes this mediation but also adopts it as a conceptual point of departure. Consequently, this ethnography reveals a diverse wealth of additional facets of wailing in its mediated form. Some are overt, and others are covert; they exist at various levels of encounter: between wailer and audience, between woman and woman, and between storytellers and the woman who documented their stories. The motif of dialogue links all the chapters like a crimson thread, and by its means we get a whiff of the authentic that flickers like a tiny flashlight from far away. We use this concept to think about the present and the past, and then we free ourselves to contemplate ritual human behavior one more time. An ethnographic posture of this kind includes a dialogue with the reader as well, it being our belief that the dialogic narrative in telling the story of the culture is exactly as necessary as the original model of the culture is inaccessible. Generally speaking, the ethnography copes with this difficulty by inventing dialogic strategies vis-à-vis the respondents and applying the knowledge accumulated thus far about women's wailing cultures. This method is didactic in that it exposes the reader to the steps taken on the road to discovery.

The dialogic point of view is also valuable in that it dissipates the otherness and the exoticness that envelop the wailing culture of Yemenite Jewish women in Israel. Dialogue has the ability to present the object being researched, to turn it into a subject, and to remove it from its display case in the museum of cultures, where it is transparent to visitors' prying eyes. Since then, the focal points in research on ethnic groups have changed; scholars now settle for partial illumination of cultural realities. One reason for this is the growing dearth of fields for community and traditional research. Another important factor, however, is the claim that this discipline's traditional preference for picturesque description of exotic societies is not free of power implications. Insofar as this allegation pertains to research on Middle Eastern cultures, the preference is firmly linked to Orientalism and is convenient for disciplining (Moors 1991). Gauging the responses of audiences at conferences, lectures, and conversations, I found that women's wailing makes an impression due to its exotic flavor. Wailing comes across as wearing a mask of sound, motion, clothing, language, and customs that conceals folk knowledge. This knowledge is visible only to researchers who forget themselves in the domain of symbols of "them." The description of the phenomenon in these audiences is impressive in its full and exotic beauty, as if wailing were an imaginary tourist site that the audience's vernacular has not reached. Yemenite Jewish women were considered experts not in wailing but instead in tradition, and just as the tradition has fallen into obsolescence, so have the wailers. Such was the case only at first, at the beginning of the description. By the end of the encounter, the power of interaction in the descriptive, cultural, and theoretical dialogue made such a strong impression that wailing came to light in a rather different way. The dialogic point of view from which I performed my observations inspired these practitioners of intellectual tourism to ask about themselves as well and to wonder, not without sadness, about the disappearance of wailing before Israel could get familiar with it. What remains for me is to hope that you will gain this welcome form of inspiration from here on as you read this book.

In chapter 1, "Wailing: A Topic That Defies Research," the Yemenite Jewish wailing culture is explored as a challenge for research. I describe the hurdles that I had to surmount in order to attend, observe, and participate in wailing events; to get to know the wailers; and to interview them. At first, it seemed difficult if not impossible for a female researcher to appear at a death event, the best opportunity to gather pictures and thoughts. The fieldwork was replete with missed opportunities due to the crisis of the death event, the respondents' forgetfulness, the terror that wailing evokes whenever it is performed, and the assortment of murky beliefs that have been attached to wailing, the song of death. Sometime later, however, after I made the acquaintance of a local ethnologist, the culture of women's wailing became a much more dialogic topic for me. With his help many of the barriers fell, and my research crossed a watershed. Chapter 1 also speaks of the contradictory ways in which my respondents described wailing as culture and as singing. As my journal sat open before them, my respondents invented clashing "truths" that entailed conceptual dialogue and interpretative delays. The chapter also reveals something of the experience of my encounter with a wailer who wailed as I interviewed her. Finally, the chapter reports the emotional price that wailing demanded of me, a one-woman audience who had come to learn.

Chapter 2, "Johara: The Mother of Wailers," recounts the image of the quintessential wailer and the respondents, all of whom stand in awe of the then-as-now mother of wailers. Johara is a mythical woman who, in her wailing and her whole being, shuttles between the world of the living and the world of the dead. Her wailing and her ways are paragons of a continuous and audacious dialogue between fertility and extinction, joy and gloom, the mundane and the sacred, and man and woman. The transitioning of the wailing performance between real and make-believe shows that Johara is a symbolic type. Her story is written in a somewhat mythical tenor. It is an overture in which cultural exoticness is portrayed via illusion—one woman's faint recollections. The chapter has another purpose: defining the substantive issues that will recur in subsequent chapters and allow the cultural jigsaw puzzle to be assembled.

Chapters 3, 4, and 5 reduce wailing to its components: text, performance, drama, and emotional power. This sense of the matter pertains to the difficulty that arises in a research process that lifts the lamentation out of its special cultural context, that is, explores it via an interview and not via observation in a house of mourners. The gift—the contribution made by passing on a tradition—is reflected in my research dialogue with a wailer-narrator and also in her dialogue with anonymous readers who need to perform a dual translation, from one language to another and from the oral to the written. The dialogues elicit a collection of lamentations that are presented in succession. Chapter 3, "Giving Words," identifies categories in the wailing discourse and draws discursive lines with which one may understand them. The categories are sorted in accordance with a model comprising four arenas of identity in which the self and the Other meet. This split presentation sheds light on the voice that the wailer works through—a representative dialogic of others, living and dead—and the gift that her wailing lyrics award to members of the community. The principal finding here is the ability of wailing to respond to a range of psychological and social needs at times of death.

Chapter 4, "The Performance Stage," describes wailing from the vantage point of the stage on which it is performed. Since the respondents repeatedly invoked theater analogies in reference to wailing, I do the same, placing the wailer on a metaphorical stage in the middle of a dramatic circle of light before an audience. The solo performance in a house of mourning is the last configuration of wailing that has survived the mass emigration from Yemen. This performance was preceded by two performative forms that are essentially dialogic, both described from the respondents' memory: the women's circle and the solo wailer whose performance is responded to in a chorus. The chapter focuses on the dramatic soloist, whose performances, as stated, are steadily dwindling among houses of mourning in Israel and describes the wailer's journey of female/maternal evolution from childhood to adulthood. The contents of the journey serve as inspiration for her wailing and an element in the definition of her expertise and her becoming a wailer. The description of the components of her expertise segues into the tracking of her performance stage by stage, from the moment she invites herself to the house of mourning until before she leaves, and probes the deep levels of play-acting in the wailing performance, in two senses: as the wailer's pretense and in her changing levels of emotional involvement. I liken the performance to a complex and multifaceted dialogue between the text and the audience's definitions of truth, a dialogue designed to induce an experience of emotional persuasion. Further on, a staged observation appears; this is the subtitle of an ethnographic experiment that clarified, after the fact, the performative point of view of expert wailers. The focus here relates to the implications of positioning a camera between a researcher and her interviewees. The last part of the chapter recounts Jews' wailing in the homes of their Arab neighbors in Yemen. The resulting tableau projects onto the nature of relations that had existed in Yemen between Jewish men and women and between Jews and Arabs and onto the play-acting dimension of the wailer's performance.

Chapter 5, "Melancholic Power," concerns itself with the melancholic power of wailing and of the wailer. First, wailing is presented in terms of the healing effect of weeping and the covert dialogues that the tears bring in train. By examining the wailer's curative intentions and the audience's performed response, I show that wailing plays a role in working through grief at two levels: first at the individual level, at which it also defines the continuation of the experience of loss in the mourners' lives, and then at the collective level, due to its ability to close in on the audience and unite it in the solidarity consciousness of a collective in exile. Further on, the ethnography demonstrates the intrinsic element of enticement in the verbal contents of the lamentation and in its performative form. These characteristics are revealed in a slow but steady spiraling dialogue between me and the respondents, including steps forward and steps backward. As the wailer performs for her audience, she exhibits "female" excitability and the dualism of a victim and an actor who controls her acting. Her lyrics send a covert message of love that everyone craves. The lyrics stifle the separation anxiety that has mounted due to the death crisis and offer the audience the consolation of a motherly embrace. In a thickened multilayered description, the lyrical monologue acquires substance and evolves into an erotic dialogue between the wailer-woman-mother and her audience. Her performance oversteps the strictly regulated bounds of modesty. Her repertoire of motions and metaphors links separation and coupling—and death and fertility—with threads too delicate for even the critical eye to see. The discussion of melancholic power reveals women's wailing as an art of empowerment whose beneficent potency serves the goals of healing, loving, and living.

In chapter 6, "Mission," the ethnography leaves behind the performative arena of wailing and illuminates the status of wailing in the class of death rituals—funeral, burial, and mourning. Yemenite Jewish wailing is rooted in the socioreligious mission of honoring the dead. The wailer's mission fits into the framework of the theoretical study of female religion, which gives the appearance of being a separate religion in terms of time, place, and symbols. Under this heading, women's narrative wailing is proposed as a contrast to and a companion of men's prayer book wailing or eulogies. As a practice, narrative wailing complements the devotional work that men perform and affirms the hegemonic basis of the Jewish faith and ethics. By representing a transition from tears to ideas, women's wailing is construed as an overt style of dialogue between the sexes. The chapter concludes by describing an ethnographic experiment in which women's wailing is set in the middle of a men's circle of narghiles. The absence of women in the circle that surrounds their wailing is found to be of methodological and theoretical value. The circle separated itself from women's wailing but also accommodated it, and the tears, initially attributed to the nature of women, recurred in the men's testimonies and also flowed in the men's own settings. The participants in the circle admitted that they had cried. Their reflective observation alludes to the dual connection in death rituals between separation and unification of the sexes, between death and the celebration of life.

The value of honoring the dead serves as a social justification for the establishment of a wailing culture. This value, however, is given thorough presentation in the concluding segment of the ethnographic story and not in its beginning. I made this choice in view of the representation of cultural reality that a text can provide. As with the other themes and sections of this ethnography, the place chosen for this chapter, "Mission," alludes to the translocation of matters from the field to the readers. By arranging the chapters in this order, I wished to imitate, to some extent, the characteristics of the persuasion that wailing applies to its audience. Thus, I wish to give over an impression of the words and then the minutiae of the performance, the discomfort attending the female temptation, and other related conscious and unconscious themes and to conclude by showing respect for the task at hand. As the respondents, including myself, listened to the wailing in its terrifying eruption, we acknowledged to some extent the existence of the cultural game being played. Nevertheless, they, like me, lowered our heads at the sound of it and were left, after the performance ended, with a sense of respect for the wailer and the mission of self-devotion that she undertook. Honoring the dead is never disengaged from honoring the person who bewails him; it disconnects itself from the deceased and moves over to her. Honor is the social cloak in which wailers wrap themselves, no matter how eagerly we wish to undress them and no matter how sincerely they wish to divulge their secret. At the next death event, too, if a wailer performs in the middle of the all-embracing misery, her mantle of honor will endure.

This argument concerning honor is especially correct in the eyes of participants in the first circle, elderly people who have been oriented in the wailing culture and its community configurations since their days in Yemen. The epilogue, "The Lament of the Printed Words," separates the message of this audience, on which the chapters of the ethnography are based, from that of the second-circle audience, the children and grandchildren of the immigrants from Yemen who participate in the performance but hardly blunt their criticism on that account. The divergence of these groups' attitudes is not total but recurs consistently and blatantly in the remarks quoted in this concluding chapter. The epilogue begins by describing the Yemenite Jewish collective as a disintegrating structure of emotion and then describes recent manifestations of the decline of this collective's wailing culture. The second part of the epilogue presents the ethnography as a text that establishes a dialogue on the topic of cultural authenticity. The ethnographic dialogue between a group of immigrants and their modern environment and between a traditional practice and a research project creates open and closed avenues of interpretation. The foregoing survey of chapters is presented from this special point of view, which analyzes the link between the ethnographic process and its inventory—the assets of a culture. The epilogue concludes by discussing possible reasons for the decline of Yemenite Jewish wailing, which mirrors that of the wailing of other Mizrahic women in Israel and women's wailing in the West overall. The objections of the second-circle audience force wailing into a confrontation with modern values of emotion, which tie into the ideal of authenticity of self that typifies our society. Many consider these values superior to those represented by the wailing culture, and apparently they have effectively defined the community's self-image and its emotional needs in death rituals. The collective remarks of the second generation have cemented the consensual status of women's wailing as a failed performance that should not be revived. Thus, wailing is doomed to perdition, and with this its story ends as well.

· 1 ·

Wailing

A Topic That Defies Research

THE TENSION BETWEEN COVERT VALUES OF CONTINUITY AND LIFE, represented by scientific investigation, and melancholy and dread of death, associated with wailing, transformed my research into a story of squandered opportunities. As a researcher, I was eager to attend places where a wailer would appear and perform. Accomplishing this proved to be a challenge and, at times, an impossible mission. Various behavioral manifestations evolved into clashes between doing and emoting. Informers came forth, expressing their willingness to tell me "at the right time," that is, when a death occurred in the community, but they seldom kept their word. When I initiated communication, they sometimes vociferously tended to recall some tragedy that had occurred—oh, how sad it had been!—a few days earlier, a week or perhaps two weeks earlier, and to note how sorry they were for having "forgotten" to pass the word. Repeatedly I was told, "Oh . . . it's a shame you weren't here yesterday. A special wailer was here; you should have heard her," "I wanted to record the wailer for you, but . . . ," or

"You would have learned lots from the wailers who were at the cemetery. . . . Yes, I really hadn't heard wailing like that in so long." When I asked them why they had not called me, they apologized, blaming a memory lapse or a negative emotional response to the death event. Sometimes they packaged these apologies with a promise to do differently next time, and round and round it went. Most of the cases that did come across at the right time—before the funeral or in the first days of mourning—related to the deaths of people who were less familiar to the informers or distant from them in geographic or kinship terms. Only in these cases could they give thought to esoteric matters that came to mind associatively and allowed me to progress in my research.

Death rituals are also crisis rituals that challenge the strength of the illusion of ontological security that society is responsible for maintaining (Chidester 1990). The death of a familiar individual strikes with waves of anxiety not only the deceased's relatives but also anyone who knows the deceased. I learned that the moment a death rumor in a small community spreads, members of the community need to adopt a degree of indifference, alienation, or strength to endure the task of passing the word.

I discovered another kind of squandered opportunity that stemmed from the research topic when I visited mourners' homes or the cemetery after receiving the coveted announcement. I found myself participating in observance of the religious obligations that belong to the rituals, that is, walking behind the deceased and consoling the bereaved. However, I was unable to observe the ultimate object of my research craving, the wailer. The rituals at cemeteries and in mourners' homes sometimes took place without a wailer's performance even though she was there, because the crowd of women consolers swallowed her up. When this happened, the informants expressed the squandering of opportunity in different ways: "That's interesting, today of all days she isn't opening her mouth to wail," or "The mourners aren't letting her. . . . They don't want to hear wailing women." These cases provided the very best evidence of the decline of wailing in the Yemenite Jewish community. One reason for the decline is that people in the community are repulsed by the emotional impact of wailing and have become acquainted with calmer mourning patterns. This tendency illuminated another facet of the tension that existed between my research needs and the essence of wailing.

Two cases demonstrate the sensitivity of wailing to changing circumstances despite the wailers' goodwill and their belief that it was important to help me in my research. In the first case, I sat among women consolers one morning and started up a conversation with an older member of the group. She told me with undisguised pride that she herself was a wailer and had regularly wailed since her days in Yemen long ago. Sensing my enthusiasm at that moment, she promised to go home and return in the evening to give the many consolers a really superb performance. To avoid the need to wait there for hours, I also decided to come back when it was "her time." I returned but did not see her; she had not joined the consolers at all. In the second case, one morning I called Rachel,[1] one of the professional wailers, several weeks after I had interviewed her in her home. She informed me that she would be visiting a mourners' house out of town that evening; her acquaintances had invited her, and she had promised to perform. I came and found her seated near the women mourners, conversing with them quietly. When she noticed me, she smiled apologetically. She related that she could not let herself wail in this special and tragic house of mourning, where not only had the paterfamilias just died but his wife had been taken to the hospital with heart failure. After the fact, my informants did not know how to explain or justify the logic behind her decision. Only indirectly did I realize the infectious power of wailing and the fear that it inspires: she was afraid that bewailing the deceased would affect his wife's health and bring her closer to death, because wailing, directed at the deceased, is perceived as "getting in the last word."

The sense of squandered opportunity also occasionally bedeviled my attempts to interview Yemenite Jewish women who were not wailers. Immediate and firm refusals were accompanied by the expression "*Allah yastur*" or its Hebrew equivalent, "*Elohim yishmor*" ("God forbid"). From the moment they realized what the topic was, the refuseniks took on grave and rigid facial features. They extended an open palm in a motion of rejection and stared at me in fear. Many of these women were familiar with the phenomenon, had taken part in it, and possessed much knowledge. For this very reason, however, they were wary of cooperating with a researcher whose choice of topic they found puzzling if not irresponsible. Other women invoked a less direct form of refusal: evasion. They elected to tell me that they had immigrated to Israel as little girls or had been born there. They said this to suggest that they were no different from me; they used this pretext to excuse their unfamiliarity with the topic or their self-imposed silence at the sound of my questions. I asked a member of a small group of elderly women who participated in a crafts group at a community center, "Have you ever seen a wailer?" "No," she replied, "I was born in Israel. I don't know any." An acquaintance of hers intervened immediately, blurting at her, "You know you shouldn't lie. You were married when you came here." "Very well," the woman replied, "I got married on the way. I'm not a wailer, not a singer, not anything." Then she clammed up totally; I couldn't get a word out of her. One interviewee who deigned to give a wailing demonstration in her home first approached the mezuza at her doorway and then stroked it with her hand, kissed her hand, and said, "May God protect my children."[2] Another woman, a member of a golden-age club, justified her refusal to wail by claiming: "If I wail, they'll take my children [my children will die]." Seeing the puzzled look on my face, she explained, "It's dangerous. If a woman wails, it's only if they took her husband or children away. Look at her [pointing to a well-known wailer seated next to her]. She wails for her son [who had been killed]."

Aside from fear in the subjects' cumulative responses, another important reason for the possibility of squandered opportunity came into sight: the lack of a distinction between giving information about wailing and performing it. Sometimes, I needed only to tell these elderly women that I wanted to "talk about wailing" or "about the wailer" to crash into a wall of refusal. They thought I was guessing about something related to their ability to wail at will, in midday and for no justified reason; therefore, they also refused to converse at will, in mundane language. When they didn't understand the Hebrew word *qina,* which denotes wailing or lamentation, I translated it into Yemenite Arabic and said that I wished to speak with them about *'eiziyyeh* or *'eidad,* about the woman who *ma'aziyyeh* or who *ma'adadeh.* Some of these women treated the sound of these words in their mother tongue as a red flag, immediately dismissing the matter and defeating any attempt at dialogue. They must have taken my inquiry as an emotional threat. However, their reaction also mirrored a nebulous difficulty in their ability to contemplate a tradition by which some of them still lived. I found that many elderly women were less willing to reflect on their wailing than were young women or those who had come to Israel at an early age and also less willing than male members of the community. Having experienced wailing as culturally self-evident, they could reflect on it only in terms of actual performance and not as a topic of commentary. This also explains the standard and somewhat laconic phrasing that several women respondents offered when asked to address the matter for the first time: "The *ma'aziyyeh* says words about the dead. . . . She covers herself with a kerchief and she has this exciting melody, and people cry." Most respondents who said something like this did so in a tone of bewilderment or with a gentle sigh, sending a semiamused expression in the direction of the researcher who wished to deal with such a well-known thing. "That's how it is!" these women tended to answer when I asked questions of "why" and "how." One of them said, "That's how they did it in Yemen. The whole world [everyone]. Why, I don't know." Another respondent, after I repeatedly primed her for an answer, said, "There was no research to know why the women behaved that way. That's how they did it, and that's that." On one occasion I pressured a respondent, asking, "Why do you think it's important for the wailer to mention what [the deceased] did?" She answered firmly, "It's important, very important, very important, very important, to say how he was, whether he went through life in sadness or in goodness." Another time, I received an answer that may or may not have been tongue-in-cheek: "A man, even if he cries, even if he cries and cries, he doesn't wail. Women wailed, and how." I asked, "Why do you think women wailed and not men?" She answered in a despairing tenor that emanated from profound insight: "What can I tell you?! I don't know. That's how it is. Women know how to cry." Then, chuckling, she added lyrics from a well-known Israeli song: "Men don't cry in the day—they cry at night." Some respondents dismissed the entire phenomenon and absolved themselves of the need to contemplate it. If I obtained variations, expansions, and developments of these themes—and indeed, I harvested rich and valuable findings—it was only due to sympathetic and lengthy negotiations that I insisted on conducting or encounters with eagle-eyed informants who knew how to reflect on their wailing culture.

Sometimes I found a tension between my respondents' perception of something that they take for granted and their ability to contemplate it. A member of a group of men expressed this conspicuously by beginning, immediately after welcoming me, to interpret my previous encounter with the group, which he had arranged. The group gathered every Friday afternoon for a *takhsina* session, a fraternal custom in which khat leaves are chewed. I found the men—about forty in number, ranging in age from forty to seventy—seated on cushions in a large circle on a spacious terrace in front of their host's home. Ten colorful narghiles stood in a smaller circle amid the cushions, next to their owners. Cups and kettles of hot tea and water, as well as the scattered khat leaves, rested on small stools. As they chewed away, the principals busied themselves in mundane conversations and sometimes stopped to listen to a *d'var Torah* (a brief comment on a religious topic) or a joke that burst forth loudly. Occasionally someone stood up to replace the charcoals in the narghile or pour others something to drink. Sometimes someone also passed the mouthpiece of the narghile to someone else. The participant who addressed me was Yossi, a teacher who, apart from being relatively young, was considered an intellectual by the standards of many of the men in the group. This was our second and last group meeting. As he took the floor, his well-trained teacher's mouth was stuffed with khat leaves, and his lips puffed smoke. He spoke gravely about the experience of the first interview, which had taken place several weeks earlier:

> You made something unique happen to us that we're not used to. You asked questions and made us do some brainstorming, as they call it, where each of us thinks about the same thing and tries to express his opinion and say what he knows about it. That's unique. It's a very important thing to do when you really want to work through some topic. Overall, I can say that you made us realize that really every topic, everything can be investigated.

> Who among us had ever thought about what wailing does to him? Or, for example, who had ever thought about what I feel at that moment when I hear the wailer? Who had ever thought about the history, where it all started, etc.? Even if we go into our biblical sources, it's something that we've never exactly thought about. You brought up a topic that seems simple, but you proved to us that, really, every topic can be investigated, approached from all sides, from the historical standpoint, the cultural, the ethnic, the whole thing. I think that overall it was a good, important meeting. It did something to us.

Yossi, like other men whose acquaintance I made in my research, typically displayed much more reflexivity about women's wailing than elderly women did. Since women considered wailing "their" custom, a practice in which men played no active role, men had a superior angle of observation. If they were members of the second generation, whose worldview was also based on academic schooling, their advantage was even greater. Yossi's remarks showed me that he was suspended between two worlds: the traditional and the modern. He admitted that he had to resort to a special intellectual act, "brainstorming," to break through the ordinary and self-evident patterns of one symbolic world and view them via the concepts of a different world.

The respondents' treatment of wailing as something to take for granted was an additional element in their emotional resistance to cooperating with me and contemplating their culture. This was one of the factors behind the failure of the respondents, many of whom were elderly women, to provide information. Amid the lost opportunities, false alarms, and empty promises, however, the process of gathering data yielded a very valuable harvest due to a snowball effect and the mediation of several devoted performers. With their assistance, I attended death rituals and gatherings in mourners' homes and cemeteries and was privileged to watch and monitor the performance of wailing women. Ultimately, I also reached respondents whose encounters with me were totally different from what I have described thus far.

Contradictions and Mystery

The sense of mystery is the product of a contradiction between two coexisting situations: ignorance versus the wish to know. Scientific research is seemingly nonpareil in its ability to represent the aspiration for and the attainment of knowledge; even so, it does not always resolve a mystery. The respondents handed me a special kind of challenge in my attempt to understand wailing as a social phenomenon: the information they possessed was rife with contradictions. As I went from one respondent to another, men and women, I collected many of the wailing themes in the form of point and counterpoint. Sometimes this was obvious, because individual respondents contradicted themselves; after all, they, like everyone else, had never reflected on the topic before. In my attempt to convert the information they had provided into knowledge, clashing and internally contradictory attitudes took shape, and the fact that the information was now being integrated blurred the phenomenon being researched and made the mystery all the more intractable.

The responses were typified by polar, almost binary, responses to the research topic. It was this polarity, however, that created an opening with which I could fill the void that the missed or inhibited episodes had created.

For example, wailing, as both a performance and a text, was revealed to me in a patchwork manner that left me unable to determine which of the respondents' clashing statements was more valid. Age and talent, the characteristics of wailing women, were presented in ways that were as contradictory as they were emphatic. I asked a wailer, "Were young women in Yemen also wailers?" "There were no young ones," she replied, "just old ones. The young women in Yemen hadn't learned yet. Respect belongs to the elderly." However, when I asked another wailer, "How old were you when you began to wail?", she replied, "Fifteen," and added, "Anyone who learned the words, even a young woman, could be a wailer." On another subject—the wailer's talent and function as a singer at weddings—one respondent noted, "[A wailer] could sing and also wail. She had a pleasant and lovely voice." However, when I asked "Were there women who expressed themselves in both rituals, mourning and wedding?", another respondent answered in the negative. "Some wailed and others sang." To her mind, wailing and singing are two types of expertise that cannot dwell inside one woman.

The respondents disagreed about additional matters, such as compensation for wailing, the length of a performance in the mourners' home, and the customary arrangements there. Some respondents were afraid to utter the word "money" when I tried to guess aloud about why a wailer would repeatedly perform in houses of mourning. They punctuated their remarks on this topic with the expression *has ve-halila*—"perish the thought"—and glorified the wailer's role by attaching the word *mitsva* ("religious obligation") to it, defining it as something that required no further compensation. "Are you considered a professional wailer?", I asked Miriam, a well-known wailer. "No, no," she protested. "Not a professional for money, *has ve-halila.* I do it on my own"; that is, her only motive was internal and value-related. Gideon, describing his mother's role, even added, "I don't believe there's any Yemenite woman who took money for this." Others, however, thought that I had guessed correctly and that payment was self-evident. "Sure she was paid," Saida noted. "Some of them are really down and out. They go to wail in people's homes. It's their profession." Another woman respondent related that "They invite her to come and wail for the dead." I asked, "Do they pay her?" She replied, "Of course. What kind of question is that? She won't come to wail unless she's paid." Some respondents even described the practice of paying the wailer "by the head of household or the head of the family, or the children." Payment was made in cash or in food or gifts that the wailer received as she performed. Some respondents emphasized the respect and honoraria that the wailer received in the mourners' home and among members of her community. Although the respondents disagreed about how wailers were compensated, they agreed that some form of compensation was given. It stands to reason that the attitude toward compensating a performer who is perceived as emotionally identified with those compensating her would be ambivalent. Caton (1990) reached a similar conclusion in his discussion of the expertise of the Arab poet in Yemen as it pertained to interpersonal relations. On the one hand, the poet's performance earns him repute and respect; on the other hand, these emoluments rule out his public acceptance of money.

The respondents also gave varied information about the duration of the individual wailing performance. Some respondents said that it lasted about half an hour from start to finish, others estimated it at one or two hours or several hours, and several estimated it at half a day.

These were only a few representative examples of contradictory attitudes among the respondents. As for how to sketch the outlines of the wailing culture and the wailer's persona, I resorted to a list of points on which the respondents agreed or consistently expressed as well-known norms. For example, they taught me that Rada'a, a major city in eastern Yemen, typically had the best wailers and that Sana'a, the capital, had expert wailers. The respondents repeatedly praised the quality of wailing that originated in these towns: "The real wailers are the ones from Rada'a," "The girls from Rada'a are Grade A-plus wailers," or, "In Sana'a it was something else." They were almost unanimous about the proper time for wailing during the days of mourning; all respondents repeated the statement "Three days [are] for crying" like a mantra, referring to the weeping that the wailer inspires. Another point of consensus was split between men and women: all women respondents identified wailing as a religious commandment, whereas men were of two minds, some describing it as a commandment and others terming it a women's custom that men privilege with religious tolerance. The respondents also agreed about several very specific points, even using the same words to describe them. In one community that I visited, for example, all interviewees recalled an outstanding and widely renowned wailer who had died more than fifteen years earlier, and they expressed disappointment with the wailer who had just completed a rather drab performance. Wishing to explain their negative impression, each respondent repeated, word for word, "She gives three or four words about the deceased, no more," and waxed at length about the absence of an emotional stimulus in her wailing.

The consensus that existed on certain points made the contradictions stand out and sharpened the enigma that typified the phenomenon. Why were there material contradictions in the information and attitudes that the respondents conveyed? I found two main reasons; both deprived wailing of its special status and lumped it together with the rest of the corpus of rituals and traditions that the Jews of Yemen had practiced and imported to Israel. First, the respondents—like the research literature—described Yemen as a large country comprising separate counties, remote from each other, where scattered Jewish communities had existed. These counties were named for their towns, some of which had Jewish majorities and others of which had small minorities amid the Muslim population (Muchawsky-Schnapper 2000; Nini 1991). In this mountainous land, major dirt roads were the main transport arteries, and motor vehicles were not used; it took several days to walk from town to town, creating relative isolation in each. People who walked from one town to another risked the hazards of wild animals and the country's Muslim rulers, who exploited their subjects' inferior status by robbing and harassing them (Loeb 1999; Hollander 2005; Ben-Zvi 1976). Due to the palpable nature of the distance and its attendant threats, the Jewish community in each town developed a distinct self-definition and cultural and linguistic attributes. As Ratzhabi (1975, 75) put it, "Provincial colorations were usually imprinted on folk songs just as they were imprinted on vernaculars, clothing, and ways of life." This explains why my respondents, when addressing this topic, repeatedly said that "In my town, it wasn't that way" or "Among us, it wasn't like them." One wailer was more explicit: "Each [town] had its own weeping [wailing] in a different form."

Netanel, explaining possible interprovincial differences in the Jewish wailing culture, described en passant a system of classes: "Each county has its own wailers, but I noticed that northern Yemen had nothing at all to do with the whole thing. People in Sharab, Ta'iz, and Sa'id had hardly heard of these wailers. They were not active. Active [wailers] were mainly in the center and toward eastern Yemen, Sana'a, Dhamar, and Rada'a." I asked, "How can you explain that some areas had wailers and others did not?" "I think a county of city people was different from the people in the north, who were more like peasants," he replied, suggesting that wailing was more common among city dwellers. "There was much less in the north because they lived from day to day; they didn't have the peace of mind for all this. . . . Central Yemen is the center of Yemen [in terms of schooling and high culture]. Some people who went to the periphery, north or south, lost their strength. There were no wailers there because they were less plugged in. . . .

The people near Sana'a were more intelligent. People with better lineage did this work [wailing]." Netanel confirmed that the capital, Sana'a, had been the religious and spiritual center of Yemenite Jewry and traced different degrees of awareness of wailing culture to class differences between town and village and center and periphery.

Differences in class translated into differences in practice. For example, when Zahara described the area in Yemen where she had lived, she said that "They have to cry; it can't be otherwise if your loved one passed away." Here she was referring to spontaneous weeping. Later in the interview, she spoke about provincial differences in the rules of expressing emotion: "In Sana'a, it's something else. I really lived their lives. They're introverted. Outwardly, they show [their emotions]. Outwardly, they show the lovely side." Zahara clarified, interpreting this style by offering a comparison. "I'll tell you, there are poor people who've got nothing to eat. You'll see them at home with a dress that's just patches over patches. When she goes out, you wouldn't believe it, she goes out with the loveliest clothing, all dolled up." Restraint of emotions and tears was typical of the Jews of Sana'a; Zahara appreciated this and described it as the style most appropriate to members of a social upper class. Such people, by implication, needed especially talented wailers, professional wailers who could inspire weeping at a time of crisis. This resolved one of the contradictions in the respondents' answers, relating to financial compensation for a wailer: different counties in Yemen probably had different rules for the expression of emotion and different attitudes toward the wailer's social role. Where emotional restraint was a class indicator, one could find expert wailers who were paid. Thus, they met emotional needs and concurrently created an impression of distance from inferiority—a distance both natural and spontaneous. Another possible reason for contradictions in the respondents' statements is the waning of wailing in Israel's Yemenite Jewish communities. Many wailing cultures around the world are facing the same fate (Holst-Warhaft 1995), becoming a muted tradition in a modern world that has developed its own ways of coping with death.

All that remains today of this grand tradition is a handful of elderly women who issue their wailing. The ritual setting for this act has also been transformed. The very waning of the tradition is confusing its message. Against this background, new attitudes toward wailing are being constructed, as are interpretations not drawn from the sources. Consequently, even wailers get the feeling that they can deviate from the permanent custom and behave as they please. Now that the wailing culture is facing obsolescence, it is being practiced in a diminished, thinned-out way. Over time, in my judgment, this has generated contrasting attitudes and contradictions among respondents. Although the respondents belong to the same ethnic group and are familiar with its rituals, they are not equal participants in and are not witness to the same traditional scene. One way to deal with this challenge is to rely on traditional Jewish sources, determine what they have in mind, and use these findings to understand practices and perceptions that had been constant in the consciousness of the respondents' ancestors and of their mothers who had lived in Yemen (Madar 2002, 2005a, 2005b). A historical reading of the relevant texts creates an anchor of sorts that complements the ethnographic point of view, which often fixates on the respondents' statements and emphasizes the forms of the cultural present.

Another way of gaining methodological insight is by juxtaposing two studies, Madar's and mine. Although this state of affairs—two women researchers of Yemenite Jewish extraction performing independent studies (a thesis and a postdoctorate) in the same field—had not been planned in advance, in retrospect it subjects the research topic to an inspection that rarely occurs in qualitative research. Madar's conclusions, her interpretations, and the documentation and translation challenges that she faced are conspicuously lacking in contradictions. The act of combining studies about a waning cultural phenomenon that has not been graced with a meaningful presence in the literature is valuable because it creates a unique and nonrecurrent opportunity to assess the reliability of the claims, the interpretations, and the nuanced manifestations. Two researchers return from a field that throbs with mystery and offer, each in her own way, "merchandise" that does not allow contradiction. In view of the points and counterpoints that my respondents expressed, I consider this fact immensely valuable.

Methodological Rigor

"Writing down lamentations is the most terrible thing, the worst thing, the hardest thing. How can you sit among women and hear and write down what they wail?! It's not so simple." So I was told by the late Nissim Binyamin-Gamliel, the Yemenite Jewish author who published one of the few books about the song of Yemenite Jewish women.[3] Binyamin-Gamliel described with precision the experience that awaited me in several interviews with wailers. I could not skip or circumvent this experience and did not wish to forgo any part of it. If an interviewee agreed to wail for me, it instantly became an experiential interview that tested the influence of wailing on me, personally, and forced me to respond. Relating to this important necessity, Turnbull (1990) claimed that those who engage in fieldwork cannot rely on traditional methods of objective reportage about a performance—not because objectivity is impossible but because performance cannot possibly be understood this way. To enter a performance situation, one needs discipline, concentration, and also submission of one's inner self, which changes its form. In most cases, after an interviewee uttered several lines of her dirge, made their Arabic endings rhyme, and emphasized and timed her sighs amid the gushing of her delivery, I could not but lower my eyes, abandon all pretense of my interviewer role, and surrender unconditionally. The sound of wailing in midinterview undermined everything, shunted aside the protective mantle of daily life in one stroke and prevented any possibility of fakery on my part. When it was over, she lifted her hand from her eyes and met my tears—a woman with a different face. Perplexed, I sought a way to tie the loose ends down in order to proceed to the next question. During a peculiar pause that often occurred at these moments, we switched roles. The interviewee, just having concluded her wailing, gave me a soothing smile and then, tenderly, asked me about my personal losses and my worldview concerning them. I thought that this reordering of the interview was the most warranted thing of all. Having demonstrated a bit of her talent, the wailer now took responsibility for the implications of her performance. She had transformed me into a member of an imagined audience, and I now wished to be a receptacle in which the sounds and effects of the wailing would be assimilated and examined (Gergen 1997).

The demanding nature of wailing as a research topic found expression not only in this welcome reordering of the interview but also in the wailer's expectations. Admittedly, wailing performances that were offered on my behalf did not always work. On those few occasions, my ears perceived them as undifferentiated singing that lacked the familiar intensity. The moment the wailer lifted her hand from her eyes, however, I knew that she thirsted to find my tears. Her eyes scanned for familiar signals from her one-woman audience that would signify the confirmation of her talent. If I did not give the desired response at the end of her performance, she would send me a questioning half-smile about my feelings. Then, with telling accuracy, she would translate my emotions into an evaluation: the sadder I had become, the surer she was that she had wailed well, and if I had shed no tears, she knew that she had not scored a ten. When a wailer found that she had managed to upset my composure, she could barely conceal her satisfaction, saying, for example, "Look, you're crying, too." Dina let out a joyous cheer at the end of her wailing performance in the presence of another woman, as though my tears told her a story about herself. Both women repeated grateful remarks that they had received in mourners' homes—beneficent words for which the tears had served as a prerequisite. Their expectation of an appropriate response was so evident that had I sent a signal of indifference, they might have been insulted and might have terminated what had been fruitful interviews. I learned that I had to impress the wailers with my desolation, that is, to imitate the role that they assumed at the house of mourning—to create an impression of grief, to put on an act in front of women who had enacted others' emotions.

I also had to produce appropriate emotional responses in my observations at houses of mourning. When I sat among the crowd of women and listened to the wailer as they did, I knew I had to be on the same emotional page; that is, I must wipe tears or, at least, lower my eyes in lachrymose silence. Here again, I rarely had to pretend; the wailing performance spoke to my heart and attained its affective objective. Occasionally, however, the duty of the anthropologist won out, spurring me to separate myself from the crowd and turn all my efforts toward documenting the information. At one mourning event, women who had come to console the bereaved pushed me back to the edge of the mourners' tent. The moment the wailer began to perform, I was so far from her that I could not hear her properly. Worse still, no older woman who could translate the lament stood nearby. Then I noticed a hidden place outside the tent and very close to the wailer's seat where I could record the lyrics in my journal. Before I stood up to move to that position, I felt that I needed special courage to do so. All the women around me were seated, anxiously listening to the melody that filled the void. Were I to move around, I would surely create a disturbance or attract undesirable attention. As I weighed my options, one of the mourners, sitting in the group of men at the other end of the tent, suddenly stood up and rushed out, head bowed. An elderly woman, sobbing, implored him not to "run away" at the sound of the wailing performance for his mother. As the women stared in the direction of the dramatic occurrence, I picked up my purse and moved from one row of chairs to the next, eyes down and lips sealed. One of the women followed me. For much time we stood outside the tent, she and I, whispering about the wailer's story and learning things about each other.

Whenever I tried to explain my outsider's role among the women consolers or my bizarre wish to hear a wailing performance in midinterview, I noted that I myself was in *sh'nat evel,* a "year of bereavement."[4] These two words ushered me into the women's support circle. This, I discovered, is how women in Yemen added their friends to a lament that was under way. Hannah described this: "They put the deceased on the floor and then the women wail. And if someone comes and she's still in her *sh'nat evel,* [one of the dominant wailers] puts her in the middle. She gives her the emotion to cry, from her words. She lets her unburden herself." Netanel responded to my personal status by explaining that "If a wailer's father or son dies and she's in her year, then she's still full and she bursts into weeping." To my respondents, my being in the midst of my father's *sh'nat evel* placed me in a special situation that warranted consideration and, in turn, cooperation. Furthermore, my respondents construed my sharing this fact with them as an invitation to enter my world. The result was the downing of several barriers between researcher and subject and the establishment of two-way outreach.

My women respondents also noted their satisfaction whenever I uttered words in their native language. By using off-the-cuff expressions and sayings that facilitated relations in daily life, I signaled inside knowledge of the deep messages of their culture. My research activity gave me a first opportunity to demonstrate familiarity with the spoken vernacular in that I communicated a message rather than just listening passively. My use of the language in its right place and time gathered us into an intimate bubble, bridged the generation gap, melded our disparate cultural worlds, and banished all tension. At the end of the encounter, which could be called an informative interview, I found myself standing at the doorway of a house of women as a changed woman, dressed in different "attire" as it were. After determining where my parents' ancestral home had been in Yemen and guessing something about the mentality that had enveloped the residence, the women revealed to me that they and I might be kin. They mentioned names of people and families in an attempt to trigger associations of acquaintance and personal connection. They were so insistent about this that sometimes I admitted some tenuous connection; then the coveted relationship clicked, bringing with it a sense of peace of mind. I parted with them as a longtime acquaintance, a welcome guest, thanking them and reciprocating wholeheartedly as they kissed me good-bye and wished me the best.

A Local Ethnologist

I encountered my most important informant by chance, albeit a chance that I had intended to begin with. Unable to find enough interviewees in one town, I went on to another. The bus driver who took me there thought it odd that I asked him to let me off at the "Yemenite neighborhood" without knowing exactly where I was heading. After I explained my purpose and goals, he decided to drive me to the last stop, where other drivers of Yemenite Jewish origin would "certainly be able to help." I got off at the stop and stepped into the drivers' cabin, intending to go on from there to the homes of several

Yemenite Jewish women whom I had never met. My appearance among the male drivers, who were changing shifts, made an astonishingly weird impression. All eyes turned toward me. Meir, the job foreman, sat there, legs propped up on his desk as he bantered with one of the drivers. Noticing me, he put his legs down in a gesture of good manners and asked me to explain my presence. What followed was a significant turning point in my research: Meir became a partner in my fieldwork. He downed many of the obstacles that had been distancing me from observations and interviews, attenuating my frustration and sense of squandered opportunities. Meir is a paterfamilias who lives in a town that hosts a large Yemenite Jewish community, to which he belongs. When we met, he was verging on retirement and was known for political involvement in his place of residence. These two circumstances coupled with his character traits quickly made him into a perfect informant. His devotion to and facilitation of my research tasks greatly enhanced my data-gathering work. I was lucky to have met him.

"He has lots of connections here," an old acquaintance of Meir's said, alluding to the man's social status. Meir represented one of Israel's large political parties locally even though he believed in a rival party's ideology. The way he explained the seeming contradiction—tracing it to pragmatic considerations—inadvertently reinforced his "personal platform," which reflected his ultimate cause: helping to advance the well-being and image of the Yemenite Jewish community. Applying this reasoning, he linked my research to his public agenda and considered it an important way to preserve the legacy of Yemenite Jewry. During his involvement in the research, however, he considered himself external to what was happening. He construed his role—so I judge from his statements on various occasions—as a string-puller, an adviser, and an aide, nothing more. This manner of involvement portrayed him as a perpetually marginal person who has a hand in everything but does not allow others' hands to touch him. Practically speaking, he postured as a busy man whenever he wished to avoid social events and as a much sought-after personality when participation served his needs. We met regularly at several nearby rendezvous points out of town, from which he drove me to acquaintances' homes where mourning or social encounters were taking place. Then, offering some banal excuse, he drove away and returned to pick me up at an appointed time. His tendency was to set things up, drive me to the place of the encounter with my respondents, and take off at once. He spoke of the exotic beauty of the tradition that the members of his community were preserving; equally, however, he distanced himself from them as if he were an observer from the sidelines. I felt that even without academic pretensions, Meir did well to participate in my observations.

With his abundant and ramified connections, Meir was able to produce contacts and encounters that were tailored to my specific requests. When I asked to interview men, he introduced me to some forty men, who, as stated, gathered on weekends for the *takhsina* rite and deigned to take part in fascinating group interviews. When I asked to interview women in small groups, he drove me to a golden-age club and telephoned the directors of other clubs. First, however, he established relations between me and the director of the club, who drew up a list of appropriate women. Given the nature of group psychology, I feared that I might face a common front of self-justifying resistance in view of the topic of my research. I was afraid of being embarrassed, of loudly dismissive statements with the backing of various people, and of the helplessness of an individual such as myself against a united front of opposition. However, none of this happened. Each group, of women and of men, treated me kindly. When individuals manifested their disapproval, others hushed them. Ultimately, disapproval was expressed hesitantly, in the manner of a minority view.

"Grade me" were Meir's first words as I slipped into his car after visiting his hometown. As he drove me out of town, he said this as an overture to his own participation in the research experience. He translated the grade, on a zero-to-ten scale that he had devised, into a rating of my satisfaction and, in turn, of his contribution that day. It was a regular ritual with which we learned lessons and planned the next visit. On only several occasions, Meir did take part in meetings, attend funerals, and visit houses of mourning, first mingling in the crowd as I did and then shifting into observer mode. When we parted, he expressed his conclusions and suggested that I treat them as food for thought. His request to be graded, accompanied with an amused look on his face, alluded to the special position that he had carved out for himself, one that signified semi-involvement, almost noninterventionist and eager to be spared from the details. The grade provided a general assessment of the data gathered and created a narrow slot through which we could exchange impressions and thoughts. However, the grade also signaled his responsibility for certain aspects of the research and his freedom from responsibility for anything related to the research tasks. He was a loyal adviser who applied his discretion and his social influence insofar as I asked for it and refrained from imposing his views.

In one of our last conversations, weeks after I had concluded my field visits, I asked Meir how he perceived his contribution to the research. He said, "I'm one of those who caught the bug of saving the roots of the tradition, the values, and the authenticity of the Yemenite [Jewish] community. You touched on exactly this thing that's close to me. I'm against seeing the community assimilate or losing its values and roots. I'm definitely in favor of integration, but every community should maintain its uniqueness. I liked that side of your research." I asked, "Was it sometimes hard for you?" "It's not right to ask whether it was hard for me to help you or not," he corrected me. "The question is whether I got satisfaction from what I did. No one forced me. I did it willingly. I got satisfaction when you got results. That's the first question that I asked you every time: this effort of driving you around, arranging a place, making time available, making sure that the task was performed in the best way possible, without slip-ups. And then, on the bottom line, the results were interesting. That's where I got my satisfaction; that's where the fatigue stopped." Meir expressed a pragmatic stance: by helping with my research, he had sought to fulfill an idea.

When I asked him what specific value he had found in his contribution, he replied eagerly that "Anyone who could help you, and whom you got help from, created a blessing for us all. I'm happy to have been a piece in this jigsaw puzzle of all the people who helped."

The theme of wailing created multiple difficulties against its very investigation at the three levels described above: the potential of missing something, contradictions in the information, and the emotional demands of the topic. To tackle the first set of difficulties, informants paved my way to arenas of information and talented women. At the second level, I was given little substance with which I could probe the contradictions that the respondents expressed; they remained unsolved at the end of the research, and this is how I shall present them in this book. As for the third set of difficulties—the emotional demands—I asked Meir in one of our final talks, "Did wailing ever make you cry?" "Never," he replied. Observing the puzzled look in my eyes, he continued, "Because I know it's a show. I'm sure the women are putting on a show. I also know it from their stories. I know the wailer has no emotion; she just comes when they invite her. They say it's all *kharta-bart*a [make-believe], all the wailers that I got to know [laughs]." Thus, it was the distance that Meir had established between himself and wailing, his avoidance of its emotional purview, that explained his ability to help me in my research and made his devoted contribution possible.

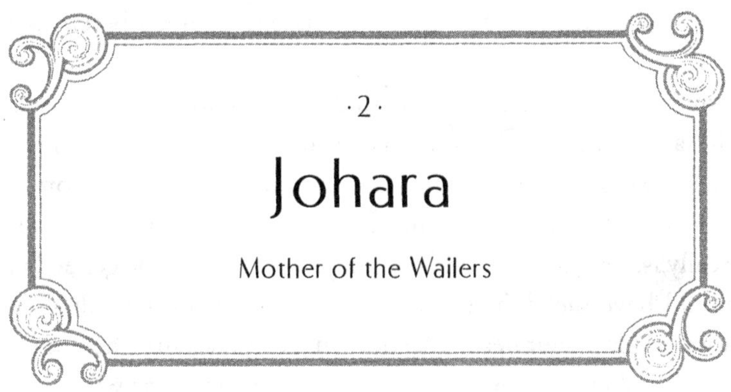

·2·

Johara

Mother of the Wailers

THEY CALLED THIS EMINENT WOMAN JOHARA. ANYONE WHO PRONOUNCED her name followed it with a metaphor of exaltation, as in "Johara was a jewel" or "Johara was a gem." Her name was uncommon in Yemen but walked before its owner like a loyal caddy and was the best-known name around.[1] They say she was born in Rada'a, the county of the great wailers. Her family belonged to the aristocracy of the towns of central Yemen. Her father endowed her with wisdom, pampering, and a coterie of servants. She loved him dearly, and his love for her and her ways exceeded the norm in parent-child relations and the standard in the impoverished landscape of those days.[2] Johara, pretty and intelligent, was the apple of her father's eye. The term "gem" fit her well, because she stood out like one among those in her community, symbolizing the loftiest of their emotions. You ought to "go far" and "aim high," her relatives said, wishing by saying this to express the uniqueness of the love that flowed to her and from her to her surroundings. If this description creates the impression of a childish sweetness or charm, it shows that thus Johara was remembered: as a living legend.

From my first acquaintance with Meir's community to the last, the name "Johara" worked its way into my journal and cemented itself there. My respondents, men and women, reached twenty years back or more to recall this nonpareil woman. "If you want know what wailing really is and what a wailer really is," one of them said wistfully, representing the general attitude, "you should have met Johara." Many respondents, in individual or group interviews nodded their heads like old-time cognoscenti when mentioning this womanly phenomenon, as if to say "You can't imagine what we've lost." The mere pronunciation of her name made their faces glow, even when said in reference to the lachrymose melody that was hers alone. Wherever Johara was discussed, unadulterated enthusiasm reigned. I learned about her from stories that ventured into deep waters of nostalgia for bygone days of solidarity and mourning. Several of Johara's relatives gave me lengthy, emotional, and highly informative interviews. Their stories, like others' brief mentions, blended into a sketch of Johara's private and public persona.

The sketch that follows, I should emphasize, was not culled from a direct interactive encounter, no matter how persistently I tried to engage other respondents in one. Instead, it is a composite of responses and comments influenced by the absence of the object of the conversation and the need to fill gaps between present-day knowledge and past reminiscences. Sometimes, by observing interviewees' facial expressions and manners of speech, I could sense the importance that they attributed to the task they had undertaken—to revive in colors and words all levels of this woman's personality and to serve it up to me in complete form. The phenomenon of distortions of memory, including the idealization of the dead and being influenced by the changing nature of the speaker's self-identity with the passage of time, is well known (Baddeley 1990). The mind plays tricks, blurring differences among facts, assessments, and interpretations and causing inaccuracies. A significant characteristic of Johara's narrated persona—her being an exceptional and complex woman, rife with contrasts of her own—made the predicament even worse. Given these difficulties, my attempt to describe Johara in a few keystrokes is viewed through the lens of her role as a wailer. My interpretation centers not on the real Johara but instead on the meanings of her persona as viewed by the respondents. In other words, I describe Johara only as an archetype that the interviewees cited to express their perspectives on the image of the quintessential Yemenite Jewish wailer. The more Johara was retold and spoken of, the better I would be able to usher the topic of this book—a wailing culture that had many participants—through the front door. The name "Johara," I found, was a code word for an inner truth that the interviewees, those who share a special cultural reality (although not fully), possess. The name is a canvas on which they sketched their imaginings and perceptions of the wailing culture without having to ponder overly direct or prying questions. In this sense, Johara, as a widely known myth, was not only an interpretive strategy but also a way of collecting data. By implication, while the question of how to represent a cultural reality by means of a narrated biography is not unanswerable, the answer proposed here should be applied with due caution. The question of representation and the discomfort attending to it are discussed at length in Bilu's (1993) biography of Rabbi Ya'aqov Wazana, which unravels its hero's life and death as retold by "references." The definition shared by both heroic and departed personalities, Johara and Wazana, may pertain mainly to them being objects of admiration and nostalgia, to their occupation with healing and with supernatural forces, and to their characterization as riddled with contrasts. The significant difference between Bilu's book and this ethnography is the extent of these personalities' centrality in the stories they tell. From this standpoint, if Wazana represents a grand hall where the readers pause at length, Johara represents a corridor that leads to the wailing culture at large.

Everyone called Johara *umm al-ma'aziyyeh* or *em ha-meqonenot* ("mother of the wailers"). At first I took this as hyperbole, but since it emanated from everyone's mouths and above all from everyone's hearts, I regretted not having met her. The impression that the sound of Johara's name made on me and the ordeal that her son recounted have something in common. "To this day," her son said, "years after she died, whenever I run into old-timers and tell them I'm Johara's son, they all hold their breath. I only have to say it and right away they want to tell me all sorts of things." The "mother of wailers" of the respondents' stories sometimes impatiently counted the days after the community's last death event, awaiting another mourning opportunity, "wanting to burst out." Some respondents said that she had considered wailing "her whole life" and "her reason for living." If she entered a house of mourning in the middle of the community rabbi's sermon, the rabbi would stop, welcome her, and wait for this "woman of honor" to take up her place. Johara the wailer was "like a Hasidic leader; she had followers who saw to her needs." In her presence, one heard murmurs of admiration, such as "That's the wailer, that's the wailer," or "Johara, Johara." Contrary to my expectations, however, respondents told me that during the shivah, for the greatest of wailers there had been no "deep sadness." Johara's relatives informed me that many members of the "crowd of people" who visited her home were unable to "remember her and cry." They remembered things that had made them laugh; accordingly, her shivah was also an occasion for laughter.

This chapter explores several overt and covert elements in the persona of Johara, the quintessential Yemenite Jewish wailer. These elements can be viewed on a continuum that parallels the chronology of her life. The first two sections, "The Dream of the Ten Dead" and "Fatma's Story," recount her youthful years, a dream, and a story about companions of sorts who called on her in the early going, before she became a wailer. The other sections, concerning Johara's wailing and character, relate to the persona that took shape later on. The sections about Johara's personality branch out but amount to a single configuration, so to speak, of the way I wish wailing to be appreciated: as a cultural phenomenon of existential significance and abstract manifestations. Despite Johara's complexity, her personality, over which many respondents wrestled, is a relatively convenient point of departure; it is concrete enough to serve this purposes and alluring in its bold colors.

The Dream of the Ten Dead

I heard the story from Johara's son. I wrote it down in the order of the events and the tone in which they were enunciated. Her son treated it as a veritable testimony that solidifies his claim that it was this event that destined wailing to Johara and Johara to wailing. Here is what happened:

> One day when she was a teenager, Johara took to bed. She lay there, depressed and weak, her eyes open as if the breath of life had fled her. For ten whole days she slept deeply. The members of her family lit candles and placed them around her. Ceaselessly they recited Psalms, pleaded, and wept. When the ten days ended, Johara opened her eyes and regained consciousness. Her parents and relatives were delighted to no end. Anguish and dread gave way to prayers of gratitude for the miracle that their loved one had experienced. They showered her with love and expressions of the concern they had felt.

According to Johara's son, however, his mother's face then was not like other faces. Although once again privileged with pampering at a level worthy of the princess that she had again become, Johara remained riveted to the memories of her lengthy dream.

> She spoke with her father privately and told him about the dream that she had experienced as though it had been real. "As I slept for those ten days," she related, "someone died every day." She recited the names of ten well-known townspeople in the order of their death. At the sound of this story, Johara's father was terrified. Although impressed by the persuasiveness of his daughter's delivery and the intensity of the event that she had experienced, he was very angry. He ordered her to shut her mouth and say nothing about the whole thing to a soul. He called the dream "stuff and nonsense" and nagged her to get back to the doings of her mundane life. Johara, however, was unable to forget her visit to the other world. Her life turned upside down. Whenever the fog lifted and new islands in the memory of her dream were discovered, she wished to share them with her father. Repeatedly she pleaded with him to admit, as her heart had told her, that she had received a genuine revelation.
>
> After she spent several weeks in total thrall of the impression of her terrifying dream, her father made up his mind and took her to the home of the town rabbi so that he would cure her of "this madness." The rabbi asked Johara to describe what had happened to her while she had been unconscious. Johara did so, listing the ten people who would be dying

> from that day on. The rabbi knew better than to dismiss her words just so. Familiar with the Jewish occult literature, he was frightened, too. The days about which Johara had dreamed arrived in order, and the first man died. He had been healthy; his death took his relatives by total surprise. Several days later, the second man died. Then everyone in town knew that Johara had been made privy to the secret of the world of the dead: "Johara knows about ten people who are going to die, and two of them have already died." With that, her father and the rabbi visited this person, who had been privileged with a portion of sanctity. They ordered her to seal her lips with bars and bolts, lest any of the names of the other eight doomed townsmen become known, even in the slightest. One of the doomed was Johara's sister. The dreamer indeed vowed not to divulge this; only surreptitiously did she observe her sister immersed in prayer in an attempt to revoke the decree. Her sister's appointed day was a bad and bitter one for Johara—her sister and her own two children died that very day; they fell ill and were snatched away with one blow of the lash of death. Johara plunged into grief; her dream had not revealed the fate of her own offspring. She wailed for many days, heedless of all words of consolation. Then, if her own agony were not enough, one of her sisters beset her with guilt for days on end. "Look, you knew and didn't tell us," "You knew and didn't warn us," "You knew what we didn't know," she blurted at Johara over the loss of her dear sister, a stunning separation that overwhelmed the survivors. Johara's triple grief was now compounded by pent-up resentment and rage—about the dream itself, her acceptance of the vow of silence, and the unbearable burden of guilt. The tragedy, compounded by guilt, led to a feud with her sister that lasted until her dying day.

Dreams wove their way into Johara's life and determined its progression. They also skewed the fate of people near and far. The Dream of the Ten Dead was recounted as a special event that had occurred in Yemen many decades ago, when Johara was young. The heroine's experiences during and after the dream were seen as transcendent of daily reality and ordinary consciousness. Eventually they turned cruelly against the person who had been crowned and honored on its account and became a tragic memory.

Johara the mother was around eighteen when she first assumed the wailer's role. Her pain did not subside as the days passed; it only mounted commensurate with the agonies that her silencing of the dream had inflicted on her. "The thing that made her cry," her son said, explaining the source of his mother's wailing, "was the vow." Johara responded to those days of strife by "vowing, you might say," to no longer participate in others' celebrations and to turn "only toward mourners' houses. . . . You might count on ten fingers how often she took part in happy events." She responded only to happy invitations from "very close family members, children and grandchildren. If you told her that mourners would be there, she'd be the first [to appear before them]." This choice of rituals and this manner of viewing her participation in them became the sacrifice that Johara offered for the sin that she attributed to herself, and these rituals gave her the catharsis that she needed to deal with the intensity of her grief. In this matter, Yemenite Jewish wailers resemble their counterparts in other cultures: these women, who elect to express their sorrow in public song, do focus on the dead but do not overcome their own suffering, losses, and distress (Wilce 1998; Benedicte 1994).

Fatma's Story

"Everyone in our home knew the Fatma story," Johara's son said. "Fatma was a story unto herself. Fatma is Johara. My mother was capable of telling the story several times a month. She'd wail to us after saying, 'I'll tell you a story that happened in Yemen.'" My interviewee's opening remarks segued to a thrilling, elaborate narrative that accompanied Johara and may have shaped the mental work behind her wailing and that of other women. For purposes of the presentation that follows, the text is as unedited as possible and preserves the order of events and the picturesque impression that the narrator conveyed.

> Once there was an ordinary family that had two parents and three children. The parents and two of the children died, leaving one boy. The uncle

pitied his nephew and took him into his home. The orphan grew up with his uncle's children and was like a brother to them. One of the uncle's daughters was Fatma, a cute little girl. When the children grew up, the uncle decided that his adoptive nephew should marry his daughter, Fatma. Fatma loved her cousin dearly but in the manner of a sister, and she couldn't imagine ever becoming his wife. Her father set the date of the wedding and attended to all the details and arrangements. Her mother hired a girl to meet all of Fatma's needs ahead of her wedding. As the wedding day approached, Fatma became anxious. Her father had not consulted her, and she knew she could not persuade him to reconsider.

In her distress, Fatma decided to run away. In the middle of the night, she climbed out of bed, got dressed, and left. From her parents' home, which was on the main road, Fatma saw a passing caravanserai being driven by black men who looked like slaves. The beautiful Fatma ran toward them and asked, "Which of you would like to marry me?" The head of the convoy, who alone had the right to answer, stared at her and said, "I would." She told him, "The price you'll pay my father is such as such." Hearing this, he immediately produced the specified amount, handed it to her, and said, "Please take it." Fatma took the money and ran to her parents' home. Silently she placed the money on the windowsill of her father's room and added a handwritten note: "Father, I'm sorry but I cannot marry someone who's a brother to me. Here is my husband's payment to you. You lack nothing; I've gone away."

Fatma's mother woke up in the morning and found the money and the note in her daughter's handwriting. Realizing at once that her daughter Fatma had eloped with an African, she felt an immense sadness. "Fatma," she said in anguish, "What will I tell your father? What will people say about us? What gossip will be said in the street?" and other sundry unanswerable questions. Thus Fatma's mother gave her father the bad news about her daughter's eloping. Realizing what had happened, he also began to sing a sad song but insisted that he did not believe his dear Fatma had left. As he sang, he became angry and wished his daughter never to have a grand wedding and never to have children. The intended groom heard what Fatma's father had said and trembled. He loved Fatma with his every

> fiber and considered her the wife of his youth. Then he, too, burst into melancholy song: "Fatma, I bought you a red kerchief. I bought it for you and someone else is wearing it. Fatma, you are the beautiful flower that I raised, and someone else has come and plucked it."
>
> The caravanserai, with Fatma now aboard, moved ahead slowly. The rear guard with his camel stopped at the edge of town to buy some more supplies for the lengthy trip. Word of Fatma's elopement had already spread through town. People repeated the lachrymose songs that her parents and her groom-designate had recited. The rear guard now caught up with the caravanserai and reported the contents of the anguished lamentation to Fatma and the men. This saddened Fatma greatly, since she loved her parents. As she heard the lyrics of her cousin's song, her love for him, the champion of her youth, reawakened. Then an immense sadness overtook her, for her act was irrevocable; she had already been sold to a stranger. She sang the misery, the sorrow, and the regret that now filled her heart. In her song, she said that her days were numbered and that she wished to be buried on the main road. When she concluded her ode of anguish, she plunged from the camel's back to her death.

Notably, the story that Johara's son told—an account passed on by oral transmission—corresponds to the character of the Arab heroine as reflected "in song, in legend, and in history" (Nicholson 1942, 76). Nicholson quotes the story of another Fatma, the daughter of Kharshev, from Arab antiquity.[3] Although the plot is different, there are perceptible similarities of motif between the story presented above and that documented by Nicholson:

> Fatma daughter of Kharshev was one of the three noble mothers who were coronated as . . . the mothers of the heroes. She had seven sons. . . . One day, Kamel Badr of Pizhar attacked Bani Abbas, Fatma's tribe, and took her captive. When he drove away the camel on which she had been riding, she cried, "Son of man, your capacity for understanding has gone into hiding. By the life of God, if you take me captive and if we leave behind the hillock that is before us, there will never be peace between you and Bani Zayad [the sons of Zayad, Zayad being her husband's name], because people will

> speak as they wish. Even an undifferentiated bad suspicion will suffice." "I will lead you," he said, "so that you will let my camel graze." Realizing that she was his captive, Fatma threw herself off the camel and died. Thus she perished lest she bring shame upon her offspring. (Nicholson 1942, 76–77)

In both stories, tragedy befalls a noble woman named Fatma, who prefers death and throws herself from a camel's back to avoid dishonoring her family. The moment she realizes that she has become a captive and may be forced into sexual relations with her captor, she unhesitatingly takes her life. Fatma is considered a heroine who sanctifies important values. It is not totally out of the question, in my judgment, that this story, like other works of folklore, has taken on and shed form over the years, metamorphosing into the Fatma story that was current in Johara's surroundings (Ben-Amos 1973).

In the story that Johara told, four characters—a mother, a father, a man, and a woman—burst into lyric song. Johara's son described the song as the libretto of a very melancholy "musical." He conjectured, on reasonable grounds, that it was a standard text that women had sung away from places of mourning in order to rehearse for a wailing performance. Johara regularly told the story in her family setting. She wailed at the segments where each of the characters "discovered" its loss. As in a musical, she delivered the connective segments between the songs in ordinary speech, and they were very short. As the structure of the story signals clearly, the characters' laments appear in sequence and at the end of the story, as the climax of a shared tragedy. By using this device, one could rehearse wailing without being disturbed by lengthy segments of speech that were extraneous to the actual performance. By the same token, this narrative style accommodated elements of rapid transition from melody to speech and back, creating the kind of challenge to emotional control that is typical of the professional wailer.[4]

Here I return to what Johara's son addressed as if it were a tautology. He said, "Fatma is Johara." By saying this, he drew a connection between the personal tragedy and the narrated one; that is, the story squares with the thinking part of wailing in ways that transcend mere structure. To the best of our knowledge, the story corresponds to the content framework of traditional song among Muslim tribes in Arab countries, which expresses a discourse of vulnerability, sadness, and self-pity. By and large, the story also reflects the emotions of love and sense of betrayal (Abu-Lughod 1986). The heroines of both stories are linked by an ostensible act of betrayal that dooms them to death. Johara and Fatma are fated to agonies of regret, and each dies a different death. The wailer trained herself to lament the bitter fate of a semi-imaginary woman, amassing the power that Fatma gave her as a reliable narrative for rehearsal purposes and inducing this show of force in the place of mourning. It was there that Fatma vowed to lament for herself due to the thing had brought the Dream of the Ten Dead upon her.

Fatma's story is special in that it has a wedding motif, one that maintains a well-known relationship with women's wailing. In many wailing cultures, and as my respondents showed me, death and marriage are two sides of one coin. One of the most extreme manifestations of this nexus is found in a lament that Danforth (1982) documented in a Greek village. Uttered by a man who appears to be on the verge of death, the lament likens death to a marriage: "Just tell them that I got married and took me a good wife. I took the tombstone for a mother-in law and the black soil as a wife" (80–81). This metaphor softens the indelicacy of death by presenting it as a state of transition that carries a person from one place to another. Nevertheless, it suggests that death has the disadvantage of being a painful separation (Holst-Warhaft 1995). Separation is something that deaths and weddings have in common among Yemenite Jews and in other patriarchal cultures. A bride leaves her parents' home and often her hometown; she moves in with her husband's parents and becomes an active participant in a strange household.[5] The fact that her parents receive a payment on her account establishes the irrevocability of the action taken. With this in the background, getting married is accompanied by a sense of crisis among Yemenite Jewish, Iraqi Jewish, Greek, and other women. Their wedding marks their first experience of elective parting from their parents and progenitors. Marryinggenerates loneliness, erects a buffer between them and their husbands, and anticipates the arrival of literal death. The connection between the experience of separation from family members and death is underscored in the wailing of Polynesian women, which describes, among other life events, the concept of burning the pain—a concept that relates to the emotions of a mother who parts with her dead child. The lyrics of these women's laments demonstrate that the event of birth, in which an initial and painful separation between mother and infant occurs, is analogous in their eyes to the experience of death (Seremetakis 1990). In marriage, too, which symbolizes fertility and giving birth, a separation-anxiety emotion settles into a fixation, and the symbolism of an abandonment amplified by death is added. A conspicuous example of the perception of loss occurs among Pakistani women, who attribute the onset of suffering in their lives to their weddings. Their story of suffering—a story of dignity—begins at the wedding and is woven into their wailing (Benedicte 1994). A male interviewee of mine made the same insinuation: "They begin to escort the bride [from her parents' home] with special songs, and what tears, what weeping, you should see the mother and father crying."

For Yemenite Jewish women, it was a twofold experience of abandonment. Leaving the home was often accompanied by suspicion that their parents viewed the marriage as nothing more than a sales transaction. The fact that the groom had to make a payment after dialogue and negotiations—behind the scenes and without the daughter's knowledge—magnified daughters' sense of abandonment by and distrust in their parents, who shipped their daughters out and kept the cash. Girls from poor families, who had to marry older men while still in childhood, were especially suspicious. Hava stressed this in the following way: "When a young girl in Yemen got married, she was very young, maybe thirteen. She'd marry an adult man. The women around her would cry about how she'd get along with him and she's just a girl, how he'd raise her, and what would become of her when he got old and died." Tsipora expressed this bitterly, sharing her marriage experience: "I got married when I was twelve. A woman in Yemen is just a servant. Her parents marry her off to whomever they want. My husband was thirty-five and I was twelve. My father would say, 'He learns Torah' [she says this derisively]. By the time I was fifteen, I already had a daughter." In one of my encounters, Na'ama drummed on the table and sang. Concluding, she recounted that she had protested to her father about having been sold to strange men. "What convinced you to sell me, Father? Tell me what convinced you. Was it the money? Was it the wheat? Or the butter or the cow?"

Biara, delivering her wedding song, said, "The daughter gets married when she's still small and has no breasts. Breasts are like roses. The man plucks her before she blossoms [develops]. She's with him for five years. She's a flower that hasn't opened yet." When a wailer was invited to sing at a celebration, she began with a very sad song—the sort that she delivered as she led the procession of women who escorted the bride out of her parents' home:

First you put your right foot ahead, then your left.
What have you still got in your parents' home?
You've got nothing left.
You're going to your husband's home.
You already belong to him.
Your parents already received the money.
They've already put the money on the scale.
And you can't do a thing about it.[6]

It is the sorrow of separation that conflates the tenor of the wedding event with that of mourning, even though the difference between them is perceived (Abu-Lughod 1993). Many respondents repeated the adage "The dead is honored with weeping; the groom is honored with singing." One of them even added, "They're different stories. If there's a dead person in one house and a groom in another—perish the thought—they go to the dead first and then to the groom. As they say, 'It's better to go to a house of mourning than to a house of drinking'" (Ecclesiastes 7:2). By articulating the contrasts and expressing them in one sentence, they show that mourning and getting married are taken to be parallel events that have similarities. The wailer Adina described her two roles as if they were one: "You have to make the bride happy and you have to cry for the dead." Rachel played a cassette of wedding songs, one of which retold the anguish of a bride who wished to visit her father's home and cries upon not finding him there. She pounds on the door, and no one answers. The bride seemingly describes the path that she takes to her parents' home, the profusion of her tears, and the emptiness, which makes "her heart burn inside her." The story in this song, the wailer explained, resembles wailing lamentation; the only difference between them is the type of melody. Indeed, the motif of searching for parents in one's childhood home and longing for signs of life and a response from them recurs in a woman's lament over her parents' death and in her wedding song. Such a parallel of contrasts is typical of wailing, which concerns itself with metaphors of wedding joy. The instrument of metaphor sets up a contrast between death and joy in order to amplify the tragedy (Danforth 1982).

Yitzhak, one of the men who deigned to be interviewed, described the wailing-wedding nexus similarly in the course of a group interview. "I think I know why women wail and not men," he began. "You know, when a woman gets married, she has to leave her family. She feels the enormity of the pain of separating from her family, because in Yemen she goes to a new family. In wailing, there's also a separation from the soul that's leaving us. A woman knows how to express this best because she's already experienced it." Thus, Yitzhak describes the gap between men and women in life experiences and cites it to explain the prominence of separation anguish in women's ordinary songs.[7] Jewish men in Yemen did not face the kind of powerful separation anxiety that women experienced. Never did men have to part from their parents except when their parents died. The expected sequence of life events set men up for a relatively easy farewell, since by the time their parents die, the men have bonded with their own families. Furthermore, men, unlike women, associated their parents' death with economic well-being and symbolic continuity due to their succession rights. This gender difference is also manifested in the linguistic structure of the wedding-and-death metaphor: at the time a woman gets married, she, the *isha* (feminine gender) parts with her *bayit* ("home," masculine gender). When a death occurs, the *neshama* ("soul," feminine gender) parts with the *guf* ("body," masculine gender). The woman, tantamount to a soul, symbolizes an element of consciousness and dynamics that death events have.

Fatma's story is one of a woman who plies her way between two lovers, her father and the person whom she considers her brother. The situation that overwhelms her pits these loves against each other and forces her to forfeit both. She is asked to convert her attitude toward a brother into an attitude toward a lover; she finds this emotionally impossible and, as a result, disobeys her father. Consequently, Fatma may be the heroine of a story about choosing between conventions of different emotional and moral weights. She is the woman who safeguards the values of her world and, by means of her choices, defends the emotional (whom to love) against the social (establishing a family at her father's behest). Confronted with both men's ambitions as described, she chooses between loves that are anchored in conventions and, more so, in values. So we learn from the beginning of the story. However, if we discuss all components of the story and above all its ending, we may see a different meaning in the betrayal: it is not Fatma who betrays her family but her heart that betrays her. She will find love elsewhere, her heart predicts. Her emotions trick her into viewing her intended groom as a brother; only at the end does she admit that he is her knight in shining armor. The tension between the situations, one a priori and one a posteriori, is so great as to be tragic. The emotional delusion, culturally expressed in the term "chaos," also finds a place in the stereotype of women versus the social order (Lutz 1988; Durkheim 1952, 1964; Fischer and Manstead 2000). The source of the flaw of this delusion is the realization that woman's emotionality carries power and the acknowledgment of its implicit element of otherness. Wailing per se, enunciated amid a crowd of people who have gathered on the occasion of a death and instilled by means of a narrative, is considered a feminine mechanism that has similar affective characteristics (Holst-Warhaft 1995).

Johara also rebelled against conventions but did so in her own way, that is, complying but in a circuitous manner. In Yemen, they say, she fell in love with her niece's husband. "She almost stole her husband," Hedva elaborated. "They hated each other." Describing the relationship that took shape between Johara and her lover, Hedva stressed that "Affairs were almost unheard of in Yemen. Johara was bestial. She took no one into account." During her life, Johara married three men and buried them all. Hedva related that "People called her a murderous woman [able to cause death] and were afraid to become her fourth husband." Ardent love and death were intertwined in Johara's driven persona and came together to undermine the convention of marriage. She followed her heart as though it were her captor, pursuing what she reserved as her own until, in the eyes of those around her, she overturned the ways of the world and overstepped their limits. In her old age, Johara wished to become a counselor and protector of young girls. She served them as a matchmaker, a sex and marriage counselor, and an interpreter between them and their husbands. At this stage of her life she still wailed in mourners' homes, where gender segregation was the custom. Her lover from bygone days appeared at these occasions, seating himself at the far end of the women's room and observing her at length as she wailed. She knew he was there. Of all the wailers, she was the only one whose voice he liked to hear. She lamented the loss of those whom she had loved, those who had died on her. To him, her pleasant voice was a veritable paean to the pleasure that he had experienced in her company. Some say that he seemed to have reexperienced forgotten moments of intimacy at these moments.

Johara's love life is inseparable from death. The last wailing situation I describe here reveals a lengthy and focused moment—a situation that accommodates all necessary ingredients of the theoretical strands that Bataille (1986) connected into a parallel between *erotique* and sacrifice. I wish to argue that at the moment of public wailing, a wailer figuratively offers herself up on an erotic alter, akin to the sacrifice that lovers make in the contact of intercourse. As the wailer unites with her audience, she denudes herself. She places herself on loan for the purpose of the catharsis of weeping, which unites those around her in a social bond of bowed heads and submission to nature. In so doing, she looks very feminine, incomparably alluring, a fantasy of unifying contact that drives the ego from memory and banishes it as if it were dead. Bataille considers the erotic an arena where an intersubjective encounter takes place. In this encounter, the barriers between the living and the dead fall—a pleasurable tumble into an abyss that occurs in the aftermath of an act of self-devotion. To my mind, one may use these very terms to describe the wailing arena: the wailer is, ab initio, only one party or entity among many entities that yearn for an erotic encounter.

The Sound

As I noted above, the descriptions of Johara's wailing were marked by wistful recollections of Johara as a person. Many interviewees, especially men, had known Johara more for her wailing than for the other facets of her life. To demonstrate this, some respondents lavished words on their descriptions of those moments when her voice rose, warbled, and gripped everyone in attendance. Some reexperienced this gripping effect so powerfully as to lose the power of description. "There was no one who didn't get goose pimples," one of Johara's protégées related. "No one could hear her and not weep. It didn't happen. She'd give words. I don't know. I can't even take apart the words that she uttered. I don't know where she got it from." Another woman respondent said, "She'd say such things about the dead that tears came up for you from under the ground. I don't know. It was something strong." Meir had only one thing to say about this: "She had a wailer's face. Sadness and weeping all over. She had a throat that issued mighty sounds." Another woman respondent, when apprised of the topic of the interview, said, "There was one who passed away; they called her Johara. God, when all she did was open her mouth, her voice was like thunder, a hollow voice of sorts that made a person cry even if he had a heart of stone."

Just as man could not withstand the sound of Johara's voice, neither could the mineral and animal forms of nature. Many interviewees described her wailing as having "made the stones cry." One of them added, "She had this voice as they say [in Arabic], *Johara t'baki a-tiyyur* [Johara makes the birds cry]. Birds cried when they heard her voice, her words." To substantiate the power of her wailing, respondents proposed men as a reference group for comparison: Johara's voice overcame the toughest of men and melted the coldest of hearts. Her son related that "I've been a boy, an adolescent, and a man. I didn't like it [the wailing] but if I heard it, I cried. Sure." He also described the responses of other men: "She could wrench tears from them. They couldn't help it. Even if they didn't want the embarrassment [of crying in public], they cried like little girls. Prideful men had to run away. Why? Because they knew they couldn't help it—my mother starts to wail, you're like glue. You're glued to your place. You're embarrassed. You just hear her voice and your tears [flow]." Several women confirmed this by asserting that Johara made even the men cry. Among the Jews of Yemen, as in many other groups, men's sexual identity is based on their restrained and unemotional nature—the polar opposite of the nature of women (Rosenblatt, Walsh, and Jackson 1976; Rosaldo 1974). Hanan put the connection between wailing and women into words: "A woman has characteristics of emotion. She expresses her pain differently, not like a man. Men are stronger. It's natural, that's how it's been ever since woman was created. That's also how it is between parents and children: the father is more demanding, the mother is more of a persuader." Johara's wailing overcame the differences and swept men and women into united sobbing. A woman interviewee recalled that "You should have seen how the men cried like babies and the women, *agha, agha* [imitating the sound of their sobbing]."

The power of Johara's wailing was translated into appreciation and honoraria, of which she received more than any other wailer. When she wailed, a special drama took place. Her son, who often escorted her to mourners' homes, related that "Today when a rabbi comes to a house of mourning, everyone goes *shhhh.* That's how it was with her. Once she got started, children didn't speak and no one made a sound. Total silence: Johara is wailing. It was something huge. They wanted to understand her words. The melody, everything was perfect, and all that remained was to understand." To explain how the situation proceeded, he put together a made-up dialogue of sorts that was factually unnecessary in the presence of the mother of wailers at a house of mourning: "How on earth can you people talk while this woman is ripping out our souls?" Then he explained: "[Her wailing] really ripped. For example, I could bring her over there and then run away, but my tears started right off, even if I didn't know who had died. She began to wail, and the game was up. Everyone was crying. I knew her. I didn't have to let her stir up my emotions right away. Even so, you couldn't get used to it." The lyrics, clearly enunciated, grabbed everyone's attention. This, Zvia said, traced to Johara's roots in the geographical culture of Yemen: "She gathered up her words back in Yemen. Her dirge was original. She was from Rada'a. They're bright, and you understand the words they say. They're words that all Yemenites would understand. Because some Yemenites have a different accent." Thus, Johara's wailing bridged linguistic differences among the various counties of Yemen and was able to affect a large audience.

It was Johara's practice to visit mourners' homes after morning prayer services or before evening services, either unescorted or delivered by relatives of the bereaved family after she assented to their request. A woman interviewee related that "First she comes in and consoles [the bereaved], using the expression, 'May heaven console you.' Then she sits down." Another interviewee continued: "She sits down strong, erect, beautiful, properly dressed, . . . and then she first talks with the people who are okay [not in mourning]." The first interviewee added, "She asks them all how they are and banters a little." I asked, "At what moment does she know when to start wailing?" "When she senses that it's quiet. When she sees people whom she knows will listen to her," the first respondent explained. The second one added, "She sat in the room where the mourners were sitting. She looked around. That's how she knew she could let herself go." Then she withdrew a small kerchief from her pocket, spread it out, and pressed it to her eyes with one hand or pulled the kerchief on her head over her eyes, and burst into wailing. A relative of hers recounted that "When she finished, she didn't stay seated. She'd straighten the kerchief over her head." Her son continued: "She'd get up and ask, 'Who's taking me home?' and say that she didn't want to stay. Only if it was a related family, then she'd stay a little more and catch her breath. She knew they'd pressure her to give another bit [of wailing], like an encore. If it wasn't family and they begged her to stay, she'd refuse, as if she were saying, 'I'm the one who counts. Otherwise, I'm out of here. I have a house of my own; I don't need to stay here.'" Then she would go home, either alone or escorted by acquaintances.

The sound of her wailing did not always stop there. Sometimes, amazingly, it resolved into the reverberation of peals of laughter. Johara, the breathtaking wailer, would issue a taunt amid the dismal atmosphere that she had created and remain at the focus of the crowd's interest. This, as I was told, happened mainly when the deceased were elderly. "After she finished wailing, she'd ask, 'Are we done crying?' And then she'd say funny things," a woman interviewee said. "You can't help but laugh," she concluded with assurance. Johara's humor was no less powerful than her wailing. At the end of her performance, she went out of her way to communicate her belief that "It's a mitsva to make the mourner happy." I asked two women, "What did she do that was funny?" She would quip in Arabic, they replied. She said things like "Hey, we're all gonna end up there [at the cemetery]" or "He just went first; we're gonna follow him, each of us when their time is up." One respondent related that "Once somebody said she'd begun to cry over someone who'd died and was already old. Enough! He already got his share [in life]. Enough, let him rest." Sometimes she sounded as if she were blessing the dead as though saying goodbye to living relatives, that is, wishing them a safe return. She would say, "Allah be with you." Those who knew Arabic well and understood the setting of these remarks laughed at the sound of this statement, lifted from its context. Sometimes Johara concluded her wailing visit by saying "Come now, let's give [the deceased] some rest. We cried for him; we said what we're supposed to say about him. Now let's give ourselves a little." Then, having expressed emotions and counteremotions, she would begin to amuse her listeners to the point of tears, thereby compensating them for the other tears that she had induced in them. Once she dared to tell an elderly woman who had lost her aged husband, "Enough, ya Shama'a [the woman's name]. May the devil be safely gone." What Johara meant was that she was giving her blessing for the journey to the devil. The devil was the old man who had died; while alive, he was known as having been mentally disturbed. The women I interviewed, rocking with peals of laughter that infected me too, noted that the mourners and the consolers had responded as we did at those moments. Johara's custom may have been surprising, especially if one perceives the wailer's job as the amplification of the sense of loss and sorrow. Here, as in her other wailing patterns, Johara overperformed; her laughter evidently reflected not only her ability to leap from one emotional extreme to another but also the perception of the meaning of these expressions of emotion—weeping and laughing—in the Yemenite Jewish culture: both are conduits to emotional release and psychological and physical solace. This functional outlook is saliently evident among the Balinese, who tend to repress sorrow and suffering in death events in the belief that they should distance themselves from bad emotions; instead, they put on a display of laughter and smiling, which encourage the bracing effect of good emotions (Wikan 1986).

"She wailed alone," Johara's relatives recounted. By saying this, they meant that she used the mourners' house as her exclusive venue of self-expression. What about other wailing women? "It was shameful to wail next to her," Hedva explained. "It's like a large man who dances. Another dancer might embarrass himself by standing next to him. There weren't many who volunteered to wail" in her presence. Johara's shoes were too large for the other women in her community to fill. She cultivated her esteemed reputation to her last breath. One of her tactics in this respect was retirement. A woman relative of Johara related that "Toward the end, she hardly ever went out to wail. It took lots of psychological energy out of her. She didn't have the strength for it. It was like a football player who quits while he's at the top of his game. He doesn't wait for people to boo him." "People never wanted Johara to stop [wailing]. Never," another woman said. "They always enjoyed hearing her, and they cried from their hearts." When asked how in the middle of her performance Johara decided when to stop, the woman replied, "She was flexible. When she saw that the crowd was really, really crying, then she felt sorry for them." Another woman confirmed my impression that "People talk about Johara as if she died only two years ago" and not fifteen. "They'll be talking about her twenty years from now," she assured me. Everyone confirmed that there was "no substitute" for Johara's wailing; in their narratives, they demonstrated that the sound of her wailing induced general anxiety.

The Metaphysic

The crisis brought on by Johara's youthful dream, the Dream of the Ten Dead, evolved into a constant and tortuous journey between two worlds: the living and the dead. The living and the dead were reflected in each other in infinite depth, like two enormous parallel mirrors. The end of life and the beginning of birth, curse and blessing, deep sadness and exultation, intermingled in Johara's contributions to the community all her life. She touched death, and her touch generated life, restored life, and created hope. The dead taught her how to predict the tonics that she would administer, and she mouthed with her lips, with infinite compassion, the secret of healing. The Dream of the Ten Dead was one of many windows through which she contemplated the timeless corridors of the soul. Her wailing magnified the sorrow of this world and clouded all segments of the corridor that led to light and darkness. In the eyes of those who witnessed her, Johara's image was wreathed in a single halo of love and fear.

With her own hands, she painstakingly carried out the religious imperative of *tahara,* that is, preparing the dead for burial.[8] She wailed not only in mourners' homes but also before the burial, as the body was entrusted to the skill of her hands and those of others. This is a wailing moment in other cultures as well (Briggs 1992; Aborampah 1999). Johara was a member of her community's burial society; whenever someone in her community died, she rushed to the *tahara* facility at the cemetery to wash and dress the corpse. As she worked, she wailed. The lyrics of her laments were addressed to the soul that had exited from its material shell before it could go too far; her wailing spoke to the dead. Johara took account of the deceased's limbs and their integrity, the agony of the loss of the contemplative soul, and the sorrow of parting with the living. She helped to immerse the body in the ritual bath, dry it off with a towel, comb its hair, trim its fingernails, make up its eyelashes, seal its orifices, apply perfume, and dress it in shrouds. She accompanied all these actions with dejected wailing that also addressed those whom she did not know and for men whose bodies had no one to care for them. Like other well-known Yemenite Jewish wailers as well as Yemenite Arab women (Meleney 1996), Johara was part of a broad cultural tableau that defined care for dead bodies as woman's work.

Researchers explain this division of labor by arguing that the preparation and purification of corpses by women are merely an extension of the duties of feeding and caring for children. These actions are associated with the fact that death in premodern societies usually took place in the home, the arena where women's skills were in evidence (Tilly and Scott 1989; Ulrich 1982).

Wailing while administering physical care for the dead was only one facet of Johara's dialogue with the dead. Her relatives and acquaintances related that Johara had, and still has, the reputation of a healer. (One interviewee even inserted the English word "healer" in her Hebrew diction to make the point.) Johara's son credited her with "healing scary things" and taking responsibility for the onset and continuation of life. Johara took care of underdeveloped babies and visited the dead for this purpose. A female relative of hers said, "She'd take the babies to the cemetery. The treatment required several visits. She'd ask the parents to bring something with them. If somebody died here, she'd ask for the water and soap that they'd used to wash him, and sometimes the towel, too. Then she'd wash the baby with the dead person's water and soap and wrap him up in the dead person's towel. She did with the baby what they'd done with the deceased. She did the whole thing without saying a word. She said nothing." Her son related that he had seen this from up close in the care of his brother, Johara's son. Johara, he reported, had covered the little boy with a dead person's towel and then passed him under the deceased's litter seven times. She performed all these essentials of the healing ritual in total silence: "She turned away to take the boy home without even saying 'so long' to the people at the graveyard."

Johara's style of healing led to cures and deliverance. The interviewees did not report it as something foreign to their compendium of cultural knowledge; instead, they recounted the gratifying results of her actions, albeit in the tenor of guardians of a purloined secret. Johara's son recalled her treatment of his brother: "Afterwards, at home, the boy slept for forty-eight hours and he got well. He woke up healthy. He ate and slept and developed like a man. He became a strong man, a tough guy." A woman interviewee said, "Those stories about treating [ill babies] are facts. You can't argue with it. I told you how Johara treated a girl who'd been born with my son, and today she's alive and kicking." One of the relatives described how women in the community remain grateful to Johara and her successful cures to this day; after all, their infants were the ones whose lives she had saved. A relative related that "To this day, whenever Rivka sees me she worships me as if I were part of Johara. You always see the gratitude in her. I myself saw two children who were sick and got better." Other women retold Johara's successful and famous treatment of someone else's child in the manner of a piece of very popular folklore: "Johara bathed the boy over the grave. She saved him. Now he's a young man. If she hadn't done it, he wouldn't have got better. Only she knew how to cure [children]. She knew. She helped everyone."

I had an occasion to interview Rachel, a woman who had been Johara's protégé and had personally been helped by her more than twenty years earlier. Rachel's story wreathed Johara's image in a halo of heroism and recalled the rituals of elders in traditional societies (Simmons 1970). Rachel went through a very difficult period in nursing, at least at first: "Blood came out of one breast. My son would throw up and refuse to eat," she explained tersely. The situation forced her to seek hospital care. Johara, however, sensed her misfortune and paid her a visit at home. "No one told her that something was wrong with me," Rachel continued. She then described the "medical miracle" that ensued:

> Johara asked me, "Did anyone visit you while you were nursing?" The moment she asked me this, I remembered that a woman had come to visit me and brought a pita with her. When she'd seen me nursing, she said she was sure I could nurse lots because I'm like a cow. You don't know what Johara did. She pulled something out of her kerchief and said, "You'll see, your baby will yet become a soldier." [Johara asked her protégé to let her visit her next Tuesday.] She brought food with her. She fixed us some *'asid* and *sman* [butter and porridge, a warm and nutritious Yemenite dish]. She asked me, "Who was the woman who visited you while you were nursing?" "It was my neighbor," I said. She went to the neighbor and said, "Do me a favor. You're like my mother. Come, let's help Rachel. Rachel's sick. You told her she could nurse like a cow. Maybe you didn't mean it, but she's sick." Johara asked the neighbor to bring some of her tattered clothing, hand her a piece of one of the garments, and to trample on the sand in the exposed ground. She then prepared incense and burned the sand and the piece of cloth in it. Finally, she asked my neighbor to spit at me. It was unpleasant. The neighbor spat at me and was asked to smear the saliva on my hand. I was asked to tell her, "*At bi-mehil*" [I forgive you]. It's a ritual that drives away the evil eye. It's called *naqas* in Arabic.[9]

> Two days later, I went to the hospital for a checkup. I couldn't believe it: there was nothing pathological in my breast; I didn't have to undergo surgery. Johara took something from the garden and some thick salt. She burned it over coals and waved it over the boy's head. She smeared it on the boy and changed his clothing. She took him to the cemetery one way and led him out another way. In the cemetery she laid him on one of the graves and bathed him. We went home by a totally different route. She asked me not to bathe him and not to feed him even if it made him suffer. Just let him drink. The next day, you can feed him gradually. I told myself that I'd give him one spoonful after another, and before I knew it he'd eaten a whole cupful. The doctors thought he might die. I took him into the hospital, and they couldn't believe it. Right away they called all the doctors from the pediatric department.

Johara sought to intervene in people's predicaments not only by wielding her curative powers but also by using the power of prediction in the domain of the living and the dead. She applied preventive intervention through the meaning of her words as warnings or as blessings. Hedva related that "Once there was this woman who had a really handsome boy. Johara sent people to her and said, 'Tell this woman that she should watch out for her son.' The woman asked, 'Who told you I should watch out for him? Johara?' And she added divisively, 'Pay no attention to her nonsense.' The boy died less than a week later." As for the ritual of blessing, Rachel had the following to say: "I loved her lots and lots. I was like a daughter to her. When I had my first period, I didn't know what you do. My mother wasn't home. I went to Johara to cry." I asked, "How did she respond?" Rachel replied: "First she took an egg and some flour and spun them over my head. Then she threw [them out] and said, 'Congratulations, now you're a woman.' She kissed me and said, 'Come to me.' I came to her and she put my hands in a bowl with some flour and some sugar and lentils and all kinds of little things. She said she did this so that I'd be blessed, so that everything I'd do from that day on would be blessed. Thank God, I think I'm blessed. I do something small and it becomes something big."

The interviewees described Johara as a woman well versed in the rules of occult metaphysical worlds. They touted her uncommon talents as a medium in various ways. One woman interviewee asserted that "She had mystical powers, like prophecy. She always knew things. She knew how to interpret dreams." A male interviewee said, "She always knew when women got pregnant, even if they didn't know." According to Johara's son, "She was something heavy." Another woman said, "She had magic powers. She could guess what a person was feeling even when he was doing fine." Johara acted in strange ways and indulged in silences; these amplified the sense of mystery that enveloped her and the impression that she was some kind of a medium. "Even when she came back from the cemetery or bathed a woman who had died, she did not talk," one woman said, indicating that she had been closely acquainted with Johara's doings. "She came home from the cemetery and washed her hands outside, in the yard, before she entered the house. I would call her, and she would gesture with her hand [closing her mouth] that she'd wash herself first and then talk." By means of her silences, Johara signaled that she had "gone away," that is, exited the ordinary world of the living and then returned to it. If, according to a certain theory (Douglas 1966), death is an ambivalent form of a woman's reversion to child care, it follows that she dirties herself by touching it (Goodwin and Bronfen 1993). Like the body that decomposes, the feminine is considered unstable, teetering on the brink, and bothersome. Death rituals are arrayed in such a way that women may first tend to the body of the deceased and then separate themselves from it. Death rituals and representations are typified by strategies that are designed to stabilize the image of the corpse (e.g., the construction of monuments and gravestones). Thus, symbolically, the body is allowed to distance itself from the destabilizing contact with the feminine. Johara's opaque and protracted silences allowed her to attain the opposite result: she wished by their means to stabilize her own image and her social affiliation whenever her forays to and from death endangered her status. Hedva's remarks reinforce this argument: "If she were alive today and you'd ask her if she had powers, she'd say, 'Nonsense.' She never admitted it, but she had powers. She was wise." I asked, "Why didn't she want to attribute powers to herself?" Hedva answered by offering a conjecture: "She probably didn't want others to know. She was afraid of the stigma of witchcraft. She didn't want it; she was afraid people would avoid her."

One of the things that sustained Johara's reputation was the absolute contrast of her silences; it established continuity between the spheres of life and death. Zvia expressed Johara's main social role pithily: "Johara washed the dead and nursed the sick." Zvia's description suggests that once Johara undertook the role of caregiver and sought to revive someone's emaciated body, she attached herself to it until his dying day and beyond, until the end of the shivah. At first, she did everything she could to effect healing with such medicines and rituals that she knew. This failing, she planted herself at the place where the person took his last breath and prepared the body for burial. She experienced the visceral transition between the signs of the imprints of life and the last indicators of the release and throes of death. Her skill in caring for the body was applied with the same devotion, the same motion, and the same tone of anxiety and sympathy. Again, her contact with the corpse included bathing, applying perfume and makeup, and performing other sundry acts of painstaking aesthetic care. At those moments, the corpse resembled a living body and received the same maternal compassion that babies and children receive. The impression of compassion was amplified by the lamentation lyrics and the sorrow that Johara expressed even before the body was removed from the house. As a healer, Johara acted as someone who might or might not be responsible for the failure of the treatment given. By preparing the body for burial, she expanded her purview. She was known as someone who had a hand in all stages, both healing and *tahara.* This may have signaled to the onlookers that healing was not a foregone conclusion. Their knowledge of this may have insured her against criticism and blame. Basically, the preparations for burial resembled and were a logical continuation of the acts of devoted care. They and their adjunct—wailing—were perceived as a way of expressing respect for a person, living or dead, and something that might console and also silence his or her relatives.

Breaker of Walls

Johara is an expression, a performance, and a reality of a type that the Yemenite Jewish culture and other wailing cultures attribute to wailing. She represents wailing in the sense of a feminine performance. From its broad perspective, this book is an attempt to shed light on the enigmatic, complex, and multifaceted phenomenon that wailing is. The same may be said about Johara the woman. "Johara is something that can't be explained. She's an exceptional personality, hard to define. It's hard to fit her into a framework and say 'That was Johara,'" her son ruled. Inadvertently but directly, his remark alluded to the essence of the wailing culture and recommended ways in which the culture could be redacted into an ethnographic narrative.

As previously stated, Johara was married to three men during her life. She was considered alluring; some described her appearance long ago as the embodiment of beauty. According to the perception of female beauty in Yemen, light skin pigmentation that emphasizes the shape and color of the eyes is preferred (Piamente 1984). A family member described Johara as "very white," having "blue eyes" and smooth, tender skin "without bodily hair." One women interviewee recalled having specialized, as a girl in Yemen, in dressing women in traditional wedding attire and having performed this service for Johara. "Johara's sister sent her a magnificent outfit from Palestine. She sat on a bed and I went up on my knees to dress her," she explained, immediately adding a bygone memory: "She was gorgeous, gorgeous." To emphasize the last word, she not only repeated it but closed her eyes as if amazed anew. Another woman respondent related that "She had such a beautiful body. She was tall and light-skinned, almost a redhead." Johara's appearance was atypical of women in Yemen, most of whom are swarthy and dark-eyed; she stood out as an uncommon ideal of the prevailing notion of beauty.

Johara's beauty—one facet of the definition of femininity—was offset by elements of masculinity that people attributed to her personality. "She was aggressive," her son related. "You couldn't mess with her at all. They called her 'a man and a half.' In Yemen, they said she also beat men. If she had to do battle, so she did." All interviewees persistently described her as a "strong woman." "If you don't respect me, I'll wipe you out," a relative said as a demonstration of Johara's state of mind. Then he added, as if summing up the matter, "That was Johara." An admiring woman respondent imitated Johara's sitting posture and facial expression to demonstrate that Johara was a straight-backed woman who projected pride. Many respondents said that she had never been afraid to say exactly what was on her mind. They called her "honest" and "straight as a rod." "What counted most [for her] was the truth," irrespective of the price she might pay for saying it. The interviewees sometimes expressed the contrast between these personae, the female and the male, in the same breath. "She was a classy woman, like a man," Shula said. I asked her, "What do you mean by 'like a man'?" "She was strong, healthy, beautiful, good," Shula replied. "I loved her as I loved my mother."

One interview brought the clash between Johara's personae into clear focus. Her beauty was taken as a constant in the interplay of strength and weakness. Hedva described it: "Everyone will tell you that Johara was strong and powerful. She always put on a show of strength. That was her image. She must have told herself that she mustn't be weak, after all, that's the reputation that preceded her. But I'd see her points of weakness. If she wailed for a relative or someone from her town in Yemen, then she'd continue to cry at home. But she did it quietly there. At home, her crying was real. Sometimes she took a bottle of *arak* to escape from reality. She'd get drunk and fall asleep. Sometimes she'd come after wailing and smoke a narghile. She wouldn't say a word; she'd sigh. At the mourners' house, she'd talk like a hero and say, 'He's dead and we're all going to be dead,' but inside she was sad. She made you believe that [the torment of mourning] didn't get her down, but she got down." The interviewees moved up and down a continuum of symbols and behavioral manifestations that can be interpreted in accordance with female and male stereotypes. One of the men bridged heartrending beauty and emotions of self-pride, audacity and the tenderness of her voice, by explaining that "Johara knew how to display strong weakness."

Where the wailing performance was concerned, tears played a role in tipping the scale of the impression toward strength or weakness. "She could wail without shedding tears," Johara's relatives revealed; others suspected this as well. One of them emphasized that "If Johara shed tears, they were real." When relatives accused her to her face of revealing her "fakery" and not really crying at all, she defended herself by asking, "Where would I bring tears from?" Countering the charge, she would express puzzlement about these women's very puzzlement about her ability to maintain equanimity while her listeners heaved with weeping. Sometimes she simply apologized, as if demonstrating the extent of her emotional distance, saying, "I don't have any tears." To convince those around her that she was crying from the bottom of the heart—so I was told—she smeared saliva on her cheeks and around her eyes. "She was a good actress, a politician, you might say," a woman relative said. "She had to make you believe she was crying. She'd persuade people." This strategy indicates that Johara sought to conceal her very ability to control their emotions and wished to stress her identification with her audience, in whose honor she was play-acting. If she shed tears, they would testify by means of their precious, special glimmers that she genuinely felt bad about the death of the object of her lament. Nketia (1969), observing Akans in Ghana, described the importance of the wailer's demonstration of emotions during the performance. His account corresponds to the accepted perception in Johara's surroundings:

> A good singer wins in emotional appeal: She moves her audience. Nevertheless, a funeral is not the occasion for mere display, though the temptation is great and many succumb to it. One of the requirements of a performer is that she should really feel the pathos of the occasion and the sentiments embodied in the dirge. Pretence is condemned and mock-sadness is discouraged. A tear should fall, lest you are branded a witch and a callous person. If a tear is physiologically difficult to shed, you must induce it by some means; but if it is physiologically impossible for you, it would be better to have the marks of tears on your face than nothing at all. (Nketia 1969, 9)

One story that I was told may upset the reckoning of truth and pretense in wailing. The story was presented in several ways on different occasions by

Johara's female descendants. The mother of one of them had died. Before she was buried and as Johara arrived to wail, several women relatives of the deceased turned to Johara and demanded that she refrain from the unwanted custom of smearing saliva over her eyes. Instead, they demanded a show of "real tears," since the deceased had been "a really special woman." It was an absurd thing to ask of an actress—that she feel and not merely create an emotional atmosphere befitting the state of bereavement. They magnified this absurdity by expressing this demand in the jocular way that, as they knew, was typical of Johara. The wailer answered in the same coin: she promised to cry but said so in the somewhat humoristic tone of voice that the grieving women used in order to level funny imprecations at Johara and absorb funny imprecations from her: "You know I loved your mother, and I'll cry for her for real." The daughter of the deceased attested that Johara "really wailed. She cried a flood." Before doing so, however, Johara made a conciliatory promise: "I'd put spit for your mother?! I'll cry for her forever. If only I had died instead of her."

If there are schemes or categories that guide our perceptions of truth and pretense, emotion and make-believe, this episode greatly broadens their limits. This collection of relatives, who ordinarily knew how to distinguish between false wailing and real wailing, between saliva and tears, no longer knew which of them was being offered. The only thing that Johara managed to promise was that the saliva, as a symbol of play-acting, would not be used in the performance over the interviewee's mother's death. Therefore, the interviewee reported that Johara "really wailed" because, after all, she could not know whether Johara had been really sad. In her just-kidding response to the women's demand, precisely due to its weepy delivery, Johara deprived her tears of the symbolic insurance policy that carried her down the course of her life. Her external manipulation (the smearing of saliva) became an internal one, with no transition from surface acting to deep acting (Hochschild 1990) taking place. In other words, her weeping did not attest to real emotion; instead, the weeping itself became a kind of show. The act that Johara was asked to perform was a high-order one, at the pressing behest of a suspicious audience of eagle-eyed women. Either way, she left her audience deceived or, at the very least, confused.

The blend of extremes in the recounted image of Johara recurred when I asked my respondents about her attitude toward religion. The religion and its canon beliefs, as well as God's explicit commandments as reported in Scripture, served Johara as items to interpret and disregard. She cultivated the appearance of a woman who scrupulously observed the most important commandments. Her relatives' remarks, however, showed that while she did not toss Scripture aside rebelliously, circumstances of temporary expediency and social sentiment presented her with a temptation that she could not resist. Girls loved to spend time in her open house and surreptitiously desecrate the Sabbath there. Some respondents described the signal that she sent on those occasions: she had no authority "to tell the young women what to do" or "forbid them" to act in any way they pleased. She depicted her religious and moral responsibilities as circumscribed by personal autonomy; concurrently, she sought to conceal the "wantonness" in her home from the public eye. Once on a trip out of town, she even desecrated the Sabbath herself by traveling on the holy day on grounds that were too flimsy and unacceptable to justify such an egregious breach. Due to indiscretions such as these—which amounted to nods of sorts to the practices of the secular Jews on the other side of the Israeli divide—many of adolescent women aligned themselves with her wholeheartedly and considered her one of them. For them, her home was a shelter from parents, a place where the girls could rebel and change masks. They remember it as being positioned between two cultures, Eastern and Western, a place where holy and profane customs intermingled.

Another account of something that happened in Yemen shows that Johara consulted only herself in matters of life and death, to the exclusion of authoritative decision makers and rabbinical decisors. Her brother came down with a serious illness. The dismayed family turned to rabbis, who ordered them to perform a symbolic sacrifice as an act of atonement. A woman relative of the brother related that "They went to Johara and told her, 'You should be his atonement.' She retorted, 'I'm going to atone for him?! Use a cow instead.' The rabbis replied to Johara, 'But he's your only sibling, all your other siblings have died, and he's male.' Johara stood her ground anyway: 'In no way do I want to atone [for him] and sacrifice myself.

God gave everyone his life. If you want, take one of my cows. She'll atone just fine.' The relatives protested: 'It's got to be a person, not a beast.' When she answered vehemently 'I don't want to!', the patient's two sisters stood up and insisted on atoning for him themselves. They circled him seven times. Accordingly, within a few hours he recovered, and they took ill. On their deathbed, Johara saw fit to tell her sisters, 'I'll wail for you [a routine expression of derision and anger]. God gave you life and you chose to forfeit it in order to atone [for someone else].'" The relative concluded that "Even when the rabbis explained [the alternate-soul atonement ritual] to her, she wouldn't accept it."

Where the sanctity of wailing was concerned, Johara also decided what to accept and what to reject. When Tsipora's uncle, a formidable religious scholar, died, his family invited Johara to wail. She duly reported to the mourners' house. According to Tsipora,

> Everyone honored my uncle and cried lots over her words. Heaven and earth cried for him. She came to wail in the morning, after everyone had finished eating. It went on for several days. On the fourth day, the people waited for her so they could cry. They said to her "Johara, *yalla* [wail already]," but she said "No, not a word." They asked her, "Have you lost your mind?!" She said, "Not a word." "Why not?" "He," Johara replied, calling him by name, "came to me last night and said, 'Johara, you did everything you had to do [wailed for me] for three days. From the fourth day on, I ask you to stop wailing. You know it's forbidden. Three days are for weeping. Not more.'"

By imposing this limit on herself, Johara reminded those in attendance of the well-known prohibition—almost an article of rabbinical law—that women should wail and inspire weeping in public for the first three days of the seven days of mourning only. By refusing, Johara not only cultivated her professional image as a performer but also applied proper limits to her performance. By divulging her dream, she absolved herself of responsibility for her refusal but enhanced her reputation as a wailer who was accepted not only among the living but also among the dead. By explaining this sweetly, Johara informed her listeners that she submitted to the dictates of the canon ritual but wished to keep them within her private domain. The impression of religious conformity, to the extent of piety, was something that Johara implemented in front of her audience before seating herself as a member of the collective.

Was Johara a religious woman in the accepted sense of the term in her community? The answer seems complex. The respondents' remarks alluded to a connection of sorts between religiosity and its opposite (e.g., her tendency to go easy and flow with the accepting religious imperatives), in contrast to other women's strict observance. In saying this, they implied that Johara had acted religiosity in accordance with the imperatives of her personality, that is, her social needs. In her casual approach to the commandments and the accepted proscriptions, Johara ostensibly drew on her access to secret sources of the highest authority. Others could pray, divine, and worship to exhaustion; she dialogued with the world of the dead. Although this dialogue could not be fully articulated, its imperatives were totally valid for her. This validity absolved her of the compulsive male religious ritualism that inhabited the world of the living. My purpose in mentioning this is to challenge the possible claim that the story of Johara's dream about the man who asked her to stop wailing is merely an act of exploitation, culmination, or cultivation of the image of the wailer. Presumably, Johara cited the deceased's request as she had indeed seen and heard it in her dream.

People are drawn to mysticism in death events. They attribute amazing significance to the contents of their last contact with the dead, dream about the dead, hear voices outside of the dream, and contemplate agape the coincidences and sequence of events that led to this moment. Wailing women know how to milk these feelings to special dramatic effect. They manage to greatly amplify the unconscious experience and give the appearance of mediating between the living and the dead. In the Akans of Ghana, for example, wailing women at funerals are totally susceptible to possession by the spirits; thus, they reenact with their bodies the deceased's experiences and aspirations as the onlookers had known them and reenact other experiences and aspirations that the onlookers had not known. To perform this drama, the wailers emulate speech, clothing, and dancing; send messages and advice to grieving family members and the community; and predict events and disasters (Aborampah 1999). "They are expiation and forgiveness for all the dead. You shouldn't think about the dead too much," I was told by Tamar, a wailer who, like Johara, also washed dead bodies. Tamar spoke of the dream as a dangerous window; her words returned me to the motif of the dream, with which I began to tell Johara's stories and with which I now conclude. I asked Tamar, "Do you sometimes dream about the dead?" Tamar replied, "Perish the thought. Nothing gets into my head even if he's standing next to me, unless I summon him: 'I want to see you, so you'll tell me at night what happened to you.' Then his image suddenly [appears]. In Yemen, my mother told me that someone had summoned someone who'd died and he came at night. I don't [summon the dead] aloud. In the dream, he comes and tells everything that happened to him. I'm all alone at home; I don't dare." Unlike the Akan wailers, who communicate with the dead in public and allow the dead to express themselves dramatically, and unlike Tamar, Johara demonstrated the breaking of another wall, that of fear. Respondents said that Johara would "go down to the dead at night in her dream." She reported the fact of the dream to those in the mourning arena and communicated something of the message calmly, rhythmically, and in ordinary language. A woman relative of hers, one of those in whom she confided, personally witnessed Johara's talent as a medium. It was evident not only in the quiet way in which she retold her experiences but also in the esoteric and minute contents that "preoccupied" the dead woman's soul: "On the second day of mourning for my mother, [Johara] woke up in the morning and gathered my sisters around. She told us that she had dreamed that my mother had come to her. Look, we didn't believe everything she said. We said, 'Stop talking nonsense. We have no patience for you. Our mother is something [that you can't talk about just so].' Then she began to swear so that we'd believe her. With that we said, 'So tell us already! What did you dream?' She said, 'In the kitchen cabinet on the right, on the bottom shelf, there's a can of paint. Your mother hadn't had time to paint the gate and asked you [sisters] to bring her the paint.' I asked her, 'Dear, when did you poke around there so that you could make up these revelations?' She answered in her regular way, by cursing. I asked my sister to go to the kitchen and check. Well, there was a can of paint right there. It was amazing. She told me that back in Yemen she'd been like a medium. In Arabic they call it *masfaleh.* She'd do the *sifl* [a special ritual performed by a medium]."

Johara's profile as a member of a small community and a reputed wailer accommodates an abundance of contradictions and contrasts. Her close acquaintances, not to mention her distant ones, were unable to harmonize her disparate traits and array them on a single linear or coherent descriptive continuum. In their stories, she broke walls. The narrators, in contrast, come across as people who, bidding farewell to her over the years, clung to conventions and relied in their lives on the strength of such walls, however sociable they may be. My encounter with Johara induced enormous outpourings of melancholy and delight that the respondents had not experienced anywhere else; however, their encounter with her had been a transitory one that they had not internalized. In their recollections, Johara remained an independent force whose contradictions sliced through boundaries and separated her from the masses. Her wishes and her profound miscalculations distanced her from convention in both directions, toward things that were clearly very proper or very improper. The power and persistence of Johara's contradictions made it possible for her to oppose the wisdom of the social order, a wisdom concealed from the eye and, it would seem, hidden in the depths of its recesses. These very contradictions brought the gamut of facets of her personality, including those on her shadowy side (Jung 1960), to general fulfillment. From the wailer's stage, it was, in a sense, an intensive theatrical realization.

One may see in Johara what Handelman (1990) calls a symbolic type, an autonomous entity totally loyal to its proclivities and usually attracting one of two responses: rejection or sympathy. Liminal connections such as a mourners' house are considered abnormal, timeless, vague, marginal, and sacred (Leach 1976, 35), fertile soil for the creation by a society of the symbolic type and the perseverance of its appearance. Basically, the symbolic type represents a set of clashing characteristics: the sacred and the profane, wisdom and stupidity, sadness and laughter, heaviness and lightness, etc. The symbolic type creates inconsistency of meaning, vague points of view, and insecurity. To Handelman's mind, the symbolic type abounds with play-acting and non–play-acting; it moves among alternative realities without resolving the paradoxes of what lies beyond and without creating an overarching message that would surmount the paradox (Handelman 1990, 242–43). Johara's persona shuttled between poles in her daily routine. It was always at the threshold of familiar social categories and enhanced the richness of their boundaries. These poles lost much of their strength during her wailing and evolved into a balanced web of messages and countermessages, within which she transported her listeners. Indeed, there is a strong correlation between wailing, as a performance, and the nature of the symbolic type. This correlation emerges from the argument that performance impels the symbolic type to be serious and to entertain, to be itself and to play-act others, to be in a trance and to be conscious, to induce results and to induce madness, and to elevate the there and then to the present and sustain the here and now, among other opposites (Schechner 1976). The persona of Johara accommodates hints of feminine weakness and manifestations of masculine strength and aggressiveness, depending on how those around her perceived them. The externalized strength and strained frivolity that she evinced in mourners' homes were shattered by the tears and the quiet that closed in on her motions in her own home. God's will, as expressed by His spokesmen on Earth, was circumvented by the force of her intelligence and in her dialogue with the spirits. She would return from this realm of the unknown to affix to herself the image of an observer of the religious commandments, as if she were like other women. Wailing served her as a safe house, where she could rummage through her overt and covert self. She placed herself on loan, as it were, to give her listeners an opportunity to glimpse the way she contemplated the human condition from one extreme to the other. Death is an event that magnifies existential dilemmas, material contradictions, and paradoxes that create a place for the wailer once she gathers them up. The typical disorder of the event and the wailer's psychological innerness may release, in the encounter with her, a great deal of energy and may translate into healing and fruitful power in terms of its potential to change the social order (Turner 1969, 1974; Douglas 1966). States of illness, like states of mourning, are perceived as deviations from a balanced and harmonic social order. Johara, both as a wailer and when she was out of character, abetted healing in both situations due to her very ability to break down contrasts and keep them in delicate balance. The nature of her actions and her strength are akin to those of shamans in traditional societies (Myerhoff 1976) and also to some extent to those of the Ajuz, elderly women among the Sinai Bedouin whose advanced age relegates them to a liminal place in the tribe but invests their allegorical performances with great influential power (Lavie 1990).

By contemplating the images of and stories about wailing women who still live in their communities, I found what the respondents found: Johara, as enshrined in their memory, represents the image of the ultraideal wailer. That is, her best-known ways mirror her wailing: her ability to bridge the gap between the living and the dead, to have compassion for people's psychological ailments, to manipulate their emotions with stunning power, and to earn their admiration. I have told Johara's story as an overture to the remaining chapters in order to hint at the possibly contradictory manifestations of a wailing culture. Her story raises issues great and small that link wailing to religion, marriage, betrayal, birth, play-acting, separation, social status, the dead body, feeling, caregiving, aesthetics, and performance, to name only a few. These and other issues, some of which I mentioned briefly and by allusion only, will merge to complete the cultural jigsaw puzzle. Additional elements of Johara's image, especially those relating to her expertise as a wailer, are unveiled and unfolded as my description of a women-led culture branches and develops.

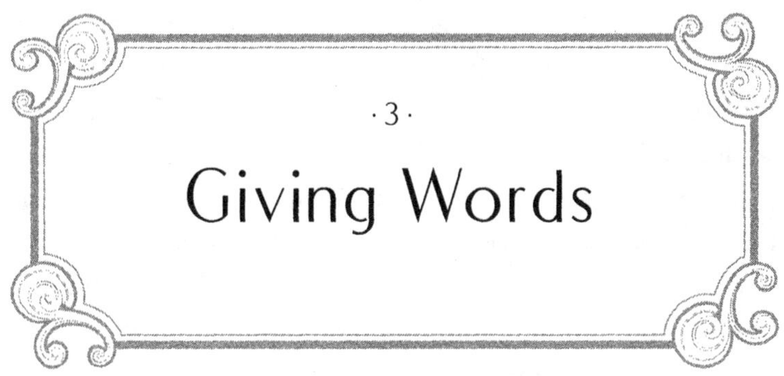

·3· Giving Words

Wailing is an outpouring of a speaker's heart, akin to a collection of evocative metaphors, and represents the possibility of transforming experience into words. Wailing crafts the experiencing of trauma, the sensing of loss, and the heartache of anxiety into a verbal art (Finnegan 2001)—a translation of tears into ideas (Holst-Warhaft 1995, 22)—and melds one word and then another into an irresistible metaphorical structure. In this chapter, we artificially separate two performative dimensions of wailing: content and articulation. The two are inseparable ab initio. In her performance, the wailer tells a story about the deceased in a lyrical singsong. One of my respondents, a wailer, demonstrated this in her remarks. "The words, the words," she began. "That's the most important thing they hear, it makes them burst into tears." But then she added, "It's the voice and the words. You just begin the melody and *everyone* [my emphasis] cries." Even though wailing makes its emotional impact by blending the two dimensions, and no matter how seriously this may diminish the representation of the "stylistic reality" (Finnegan 2001, 177), the analysis that follows cannot treat them as equivalent. The vocal dimension, fundamentally experiential, is analytically obtuse; the verbal dimension, which I discuss as a complex and categorical discourse, is not. In accordance with this distinction, I treat the melodic or singing element as a theme in the respondents' attitudes in the chapter 4, "The Performance Stage."[1] In this chapter, I present, describe, and analyze the lamentation lyrics. The wailer's words, it turns out, have a representational status because their contents are of interest to the full range of participants in the death event. The words used by the wailer also correspond to rhetoric that has the effect of working through the mourning that is taking place, a process so necessary at a time of crisis. We will see in this chapter, as a text per se, that the separation of words from melody is not the only separation that takes place.

My respondents often spoke of "words" and attempted to describe and wax nostalgic about them. Sometimes, several women doubled the term "word," creating the expression "*milim-milim*" ("words-words"). They accompanied the repetition by rubbing their fingers against each other and then touching their lips with a kiss, as if to say that one can derive pleasure from the words. The words were only one facet, albeit a very creative one, of the splendor of wailing. Words-words are what respondents noted when relating to the reputation of the lament or the wailer. This accepted coinage sufficed to define wailing as an aesthetic experience. To some extent, the term resembles the impressions that art critics, who may be effete but are also uncompromising and ungenerous, are known to report. Literature describes the aesthetic experience in a way that allows us to detect the meanings of the message that the men and women in my study expressed after having experienced something like textual gratification. The aesthetic experience is a unique one, exceptional in its ability to induce pleasure and often suffering and pain, but foremost it is an experience that cannot always and easily be experienced (Findlay 1967). Our minds, normally able to probe, praise, or condemn, are totally conquered. Our imagination is taken captive by the enchantment of words that we see or hear; they affect our minds as though we ourselves had pronounced them and really meant them. They create change across a broad range of thinking habits, outlooks, and values. We not only agree with them but also identify with them, as though they are truly ours (Meager 1964).

My respondents combined the painful and pleasurable sweetness of the words into the concept of giving. They often described wailers as "givers of words" about the deceased and perceived this act of giving as the quintessence of the kindness that the wailer does for the dead: a personal eulogy, so to speak, that she composes in his or her memory. This giving is also directed at the audience; its purpose is to rupture the dam that holds the anguish back. Rina, a wailer, explained with emphasis: "gave *words.*" Then she established the connection between the means and its end by adding, "She'd literally make the whole world cry." The Hebrew words *matat* or *matana,* both denoting "gift," do not allude to sources of inexhaustible wealth or self-evident access to something good. Instead, they relate to something of value that passes from hand to hand or, in this case, from mouth to ear. The gift of wailing was transmitted from wailer to audience—and from woman to woman—before a given performer appeared before her random audience. It was not necessarily the case that the women in the audience would accept the words as a gift that they would pass on to others. The encounter embodied in the interview, where the women were asked to utter words, revealed the element of giving that was intrinsic to the words. The women, wailers or not, thought that I was asking them to "give words" as if they were in a house of mourning and I were an audience on the edge of its seat, expecting to hear them say something. My dialogue with these respondents sometimes became a negotiating session in which the words, whether ultimately revealed or concealed, became objects.[2] "What can I tell you? I'm willing to sing, but . . . ," one of them said with a smile. Wishing to ease her embarrassment, I asked her, "Do you feel uncomfortable? Would you rather keep it to yourself?" After a moment, she straightened and answered firmly: "No, I'll give you a few words." Another respondent, wishing to honor my request and deliver a recitation in the manner of a speech, preceded her performance by granting me permission: "You can take the words." The words became weighty when one woman described how she "brings the words to the dead," specifying his first name, thus making him the object of a lament that she knew well.

To provide a clear presentation of lamentation lyrics that originate in Arabic, translation is necessary. This chapter takes up the translation issue in two forms that are typical of oral tradition: from one language to another and from the oral to the written. The claim that translation is somehow impossible has become axiomatic in research literature (Feleppa 1988). The problem of representing one language in another is especially complex in poetry and when the source culture is the subject of affective stereotypes (Finnegan 2001). To tackle the representation problem, the translator has to choose a model that is tailored to the linguistic and cultural circumstances of the research population and take into consideration the contents of the arguments that he or she is making. In the latter respect, the assumption is that a distinction exists between a translation that focuses on actual contents and one that emphasizes a collection of ideas. On the continuum between these emphases, the point of view in this chapter is closer to the second possibility, that is, presenting wailing with its patterns of meaning and its nature as the configuration of a discourse. This perspective, one may say, mirrors the anthropological view of translation as more a social than a technical endeavor. In this sense, by presenting the translation as an ethnographic text, I may be able to contend with a range of questions, such as: Are there specific translation patterns that women who perform or translate the lyrics find acceptable? What role is assigned to the audience for which the translation is performed? As Schulte (1987, 2) says, translators do not merely plant words in paper; they transfer situations from one culture to another. Accordingly, the ethnography here focuses on an interactive connection between text and context and views metatext as social interpretation.

While the wailers whom I interviewed were fluent in Hebrew, I—a second-generation Israeli immigrant of Yemenite Jewish extraction—am very poorly versed in Arabic. For this reason, the lamentations that I present below were translated into Hebrew by the respondents. This interactive connection overcame not only the deficiencies in my knowledge but also, to some extent, the problem of representing Arabic and its levels of meaning in the Yemenite Jewish wailing culture. Furthermore, the final rendering of a text by native speakers surmounts a problem originating in the notion that translation is a forced act that rests on ideological props. In this last-mentioned matter, and insofar as a research project represents an intercultural encounter, Glassgold (1987, 20–21) offers some apt remarks. There is a direct connection, in his view, between politics and translation. In the discussion of cultural dissemination, we adopt a liberal political point of view, stressing progress and the free and unrestricted flow of ideas. While Glassgold considers translation the only hope for a truly democratic "global village," he defines translation and near-translation as facile ways to sow confusion and transform facts into propaganda.

Thus, straddling two cultural worlds, the women translated their works into Hebrew and interpreted them in accordance with their estimation of how well the audience—represented by me, the researcher—could comprehend them. Their act of translation came across as a special and possibly nonrecurrent communication process, as Galit Hasan-Rokem (1993) defined it in her discussion of the translation issue in her research.[3] In anthropological terms and in comparison with Hasan-Rokem's unique strategy, my approach reflects greater dependency on the respondents' perceptions. In my estimation, there is ethical and methodological value in this approach; it treats the wailers as hosts who share the language of the critics of their culture and treats the printed words of the lament with respectful and weighty responsibility. Therefore, the discussion that follows will not wrestle with translation issues in the manner typical of studies of the kind presented here but instead will describe the translation challenge that the respondents faced and will reveal something of their cultural essence.

The respondents were challenged by being asked to "give words"; sometimes they responded in a forced manner. This made the presentation of the texts in this chapter a complex task. In the presence of a researcher who faced them with a recording device, a notebook, and a writing implement, the respondents' eyes alternately smiled, turned serious, and swiveled about in search of an opportunity to transcend the moment or to defer. As it turned out, the words produced had natural life in the right context only, that is, at a Yemenite Jewish house of mourning or a cemetery where a large congregation gathered. The interview situation represented what Goldstein (1964) defined as an artificial connection of the sort that a researcher organizes, for better or worse, when seeking to capture a phenomenon in its last moments (Finnegan 2001).

Wailing Words

Below I present nine lamentation texts. Several of them are segments of complete laments, presented in this manner when I asked respondents merely to give a demonstration or because they found the entire lament difficult to perform for some reason.[4] The first six were gathered from women who participated in the study as interviewees or as performers at death events. The laments exemplify several variations of the researcher-wailer encounter (personal, group, indirect, and direct), the wailer's relationship with the object of the lament (mother, relative, member of community), types of laments (personal, impersonal), types of wailers (professional, amateur), metaphorical style (rich, sparse), and performative settings (private home, cemetery).[5] The last three laments come from literary sources. I present so many texts with two goals in mind: to demonstrate one of two performative dimensions of wailing as a complete ritual (the verbal dimension) and to provide raw material for the content analysis that will follow.

1.

This lament was given over by a professional wailer whom I interviewed in her home. "When I begin [to wail in a house of mourning]," she explained, "I talk about the soldiers, about important people. If he was young, I give the words that he deserves. If he was a big religious scholar, I give the words that he deserves." She recited the words that follow for her firstborn son, one of her ten children, who fell in the Yom Kippur War:

Welcome
for having come to honor us.
Welcome, you who came.

It's a death, not a celebration,
No singing, no drumming.
Death, take the elderly
It's better that an old man, already blind
die and not suffer.
Leave the young men alone, let them enjoy themselves;
[The deceased] was like a baby;
he should have been given a chance to enjoy life.
I have white papers to tell relatives and acquaintances.[6]
My sisters, help me cry.
It's a death, not a celebration,
No singing, no drumming.
You should cry together with me.
After all, we're all going to die.

2.

The following lyrics are about the brother of a woman who, while knowing how to wail, is not considered a professional wailer. She is a relative of mine; I interviewed her at a family get-together. She wept in the middle of the lament and at its end, and she concluded by noting that "There's lots more to say."

My brother, son of my mother,
where will I look for you?
Where will I see you?
You are lying in the sand,
in the clutches of darkness.
I have no friend in the world.
You have left me alone,
without father or mother.
You are in the dark,
in the soil and water.

Where will I look for you,
in morning and midday?

3.

Zvia, the informant cited above in my description of the research field, wished to encourage an acquaintance of hers to wail for her (Zvia's) mother for the purpose of the interview. Her idea in doing this was that the acquaintance would reconstruct what she had said "back there," that is, at the house of morning. It was an artificial attempt; the woman could not find the words. She apologized, saying "What can I tell you? I forgot the words. I don't have a feeling for *la'azi* [wailing]." Only after the two women exchanged a few words about the deceased, whom they had loved dearly, and recaptured something of her personality did the woman cover her eyes and disengage from both of us:

Oh mother Gazel,[7]
I will bewail you aloud.
Oh, my mother,
how sad it is that you have departed.
Celerity was your way, generosity your hand.
What did the Angel of Death tell you?
Oh mother, what a pity for you,
You are like a bounding gazelle.
Oh mother,
You are like fine glittering salt.
What a pity for you.
For you I truly weep.
You are like a fresh flower on a rooftop.
You give and do not say, "I have given."
Zvia, did your heart prophesy
that your mother has died?

4.

The following lyrics were recited by an elderly woman. The object of the lamentation was her son, who had died of a serious illness at the age of forty. The poem expresses her loneliness and her severe yearnings for the deceased.

How did you leave home?
[The house] will be sealed now that you've gone.
God, may He take the elderly.
If only I had gone to the grave.
If only I were a maggot in the ground.
Father and Mother,
if only I had someone to tell the story to,
if only he were alive; if only he'd knock on the door.
The wind knocks on every door;
take my letter
to my son, who has departed,
and bring me a reply.
He went to the grave
without saying goodbye.
If only I were a maggot
That would go into his grave
And I'll think of him
that he will return to life.
He cannot rise;
he's already covered by a mound of stones.

One of the women who wailed for me first mentioned another wailer, a well-known one, who, she said, "uses a different melody and finishes the whole thing in two or three words." Then speaking about herself, she said, "I have lots of words. I [wail] for three days." The lyrics that follow are for her son, who died of an illness three years before the interview:

How did you leave home?
It will be closed now that you've gone.
God, He should take the elderly.
If only I had gone to the grave,
If only I were a worm in the ground.
Father and Mother,
If only I had someone to tell,
If only he were alive and knocking on the door,
The wind is knocking on every door,
Take my letter
to my son, who has gone,
and bring me an answer.
He didn't say goodbye
and went to the grave.
If only I were a worm,
that would go into his grave.
And I will think about him,
so that he will return to the living.
He cannot stand up;
a mound of stones is already atop him.

5.

The following lyrics were recorded at the cemetery as the wailer prostrated herself on the grave of her son, who had died at the age of forty. After her powerful performance, she washed and caressed the tombstone and murmured, sobbing, "You were a fresh flower. What a pity for your eyes. A pity for the face, the lovely tallness, a pity, a pity."

You're gone; you were like a sapling.
Who will finish your work?
You were the light of my eyes, my father and my mother.
Everything has closed in our faces;

Our world has fallen upon us.
The stars pass in the night
From place to place.
I'm already ill
Because I remember you only in tears
And you didn't deserve it.
The heavens are rent asunder
From the sorrow in our hearts
And we accepted the decree
However hard it was.

6.

The next lamentation was performed during an interview that I conducted in the home of a wailer who was about sixty years old. She composed the text after recalling a recently deceased member of the community for whom she had not had an opportunity to wail in the mourners' home.

Woe, woe,
I bewail the loss of Shalom.[8]
My mother and father
It's a shame about him
My heart aches as I lament you.
My heart aches as I lament you.
I entrust you to God,
go safely
Shalom, have a good evening
From me and from your children
And from your mother's children.
Your wife is greatly saddened
Her heart aches,
she pleads to God:
Why have you gone?

It causes her grief.
There were ten men in the synagogue[9]
and now you are missing.
The Torah scrolls will bemoan you.
Woe is Mother,
the candle of the home has been extinguished
and it was yet filled with oil.[10]

7.

The following lament, about a woman named Zahara (Sarah), was reported to me by the author Binyamin-Gamliel.[11]

Zahara, oh gazelle of the dawn,
Did they find you a cure?
No, they did not find you a cure.
Oh Zahara, oh white flower,
A tifrahat al-kadi,[12]
Your sloufa[13] *is a whole meal for me.*
Your home expects your arrival, your kitchen is waiting for you.
Zahara, you are a mother to all comers.
What more can I say about you, my mother?
Your lahouha[14] *is a meal for me*
Your sloufa—*a magnificence.*
Oh fragrant flower, oh white one,[15]
Oh mother to all comers.
Always walking and smiling
at the young, the old, the suckling,
pleasant and cheerful of character
at home and in the street,
to men and women.
Zahara, oh I was careful, my mother.
My heart thirsts for you all my life, night and day.

I will never forget you.
Oh Zahara, oh my sister.
They open your home and no one is there.
I call your name and no one answers.
I go into the street
thinking I'll find you, and I do not
until I follow you to the land of the spent.[16]
Oh I was careful, what a pity for the pink cheeks and the fresh forehead,
and the lovely youth.
Zahara, a pity for your girlhood.
You were the little one in the cradle.
Who burned you? Who consumed [you] with a dry flame?
Was it the evil eye, or was it a mistake,
or might it have been the mehaneh *[claiming his portion]?*[17]
Zahara, my heart burns for you.
until I follow you, my sister.
There is none who resembles
this one, the Jewish woman.
But it is a falsehood and a deceit:
people are not equal.
The good are not long-lived.
Don't tell, don't say
that others are my mother's equal.
Zahara, you are the gazelle of the dawn,
who appears in her splendor.
Oh Zahara, stand up and speak with me.
Haven't they found a cure for you already?
I'll send it from here.
She is in mehil *and in a thousand mehils.*[18]
Her resting place is in the Garden of Eden,
now and forever.
Like that Jewess, there isn't much, there's nothing.
The likes of her will never be attained again, ever.
Say what you like, there's no one like Zahara.

No one, no one.
However far I searched, I did not find one. There's none.

8.

The following lyrics are about Hoyda, a distinguished woman member of the community. In this lamentation, the wailer recalls the good deeds of the deceased and cries out to her husband and children.[19]

Oh my mother, oh my father, oy, it's a shame
My mother, my father, Hoyda, it's a shame
My mother, my father, Hoyda, it's a shame
Oh my dead mother, among the living.

My sisters, today is lamentation day
Oh my mother, he who mourns will cry
O my father, he who rejoices will hear
O my father, O my father, Hoyda, it's a shame.
Oh my mother, a fragrant herb on the roof[20]
Oh my mother, it is irrigated without water
My mother, of the clean hand
My mother, mother of righteous deeds and commandments
Oh my mother, a silver bell with the polishing tools[21]
Oh my mother, your daughter does not know how to lament
Oh my mother, I will lament and bewail you, so I will
My mother, I will cry for you and so inspire women to cry.
Oh my mother, O my father, oy
Oh my mother, it's a shame about Hoyda
My mother, everyone has already bemoaned you
My mother, the close ones have already complained.
My mother, how quickly you have gone to the grave
My mother, in the brown soil
My mother, is it light or dark where you are?

Tell me. Where I am, it is bad and dark.
My daughter, the worms will consume your flesh[22]
My daughter, the worms will consume your flesh
My sisters, the wailer has wailed and gone
My brothers, the fire resides in the place where distress lives.[23]

9.

Hoyda, the woman about whom the previous lament was composed, wails for the patriarch of her extended family.[24]

Indeed, it is so;
rot rises from the mud.
A pity for your dignity, a pity.
O you generous soul
This is my outcry.
If your voice may yet be heard,
give your guest, who stands at your door,
a blessing.
Do not show the back of your neck.
The door will collapse in your absence,
when guest's feet step in.
My tears will flow like springs
and my heart will issue blood.
A pity for your dignity, a pity.
A corner of the synagogue has fallen in,
and the minyan[25] *is short on your account.*
How sad for you, how sad
Oy, for your toil and your reward.

Discursive Outlines for the Understanding of a Lament

Song, in the opinion of Abu-Lughod (1986, 187), is a discourse of vulnerability that expresses sentiments of sadness, self-pity, and betrayal or, in the case of love, a discourse of profound connectedness and emotions. In one of her works (Abu-Lughod 1993), she views Muslim wailing as a gender discourse about death. Ratzhabi (1987–88), discussing Arab motifs in Sephardi Hebrew wailing, described the lament as a highly refined form of discourse that includes a monologue of the deceased and a dialogue between living and the dead. I contend that these approaches, based on painstaking content analysis and the detection of differentiated themes in wailing, support the analytical point of view that I am about to present.

The classification that follows was inspired by my respondents' reflective attitude toward the wailer's role and performance. When they spoke about wailing, they alluded to the centrality of the wailer in a context share by several discussants, some present and others absent. Meir offered an impression that was very typical of the responses I received: "[Wailers] begin to describe the history of the deceased from the day he was born, and the whole story of his life, in milestones. They say, 'How respected you were, how beloved you were,' and then they press the sensitive buttons of everyone who'd been around him. The wailer gazes at each of them and wails for them: 'Where's your father gone? Where's the man who supported you?'" Netanel's impression of wailing sheds light on its being a discursive opportunity: "The moment someone dies, the wailers exploit it and come there to cry about their own bitter fate. They turn things inside-out, you might say. They turn to the dead person so that he'll give their relative, who died a year ago, a message of some kind, and then they begin to make all sorts of connections about their problems and other problems. They wail, but it's no longer for the person [who was just buried] but someone who'd died before, and they mix the two together." One of my wailer respondents spoke about this intermingling of domains: "They go to the mourners' house, they remember the dead, they remember the living, they remember the troubles, they remember the whole house, anything on earth."

Thus, as the texts in my possession show, the wailer mentions individuals and groups interchangeably: she turns to the dead, the audience of consolers, the bereaved, other wailers, death, God, and even herself. In addition, as I show below, wailing contains both direct and indirect speech, the latter on behalf of several personae.

CATEGORIZING THE WAILERS' DISCOURSE

My survey of lamentation texts illuminated ten categories of discourse, concise examples of the things that wailing women say. I specify these categories below in excerpts, and then I present a complete lamentation text to show how several categories may be included in one text.

Category 1: A narrative about the deceased. The wailer describes, step by step, how the deceased met his or her demise and retells the person's story in the context of significant life events. She also lists the deceased's physical and personality traits and lauds his/her virtues. For the most part, the contents of the narrative are associated with the deceased's religious merits in worship, faith, and daily actions. Here are some examples:

- He had just gone out without asking his mother's permission / Thus death, randomly passing by, tugged him by his sleeve.
- He would learn Torah / His mouth produced gems of wisdom / His eyes radiated light and holiness like sunbeams / He would stand at the [prayer leader's] lectern in the synagogue like an angel / and the poor know how much charity he gave.
- She was a woman of valor / raising orphans and giving charity / What a pity it is that this righteous mother [has passed away].

Category 2: A narrative on behalf of the deceased. The wailer conducts a "dialogue" with the deceased and gives him or her an opportunity to respond.

The deceased's "answer," as the wailer reports it, describes the deceased's fate before or after death. Examples follow:

- The wailer "asks" the deceased woman: "What was your disease called?"
- And the deceased answers: "It was an incurable disease."
- The deceased woman "says," "My daughter, I'm going to be eaten by maggots."

Category 3: A narrative on behalf of the living. The wailer conducts a "dialogue" with the deceased on behalf of the mourners. She tells the deceased, on the mourners' behalf, how sorry they are to have parted with him or her. Examples follow:

- Shalom, good evening to you / from me and your children / and your mother's children. / Your wife is very sad. / Her heart aches. / She pleads to God. / It's causing her pain.
- My mother, everyone is already crying for you / my mother, and the relatives are already complaining.
- How could you leave your wife behind with a young child and go away?

Category 4: A personal appeal to the deceased. The wailer addresses the deceased directly and tells him or her how anguished she is after having lost the person. The wailer has become a mourner and describes her daily expectation of the deceased's return and her dismay over his or her death. Sometimes the wailer makes special requests that only the deceased can fulfill. Examples follow:

- Mother, we haven't seen you. / You have disappeared from us. / We imagine how you're laughing and our hearts cry. / Mother, when will you have us as your guest? / Won't you caress us?
- Pray up there for us, the soldiers, and the State [of Israel].
- They taught your daughters that you've gone to Heaven / that you're handsome. / I'm waiting for you to come in through the door as you always did, and you're not there.

- Oh, my sister, to whom shall I cry? / Who murdered you? / Where was your husband? / If only you could hear my outcries and come to me.

Category 5: Greeting and addressing the consolers. The wailer usually begins by expressing her gratitude and appreciation of the consolers for visiting the home. This initial statement typically apologizes for the guests' presence in the home of the bereaved instead of some other place where happiness reigns. Sometimes the wailer asks questions that are appropriate in view of the family crisis occasioned by the death and its expected implications for the state of the bereaved. Examples follow:

- We welcome our visitors. / If it were a happy occasion, we'd be celebrating / but you have come and we are sad. / All these visitors are too much for me.
- We welcome you for having come to honor us. / This is death, not joy. / No one is singing and drumming.
- What will become of the family now? / Who will support the young children? / How will the wife [calls her by name] survive alone?
- Woe is Mother. / She's alone now. / The lamp of the household has gone out / and is no longer filled with oil.

Category 6: Addressing the mourners. The wailer addresses the mourners directly and tries to impress them with the immensity of their loss. She hints that their agony will become even worse after the mourning period and drives the point home by referring to important events in their lives. Examples follow:

- How will you give birth to your child, now that your father has gone?
- From now on, your home will be filled with darkness. / Morning comes and he's gone; evening comes and he's gone. / Your cherished one has gone, never to return. / Don't look for him and don't call him by name anymore.

Category 7: Personal story. The wailer assumes the role of a member of the group who wishes to retell her woes, losses, and bitter fate. Sometimes she plays the role of a mourner. Examples follow:

- What has happened to me? / What woes have befallen me? / What will become of me?
- Rain has come but my tears are greater than rain. / The camel suffers but I suffer more. / The camel sighs but I sigh more vehemently.
- My husband has left the home. / The light has gone out and nothing remains. / If only it were the man who remained and not the darkness.
- My son went to work this morning. / In the morning he went to work and in the afternoon my son is no more.

Category 8: Addressing other wailers. Often several women sit in the home of the bereaved and wail while listening to each other. One of them may conclude her lamentation by requesting, or by accepting a proposal from the others, to allow the wailing to continue in the manner of a chain. Examples follow:

- My sisters, help me with my sobbing. / This is death, not joy. / They are not singing and drumming. / In wailing together with me / each of us will die.
- Thank you, you women who've come to weep for my mother, my father, and the close ones.

Category 9: Addressing death. The wailer addresses requests to death, which she personifies. The requests pertain to the cause of the particular death that has occurred. An example follows:

- Death, take the elderly. / It's better that an old man, already blind die and not suffer. / Leave the young men alone, let them enjoy themselves; / [the deceased] was like a baby; / he should have been given a chance to enjoy life.

Category 10: Addressing God. The wailer mentions God mainly in expressions of gratitude and acceptance of judgment, supplication, and the asking of unanswerable questions.

- You are God the healer / Who cures the illnesses of all flesh. / O for your deliverance, Creator. / Pity the oppressed / pity me and cure my illness. / Oh, I have neither mother or father / but only You, Master of Heaven. / Let us thank You, my God. / Had it been an enemy, we would have fought him. / Had it been locusts, we would have run away from them. / But this was a decree from the Master of Heaven.
- Why did God hand down this decree? / Why did the deceased leave his children and go away?
- Avraham, what is it that happened to you? / Was it the evil eye, or perhaps a mistake? / Or perhaps the mehaneh *has come: / a decree from God.*

Below is a complete lamentation, performed by a wailer in a cemetery, at the tombstone of a deceased woman in the presence of mourners and consolers:

> [Addressing the deceased:] Rachel, you'll be amazed who's here. / Your daughter is here. / Good evening, Rachel, how are you? Do you have a candle in hand? / [The deceased "replies":] I haven't got a candle. / I'm a prisoner of darkness. / [Addressing the bereaved daughter:] Your mother has died. It's good for her that she died in your daughter's home / in bed, under the blanket / and not among strangers in a hospital. / [A story about the deceased:] She is like a flower on the roof / that needs no water./ [Addressing the bereaved daughter:] Make a cradle for your bereavement; / let it dangle from your right hand. / That way, you won't forget your mother / [The story of the death, in some distant location, of the son of the daughter who is grieving for her mother:] David was unique; / he was like the waters of a spring / [Addressing the wailers:] My sisters, weeping won't help anymore, / neither will the sound of wailing / It's all over.

IDENTITIES IN THE ENCOUNTER

We can sort wailers' rhetoric into four main fields/arenas of encounter that correspond to the model of self-other identities that I developed in my previous study (Gamliel 2001).[26] The fields of the encounter reflect the point of view of the wailer, who serves as a junction of interests, needs, people, and realities.

Field I hosts an encounter between a living self and a living other (living-living)—two people who may be experiencing, together, the illusion of the absence of death in life. In Field II, two people, a living self and a dead other (living-dead), come together: the living isolate themselves from the symbols that the dead represent. In Field III, two people, a dead self and a living other, confront each other; the former isolates him or herself from the symbols that the living participant represents (dead-living). And in Field IV, the encounter is between a matched pair: a dead self and a dead other (dead-dead) who have a common identity and fate. The encounter is effected in what has been defined as the tendency of postmodern anthropology to deal with the structured nature of cultural perceptions by presenting examples of types of discourse (Clifford 1986). If we contemplate the ten categories in wailing presented above, we can easily understand that wailing contains elements of both direct speech and indirect speech, that is, speech in someone else's name. The assortment of verbal expressions appears to sort itself into the four fields of encounter, although it then becomes necessary to interpret who and what the words "living" and "dead," as well as "self" and "other," symbolize. The four fields correspond to images of reality based on the wailer's message. Those in the audience are in the thrall of whatever it is the wailer says. She passes them through several perceptions of reality, and the fields are their imagined experiences in view of their identification with the wailer as she performs.

The model, with its four fields, represents a seam in the individual's identity, along which perceptions of life and death that are attributed alternately to the self and to the other are connected (see p. 126). The inclusion of these contrasts befits the timing of the wailing act along the continuum of mourning rituals and the mourning period. Wailing is conducted at a liminal stage in terms of the status of the deceased, the mourners, and the audience (Radcliffe-Brown 1964; Danforth 1982). The in-between status in the model, denoted by the expressions “neither living nor dead” or “between life and death,” is translated by the model into positive categories of both life and death, which give the participants in the wailing event a dual awareness—an inseparable union of absolute opposites. Life and death touch each other and overlap slightly due to the swapping of masks. The blending of contrasting elements that wailing creates by blurring the self and the rest of the world is related to common metaphors of motherhood, in which the existential elements stand out. According to these metaphors, women, whose bodies and thoughts are enslaved to fertility, are linked with nature. Accordingly, they represent irrationality and anomaly—the polar opposites of culture—of a male world in which everything is clear; accordingly, too, they are like signs that warn of the danger intrinsic to these representations (Rosaldo 1974; Douglas 1966). Nature is the unrestricted arena in which birth and death events take place, and woman, who is likened to Mother Nature, attains her existence within her culture as the product of this tangle of symbolic ambivalence. Accordingly, as Turner (1967, 96) says, in many cultures the symbols that represent the liminal persona are taken from the biology of death, decomposition, and other physiological processes that have a negative connotation, such as menstruation. In the deepest recesses of the “forest of symbols,” for example, Turner describes the menstruation ritual of the Ndembu girls as a coming-of-age ritual that carries messages of the color of blood: fertility, carrion, murder, and death. If so, one would almost have to say that a model accommodating life and death in harmony expresses a feminine scheme of things.

Textual categorization is a familiar tactic in research on wailing cultures; many researchers find intersubjective connections in the words themselves. Feld (1995, 95), for example, describing the dialogic and nondialogic possibilities that the wailing discourse offers, claims that wailers speak to the interest of the deceased, of other wailers, and of the collective, expressing themselves in a way that presents them as performers in a cultural arena. However, the mapping of categories in the model takes the analysis one analytical step beyond the interpretations offered in the literature: it construes wailing not

FIGURE 1. DEATH-LIFE MODEL:
CATEGORIES IN THE WAILER'S DISCOURSE

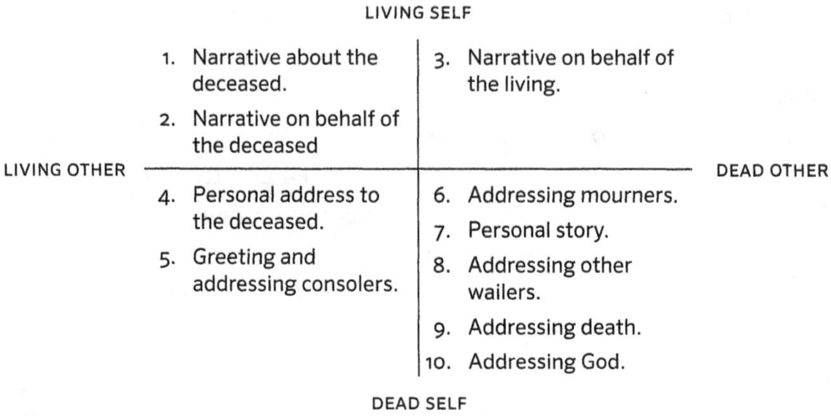

	LIVING SELF		
LIVING OTHER	1. Narrative about the deceased. 2. Narrative on behalf of the deceased	3. Narrative on behalf of the living.	DEAD OTHER
	4. Personal address to the deceased. 5. Greeting and addressing consolers.	6. Addressing mourners. 7. Personal story. 8. Addressing other wailers. 9. Addressing death. 10. Addressing God.	
	DEAD SELF		

as a text per se but as a representative voice that sets up an encounter among identities that may exist between two subjects, one living and one dead. Schieffelin (1985, 722) supports this approach to the findings. A performance, he says, derives its objective and social validity from the participants when they share in its action and intensivity, irrespective of what each individual may think on his or her own. By and large, he states, the symbols and the ritual itself acquire their meanings in midperformance and surface in the participants' imagination in the course of negotiations between performers and participants.

My interpretation is predicated on textual logic (expressions that denote direct speech, narrative, and reported speech), the respondents' creed (e.g., the need to honor the dead), and my experiences as an anthropologist who was not a total stranger to the situation—a Yemenite Jewish woman who attended the wailing occasion as a participant-observer. The ten categories in Yemenite Jewish women's wailing are sorted into the four-field model (see figure 1). Below I examine each category accordingly.

The first of these ten textual categories uses very positive messages to craft the image of the deceased. They emphatically reflect the official goal of the women's wailing, the one routinely expressed by all respondents: honoring the dead. Some drive the point home by quoting an adage: "The groom is honored by singing; the dead are honored by wailing." The substance of the honor is the wailer's use of descriptive honorifics about the admirable appearance, behavior, and actions of the deceased while he/she had been alive. If those who are deceased had been pious, if they had raised their children to be religiously observant, and if they had given charity, their biographies would probably be especially effusive in praise.

Wailing is a defensive method of ex post management of an individual's death for the sake of members of the collective. Thus, wailing makes the deceased a hero in the eyes of those in attendance. Interviewees also credited this type of text with the ability to console and encourage the mourners, who are not fixated solely on their loss but are also especially sensitive to gossip from members of the collective about the deceased's image. Thus, wailing is a representative voice for two wishes. The mourners want the death that has claimed their loved one to serve as a focal point of reference; the consolers desire an act meant for a worthy person in order to justify their presence in the home of the bereaved. The wailer's representative voice creates a coordinated encounter between mourners and consolers as partners in a living community. This voice lauds the persona of the deceased, temporarily aggrandizes and revives it, and renders it worthy of emulation in the future. Accordingly, the biography of the deceased, represented in Field I (living-living), creates an encounter among living subjects—mourners and consolers who are positioned on either side of a familiar person and are forced, by the report of this person's death, to renegotiate.

In the dialogue with the deceased that appears in Category 2, the wailer asks pointed questions about death and other existential mysteries and answers them in the voice of the deceased. This basically imaginary dialogue, the product of invention, expresses the existential curiosity of those in attendance as a counterweight to the deceased's advantage of knowledge. The remarks stated on behalf of the deceased allude to the attendees' belief that the deceased cannot speak but can hear the wailing and to their basic belief in the afterlife. Since the deceased cannot respond, the wailer responds for him or her. The wailer mediates between those in attendance, consolers and mourners alike, who live in this world, and the deceased, who lives in the afterworld. Accordingly, the "on behalf of the deceased" category should be represented in Field I (living-living).

Another aspect of dialogue with the deceased occurs when the wailer represents only the mourners, who bemoan their abandonment and express their grief over his/her departure. The wailer speaks on behalf of the mourners, who are living and who acknowledge the death of their loved one but find it difficult to make peace with the fact. In this third discursive category, the deceased is not expected to reply. The wailer describes the mourning situation with intensity, articulating a state of melancholy that the mourners cannot express by themselves. Her very emphasis of the sense of grief creates a buffer between the living mourners and the dead. Thus, her discourse on behalf of the living should be placed in Field II (living-dead). The final aspect of the dialogue with the deceased is manifested in Category 4, in which the wailer takes on the role of a mourner and her lamentation expresses her own pain. The manifestations of grief are especially intense in the Category 4 lamentation, since they transcend a representative voice or the wailer's empathy with the grief of others. The impact of abandonment by the deceased is amplified to such an extent that it portrays the self as distinctly helpless. The deceased has plunged the bereaved wailer into poignant nostalgia. She imagines him returning and yearns for him with bated breath. She almost believes that he could change her situation for the better if only he would deign to retrace his steps, come in through the door, or pray for her in heaven. Her helplessness in comparison with him gives one the impression that she has died in view of his advantages; thus, relative to her, the deceased lives. Therefore, the wailer's appeal to the deceased can be represented in Field III (dead-living).

The mourners' acute vulnerability is clearly manifested in Category 5 (greeting and addressing the consolers). The wailer identifies with this vulnerability and uses it to help differentiate between the mourners' state and that of the consolers. The latter are deemed to be doing a kindness by the very act of visiting the home of the bereaved, which everyone considers an inexpedient place to be. The wailer also alludes to the virtue of kindness by asking pointedly about from whence the abandoned mourners will obtain social and material support. The wailer does not volunteer members of the community to provide this support, but she enunciates her questions loudly and presents them as a moral challenge that some of members must tackle. Since the mourners are socially dead, the situation is not limited to the seven-day mourning period; instead, it continues afterward with even greater intensity. The consolers, collectively, are considered the holders of resources and are responsible for providing them in the immediate present and in the future. The consolers' advantage is underscored in view of the mourners' inaction and distress. Thus, the discourse falls into Field III (dead-living), with consolers as the living and the mourners as the dead. The mourners' vulnerability is further underscored by the wailer's direct communication with them in accordance with Category 6 (addressing the mourners). Whether she asks rhetorical questions or describes their situation as she views it, her words ordain an equality of fate between the mourners and the deceased. The fate of death is a matter of profound psychological significance; the assumption is that togetherness with significant others is an essential condition for life—a condition that no longer exists for the mourners. From the moment their loved one died, as several interviewees expressed it, "The lives of those left behind aren't life any more." The absolute death of a family member projects onto and severely diminishes the livingness of his or her relatives. Such an equalization is represented in Field IV (dead-dead).

Categories 7, 8, and 9 are also represented in Field IV. They reflect an intensification of the universal sense of existential helplessness with which everyone present may identify. The wailer achieves this effect by baring herself at the psychological level—revealing her suffering frankly and in public view. She does this conspicuously in Category 7 (personal story) by playing the role of a woman who has come to console the mourner or is herself a mourner. She neither conducts a dialogue with the deceased, as in Category 4, nor addresses a veiled message to the consolers. Instead, she tells a story of her own. Her narrative places her in the center of the sense of melancholy that those in attendance recognize readily. The wailer's story about herself parallels her narrative about the deceased (in Category 1), except that here the deceased is the hero and the narrator is helpless. As stated, everyone is considered alive, in contrast to the narrative about the deceased, whose dignity is upheld as a service to him/her. A narrative that focuses on the wailer's own hardships, as in Category 7, stymies wishes and interests and focuses attention on a human immobility that lacks all heroism and utility. Thus, the wailer stations herself alongside the deceased as a subordinate persona, the other null side of human realness. Those present seems to identify with the account by giving up; the wailer's account of her own suffering alerts mourners and consolers to their own doomedness and the disutility of any presentation of a comparative advantage over others or of reasons to take pride in themselves. The wailer's "death" projects onto the situation of everyone present in an undeniable partnership of fate.

In Category 8, when she addresses other wailers in attendance, the wailer continues to play the role of the dead. She asks for help or agrees to accept help because the display of suffering itself has sapped her strength. From the moment the function is transferred to another wailer, the latter also adopts the persona of the suffering woman. Therefore, it cannot be stated that the second wailer wishes to demonstrate her advantage over the first one. Furthermore, the transference of role usually takes place in the midst of the lamentation, as the two wailers exchange blessings. The circle of wailers generates a sense of collective doom that helps consolers and mourners to commingle temporarily in a collectivity of the dead. This tendency is reinforced by the wailer's performance in Category 9, due to the very fact that she addresses death. Death as a universal vanquisher is considered an enemy for those who, in their moments of wailing, plead and genuflect to it. Death, over which no one has dominion—no one can decide who will be taken and when—renders everyone present absolutely equal. All are like the dead in Field IV (dead-dead). Seremetakis (1990, 492) termed this social state "a collectivity of subjects in exile."

The reality of exile is unique in that it unifies those involved in social death and shared anguish. The wailer's performance in Categories 9 and 10 strengthens this reality by the very act of addressing death and addressing God. Death, the reality that defeats all other realities, is considered an enemy by those who, in wailing moments, address it in supplication and genuflection. Death, which defers to no ruling power—it takes whom it wants, when it wants—establishes total quality and unity among those present.

In Field IV (dead-dead), everyone is "dead." In contrast to the begrudging of death, an appeal to God signals acceptance of the deity's judgment; this perpetuates the stationing of human beings in Field IV. The difference in the messages and the relative textual poverty of Category 9 attest to the avoidance of challenging God and the humanization of death by treating it as the target of complaints. The contents of Category 10 appear last in the conventional wailing sequence. The reference to God's will signals the end of the lament and attests to the supremacy and definitive importance of the religious message. As Abu-Lughod (1993, 200) says, this message is the "last word"; it creates meaning and ends the speculations and musings that the lament has evoked. Categories 9 and 10 reflect the essence of the tension between religious faith and the need to express pain over one's loss by portraying people as perpetually prone to the deity's uncompromising surprise decrees. Helplessly doomed to death, they must bow their heads in submission and thank God for the bad, just as they do for the good.

This interpretation sheds light on the wailer's tasks at death events—forms of giving that are evidenced in the words alone. The wailer uses her words to outline the needs of the deceased, the mourners, and the consolers whom the community has sent. She is tasked with managing the individual's death in view of the religious imperative of giving respect in its well-known sense as the last kindness. Her rhetoric creates—reshapes, to be precise—the personality, ways, and physical features of the deceased. She describes the specific image of the deceased as she sees fit, and it is this image that the listeners are to remember and commemorate. By giving in this manner, she addresses—on a public performative stage—both the mourners' despondency and the objections that anyone in the community might have. By aggrandizing the deceased's persona, she creates a soothing and encouraging effect and dismisses the prattling of gossips. In particular, she appears to be wallowing in the agony of bereavement and loss; first she recounts the mourners' anguish as they maintain the muteness that their encounter with death has imposed on them. I have shown that by doing this, she defends their images in society from the very fact of their emotional and family connection with the deceased. The painful process of grieving and the sense of emptiness that surface after the seven days of mourning give way to the resumption of daily life, which also finds guiding and empathetic expression in the wailer's words. She sometimes expresses her awareness of the family's financial situation by encouraging members of the community to support the family; by doing this, she expresses farsightedness and notes the aspect of death as a material crisis that has lasting implications. She boosts the mourners' morale in additional ways that relate to the cultural outlooks of the community at large, as manifested in the creation of senses of identification and human partnership in fate and acceptance of divine judgment. The display of helplessness within the confines of a cosmic order is a narrative that invests death with meaning.

The giving of words in wailing reflects the belief that talking is essential in the state of bereavement. Some researchers claim that this traditional outlook has been dislodged by the modern conspiracy of silence, which enjoins the bereaved against expressing their anguish in public and defines such expression as the violation of a social taboo (Bauman 1992; Aries 1981; Gorer 1976). This is not the place to dwell on historical or cultural attitudes toward the right ways for grieving people to respond,[27] but I should note that the recent literature has much to say about the meaning of the speech response in its nontraditional form. Walter (1996) is one of the main proponents of an approach that attributes definitive importance to speech in the adjustment process. This approach challenges the widely held conviction in psychology that mourning is merely internal emotional work that aims to disengage the bereaved from the persona of the deceased. In Walter's opinion, the purpose of mourning is to construct an ongoing biography that allows mourners to integrate the memory of the deceased into their lives. Conversing and repeatedly talking with people who knew the deceased are the crux of the healing process. Walter also believes that the Jewish custom of shivah, designed to demonstrate commiseration and exchange memories of the deceased, allows a common portrait to be produced. By telling stories about the deceased, the living informally write the last chapter, the most meaningful one, of the deceased's life. Interestingly, Walter does not cite the custom of wailing as an example of his arguments. However, wailing is mentioned elsewhere, although less than it should be; it surfaces among the components of Jewish ritual that address psychological needs associated with the various stages of mourning (Stroebe and Stroebe 1987). Above, I listed the ways in which lamentation lyrics may show consideration of mourners' psychological and social needs; I also suggested that the wailer's voice, representing the audience, is tasked with constructing a common memory of the deceased and giving this last chapter its contours. The wailer addresses those in attendance directly and speaks in their name. Her verbal performance describes the deceased from diverse points of view, depending on the individual being represented and his or her connection with those present. One reason for the difficulty that contemporary people have in speaking about the dead is that family members may express their bereavement in many diverse ways and intensities and may object to others meddling in their intimate relations with the deceased. This, in Walter's opinion, prevents the formation of a consensus about the role of the deceased in the family narrative. As she plays her role, the wailer seems to overcome both phenomena: the variance of response and the barrier of intimacy. She mediates among mourners who cherish the deceased. She creates emotion by dwelling on the depth of meaning in the relations—between father and son, between man and wife, and so on—that are subject to her conjectures. In her changing representations, the wailer induces communication about the dead and about death. In fact, she shows her listeners what talking about the dead should be like.

I conclude this chapter by paying another visit to the four fields. The frame of analysis in my model shows that wailing creates blocs of references and meanings that pertain to self and collective identities in reference to life and death. Given this conclusion, a question should be asked: What is the value of an analytical presentation of wailing as a configuration of several kinds of discourse? Abu-Lughod's (1993) reply suggests that such a presentation mimics the wailer's work by seeking, in midperformance, to include the largest possible number of responses to death. The premise is that by expanding the range of responses, individuals involved in the experiential contents that the lament recounts are better able to identify. Abu-Lughod lists four discursive themes in Muslim wailing and attributes each to a social context that constitutes a living space in the listeners' lives. Urban's (1988) analysis of Brazilian wailing elicits another form of this multicomplexioned representation. Urban believes that wailing has no defined address and is performed as a monologue in which the contents reach the audience's ears by chance. This gives wailing the latitude to deal with personal matters from different angles and thus assures the identification of those in attendance. Briggs (1992) goes beyond the function of inducing audience identification with the wailer's words; he regards the types of discourse included in wailing as alternative ways of contemplating people's existential and social interests. In Briggs's thinking, wailing, paradoxically, furnishes a provocative reading of the "truth" by revealing its contrasting representations.

As my model suggests, the confirmation and juxtaposition of clashing attitudes in wailing may support the notion that the subversiveness of wailing is manifested in the challenging of social truths. In other words, the offering of interpretive alternatives to reality on a single plane undermines canon truth and ontological confidence (Giddens 1990). In this special interpretation, the wailer comes across as a symbolic type—an autonomous persona in a context that circulates freely among contradictory messages (Handelman 1990). This is not to say that such an interpretation clashes in any substantial way with the contents of the ten categories that I presented. However, by sorting them among the field of the living/dead model, I showed that they are directed toward a profound existential meaning that transcends the words. The model points to a contradiction and a dialectic at the level of the reality that the text creates, especially given the juxtaposition of a community of the living (living-living) and a community of the dead (dead-dead). One may observe this in Fields III and IV (living-dead and dead-dead), in which the familiar nexus of otherness and selfless, in which the other is rejected and the self is gladly received, is reversed. In other words, it is the dead who become "living," whereas the wailer and the mourners are likened to the dead. Importantly, too, I base the validity of my interpretive arguments in these fields on the experiential dimension of wailing, that is, its capacity for emotional activation. The connection between words and vocalization, with which I began this chapter, is inseparable and creates a blend invested with the power of melancholy.

·4·

The Performance Stage

Women's wailing is a creative act embodied in performance. For it to be brought to fruition, it needs not only the giving of words but also the voice of someone mired in looking sad and the dramatic movements and gestures that she makes. The lament, expressed in melodic form, finds manners of expression, pathways so to speak, of activation within the female body. The wailer emits melodies and words and accompanies them with movements of her head and hands, causing the verbal elements to be experienced and the anguish to reverberate. This chapter dwells on the events and processes that become reality in a wailer's motions. Importantly, they can be likened to the main components of a dynamic whole that is termed performance, only some of which are constituted in the persona of the performer. I alluded to other components of performance by using the word "stage" in the title; it serves as a spatial metaphor for an encounter among the role players. The chapter also expands on what accompanies the performance onstage, that is, its cultural undergrowth. The wailer's motions embody a cultural wealth that is poured into the dramatic circle of light and exists outside it as well.

Performance, a popular concept in cultural studies, reflects the recent transition from questions about *what* to those focusing on *how.* I base this observation on the view of performance as whatever is done to a text in its context (Blackburn 1986). This perspective emphasizes the importance of the text; in its plain meaning, it may confirm the division of labor between this chapter and chapter 3 above and also the sequence of the chapters. Chapter 3 dealt with words, with text; this chapter, in contrast, focuses on the context, in the sense of it being a social situation in which the folkloristic element is put into practice. The wailing performance as an aesthetic-expressional event that is separate from daily life, that evokes emotions, and that forces participants to experience reality in a special way. The performance splits into forms of encounter that correspond to the relations that exist between the wailer and everyone else present, relations that may strengthen or weaken the balance between performer and audience—two typical categories in the field of performance.

Averill (1982) terms feelings "cultural performances," a telling turn of phrase in a discipline that studies emotions from a sociocultural perspective. Many scholars share Averill's conviction that people are not prompted to act by their pent-up emotions; rather, they perform emotions much in the manner of acting out a scene onstage. To activate their emotions, people mobilize biology and their bodies much as an actor has to elevate his blood pressure to deliver a convincing portrayal of King Lear's fury (Rosaldo 1988; Hochschild 1983; Clark 1990). Accordingly, a wailing performance is more than a sociobehavioral arena for the expression of emotions; the performance itself is a configuration of emotional activation. The wailer puts on a dramatic and overt demonstration of people's use of cultural codes to impress others about their feelings and also—like actors—to inspire themselves to feel.

It is common to invoke the metaphor of the theater—a set of symbols—to describe a performance (Turner 1982; Carlson 1996; Hare and Blumberg 1988). This basic metaphor is also valuable in understanding wailing as a performance embedded in the context of a religious culture. By making associations with the theater, one may recount the inherent logic of overt and covert gestures, reveal cultural codes, and speak in a language familiar to the reader. Above all, metaphor allows us to repay the debt, so to speak, of having to define the performance and fill it with performative indicators that may converge to form the wailing picture. When we describe a wailer as being onstage, as stepping into and out of a dramatic circle of light, and so on, we are merely using metaphors. They should be considered symbolizations of a situation and a relationship that have neither a stage nor spotlights in their literal sense.

One of the differences between performance and theater draws the reader very close to the position of someone attending the theater. Rapp (1973, 76) defines theater as an art of sociability with a transcendentalism that turns itself around, that is, into self-reflection. Conversely, performance is considered a cultural instrument that rids the world of theatrical representations by deconstructing the symbolic potency, the codes, and the structures of the theater. Even though performance consciously starts out with these materials, as does this study, it breaks up the subjects and the objects, which intermingle in their meaning and their representations, to allow a flow of experience and craving. Thus perceived, a performance does not show us the object that we are supposed to understand, about which we are to make inferences, in a cerebral way. One may liken it to a galaxy in which many types of transitional objects represent only the failure to represent (Feral 1982). Unlike the world of the theater, the performer and the audience who take part in his or her performance are not expected to engage in metainterpretation and, ab initio, are not typified by it. Carlson (1996) left this pursuit solely to the ethnographer, who wishes to be drawn into the performative experience without losing his or her way. Following this distinction, the experiencing of a performance is fundamentally different from the experiencing of the theater. From the audience's standpoint,

> As theatre moves more in the direction of performance art, the audience's expected 'role' changes from a passive hermeneutic process of decoding the performer's articulation . . . to become something much more active, entering into a praxis, a context in which meanings are not so much communicated as created, questioned or negotiated. The 'audience' is

> invited and expected to operate as co-creator of whatever meanings and experience the event generates. (Carlson 1996, 197)

What we have said thus far makes it clear that the theater, a repository of roles, limits, codes, and other formal arrangements, is a necessary metaphor for understanding performance not only by affirmation—that is, the way one arena matches another—but also by negation or mismatch. This chapter deconstructs wailing into segments of performance as if both onlookers—the researcher and the reader—are already about to walk out of the theater and reflect.

In accordance with the appearance and the matrix of interactive strands that make up a performance,[1] the expression "Yemenite Jewish wailer" denotes three types of wailers: those who wailed in the past, a wailing woman, and one who has earned the lifetime sobriquet "the wailer." Visiting a house of mourning one day, I observed a woman who fit the first description; that is, she seemed merely to have wailed or to have tried her hand at wailing. After the fact, and insofar as I use this word to denote a phase in the processing of my data for this study, I doubt that this woman should be considered a wailer. The example of her appearance may shed light on the theme of this book and also highlights other themes that are not easily defined. I wish to say that the woman's performance that I am about to recount is a negative—an antiscenario if you will, an inappropriate rehearsal before the big show—that centers on the performance of the wailer, for whom the stage lights come on and the curtains are raised.

> She sat next to the entrance of the tent, at the end of the row of grieving women. She was an old woman, possibly in her early seventies. In blatant contrast to her younger mourning nieces and sisters, she used an upholstered armchair slightly higher than their seats. From this perch, she could observe the goings-on in the women's tent and in the man's tent next door. An expression of sorrow was pasted on her face. As the day went on, she nodded now and then, as if to herself, clapped her hands, and muttered strange things, not always clear, about her sister's death.
>
> On one of the first evenings of the mourning period, the place filled

> with consolers. The sound of Grace after Meals resonated from the men's tent. In the middle of this service and as the women stopped chattering, the woman began to hum aloud. Her melodic voice rose with each passing moment, and she swayed her head, her eyes half-shut. Hearing her, several women stood up and hurriedly silenced her. They grabbed her arm, which was swinging back and forth, and asked her to stop. They reminded her that she should join the others in saying "Amen." She disregarded their entreaties. Realizing this, the women adopted a conciliatory tenor and promised her that she could wail at the end of the service. The woman forcibly withdrew her arm from their grasp and continued as before, now inserting words into her melody. For a moment it seemed as though she had been sucked into the wake of the anguish and could not restrain herself. Around and with her, as though without her knowledge, a little struggle to gag her went on for a while. One of the men, glancing at these goings-on, stepped out of the nearby enclosure and headed in her direction. He ordered her to cease her untimely conduct and be silent. When the woman detected his tone of voice, her wailing turned into disgruntled mutterings that finally stopped as well. The man returned to his place; the women reclined on their seats as before. Shortly after the welcome moratorium, Grace after Meals ended. The men erupted into raucous conversation. Just then, several women turned to the grieving woman and encouraged her to revive her dying wailing performance. Now's the time to wail, they noted; now you may wail to your heart's content. She took this in with a distant and subdued facial expression, not opening her mouth. Her introversion touched off a crescendo of puzzled whispering among the other women: How had she wanted to wail at the wrong time, and why was she refusing to wail at the right time, which had come at long last? The woman held her silence until late that night. By then, the crowd of consolers had dwindled severely; only a few people remained, including the researcher until she, too, took her leave.

We should note the commonality of the performative expert, with emphasis on *the,* and the example of this woman's appearance in the mourners' tent. A woman who is considered the wailer also utters words in a melancholy tune, sometimes chooses to sit next to the mourning women on a raised chair as though she were their spokesperson, and may even belong to the group of mourners. These similarities, however, do not ruin the impression that the woman's behavior in this story represents an unsuccessful application of the rules of the Yemenite Jewish wailing tradition. Perhaps she lacked the experience to appear in public. Perhaps, too, the gravitas of her outpouring of anguish sufficed to cheapen the binding dictates of this kind of performance. Either way, my observation inside the tent shows that the empathy she deserved had nothing whatsoever to do with the performative ideal; all she got for her trouble was anger and bewilderment. The sound of her wailing moved no one to tears. Her state of disconnect violated the customary performative path from the first moment. And it is only the customary path that ends in people's hearts.

Women's wailing has several performative dimensions.[2] In the account of the wailer's conduct that I just presented, the importance of the time dimensions stands out: she raised her voice at the wrong juncture of the mourning sequence and for this reason deserved to be censured and silenced. She risked the attraction of negative associations by insisting on stepping out of order once again, by refusing to respond in the customary way to the encouraging voices of the women at the right moment. Her appearance was so anomalous that it turned attention to a disruption that occurred in a different performative dimension: the performer-audience relationship. The woman's reactions set the audience against her to the extent of rough physical contact, addressing her in the imperative, and gossip. The audience wished to distance itself from its role as an audience. By restraining and lecturing her—actions that affected her after the fact—they refrained from hearing a lament that threatened to compete, in word and in sound, with another text (Grace after Meals). Thus, the audience's assessment of the performer's ability seems to be a crucial dimension of the performance (Bauman 1977; Hymes 1975). The normally formative boundaries between an individual wailer and her audience had been totally breached. The exchanges of words even turned matters on their heads. The performer showed no evidence of authority over the audience that surrounded her; she even had to succumb to the pressures of the cognoscenti. When given the opportunity to wail, however, she transgressed in a matter that requires performative sensitivity—demonstrating compassion and consideration. In other words, she did not put on the mask that would command everyone's attention—that of the wailer, who pretends by the look on her face that she has acceded to others' entreaties that she wail. Thus, the distance between her and the others in attendance, something that the wailing culture translates into a gesture of respect, was challenged again.

In addition to commonalities among types of performers, there is a set of commonalities among performances. Taken in the aggregate, these elements may evolve into a nonrecurrent performance, that is, a pattern of relations that does not recur in other houses of mourning. I will use the high ground of the stage as a metaphorical place to begin mapping the performative patterns. I intend to interpret women's wailing in accordance with the metaphor of stage and offstage and the elevation of the stage over the audience's heads. There are low stages, attesting to intimacy between a wailer and her audience; this intimacy fractures the ritual scheme of relations. But then there are high stages, which firmly circumscribe the role players and stabilize the boundaries between them as if everything is staged and foreseen. In the wailing story above, I showed that the woman who wailed showed by her appearance that she was aloof and indifferent to the audience's needs; the audience, in turn, denied her the right to be alone. This is an example of an anomalous appearance on a very low stage, in which the rules of the performance were disrespected.

In addition to the wailer's solo appearance, the wailing culture has a group performance that the distinctions presented thus far do not fully accommodate. Although the group type of performance fits the category of low stage, it does not disrupt the wailer-audience relationship in any way. The definition of these relations is totally different here; it demonstrates how complex the cultural variations are in comparison with the simplicity of the metaphors. In this case, "low stage" takes on a special meaning. My presentation of the women's wailing circle follows.

The *Diwan*

The *diwan* is the largest room in the house; in Yemen, it was upstairs. My respondents described it as "something like a family living room" where guests were hosted on Sabbaths and festivals.[3] When it came time to mourn someone, the women and their wailing circles took possession of the *diwan.* "The men gave up their place to the women," Netanel noted. The *diwan,* a spacious high-ceilinged chamber designed for hospitality, is associatively connected with generosity. This characteristic signifies not only the chivalry of the men, who surrendered the *diwan* during the seven days of mourning, but also the women during those days, who in greater part, like the men, had gone to this house in order to be hosted. By inference, the *diwan* is a front for the traditional image of women because it is a place where emotional warmth and camaraderie may be demonstrated.

A circle of wailing women is a type of performance that was common in Yemen and lingered in Israel to some extent after the community immigrated. When Yemenite Jewish wailing began to decline, this circle was the first part of the culture that waned and disappeared. The formation of the circle in a death event is connected with the exclusion of women from the cemetery. "No woman follows the litter of the deceased," Tamar said. "Burial is men's business." This injunction, upheld rigorously in Yemen, lost its vehemence in community life in Israel. Women who took part in my research affirmed the implications of the religious restriction even though they no longer heed it. Today, even the older women enter the cemetery and spend as much time at the graves as they wish. The gender exclusion that had been practiced in Yemen, I believe, was passed through to the circle of wailers, that is, into equally weighty organization on the women's side. Being barred from the cemetery is a significant element in the ritual pattern that pious women transmitted and imposed on themselves. Against this background—past and present—one may understand how the female solo performance endured while the group performance did not. I obtained my findings in accordance with these circumstances, that is, in the absence of the original circle; most of my information about the wailers' circle originated in my respondents' memories. On several occasions, however, I had the opportunity to detect elements of the circle while observing women in the cemetery. Here I describe the wailing circle on the basis of these sources and describe some of these elements as they were revealed in a group interview with some of the women. My ethnographic aim in doing this was inspired by the notion that the circle is the original spatial form of all events of theatrical nature.

Whenever a death occurred in Jewish society in Yemen, the women stepped into their ritual roles. I asked, "When did the women begin to wail?" "They began the moment a man died," a male respondent said, adding, "Before [his corpse] was removed from the house, they were already wailing for him. The men were alone because [the women] had to wash the body. The men stood there and lit candles on the floor. The women sat in the *diwan* and wailed." The requisite actions to prepare the body for burial must have demanded the attention of only a few women; away from them, a large group of wailing women quickly formed. "Sisters, mothers, women relatives," a respondent noted, describing the kinship relations between the participants in the circle and the deceased. She added, "You don't leave strange women crying. They stay as a group." The women who joined the wailing circle and those who surrounded and observed them were mobilized to help feed the mourners and consolers from the first day of the shivah. The chores of procuring, preparing, and serving food each day were their total responsibility. These actions created relationships among them and reconfirmed their archetypical image as agents of beneficence at times of transition (Neumann 1974). Their role as caterers created a motherly circle that symbolically overlapped the circle of wailing and cast them in the role of caregivers who provide mutual support. In whatever role they played, the women stayed as a group, whose duality of circles closed in from all sides. They were synchronized in the minutiae of everything that had to be done and maintained the relations of solidarity that are unique to women (Ruddick 1989). The noblest aspects of this solidarity were fully manifested in the wailing circle.

After the burial and during the shivah, the women of the community gathered at the house of mourning. In the middle of the *diwan* stood a large copper tray with glasses. It was the custom for one woman to serve all the others. The women sat on rugs and cushions in a circle.

The respondents alluded to a close relation between the human (female) circle that formed as they sat down and the very act of drinking coffee. Few of them, however, dwelled on the meaning of this relation, as indicated by the brevity of their reference to it. One of the women recounted that "They'd drink coffee, and the wailer would arrive." Another said, "They sat in a circle with coffee." A male respondent recalled that "In Yemen, the *diwan* filled up with forty or fifty women in the afternoon, and you would hear. . . . Each of them would take a cup of coffee." Thus, one knew that a woman had joined the wailing circle by observing her drinking coffee. The act of drinking seemed able to signal a woman's commitment to the circle and everything taking place in it. One of the women captured this simply: "They would drink coffee . . . all of them." Seremetakis (1990) views the sharing of food, shelter, and work at a time of crisis as an exchange that entitles each participant to bewail the dead. One of my respondents expressed an approximation of this insight: "Nobody would dare to pass the other one without wailing." Whether this was an entitlement or a duty incumbent upon every participant, the accepted drinking of coffee, the public introduction of the beverage into the body, carries a symbolism of consent and involvement that we should not lightly disregard.

Some women brought their sewing and knitting; as a result, they were found to be drinking coffee and knitting together. In an interview with four women, I asked in bewilderment, "Doing craft projects in a house of mourning?" "Yes," one of the respondents said. "They want to pass the time of day." She continued, "[We women] eat at home, take a shower, change [our clothes], and go to the house of mourning all dressed up." As the women conversed, I discovered that an almost ordinary social encounter took shape in the *diwan,* a pleasant get-together of sorts accompanied by mundane conversation between episodes or cycles of collective wailing. In this gathering, an invisible but sturdy buffer stood between the two situations, that of weeping and that of talking. The woman who spoke of getting "all dressed up" and also responded with "We go, and after that all the crying," enunciating the last three words, contorted her face and then concealed it with her fingers, alluding to the intensity of the feelings experienced in the wailing episode and also revealing the *diwan* as a place of contradictions.

FIRST TEARS

The circle was completed and the strength of its links was attained when the first voice sounded. At that moment, the women placed their knitting behind their backs and set their cups of coffee, darkened at the bottom, in front of them. The women wailed in the order in which they sat, each awaiting her turn or obeying an empathetic logic of consideration whenever someone wished to jump the queue and unburden herself. As for the identity of the woman who would start the chain of wailing and establish the beginning of circular time, the interviewees proposed three accepted images: a grieving woman in the house of mourners, a woman known to be an expert wailer, or a woman who was "within the year," that is, who had lost a relative within the past year.

First-degree relatives of the deceased came first in this setting, as one respondent explained: "If the husband died, his wife begins, and if it's a son, heaven forbid, the mother, or, if there's no mother, then the sister begins, and they begin one by one." Another woman related that "They sit and wait for the woman of the house to cry first so that they can let it out, too." The first words uttered by this mourner, who is often called the "woman of the house," denote the welcoming or admission of guests into the group of men and women consolers. "Welcome to our house," one of the respondents quoted. "If this were a happy [occasion], we'd do something nice, but you've come and we're sad. Everyone who's come is on my head [has given me a chance to honor the deceased even more]."

In the course of an interview, Dina remembered her first tryout in wailing, an episode in which, while mourning for her mother, the other women in the circle pressed her to begin the wailing. She recalled the expert wailer nudging her with her elbow and telling her that the grieving daughter should begin. The wailing was delayed at length until Dina, who had never spoken in public, overcame her embarrassment. "I had only two words," she said. "I didn't know what to say. Those women came from so far away." She described what she had felt at this moment: "I have to start the wailing for my mother." To encourage her, one of the women turned toward her compassionately and uttered a few tender words. These words recurred in my research and turned out to be standard coinages: "May it atone for your lips," she pleaded. "Just say two words and we'll help you." I asked Dina, "What were the first words that you managed to say?" Her reply suggested that they connoted a momentary effort to appease those present and be accepted into the circle—a greeting of sorts for her guests and an attempt to express a general truth. She translated what she had said into Hebrew: "I said, 'Forgive me for not knowing the words. I welcome everyone who came to wail. There's nothing in the world like a mother. She's like a flower in the Garden of Eden. She gives and never says I gave.'" Dina wound up her account of this debut: "I began and they carried on." She grinned as though she had been put to a normative test that she had finally passed.

In another case of a mourner who had no idea how to wail for her deceased mother but had to set the circle in motion, the nagging women took the extra step of providing her with the right words. Recite the words with us, they ordered as she sobbed. "'Say this, say that,' they'd tell me," Naomi related. "They knew I had no experience in wailing." Zvia, the informant, reported a different kind of incentive for group wailing. She recalled the day of her mother's burial. When Zvia stepped through the gate, she found the house "full of wailing women." A heartrending scream—"Mother!"—escaped from her throat and filled the void. A scream, along with being the outcome of exhalation and the emission of sound, is also perceived as a metaphor for the violent transition of the self into the realm of loss, separation, pain, and death (Seremetakis 1990). Zvia related that her scream had the effect of admitting her to the "club"; it was a first signal to the women who had grouped in her home and had been silent until that moment. "It gave the excitement."

As stated, even a woman known as the wailer might start the wailing in the circle in her profound agony. "Everyone drinks coffee, and everyone knows that the wailer should be coming, and then they were all ready," one woman related. Some described the wailer as a "schoolteacher" who gives a lengthy signal for the extended and relatively pallid continuation of other laments. Others described her as a person who arrived "at regular hours" and raised her voice immediately after finishing her coffee. Meir's description of the wailing circle that formed at the grave site substantiates the role of the wailer in instigating the wailing: "Then, as all the women sit around the grave, then something has to be done, some [woman] has to stir things up. Somebody who's sociable comes. She seizes the initiative. She has power." Also, as stated, group wailing could be launched spontaneously by a woman in need who, in terms of her relationship with the deceased, was somewhere between a bereaved first-degree relative and the wailer. "If a woman lost her father or son and she's in the year [of mourning], she was still full and she burst into tears. She covered her face and began," one of the women related. A woman "in the year" had priority even if she joined the wailing circle late. Her presence revised the order and focused attention on her. In most cases, the professional wailer assumed responsibility for passing the metaphorical wailing baton to her as quickly as possible, thereby affording her an immediate release. One respondent explained that "If someone comes and she's still in her year of mourning, then the wailer puts her into the middle. She gives her this emotion to cry [wail]." Another said, "There's someone in pain, and she wants to express herself in front of everyone. So they let her cry. She has something inside."

The perception is that a sense of partly worked-through grief creates a state of surging anguish that the circle should accommodate. One wailer related that "If relatives are mourning, I have to go [there]." I asked, "Why do you say 'have to'?" "My heart lets me go, since I'm in the year and I want to unburden myself." One method that the group used to accommodate one of its members, it seems, was the yielding of right-of-way. Sometimes, however, primacy was determined or taken on the basis of the wish of a woman who had a kinship relation with the deceased. She could open the wailing even before she really joined the circle because, as a respondent explained, "She already starts when she's standing at the door [of the house of mourning] and sometimes literally outside, in front of the door. And sometimes she wails while she's on the way." The way in which the woman begins attests to the power of her anguish and entitles her to the other women's response.

CHAIN OF TEARS

Just as the first voice expressed an empathy that was unrelated to hierarchical relations, the continuation—the chaining around the circle—did much the same. Miriam explained it in a nutshell: "When she's reminded of the deceased, she starts to wail in front of everyone, and it proceeds in a queue, not just one." As one wailer finishes up another starts, and when the latter finishes the next one starts, the wailers related, many repeatedly using the word "queue." The sequence was sometimes determined by the order in which the women sat and sometimes in other ways, for example, willing deference to someone who appropriated the right to determine the queue. The act of determining the queue resembled the insertion of a small link among large links. The wailing chain was neither violated at all nor silenced for a moment; the performance could continue at length until the circle was completed. This continuity, an invaluable feature of the wailing practice, was attained mainly in the vocal dimension. Its significance was the disapproval of discontinuous rhetoric—the grammar of the poverty of daily life—and its pernicious effects. The continuous warbling melody produced by the collective of seated women created a flow. Weepy eyes sought each other out. Instead of trying to say something, a performative circle attempts to cultivate aesthetic relations among those present (Feral 1982). Such a performance steers the participants' experience toward a situation in which act and awareness become one (Csikszentmihalyi and Csikszentmihalyi 1988).

The inviolate rule was that they don't bother each other and that jumping the queue should occur with great delicacy and a demonstration of motherly solicitude. How could this be done without triggering resistance? The form of performance in the circle attested to the wailers' great sensitivity for each other's place in the queue and to the effect of the uninterrupted continuation of the despondent melody. Thus, as one woman wails, "The second one comes over and sees that she's choking on her tears and having a hard time. Then the second one says in a weepy voice, 'Let it be your atonement, let me help you now.' Then she continues. The third one and the fourth one do the same thing, a whole row." The women determined the queue by demonstrating need. I asked one of the wailers, "How did you let someone else know that you were tired of wailing?" She replied, "They could sense it by the way I cried. I didn't tell her to continue. One of them said, 'I'll help you cry, my sister.'" It was the vocalization and, at times, the quality of the wailing that signaled one's wish to stop. Even if a woman found it hard to continue, she did not initiate the transfer but instead paused in midperformance, waiting for soothing words that would relieve her of the responsibility for maintaining continuity. Each participant had to be keenly attentive to the words and to changes in the tones of the others' voices. Concurrently, she had to discern the impending wish of other women to cut in front of her and express their anguish. Before the baton could be passed, the participants had to weigh interactive symbols amid structured willingness to defer. Furthermore, no one could take over the leading role without displaying pity toward the counterpart who was about to step down. Thus, wailing showed itself to be a "code in female communication" (Caraveli-Chaves 1980, 146). The circle was an arena of sublimation among the women.

It could not be otherwise, at least ab initio. The chain of tears set up a special arena that encouraged its participants to come together. In the women's eyes, wailing, as a dialogue of doom and agony, could not be done on the basis of a structure of levels of importance.[4] "The women gather like brothers," Rina explained, immediately continuing: "They wail. They give [each other] coffee." The soothing and consoling remarks that emerged within the circle sustained the sense of partnership throughout. Like the deceased's wife, everyone needed consolation for the woes that they had accumulated in daily life.

The women demonstrated intimate acquaintance with the story of the loss, the effort that it took to perform the lament, and the need to unburden. One of the group interviews yielded clear elements of this—elements that, in my judgment, are the sole vestiges of the original circle. I asked one of the women to give me a demonstration of wailing. The moment I made this request, the five other women in the interview began to prevail upon their friend to accede. "You've got to know," one of them told me, "that Sa'ada [a pseudonym] knows lots about wailing, but she doesn't want to." When Sa'ada persisted in her refusal, several women tried to encourage her to perform by forcing appropriate words into her mouth. "Say 'It's a shame about my father, you've gone away and left me,'" one of them suggested. Another one proposed "I've been left behind alone in the world." As they pursued these attempts at persuasion, the women turned to me apologetically: "Sa'ada hasn't enjoyed life. It's a good thing that she's held on.'" "Wail for Yona," another woman proposed to Sa'ada. "Say 'Yona, I'm your atonement, my daughter's gone.'" "When someone cries, he's relieved of the pressure," another woman offered. This gambit also failed, even when the women reversed their custom by stepping out of the room, wishing to leave Sa'ada alone with me. "Look," Sa'ada began, admitting frankly, "everything the girls told you here is right. I remember." Then, pointing to her abdomen in a profound sadness that she hardly seemed able to contain, she said, "So it's already there, all of it."

The group performance breached the autonomy that had kept the women separate from each other. The reciprocity of their acquaintance sent a signal of "My pain is yours, your loss is mine." The joint performance exposed something of an I-You relationship (Buber 1959, 1965). As a woman spread her hands over the fresh grave of her deceased mother and wailed, the wailer did the same. Dozens of women stood all around, weeping silently. The deceased's daughter wailed bitterly and sometimes erupted into enraged speech, asking her dead mother how she could have left her, the daughter, behind. Witnessing these outbursts of fury, the wailer fell silent and allowed her counterpart to discourse to her heart's content. When the grieving daughter fell silent, the wailer embarked on a melodious lament that encouraged her to forget herself, using a metaphor that expressed a large dose of empathetic truth: the bereaved, she said, was carrying "a burn that cannot be cooled." As the wailer performed, she spoke about the deceased mother, mimicking the wording of her counterpart's agonies. Before the grieving daughter rose from her crouch at the grave site, several of the women who had clustered in the vicinity joined in to soothe her. "That's how it is when someone departs," one of them said. Another added, "There's one mother in the world. May her soul be in the Garden of Eden." Then they encouraged the daughter to enrich the account of her mother's death with details. She acceded, telling the women, "She died after she'd had supper."

The women in the circle deferred to each other as they wailed. By wailing in sequence and taking turns, they obviated the possibility of performing several laments at once. Simultaneous wailing in different voices and with different texts would have canceled itself out and encouraged rivalry. The scanty findings that I was able to gather on the topic suggest that a standard group lamentation of solo-and-chorus nature existed. This style, discussed in the next section, seems less characteristic of what remains of the Yemenite Jewish wailing culture and almost certainly has some specific implications. In the group performance as described thus far, each lament had the privilege of being listened to, and parts of it were objects for the expression of shared awareness. Some scholars view listening as someone's discourse multiplied over; where it does not take place, a situation akin to a quiet and asocial or so-called bad death ensues (Seremetakis 1990). The element of listening, I believe, yielded a form of performance in which the women maintained a delicate balance in the self-collective relationship. The circle was not meant to generate synergy in the sense of a whole that exceeds the sum of its parts, as the power of rituals does in Durkheim's (1965) theories. Neither was it an arena in which this intention created a whole that nullified its parts and silenced its voices. A circle of the kind described is typical of terminal doom situations in which selfness finds itself (Gamliel and Hazan 2006). My respondents repeatedly described the circle as a place meant for emotional release. "She came to release herself," many of them said. The recurrence of the word "release" alluded to the specificity of the encounter: the encounter was a setting that created the reality of a doom demarcated by time. In the hourglass that delimited the encounter, the trickling sand represented trickles of release. Once accomplished, this release replenished the participants' strength, a good thing to do before the return to ordinary life. A subtle ongoing dialogue took place between those in the intimate chain of wailers and the reality that would soon force them to part. The stage that each of the wailers received is symbolic of a unique place in the world. To bring this meaning into clear focus, I offer an example that pertains to willingness to deviate from strict practice. A woman who, to everyone's surprise, refused to calm down when it came time to desist from wailing for her sister blurted between sobs, "The world's horrified, the world's horrified." By saying this, she showed that by means of the stage that she had been given for the moment, the doom that she was experiencing was something like an object that she owned, so to speak—something that could not totally drive away the demands of the self. The *diwan* was a place where the circle, a symbol of the female archetype (Neumann 1974) where selfness is present and also merges units into the presence of other women, became real.

SOLO AND CHORUS

Several men described wailing performances that took place in solo-and-chorus form. These accounts, more than being indicative of the commonness of this manner of performance in Yemen, seem to illustrate its scarcity in Israel. For this reason, I cannot describe the performance in the far-reaching, detailed manner that one encounters in other ethnographies (Seremetakis 1990; Feld 1995; Briggs 1992, 1993). However, I would like to dwell on the gender significance of the source of information about this performance. The performative category of solo and chorus in wailing should be viewed as an in-between configuration—the chain of tears on one end and the solo wailer on the other. As Meir put it, the solo wailer "introduces the chorus," and the other women "respond." Various sources described women's wailing in terms such as "What's torture? When they all answer in unison. What's wailing? When one talks and the others answer after her."[5] "It's amazing," Meir said, "All of them . . . together . . . as if someone had pounded them with a hammer." I asked, "Isn't the wailing handed from one to the other?" "No," Meir replied, "it's all of them together. It's like a chain where [the wailer] says a sentence and gets to the end. It ends clearly. The sentence ends and then you hear everyone crying, and then it starts over. It repeats that way." Another account of this form of performance was given by Shlomo, who focused on the standard rhyming: "They respond after her, but she rolls the word around. Even if the word isn't consistent with the meter of the song and doesn't exactly fit, she makes it rhyme with a previous word by turning the 'ee-ya' or the 'o-ya' around." In the solo part of the performance, it is mostly the wailer who makes up lyrics and leads the rhyming. However, she depends heavily on the chorus, that is, the other women in the circle. This dependency is crucial for this kind of performance from the emotional standpoint as well (Briggs 1993). Some respondents described the collective and marvelously synchronized weeping as "heartrending" and especially shocking in its effect.

Meir emphasized the dimension of control in relations between the wailer and the other women. His conclusion verges on that of Seremetakis (1990), who found among the Mani separate names for the circle of wailers and the individual wailer and who recently discovered that there is a leader, an expert in generating especially intensive pain. Meir opined that "She has the power of melancholy." When melancholy speaks from the throat of the wailer, its power is translated into social power: "'Now I want to hear a chorus of wailing,' that's what she wants." Asked to define the objective of this wish, Meir explained that "The wailer is really pleased that everyone answers her in a chorus. It gives her satisfaction, it answers an inner craving: she's influenced them. You can't imagine the effect it has when she finishes the sentence and strikes this concluding pose, 'ay . . .' and everyone says after her, 'ooh, ooh, ooh.'" I asked, "What effect does it have?" Meir replied that "It's like, 'I'm the leader and you're all following me a like a flock of sheep, and you'll behave as I dictate and at the pace that I choose.'" Insofar as this concept is valid in regard to a collective melancholy performance, it indicates that power is attributed to the wailer and that she is afforded a high stage. In a solo-and-chorus performance, the wailer has two types of audiences: the chorus of women and the eavesdropping men. Her performance is a focal and easily identifiable example, at the behavioral level, of one woman's control of a group of people. Meir's remarks give the impression that the wailers whom he observed occupied a very high stage. In the patriarchal society of Yemenite Jewry, it is quite audacious to put on a show of unusual vocalism. A polyphonic performance at a death event may be suspected of challenging the social order (Briggs 1992, 1993). In a performance of this kind, Briggs believes, women mimic the use of political rhetoric. Correspondingly, a situation that attributes high-handed conduct to women may easily be translated symbolically into a scene of an elected official delivering a speech. To this should be added the men's appreciation of the complexity of the performance, that is, the hard-to-follow verbal acrobatics and the rhyming maneuvers. From the men's standpoint, the element shared by the women is a foreign language. By implication, their collective performance contains a message that challenges the perception of gender relations. In the men's depictions, the solo wailer counterweighs her chorus in a way that ignores the physical reality of the circle. When such a performance is given, if a women's circle exists at all, it is noteworthy only for its power to exclude. If so, the audience of men first contemplates the chorus of women and then turns around, bewildered, to contemplate itself.

A Woman in Her Wailing

In Yemen, solo wailing performances took place in both forms of the circle described. In Israel, they remained common among Yemenite Jews from the time the community immigrated until recent years. The eruption of an individual woman's voice from the women's area of a house of mourning still occurs. My respondents spoke a great deal about this kind of wailing. In the course of my interviews and conversations, they repeatedly expressed their awareness of it—sometimes from up close and sometimes from far away—and invited me to observe its manifestations. This can be considered solo wailing, even if more than one wailer appeared in a house of mourning and whether she did so on day one of the shivah or on other days. One wailer might wail on the day of the burial, and another might do so immediately afterward, unless she waited for the second or third day. Either way, they wailed in the presence of women, standing or sitting in the imagined form of a closed circle. The wailer's uniqueness and prominence are characteristic of solo wailing, a form that does not require queuing and is not requited by other voices. In comparison with the other performative forms of wailing, this form has an identifiable stage on which a protracted ritual happening unfolds (Finnegan 2001, 101). Wailing of this kind is often rewarded with words that transcend the unburdening of the anguish heart—special words from the audience, some wishing to urge the wailer on and others pleading with her to stop.

THE MAKING OF A WAILER

My women respondents told dramatic stories and used picturesque metaphors to describe the making of a wailer. These stories illustrate an insight that Johara's son offered: "She remembered what put her in the situation of being a wailer to begin with, and then she had no problem wailing." By and large, a woman becomes a wailer, or *the* wailer, in a circle or solo, due to the persistence of a tradition generations long, the hand of God, or the all-defeating power of grief. Wailing women told me that they had acquired their knowledge from elderly women whom they had heard in their youth—"the giants," they called them. The wailing women did their learning in the company of women in the outer rings of wailing circles in houses of mourning and described having listened or "heard" in this context and having "drawn the words from the air." As I have shown, a woman may have taken her first stab at wailing as a mourner who was committed to the observance of a normative obligation. Between these two possibilities—random listening and social imperative—lay a third possibility, direct training, with the elder guiding the younger. "I had a neighbor who was a wailer," Rachel, an expert wailer, related. "She was a grand and special mother. When my mother-in-law died, she told me, 'You sit there and start [wailing]; I'm here to help you.'"

Sometimes a mother personally paved her daughter's way to becoming the wailer. Ora recalled having witnessed her mother wailing in daily life whenever the latter remembered her late father: "She would sit with the narghile, and all of a sudden she cried. I would hear her, and it terrified me. I remember her words to this day. I grasped each and every word." Eventually, Ora noted, she herself became an expert wailer and a washer of the dead. When I asked her about the value of these occupations in her life, she defined them as "very, very important to me." Netanel told me about his sister, who became a wailer of repute in their mother's footsteps: "She had never wailed, but she picked it up from Mother. She trailed Mother like a shadow. She went everywhere [to mourners' homes] with her. The moment Mother was gone, passed away, all at once she set to doing it herself. Suddenly she began to wail." For her, too, wailing became a way of life, or, as Netanel added, "She whipped it out wherever she went. Where didn't she? 'Do it, do it' [imitating people expressing their expectations]. You could tell that someone [an expert wailer] had come."

Another account of the making of an expert wailer alludes to the symbolism of the injection of a wailing performance into a daughter due to her intimacy with her mother. Haviva's wailing debut was halting and weepy. She delivered it to herself; no one could overhear her except—so she believed—her dead mother. Before surrendering her soul, in a long intimate moment, her mother had made her swear that she would wail for her. While the two of them remained alone, she added a warning: take care of my body and prepare it for burial. This administering of an oath had been preceded by days or weeks in which the mother gave her daughter some words and trained her in the wailing chant. Finally, as the mother closed her eyes, she left behind a terrible threat: if you fail to do it well, I will return from the dead and take away one of your children. Even before anyone knew about the mother's death, before the house filled with people, the daughter wailed, her hands caressing the corpse. She addressed her mother in what can be called a prelament lament and said, "Look, I'm keeping my vow, I'm wailing, and I'll wail for you for many days to come." Those few moments marked the beginning of Haviva's career of visiting other people's homes and bewailing their departed loved ones.

The dying mother's threat connected two loose ends—the beginning and the end of life—in a cruel way. Stabbing the daughter's ears like barbs, their importance was that "If you don't wail for me when I die, you'll be wailing for one of your children." One may wonder about the absence of sadness in those final moments of life and how acceptance of death became a violent and incomparably difficult commandment, especially in view of the prevalent belief among Yemenite Jewish women in the existence of spirits and the harm they can cause (Tzadok 1967, 157–58). This puzzlement, however, gives way to a different meaning of the message that reverberates between the lines and in the existential space that every mother and daughter share. "If you don't wail for me"—that is, if you fail to express your sorrow aloud, to say that you sustain the image of the person who got pregnant with you, raised you, protected you, and shaped your very being for your own pregnancy—"then you have repudiated your motherness, me, and the life-creating reality that we share. If you put me to death in this sense—something that death per se cannot—you will have marred your purpose in life and your ability to give to posterity." By putting these words in the mother's mouth, I offer my own monological expression of theoretical arguments about a configuration of attachment originating in pre-Oedipal development. This attachment gives priority to—and in fact singles out—the mother-daughter bond over any other. During the life span, relations are defined in hypersymbiotic theoretical terms, in the sense that a mother cannot distinguish her daughter from herself and that a daughter identifies with her mother at deep levels of values and personality (Chodorow 1974, 1978).

Nehama, who wailed only once in her life—in a wondrous event—testified as to her mother's ability to return from the dead and demand that she wail. Although the deceased had not been her biological mother, the two of them had had a mother-daughter relationship. Nehama had stopped at the ritual ablution facility and stayed there at length as other women administered to the old woman's body. She felt that she could not open her mouth to cry or express her distress in any other way precisely when such expression was so expected. Her sense of muteness persisted until a strange and violent thing happened: "You won't believe it. Someone slapped me and I turned around. I felt I'd been slapped. Believe me, I experienced it in my flesh. Someone punched me here [pointed to her chest] and then tears poured from my eyes like from a spring. I began to cry. She was ready by then. She was already dressed; we'd dressed her up. I opened a spigot [of tears]. I said [in my lament] that she'd been my mother and if I hadn't come she would have begun to search for me." Nehama dwelled at length on the mystical experience. The dead woman's spirit had been present at the washing facility and had delivered a powerful blow to her chest to inspire her to wail. The separation of daughter from mother had not happened at all. The surprise of having being punched in the chest became an indelible memory. The supernatural, miraculous form of the attachment placed the mother's messages outside the bounds of time and bridged the separation.

My respondents' tendency to phrase the mother-daughter relationship in the context of wailing led me to several theoretical reflections. Different vocal timbres and choices of types of metaphors make every wailing performance unique. The very possibility of this reinforces my contention that it is the performance, replicated with precision by the daughter, that cements the daughter-mother attachment. To my thinking, the lamentation acquired in this manner constitutes a symbiotic mechanism that shapes women's identity as a function of the strength of the attachment. While houses of mourning do represent repeated demands for improvisation that express an individual's singular identity, it would seem that the dead, in the eyes of the wailer, are the mother's carriers, passing by in procession. The situation resembles what Freud claimed about the poet: a powerful experience in reality triggers the memory of a previous experience in the poet's life, chiefly a childhood experience, releasing a desire that creates its own satisfaction in the poetic work. The poetic work itself carries signs of both the fresh pretext and the bygone memory (Cohen 1991, 9). "Mother" represents a psychological yearning that never ends, especially when separation from her oceanic being is impossible. Chodorow (1974) notes that the mother-daughter attachment in patriarchal parochial traditional societies is shaped by the memory of a mother's separation from her own mother upon her wedding.[6] In other words, mothers who expect a similar separation from their daughters identify with them profoundly and develop a special attachment to them, an attachment that leaves the daughters unprepared for events to come. From the moment the daughter is born, the mother is shaping separation from her as a traumatic event. Several respondents shared this lesson with me, either by using this expression or by weeping at length during the interview. Mothers' consistent violation of separation processes cannot lead to the individuation of their daughters. Often, a daughter's only resort is to become like her mother and her grandmothers and to alleviate her nostalgia by wailing. This kind of attachment, lacking in separation but ending with abandonment, is the daughters' tragic lot. Once the mother has departed, and insofar as one can compare the outcome of this event with the experience that sons go through, the daughters fall from a great height. This form of attachment, which consists of identifying with and then letting go, takes shape in daughters like a burning pain—an urge that pierces the silence of the nostalgia metaphors and is manifested in them in verbal exhalations. If so, wailing may resemble various types of religion or art. Wailing is a career that unifies.

Given what we have said thus far, the reader should not be amazed to find that wailing traces its origins to deep and intertwined levels of the psyche. My respondents' descriptions substantiated this perception by offering metaphors that focus on body and amazement. One respondent described wailing as "sounds created in the human body." Another woman suggested that "The words come from the heart. They emerge from the soul; they are sown in the heart." A third respondent demonstrated the distribution of thoughts and emotions: "It's all written for [the wailer] here," pointing to her head with one hand and to her breast with the other. Sometimes wailers hesitated to say that they do not fully understand the performance, to admit that they do not know where the words come from, and to acknowledge that the words tumble from their mouths without their control. The remarks of several women revealed the making of a wailer as an unconscious process in which they place themselves in a permanent state of sacrifice and submission. In addition to the metaphors already mentioned, the women referred to God as an entity of depth and emanation, an entity that shares its power and makes use of the appropriate bodily organs. Several expressions illustrated this: "God opened the heart," "God gives ideas," "It came to me all of a sudden from Allah," "I sleep and in the morning I wake up with words," "The words come from God; I don't know how," and "The words come out inadvertently, from the head, from the heart, from everywhere. As if someone gave me something to drink and I let it out." In terms of my interpretation above, these respondents may consider God a mediator between a woman and the object of her nostalgia, that is, an entity that unifies. Some would say that the word "God," when spoken by wailers, represents an infinite and indefinite beneficence, a representation rooted in their belief that it is a kind of transcendental projection of their nostalgia for the maternal kindnesses that preceded the separation (Marcel 1965; Jung 1960; Rank 1958). The heart and mind of a wailer are tantamount to conduits that lead to goodness; they transcend the gender symbolization that separates emotion from thought and symbolize the unity that the performance requires—the emotiveness of tears and the wisdom of words. The performance, we find, is related to that which is not understood, is inadequately known, from which no separation is possible.

An additional level in wailing comes into sight from the direction of the maternal bond. Rina described a motherhood that may be cut short in childbirth. Although the respondents did not dwell on the phenomenon of infant and child mortality in Yemen, several interviews shed some light on it. Rina noted the death of a birth giver specifically, describing it as a predictable if premature event due to the dictates of nature. Unlike the forced separation that occurs when a daughter gets married but like a mother's death in old age, a mother's separation from her fetus is considered a natural one. This association leads to the goddesses and the birth-giving women of mythology, who liken their wombs to tombs. The symbolic meaning of this tautology is the metaphor of the uterus as a container in which the fetus dwells in a unity of nonexistence (Scholem 1961). This death is attributed to a reality that unfolds within the womb and differs from what the owner of this womb expects. As for the pregnant woman, the abstract symbolism of womb-tomb loses its potency because a different kind of death—a real and terrifying death—threatens to defeat her in her contortions. The remarks that I quote below connect an oral tradition, the individual's own efforts, and divine assistance with the nexus of wailing and birth as developments that crest and leave their performative imprints at the stage of a woman's adulthood. Thus, Rina relates:

> Even since she gave birth, the wailer pleads that she should remember the words [of the lament]. God puts the memory in her ear. She heard the words when she was six years old, and she has to repeat them when she's twenty-six, thirty. She wants to repeat those words. God gives memory. . . . You don't wail when you're young. From age thirty, thirty-five, after she's already had her first child, her second, her fourth. The wailer begins

> to wail when she's well up in years, when she begins to understand life, to understand sadness. She has given birth, she knows what sadness is, what torture of the soul is. She began to plead to God. She contemplates and pleads for herself. There are girls who died in their first childbirth, there are girls who died in their second childbirth, their third childbirth, even in their fifth childbirth they suddenly dropped dead. It's dangerous. Then they began to contemplate themselves. "What's going to happen? Who will save me? The One Who created me, He'll save me." So they began to pray and wail for themselves. You need to have this contemplation; with this contemplation, God allows her to listen to the whisper in her ear.

The womb is the cavity of the woman's tomb. It is the death that lurks inside her for time when she grows up and becomes a mother. In the making of a wailer, the lament begins with prayer and entreaties: a helpless woman utters a prayer and expresses the metaphors of her loss in it. Consequently, wailing has to do with grieving for oneself. Childbirth is an occasion at which the body is totally subject to the kindness, or the wrath, of a divine power. The wailing performance, consisting of bodily motions and heartrending keening, reconstructs the situation of childbirth and presents it as a situation of sacrifice. Wailers recall birth giving in their recurrent use of the expression "my mother, the birth giver." Unsurprisingly, they use this expression as incidental to mentioning people whom they have lost—a mother, a father, a husband, or a sister. Wailing occupies itself with losses that a woman experienced in her life. As one of the wailers expressed it, "Whenever I wail I remember what I've gone through, it makes everything new again. Life was bitter." Lamenting the death of loved ones in the midst of the wailing performance, as a consequence of having mentioned childbirth, appears to be a variation of the articulation of the wailer's own grief. One of the women captured this succinctly: "As they say in Arabic, whoever cries, cries for himself." Two wailers who met with me together said, "We are wailing for our soul." A fourth respondent said, "This weeping I do for me. For myself. 'Why did he leave us, and I'm all alone in this world?'" The wailer laments her selfness, which has been rendered deficient and empty by the death that has claimed her loved ones, the interactive and dependent assets of her selfness. The wailer cries for them/for herself because she is geared to relations, to mothering; ever since she gave birth, she considers these relations an anchor that stabilizes her existence (Chodorow 1974, 1978; Jonte-Pace 1987). Studies supporting the claim that women tend to cry more than men do show that their ability to empathize and be involved in relatives' lives makes them more sensitive than otherwise to events that befall them (Turner and Avison 1989) and that typical events in their life cycle are experienced as acute stressors (Vingerhoets and Scheirs 2000).

A wailer, especially an expert one, is generally an older woman who has passed fertility age and has entered the postchildbirth stage of life (an age of transition).[7] As I have shown, one reason for this is that the wailer mentions her accumulated personal losses and uses them to induce weeping in others. In other words, as one wailer explained, "An old woman has already gone through lots of troubles, and what she says is truer." This insight is much older than a recent direction of research that posits that the grieving of elderly women in Western society is influenced more by prior personal losses than by losses associated with aging (McCandless and Conner 1997). The mourning style of women is influenced by memories of the death of family members, fetuses, infants, husbands, and parents.

McCandless and Conner (1997), which does not necessarily distinguish between Eastern and Western cultures, also argues that menopause is a loss—one that takes place in adulthood, even before old age, and that serves as a catch-all for other losses. Menopause, associated with hormonal changes, is described as a change that affects the psychological state of women and, as one of its byproducts, impairs social relations. Menopause symbolizes the end of a major role in women's lives. Once it happens, a woman is tempted to think that she will never again feel like a woman. She realizes that the possibility of renewing herself by mothering yet another child no longer exists; the irreversibility of her situation causes her pain. I believe that menopause represents the end of a woman's ability to maneuver against other losses in her life. For a woman, the act of creation in childbirth is a significant mechanism of compensation and consolation. A woman issues live fetuses as a way of countering the predatory nature of death. They are her assets; they broaden her psychological hygiene in view of her parents' deaths and the other deaths that must follow soon. She may regard her children as representations of control of death and of her personal faith. The biblical account of the struggle between Rachel and Leah for Jacob's affection is an extreme example of this. Their craving for his love is bound up with craving for motherhood and translates in them into proliferate birth giving. They name their babies in accordance with the extent of their appreciation of the newborn's extrication from their hips:

> And when the Lord saw that Leah was hated, he opened her womb, but Rahel was barren. And Leah conceived and bore a son and called his name Reuven, for she said, Surely the Lord has looked upon my affliction; now, therefore, my husband will love me. And she conceived again and bore a son, and said, because the Lord has heard that I was hated, he has therefore given me this son as well, and she called his name Shimon. . . . And God remembered Rahel and hearkened unto her and opened her womb. And she conceived and bore a son, and said, God has taken away my reproach, and she called his name Yosef and said, the Lord shall add to me another son. (Genesis 29:31–33, 30:22–24)

Menopause denotes the absolute dispossession. It affixes a final imprint to the reality of noncontrol to which a woman transitions. Such an imprint, however, may be applied earlier in life, in the state of barrenness. An infertile woman is viewed as having the ultimate lacking—a response equal to the threat of death. We can surmise that the timing of menopause, preceding old age, has something to do with the change in a woman's status and her transformation into a wailer. Then and only then does she become aware of the profundity of humankind's helplessness. Her lament is the story of the loss of the symbol of her most rewarding and welcome endeavor, which had sustained her in hard times. Those hard times included the brutalities of diseases in Yemen that terminated the lives of fetuses and sucklings. Such diseases served as backdrops for protracted mourning among many women, as "funerals were a daily spectacle and the laments issued loudly from homes and from every rooftop" (Binyamin-Gamliel 2002, 109). Fertility countered mortality and filled a woman with occasional joy. In contrast, she discovers the loss of her ability to conceive at a late stage of her life: it ripens inside her in the form of protracted weeping, identifies with others' incapacity, and insinuates itself and makes itself heard in mourners' homes.

Elderly women have a special status; it is this that makes them into wailers. One of my respondents alluded to this: "Young women in Yemen don't learn yet; respect is for old [women]." The social position of women of similar age in other wailing circles corroborates the distinction she draws (Aborampah 1999; Danforth 1982) in the broader context of feminine religion and rituals involving both sexes (Sered 1994; Gutmann 1994). In several cultures, the timing of menopause carries additional significance: this period in a woman's life symbolizes a passive and belated cleansing of the self. The end of menstruation stanches the potential of defilement, possibly drawing women closer to the ritual status of men. Even though this is also true among the Jews of Yemen, the emphasis is on a partial convergence of status, not full equality.[8] "A woman does not put tefillin on her head," Rachel noted. "Why not? It's because she has this dirt [menstrual blood] that she gets, and by the time she's done with it, she's fifty. But at age fifty they won't let her wear the tefillin on her head because she hadn't done it from the beginning." Thus, Rachel explained, the "dirt" can fade but cannot disappear. However, women respondents also alluded to a connection between menopause, a phase that signifies that the woman has passed fertility age, and the easing of the intrinsic threat of her sexuality. "It's simple," one respondent explained. "If she's young, she's embarrassed; she can't wail. Even me, then my children yell at me. Society frowns on it. But when a woman is old, everyone accepts her. They don't pay attention to an old woman anymore." If so, wailing is a sort of ritual leadership, a practice that grandmothers perform for the sake of and in the presence of mothers (Sered 1994, 78). Women's transitional age and old age are parts of life in which they are unshackled from behavioral and affective norms. Elderly women feel unobliged to codes of shame and concealment (Gutmann 1994, 161–63). "It's courage," Zahara stated, "to express all this both from the heart and also about the dead. How to express the word, [the wailer] has courage. It comes to her when she really feels the people around her. Say there are women, even when it's for their loved ones, they're embarrassed. [A woman who doesn't wail] can cry inside, with tears and everything, but to wail, she has [to overcome] this inner shame that keeps her from shouting out. Without courage, you can't do it [wail]." A wailer's performance hinges on freedom of expression—it cannot engage the audience's emotions unless it contains some extent of letting go. The wailer accomplishes this at a time in her life when she appears to be beyond temptation.

Before I conclude my discussion of the making of a wailer, I would like to describe the wailing performance as accumulated knowledge. Successful transmission of this oral tradition is based on two stages: hoarding and hatching. In terms of learning and retention theories, these correspond to stages of acquisition and storage, both of which may be detected in the wailers' stories (Gleitman 1983): women hoard knowledge and allow it to hatch inside them until the right moment—the moment of retrieval from memory, the moment of the performance—arrives. This process may span several stages in life, from childhood to adulthood. The performance is brought to fruition at some moment of maturity on the curve of psychosocial development, which may have completed its ascent and begun its descent. For example, an expert wailer returns to a detail of memory from her life in Yemen, one that had been unique and significant from her perspective as a girl and one that she had used to establish the beginning of her self-image. "I'd hear my grandmother," said the expert wailer. "They'd wrap a sheet around her so she wouldn't get cold [when she arrived at a mourners' house to wail]. She was important to everyone. They were afraid she'd get cold." Asked about the timing of her first wailing performance, she said that it happened only after her son had been killed in the Yom Kippur War, more than two decades after her immigration to Israel.

Another story retold by an expert wailer, a special story, attests to the stages of her wailing career that I laid out above. She made her debut during the shivah of her aunt, a degree of kin for whom Jewish law did not require her to mourn. She did not know that she would wail until she surprised herself at that moment. She had invited Johara, the ultimate expert, to wail as a gesture of respect for the deceased. "I sent her [an invitation] to come," she began the story. "She came and gave two words. I told her, 'Your friend of all people, whom you say you loved. Two words, and that's that?'" Thus my respondent described her immense disappointment with Johara's refusal to deliver a lengthy lament; the respondent took this as an unexpected refusal and considered it deviant behavior. Wishing to make amends and ease her sense of indignity, she responded right away: "You know, at that moment I moved the sheet [between the corpse and the people in the house] and I went in there and sat down to wail. No one knew I was. They said, 'Who's that? Who's that?' Then they came over and saw me next to the deceased, wailing." I asked, "Did you know how to wail?" "Yes," she replied. "I don't know how it came to me and how I did it." "Had you heard other wailers before?" "Sure," she answered. "I would hear but I was embarrassed. That time, I just erupted for my aunt [who had been denied the privilege of appropriate wailing] and I've been a wailer ever since."

The twists and turns of the psyche and women's associations with their place in the existential space of motherhood and society are connected with their predisposition to wail, to collect and retain, and to be part of the next generation of the wailing tradition. My respondents transformed the origins of the wailer persona into a complex specification. From their remarks, one could imagine how the complexity started in childhood and developed further in the wake of events in adulthood. My remarks in this section of the chapter describe the making of a wailer as a prototypical figure—something like a rounded figure assembled from a collection of existential and social desires. I have interpreted these desires in relation to the accumulated knowledge about the human psyche and the cultural conventions that determine the ways of Yemenite women. By implication, a complete explanation is still lacking—one that distinguishes between women and women, between a general class that shares the consciousness of cultural suffering and the minority among them who became wailers. The consciousness of suffering, I should emphasize, bonds all these women to each other by common custom and makes them co-owners of the inner secrets of a maternal discourse. It places even the last of them under the umbrella of the lament in its weepy presence. However, it is not clear how the contrast of the performer's activism and her listeners' passivism is established. My respondents hinted at a perception that would make this distinction by attributing courage to the wailer and shame to her female audience. To complete and substantiate this explanation, an investigation that oversteps the limits of the current study is needed, one that probes one personality among all the others—the one that chooses to pursue its destiny on the stage.

A DRAMATIC UNIT

Once a woman has become a wailer and is presented with wailing opportunities, she performs. She shows that she is a dramatic unit by appearing at cemeteries and, above all, in houses of mourning. Several of the ideas mentioned above—about becoming—combine to present the wailing performance as merely a vehicle that the wailer uses to express her emotions. By implication, in an emotionally charged socialization process, women learn to regard wailing as a valuable tool. The missing piece of the "becoming" puzzle is the stage, that is, the importance of performing before an audience. We do make suppositions about the feminine/motherly motives of a woman who performs, but we do not put her on a public stage. In this matter, it is important to distinguish between an audience and a circle of wailers. As stated, a circle of wailers is a group of women who establish egalitarian and mutually supportive relations. A circle of women is easily interpreted as a tangible configuration of motherly projection. The story of the making of a wailer leads to and fits into such a circle. As noted above, the common form of wailing in Yemen, the one that should be considered the original mode of the Yemenite Jewish wailing performance, was the communal one. Solo wailing, in contrast, is a stripped-down, diminished model, so to speak, that was relatively uncommon in Yemen and took hold in Israel. The audience of a solo wailer, mainly in recent decades, includes men and women; it takes shape spontaneously and falls apart spontaneously back and forth. Happenings involving this kind of audience occur all the time, with women remaining close to the performer and men situated on the other side of an imaginary separation line. Even though the women can easily and consensually interrelate as the performance takes place, the wailer performs for one audience irrespective of the distance among its members. In other words, she stations herself in front of the audience and appears on a tall stage. If so, the term "dramatic unit" with which I headed this section of the discussion, leading to descriptions of a performative archetype, is a metaphorical leap of sorts. Previously, I described wailers as being controlled by subterranean flows of consciousness and by a powerful existential craving that is stronger than they are. From here on, I portray them as people who pour emotions into performative molds and then seek to control the audience's emotions. None of my respondents, male or female, spoke about this disparity. This ethnography, devoted mainly to tracing their ideas and showing how they are expressed by presenting selected wordings, illustrates the reflective deficiency. Wailing women did not admit their need for an audience. Instead, their remarks revealed a consciousness of values: they provide the audience with a service, satisfy an obligation of respect, and carry out a religious imperative. "It's unpleasant not to [wail]; you have to give respect," said one of the wailers in justification of her role, adding, "People come from everywhere. Two hundred to three hundred people every evening." Another wailer said, "Sure, they honor me, they treat me nice, 'Thank you very much,' the whole thing." However, she assured me, "But I pay no attention to it." My comments from this point on will reflect the wailers' disregard, or perhaps their selective introspection, in this matter. From here on, our discovery of the wailer's need for an audience will originate in critical perceptions expressed by members of the audience, that is, male respondents and nonwailing women. Also, I will describe the characteristics and sequences of the performance in terms of the wailer's projection of internal control onto the audience.

CONSPICUOUS IN HER EXPERTISE

When I asked an elderly wailer, her vernacular laced with Yemenite Arabic, why mourners and consolers do not content themselves with their own spontaneous weeping and need a wailer, she replied that "There's weeping and there's weeping." I belabored the point: "But what's special about a wailer's weeping?" She said, "Our [wailers'] weeping is one thing, and theirs is another." She neither delved into the nuances of the uniqueness of her performance nor used the word "expertise," which her vocabulary seemed to have overlooked. Clearly, however, she saw it as a matter of expertise. Her response was geared into our understanding of expertise as something acquired by experience and a form of social functioning that wields an acknowledged influence.

Some scholars hold the view that expertise typifies modern economies (Sills 1968). Giddens (1991) regards the confluence of expertise and social relations with the reactions of the self as an outcome of the modern project. Indeed, respondents who had adopted Hebrew as their dominant language and appeared to have assimilated concepts from the modern Israeli world of work used this word to describe the wailing performance. They also broadened their metaphorical comparisons to something beyond wailer-singer and transplanted the traditional into well-known recent systems of understanding. One respondent distinguished between a first-rate wailer and a third-rate wailer. Mazal explained that "A wailer has to be built for wailing." Then, to help me understand, she added, "It's like you're built to be a PhD." The respondents attributed talent and knowledge to the wailer as one might attribute credentials to a schoolteacher or a professional who keeps office hours. Meir expressed the conventional wisdom about expertise and its importance: "Johara was the greatest of the wailers." I asked him, "How does one determine who was the greatest of the wailers?" He answered with a question: "How does one determine who's a good university lecturer?" By invoking concepts such as "teacher," "lecturer," and "PhD," the respondents demonstrated their awareness of a reality in which society certifies its members and institutionalizes their expertise (Collins 1979).

Rivka carried her comparisons all the way to a quintessentially modern area of expertise: psychotherapy. "[Ritual wailers] could be great psychologists. They're really smart women. They didn't go to school, but they have knowledge of life." Elaborating on the special wisdom that she attributed to wailers, she said that "The wailer has to have character and pure devotion. She has to have intelligence and emotion and has to understand what's going on. It's on the basis of those things that she [wails]."

The likening of wailers to psychologists attests to the depth of the respondents' understanding of expertise because it originates in the perception that psychotherapy is a recognized system of expertise. According to Giddens (1991, 180), this expertise is firmly planted in the reflective propensity of the self. This means two things. First, expertise is intertwined with the needs of the self and fulfills them; second, and closer to the topic at hand, the respondents' self-contemplation allows them to identify a variant of psychotherapy and call it an expertise.

Gavriel used the terms "expertise" and "profession" in ways that partly overlapped their familiar meanings. He considered the wailing performance a profession and supported his view by citing the Jewish sources: "We recognize wailing from the Bible, where the prophet says 'Summon the wailers and let them come and weep for you.' It means that the wailers had the status of wailers; it was their profession, you might say. If you called them, they came; if you didn't, they didn't. That's a profession. If you call a professional, he comes and gives you the service. If you don't call him, he doesn't come. It was a kind of profession and so it's been for generations, more or less. Everywhere, in every generation, every community has wailers who make it their profession." Then he drew a distinction between profession and expertise: "The difference between a professional wailer and an expert is that a professional will come and wail and make up rhymes for anyone [who died]. The expert just knows how to wail and does it only when she's in the mood, if she feels like it. Even if they invite her but she wasn't a friend or a relative of [the deceased], she'll wail less." Gavriel concluded flatly: "An expert is influenced by the surroundings. A professional wails in any situation."

Expertise is also defined as broad command of the content and essence of a given occupation. An occupation denotes a line of business, a vocation. Gavriel's remarks relate to three elements: knowledge, status, and livelihood. The special knowledge needed for a wailing performance is linked to social status. Furthermore, the description of wailing as a "service" delivered by a professional and of the professional wailer as one who "wails in any situation" alludes to the importance of the economic element. The respondents were typically unanimous about the element of knowledge in the definition of expertise. From their perspective and as I show below, a worthy wailing performance requires knowledge. However, notwithstanding Gavriel's outlook, obviously the expert wailer has no distinct social status. As for the third element, a wailing performance is not always paid for. Such consideration is not given at houses of mourning in Israel. As for the custom in Yemen, the respondents provided a complex picture: there was some kind of material consideration, including money; this depended on customs that varied from district to district.

Where does the wailer stand on the social scale for her public performance? As stated, allusions to status are altogether missing. Instead, I found allusions to and symbols of a wailer as a person who has a reputation. Her reputation, associated with death, neither follows her nor precedes her as she enters social circles. It is a reputation of crisis that comes to the fore only when a family or the community is in a bad way; it surfaces in view of a very painful necessity. In ordinary life, the wailer is one among many, "like everyone." Only within the bounds of the event, when the house of mourning needs her performance, is a special place set aside for her. Johara's son related that "When she entered, everyone knew she was worth something so they let her sit in the middle." In cemeteries, as throngs of women form a perimeter around a fresh grave and create circles around those among them who are in mourning, the crowd breaks up easily and clears a path for the newly arrived wailer. It takes her only a moment to reach the grave and only another moment to find a place in the middle to sit. There is no delay, no protest. "The whole community comes here and drives me to the bereavement home specially," Banya, who lives in town, related.

Once, when ordered to stop a wailing performance due to the sensitivity of the deceased's children, Banya thundered, "If you don't want to hear me, I'll go home. I won't wait around." Then, mindful of the importance of her status, she immediately carried out her threat. The affair ended well, commensurate with the strength of her reputation: "You know," she told me, smiling, "they sent me a car especially to take me back." When a wailer was said to have had "a reputation for [wailing]," one of several respondents who elaborated on the point explained that "She's like a singer who gets up on the stage and attracts attention." She was also likened to an "Arab sheikh," but only in the narrow sense of someone whom everyone wants to hobnob with at a social event. Sometimes a wailer hears about a death event and shows up on her own; sometimes she is invited. They send her a message: "Come, he's dead. We want you to come." Verbal and nonverbal expressions confirm what many of the respondents said routinely: "The wailer is respected" and "They give the wailer respect." One woman respondent specified that "They give her respect in the heart." In daily life, the wailer's reputation is repressed; the will to live takes precedence. When the right time comes, however, it is translated into signs of respect at the time of the performance. The whole strength of this approach is that it allows the wailer to demarcate her setting and leave an imprint on it (Clark 1990).

Before I move on to the essence of the performance—the knowledge that fills the perception of expertise with content—I should dwell briefly on the question of material consideration. Respondents expressed vehement pro and con views, using locutions such as "Heaven forbid, they don't pay her," "What on earth?", and "Sure they pay, what kind of question is that?!" Thus, relating to two accepted forms of material compensation—money and food—one woman respondent stated that "They say you should bring a wailer who won't eat and won't drink, who'll just cry, and pay her for it." A male respondent, in contrast, recounted that "They didn't pay her officially, but they'd give her something, they'd satisfy her, invite her to meals, offer her some dates or raisins." Another woman, a wailer, added something new to the list of accepted rewards. I asked, "Did they pay you?" "No," she replied, "but they did something. They covered it. For example, a nice piece of clothing. Something good, not a rag, a dress or a pair of pants. Or some food, something to keep you going. There's lots of food there, so they give." Views about the form of payment were divided, but everyone agreed that the mourners owed the wailer something, especially since often the mourners and their relatives had invited her. The nonmonetary debt is paid back not only in verbal honoraria, such as "You deserve such respect for the words that you gave," but also in material gifts that symbolically correspond to her contribution and compensate her for the real presence and the real tears that her appearance caused to flow. A house of mourning is packed with other people's food—brought from close and afar—and the mourners feast on it throughout the shivah. The exchange of favors acquires a regular and consoling appearance in the form of food; even if the wailer receives a few coins behind the scenes, the performance ends with a pointed silence. It overwhelms the plenitude and expresses a demand of its own: make a special offering.

I now continue by probing additional elements of expertise. Weeping is elicited by a special combination of words and melody—a knowledge that expert wailers maintain. "It's the voice and the words," respondents reiterated, indicating that the content of a performance comprises words set to a tune. "You have to know how to get people excited," Simha, a nonwailing woman respondent, said. Then, however, she made an adroit observation: the audience is also part of the description of the performance. "[Wailers] say words that can sink in. It's not just hysterical crying. It's crying with words that you have to understand. It's a special melody. [The words] rhyme just right, not grabbed from here and there." Mazal expressed the wailing formula in different terms: "Everyone knows the words, but they have to be planned and [delivered] in a special voice." It was often said about Johara, the mother of all wailers, that she had "her words, the melody, she had a pleasant voice." In contrast, referring to a wailer who was an expert in her own eyes but in no one else's, they said, "With her, wailing is like singing," that is, her melody is hollow, lacking in lachrymose depth.

Lamentation lyrics that demonstrate expertise are comprehensible, varied, and original. If a wailer's performance elicits judgments such as "She's got two or three words," she is obviously no expert. Metaphors gathered back in Yemen and tailored to the deceased were employed at a high level of expertise. Johara was known not only for her voice but also for her innovations: "She'd bring in all sorts of unexpected things." Her son described her performance as special in regard to the lyrics, too: "In every house of mourning, they felt she was inventing something new." Some likened Johara, the great expert, to Aharon Amram, a popular singer in the Yemenite Jewish community, because "She has lots of words." In the middle of the cemetery, Zvia contrasted two wailers who wept their hearts out over one gravestone. She described one of them as "crying for herself" and "actually telling her dead one a story" about recent events in her life. Although the woman sounded like a wailer, her performance failed the test of expertise due to its nondescript melody and simple lyrics—a personal rendition devoid of metaphorical inspiration. The other wailer, Zvia said, was an expert at least in one sense: "None of her sentences repeated." Gideon, summing up the matter, said, "They specifically called [Johara] to come and wail because she had a voice that really made hearts tremble, and she also made up rhymes, put together special sentences." Melody, voice, and words intermingled inseparably in the perception of expertise. The weeping formula has an amazing effect on securing and influencing the wailer's reputation as an expert. The formula creates a version of identity that earns the wailer renown and a permanent place at death events. Within the creative whole, the wailer stands out and becomes a rhymester who is worthy of respect and honors.

The Performative Sequence

A solo wailing performance is not an inchoate outburst that feeds on the wailer's own energy. In the encounter between the wish to appear and the audience's needs, the performance follows an orderly sequence of practices in several stages. This perception of stages places wailing in the category of restored behavior—behavior that should be contemplated in the way a stage director contemplates a film script (Schechner 2002, 28), that is, a chain of systematic behaviors independent of the self. In the wake of these phases, the performer comes across as someone else who acts outside of herself, as she has been taught to act.

PHASE I: PREPARATION

The wailer prepares her performance before she enters the house of mourning. She is conscious of her accepted image in the wailing culture. The respondents expressed this image in various phrasings: "You call them, they come; you don't call them, they don't come. It's a profession. If you call a professional, he comes; he does the service for you. If you don't call him, he doesn't come" and "Anyone who has a profession has to build himself up so that it fits him. A wailer is like a singer. For her, it's just a thing.

Also, you can't expect a wailer to feel the same way about everyone who died when they invite her to wail." Even at this stage, the wailer behaves carefully to avoid confirming the image of wailing as an arbitrary one-size-fits-all performance, especially if she never knew the deceased, as often happens. She prepares by establishing an appropriate appearance, briefly determining the phase of mourning, and gathering some information about the deceased.

I accompanied an expert wailer who visited different houses of mourning within one day. The first house was in her hometown; she knew most of the people who were there and carried out her wailing performance in front of them. The second house was out of town, and the people there were strangers. They had not invited her to wail; when she visited, she asked only to console the mourners and to appear there "like everyone else." Before accepting a ride from others who were heading for the second house of mourning, she asked them to let her go home briefly in order to change her appearance. When she returned to the car, it was evident that she had taken off her "wailer's mask." She had put on strong perfume, earrings, a festive skirt, and bold lipstick. These embellishments gave her a gaudy appearance. I asked her why she had not dressed this way at the house of mourning where she had wailed for everyone present. Her answer indicated that the ostentation of jewelry and makeup might impair the impression of sadness that a wailer should project. "There," she stressed, pointing at the first house of mourning, "it's inappropriate . . . unpleasant."

An expert wailer performs at houses of mourning even without invitation. For this reason, she does not always know when the burial has taken place and has to find out whether the mourners are within their three days of tears. If she wails outside this time frame, she shows that she is a stranger and elicits responses of protest. To strengthen the impression of having known the deceased and of expressing a personal attitude in her wailing, the wailer finds out the name of the deceased and asks his or her acquaintances to furnish special biographical details. "The wailer," one of the experts said, "already knows how to prepare the words, what she'll say about the deceased, a man or a woman. She knows in advance." However, the wailer does more before the performance than prepare the unique contents.

She also works out a behind-the-scenes strategy of associative memory that will help her to keep the lament flowing from line to line. The wailers in my study described three main mnemonic strategies, or plans: (1) "to bring out the deceased from head to toe," that is, to describe the beauty of the his/her organs one after another; (2) "to describe his life," that is, to present a biographical account; and (3) "to describe how he'd learned Torah, how he'd given charity," that is, to recount how the deceased had performed a familiar set of religious commandments. The wailer unfolds the story in a chain, a regular pattern of lament.

PHASE II: WARM-UP

The warm-up phase immediately precedes the performance. At the propitious time and place, the wailer realizes that she wishes to wail. Although this realization is largely introspective, it is also expressed outwardly. At this phase the wailer assures herself, as one of the respondents said, that "I'm going to do this. I'm going to make the people cry, to let them cry, to get them sad." The wailer manifests her sensitivity to the emotional state of the audience at this phase. She determines exactly when to begin the performance (Phase III) in one of three interactive ways: by identifying agreed signals, by imposing the new situation on the audience, or by responding to requests from the audience.

The subjects described the agreed signals. The wailer sits in "the room where the mourning women sit" after greeting those present and telling them "May heaven console you." Then she looks "left and right" or "around the room . . . and according to that she allows herself to wail." The respondents also specified what the right timing was. "When the people should cry, they cry," one of them said, interpreting this by negation: "Not when they're praying, not when they're saying a blessing, and not while they're eating. So that everyone will hear." The wailer waits for the audience of men to stop what they are doing. Even after the room has fallen silent, however, she still needs to choose a moment of no return. If she chooses badly, her performance may be considered an embarrassing eruption. "Usually they look forward [to it]. . . . The eyes turn toward the wailer," a respondent said. The eyes and the silence encourage her to begin.

The wailer may impose the new situation on the audience if she realizes that much time has gone by without anyone lamenting the deceased. She may demand the audience's attention and unequivocally convert their conversation or hushed weeping into her performance. In such situations, the wailer assumes the role of an agent of the value of honoring the dead. "They talked, talked, talked," a woman recounted her wailing performance in the presence of a large number of women. "I said, 'What are you doing?! Did you come here just to talk?!' I began to wail." The moment of the beginning of the performance is determined in a similar way when "the women sit at the grave all the time." A male respondent related that "Then, when all the women are seated, then something has to be done, someone has to wake everyone up. A sociable woman comes over, takes the initiative, and begins to wake all the women up. It's as if she's saying, 'Stop crying silently, for no purpose.'" Another male respondent explained that "The wailer sees them crying silently, and she wants to say, 'People, we didn't just bury a cat! It's serious! Wake up!'"

Sometimes the audience decides when the performance should begin. This reversal of roles is reflected in a mild way when one of the bereaved, choking on her tears, approaches the wailer and "demands [that she wail]." The women in the audience may demand it explicitly by saying "Make it an atonement [for your sins]," "Say a few words," or "We want to hear you." The entreaties generate pressure on the wailer, prod her to take action, and make sure that she will perform. If she has not prepared previously, they focus her thinking. The gradualness of this persuasion is evident in the change that takes place in the pace of the wailer's breathing. Her initial expression of refusal breaks down. Her bodily movements say "Yes." The audience's conversation about the deceased and the death has a transference effect in terms of the performance. The wailer's response shows that she is conditioned on a discourse that, in terms of its contents, resembles wailing. In one of the interviews, I asked a woman to wail. She expressed doubt about her ability to respond. However, she began to recount the death of a relative of hers. She recited segments of her lament until a moment at which she admitted "I'm getting excited" and immediately burst into wailing. The transition from recitation to melody was sudden. The metaphoric speech with which she began shifted to recitation of the lament, which in turn set the performance in motion.

PHASE III: PERFORMANCE

An Observation

Before she goes over to her "wailing voice," the wailer withdraws from a dress pocket a small kerchief that she has placed there in advance and spreads it over her eyes with one hand.[9] Her back sways gently from side to side or forward and backward in tandem with the wailing melody. Her other hand moves in circles and in motions that illustrate the story that she tells. Sometimes she shakes her head slowly, reinforcing the impression of being detached from her surroundings. She sits straight. Her legs are slightly splayed, her dress covering them almost to the ankles. The contrast of her swaying back and her motionless pelvis and legs creates the impression that she is trying to avoid some misfortune. The wailer occasionally taps her hips with her moving hand as a sign of sorrow. Sometimes she lays her hand on her chest. At times she makes a choking sound, as if gasping for air. The choking sounds keep pace with the general tempo and correspond to the pattern of the lyrics. In all, her motions are small, limited, and repetitive. The result is a harmonic performance in which bodily motions, breathing, lyrics, and melody are coordinated. This lasts for about half an hour.

Tears

The explicit purpose of the wailer's stage performance—to make the audience cry—leaves no room for her own weeping. Her attention is consumed by the audience's emotional needs. If she weeps, a male respondent explained, "She'll mess everything up." The wailer is skilled in pretense. "The wailer is an expert. She doesn't get upset," one of the women declared. One wailer related that "There are lots of [dead people] whom I don't cry for. I perform like I'm on a stage." The respondents used various expressions to describe this performative phenomenon of wailing without crying. For example, "Her weeping isn't real. It's artificial. She only knows how to express it, how to set the tone"; "She cries with her mouth but not with her eyes"; and "She's not broken-hearted about the fellow who died. It's her job." One respondent said, "[The wailers] are already used to it, it doesn't hurt them deep inside. They just let the people cry. They themselves are strong. And when you tell them, 'That's enough, drink some water, you've done enough [wailing],' then they're OK. After a few minutes it's like nothing happened."

The respondents attributed three dramaturgical functions to the custom of covering the face with the kerchief. First, the wailer has to do this "so they won't see that she's crying." A male respondent explained that "The moment you cry, you contort your face. . . . You shout, weep, twist your face." The wailer, it was thought, would be embarrassed if seen with her face contorted. The second possible function of the kerchief is the opposite—to conceal the fact that the wailer is not crying. A wailer quoted a question that friends had asked her: "Tell me, why don't we see your tears coming down?" She answered, winking, "But I've got this kerchief and I'm drying [my eyes]." A woman respondent who was not a wailer explained that the wailer covers her face "so they won't see whether she's crying or not." She added, "She goes like this [demonstrates the application of the kerchief], but she doesn't cry. I was there." The wailer uses the kerchief to create uncertainty about her emotions. A wailer, pointing to the kerchief, said, "You make it look as if you're *really* hurting." Sometimes the wailer does not limit herself to a kerchief; she creates the effect of weeping before the performance by applying saliva to her eyes. The kerchief is not always used to conceal the inappropriateness of the wailer's emotional state. Sometimes it serves as a mask that allows the wailer to avoid the audience's eyes and do her own emotional labor. "She'd cover her face with a kerchief so that she'd cry [wail] and say things that have emotion," a woman respondent explained. Some called this "intimacy" and likened the wailer to "an artist who wants to be alone." Another woman said, "She lets herself talk and talk and talk [wail]. She sees no one, and no one sees her. They just hear her. . . . It makes her more confident about talking." This self-imposed isolation steers the wailer toward an encounter with an inner truth and gives her the confidence to express it.

We know that noticing the presence of the audience is bad for performance (Myers 1988). "If the artist sees the audience," a woman respondent said, likening wailing to the theater, "it shakes her up a little. But when there's a projector, she doesn't see the facial expressions of the audience and doesn't relate to them." If so, the kerchief is not solely for pretense; it also serves the cause of intensive emotional labor.

Bodily Movements and Breathing

The wailer's bodily movements and breathing take place in accordance with a dramaturgical rule: the less there is, the more there is. Her head, arms, and upper body are allowed to make small movements. The wailer could stand up, make herself fall, wave her arms energetically, or bend over fully. Instead, she limits her movements. By so doing, she protects her own special power as an expert who circulates among houses of mourning. Her limited movements probably create a more reliable allusion to inner tumult than would exaggerated motions. The wailer applies the principle of pragmatic paradox, in which the actor must not emote to stir others' emotions (Diderot 1957).

The wailer's choking reflects a sense of "I can't" amid the make-believe crying. This suggests that the wailer is about to suffocate, is so anguished that she cannot continue, and has come to the end of her emotional rope. I witnessed evidence of choking during my interviews. I reacted with shock each time, begging the wailer to stop the performance at once and beginning to apologize for having caused her such agony. For the most part, however, the wailer carried on after pausing briefly to catch her breath. I was a misleading audience in this respect; I was more sensitive to the time-out, denoting helplessness, than to the continuity of the performance, denoting control. In this matter, too, the principle of less equals more is at work; the wailer does not need to shriek in anguish to give over the impression of being in emotional distress. Such a strategy would be less effective than the one she actually adopts. All she has to do is choke. A woman respondent asked, "Why does the wailer cough like that in the middle of the wailing?" "It's a coughing fit," the wailer replied. "It's like saying that I'm wailing so much that I can't breathe."

Words, Metaphors, and Vocalization

The wailer's uncommon talent is evident in her combination of vocal qualities and intelligent use of words and metaphors. This combination, the informants explained, enables her "to touch the sensitive points," "to cause shock," and even "to touch the dead." "Wailers speak words that can be absorbed. It's just not hysterical sobbing. It's sobbing with words that have to be understood," an informant related. "It's a special melody," someone else said. "Those precise rhymes, she doesn't grab them off the shelf. . . . Sometimes she explains something in words by her wailing. Those who can understand her do so. Ignoramuses don't understand. The wailers know exactly what to say." When I asked a male respondent to dwell on the matter of excitation, he added that the wailing woman uses "a technique of the voice itself." He and several additional respondents believed that "People get more excited by the voice than by the words themselves." When I asked a woman what a wailer needed to know as a measure of her expertise, she replied that "She has to know how to fit the right words to the tune in order to create such sorrow."

Where do the verbal contents of wailing get their capacity to elicit and stimulate such lachrymose feelings as to make the listener burst into tears? The wailer expresses the anguish caused by the specific death and demonstrates how appropriate it is to express this anguish. She reinforces the message of justified sadness by describing the spiritual and physical virtues of the deceased. In her lamentation, she employs a wealth of words that have vast descriptive and persuasive power. The words refer to the deceased's organs, from head to toe, and explain the relationship between each organ and the performance of religious commandments in daily life. The deceased's mouth generated words of religious wisdom, his legs ran to perform religious commands, his hands gave charity, etc. The deceased is often described not only as a nice person but also as handsome or physically impressive (e.g., a person of aristocratic eyes and face, tall body, flowing hair, etc).

Additionally, the lamentation briefly retells the personal biography of the deceased and recalls salient characteristics of his or her lifestyle. As she relates this information, the wailer may address the deceased and his or her relatives in the first person. A woman who performs ritual ablution of the dead informed me that she wails as she prepares bodies for burial. "I talk about the person's life, how it was at first and in middle age, how they raised the children, how she lived a good life, and how she ended up this way [the cause of death]." An informant who had kept track of the custom of women's wailing since childhood "out of curiosity" described the script that he had heard such women recite: "They begin with the history [of the deceased] from the day he was born and tell his whole biography, including landmarks, and touch upon the sensitive points. That is, how you held a respectable job, how people loved you, how you progressed, and how you were a special man. Afterward they refer to the people around him, that is, whether there was someone whom the deceased supported, who his father was—not his biological father but his spiritual father. Then she looks at [the living person] and wails into his face: 'Where has your father gone? Where's the man who supported you, who helped you? The one who was your father?' He cries, he goes crazy, because she's pressed his most sensitive button." I asked, "Then she turns to the living?" "She turns to the living," he confirmed, adding, "She turns to people in the room who were close to the deceased and wails. She sees [the deceased's] married daughter, notices that she's pregnant, and says to her, 'How will you give birth to that child and your father's gone?' She breaks peoples' hearts." Whether she herself shares in the bereavement or is uninvolved, the wailer is able to address the deceased and sorrowfully ask him or her "How could you leave me?" and "Where are you, my beautiful son, who has drowned in the sea?" She concludes with "The great eagle is lamenting you, my beloved."

A crucial component in defining the Yemenite Jewish wailer's emotional expertise is the assessment of the truth that the text represents. The wailing culture of the Waraos stresses the same factor (Briggs 1992, 1993): "*Sana* [laments] serve as a central forum for establishing the 'truth' about the deceased, the circumstances surrounding her or his life, and any other factors that can be construed as having contributed to the death" (Briggs 1992, 341). One of my informants praised an outstanding Yemenite Jewish wailer in similar terms: "She would tell [you] who the deceased was, how he went about his life, in words that penetrated the soul so deeply that no one seated next to her wouldn't cry. She told only the truth. For her, the truth was the most important thing. She was honest." Another woman said the following about an admired wailer: "She said a few good words [about the deceased]. She didn't go on and on because she didn't want his critics to be scornful, to say 'Look, she's saying things about him that aren't right.' If they do that, it's humiliating." The text of an expert wailer translates into a response by the audience that attests to affective persuasion.

PHASE IV: COOLING OFF

The cooling-off phase signals the end of the performance. Here, as in the warm-up phase, three interactive paths lead the performance to its conclusion: the wailer picks up hints from the audience that it has had enough, she winds down on her own counsel, or the audience directly encourages her to conclude the performance. The third path is the one most frequently taken. Women address the wailer and ask her emphatically to "calm down." They couch this in empathetic terms, such as "That's enough now" or "Oh, by my dear parents!" In this fashion, they confirm that the performance was convincing and that they were impressed that the wailer's distress matched the mourners' anguish so fully that she "forgot herself." The wailer moves into a decrescendo, and the torrent of her script separates into separate words until she agrees to respond to remarks from the audience with remarks of her own. She joins a conversation about making peace with the loss, which boils down to statements such as "What's gone is gone for good" or "There's nothing we can do about it."

PHASE V: AFTERMATH

After she makes a demonstrative gesture of wiping away her "tears," lifts the kerchief from her face, and establishes eye contact and speech contact with the audience, the wailer stretches in her chair, sips some coffee, and tastes the refreshments that have been placed in front of her. At this phase, she

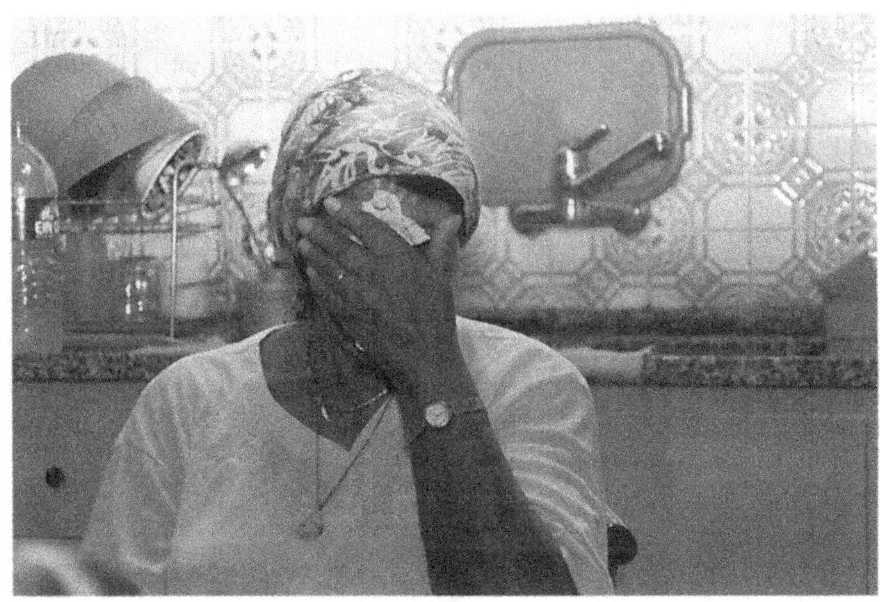

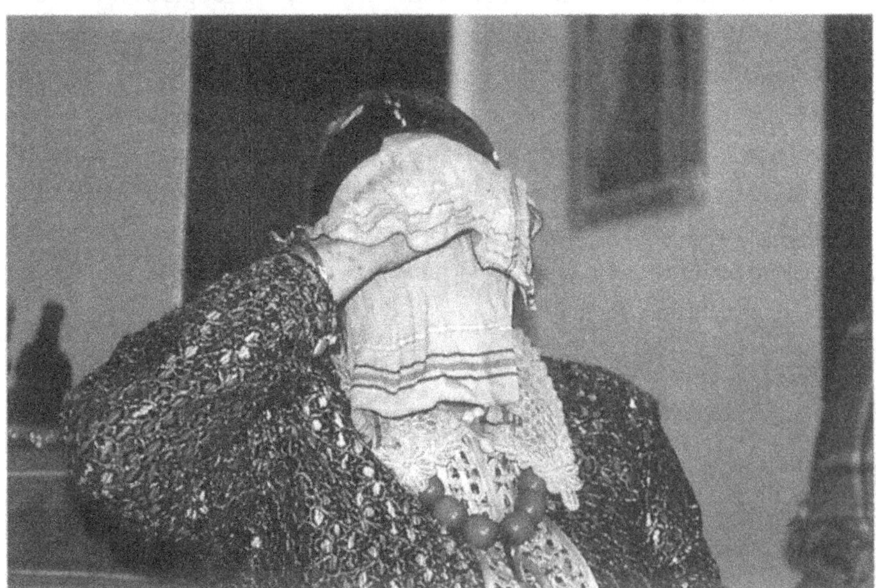

This page and opposite: A wailing woman in midperformance.

may have a surprise in store. A male respondent reported that "A wailer may finish the lament and start to laugh, smile, and move on." Indeed, wailers relate that they tend to "joke around" at the end of their performance. "I give the word and they laugh," one of them said, adding, "They know I'm a comedienne." What is the function of the laughter at this phase of the performance? Laughter signals the completion of the performance, a phase that is considered desirable as soon as a lengthy lament has ended. One women respondent seemingly answered for several: "Wailers want people to cry and to be happy." Furthermore, making the audience laugh, like making it cry, is included in the religious imperative of consoling the bereaved. The laughter of the bereaved and the audience, even for just a moment, signals to the wailer that the original purpose of the wailing performance—emotional release—has been attained. In stage terms, indications of comic relief among the audience, like cheering and applause, may confirm that the wailing has attained its emotional goal and mark the end of the complete performance.

In the totality of her performance, the wailer shapes the first response (tears) and then its opposite (laughter), both plainly manifested in the audience's faces. For this audience, which is well versed in Scripture and studies it regularly, the wailer's actions evidently echo the personal and collective prayer that appears in Psalms 30:6, 12: "[God's] anger endures for but a moment, in his favor is life: weeping may endure for a night but joy comes in the morning. . . . You have turned my mourning into dancing; You have loosened my sackcloth and girded me with delight." The wailer creates a reality of mourning and converts it into dancing. She demonstrates an emotional occasion and oversees its conversion. By doing so, it seems, she wishes to signal to the mourners a miraculous future event arising from the distress of this moment. The totality of her performance symbolizes what one may look forward to as the mourning period continues. It is a symbolic tool that she wields to inform those present that the outbursts of weeping that typify this period will wane until they stop altogether, whereupon the light from the depths of the heart will make its appearance. Her momentary laughter suggests to everyone present that the crisis is not absolute, that healing will erupt after the sorrow has been adequately expressed, and that there is hope. Signs of relief and grinning lightheartedness in the audience emerge from the message and conclude the performance. In terms of the theater, these signs are a special configuration of the cheering and applause that break out as the lights dim and the curtain falls.

Game-Playing

The following observation by Burns, although addressed to stage actors, may pertain equally to the wailer in her craft:

> The dangerous qualities inherent in acting are those qualities inherent in human nature: deceit, irrelevant mimicry and the power to arouse in others passions and emotions normally controlled. In ordinary life these subversive powers are not usually manipulated with much skill. An actor, however, is trained to develop them and to regard his skill as an art. To some extent he comes to look upon his voice, expression, gestures and movements as instruments external to and separate from himself, like the painter's brush or the musician's violin. (Burns 1972, 151)

The wailer's role onstage is to make the audience cry. In view of this goal, she herself does not cry; the audience's crying is central among her concerns both literally and figuratively—intellectually and in her craving for weeping as well as in her inner resources whereby tears are shed inside her but are hidden from view. We now know what takes shape deep in a wailer's psyche but also, although not fully, how she is perceived as a dramatic unit. This part of the discussion focuses on manifestations of the tension between innocence and cynicism. My argument is that to serve the audience, the wailer has to play a complex inner game that proves to be one of external impressions. I use the term "game" to refer to two interdependent things. First, there is an inner game that consists of motion across vectors of image that determine the extent of the wailer's emotional involvement; I deal with these later. Second, there is an external game, a pretense that the wailer needs to maintain as long as she is onstage. I start the discussion with pretense, a crucial ability and a mode of performance.

PRETENSE

Respondents used various expressions to make the point that a wailer does not cry as she wails: "Her weeping isn't real. It's artificial. She just knows how to express, to set the tone." "She cries with her mouth but not with her eyes." "She isn't heartbroken about the person who died. It's her job." One of the women said, "They're used to it; it doesn't hurt them deep inside. They just let people cry. They themselves are strong. And when they're told 'That's enough, drink some water, you've [wailed] enough,' then they're OK. After a few minutes, it's like nothing happened." Rapp (1973, 51) describes the necessity of this approach on the wailer's part as an artistic fundamental, one that may be rephrased as follows: If "truth" resides at her inner level, she has to establish some distance; otherwise, her wailing cannot appear as separate from her. Diderot (1957) also describes the importance of emotional distance: if one loses a friend or a lover, would one write a song for that person while he or she remains prostrate on the deathbed? Absolutely not, Diderot rules: woe unto anyone who harvests the fruit of his talent at such a moment. Only when the great anguish passes, the terrible excitement loses its sharp edge, and the disaster recedes into the distance does the psyche find solace. Only then does one remember the delight of yore and correctly assess the loss. Only then do memory and imagination merge. The former reconstructs and the latter amplifies the pleasantness of those irrecoverable days; only then does one control one's mind and express oneself well.

To wail properly, one must avoid stuttering and pausing. The words must sound as if flowing from a spring. Netanel described two emotional situations that may overtake a wailer. In the first situation, she has to restrain herself; in the second situation, only the audience tends to weep. The performative justification for the absence of tears in the wailer's eyes figures in both. In the first situation, the question is how the wailer can keep her words orderly and controlled in view of her tendency to weep. In the second situation, the question is how the impression of weeping is made despite the orderly nature of the words.

Wailers are the ones who interpret the making of tears into ideas, according to Holst-Warhaft (1995, 2). How does the ostensibly impossible—the enunciation of words amid emotional agitation—become possible? "It's not hard," an expert wailer stated. "She has to prepare words more than she has to weep. I also weep, but not like the men. Yes. I have to get the words out. You have to concentrate for everyone." Another wailer added that "When a woman wails for someone, then she cries and talks. I overcome it. It's like when someone gets up to sing. How does he get up? He gets emotional, but as he sings he slowly gets stronger." Both women attested that they cry as they perform. The device that the former employs is the rushed enunciation of the words that allows them to imitate sobbing. This ruse is stronger than the mechanism that makes others weep; having a ready-made story to tell, the wailer knows that the craving for self-expression will surmount the need to cry. In contrast, the other woman described a process of persuasion and self-confidence that gathers strength steadily as soon as the first words of the lament are successfully pronounced. Neither explanation suggests the perception of a significant contrast between tears and words. The eagerness to express oneself reflects the value and priority that are assigned to a text that has meaning. This motivation pushes a path through the tears to the words and the ideas. With such performative tricks in use, pauses and recovery of composure are hardly needed.

I also found devices that are designed to set up a presentation of lachrymose emotion. In regard to the question of how the impression of weeping is created despite the orderly nature of the words, these devices reflect relatively systematic emotional work that has nonverbal external manifestations. This emotional work obeys rules of expression that denote the presentation or masking of emotions (Hochschild 1983, 1990). The wailer moves in special ways, as described above, and puts a choking look on her face. True to the rules of emotion that require the tears and melancholy to correspond appropriately to the event, her body moves in a melancholy way but not in response to an inner state (Hochschild 1983, 1990). Below I will show that the wailer exploits the kerchief that she drapes over her face for this purpose. The mask turns out to be a vehicle for the expression of the true raw materials of the game. In addition, unlike other singers, she does not need to swallow her spit—her saliva serves her dramatic aims. This approach to the expression of emotion corresponds amazingly to the perception of the Akan wailers in Ghana (Nketia 1969).[10]

The bodily movements and the breathing appear to be performed in accordance with the dramaturgical rule of the less there is, the more there is. The upper body, the arms, and the head are allowed to move in minimal patterns only. The wailer could stand, fall down, wave her arms powerfully, or bend over fully. Instead, her pelvis and legs station her in her place, keeping her motions moderate and limited. This measured approach, which recurs in different houses of mourning, is ostensibly meant to avoid the necessity of forced expression. Probably, however, it may offer a more reliable hint of inner turmoil. Given the emotional expectations that arise at a time of crisis, high-mindedness generates a subtle threat. This affects the audience in accordance with the axiom that nothing is more thundering than silence. The wailer applies the principle of pragmatic paradox, which posits that to induce emotion in others, one must avoid emotionality in oneself (Rapp 1973, 199–200); thus, the wailer controls the impression of anguish that is attributed to her.[11] By going through her measured motions, she pretends to be restrained, averse to making an impression by carrying her anguish around. Her success in giving over this impression—which suggests in essence that she is not onstage and has no audience—convinces the audience that she is emotionally involved.

By choking, the wailer stresses the quiet side of her ersatz weeping, the necessary pause. This signifies a state of near suffocation, a stoppage that follows the intensity of the melancholy, the reaching of the limits of her ability. In interviews in which women agreed to wail, I witnessed this self-induced suffocation. Whenever it happened, I hurriedly entreated the wailers to stop at once and began to apologize for the crisis that I had caused. By and large, however, the wailer resumed after momentarily coming up for air. It was a moment of spiritual violence, one that originated in a game that the performer can play as she wishes, one that forces her audience to respond to her with full gravitas (Goffman 1976). In retrospect, I was a misleading audience, more sensitive to a pause of helplessness than to the performative continuation of control. Here again, the principle of minimalism is at work—the less there is, the more there is. The wailer need not raise her voice in raucous agony to create the impression of emotional distress; this kind of strategy, as stated, would be less effective. All she has to do is choke. Zvia, demonstrating this special cough, asked a wailer, "Why does the wailer cough that way in the middle of wailing?" "It's a coughing fit," the wailer replied. "It's like saying that I'm wailing so much that I can't breathe." Another wailer answered the same question differently: "Someone who has the words has to push the air out, and it comes out like crying." Johara, as her son attested, excelled at channeling her suffocation in a way that would not only hint at a level of anguish that denied her the ability to express herself but would also serve as a successful mechanism that would camouflage the act of retrieval from memory:

> She would make a pause of silence in almost every song [lament]. It was part of what she did, part of the performance, like coming up for air between the ideas of words that she brought up, because she built the sentences on the spot. It's not as though she came from home and wrote them. She was illiterate. She had some advance knowledge and had to get words out from it. She couldn't plan the whole thing. She had her pauses. It was as though she took a breather, took her time, and then had to put together a stanza real fast.

The wailer's custom of covering her face with a kerchief is explained by the logic of oxymoron, a logic that may distinguish between a naive audience and a bright one. The former kind of audience reasons that the wailer has to cover her face so that we can't see her cry. A male respondent explained that "The moment someone cries, he contorts his face. He shouts, sobs, twists up his face. He isn't himself anymore." Another respondent described the wailer's unwillingness to reveal herself "in her facial movements, which she doesn't want." According to the contrasting reasoning, the wailer wishes to hide the absence of her tears. Miriam, a wailer, quoted a question that friends had asked her: "Hey, why don't we see your tears dripping?" "Look," she answered me, winking, "I've got this kerchief and I wipe them off." Mazal explained that the wailer covers her face "so they won't see if she's crying or not" and added that "She goes like this [demonstrates the positioning of the kerchief] but she doesn't cry. I was there." The cloth mask helps the wailer to create uncertainty about her emotions. "You show," a wailer said, pointing to her kerchief, "as if you're *really* upset." Sometimes she does not consider the kerchief enough; before performing, she arranges moisture that can drip from her eyes. A relative of Johara recounted something that once happened at a house of mourning:

> I went outside with her and said, "Aren't you ashamed?! Aren't you ashamed?! An uncle, a grandfather has died and you put it in your eyes?!" She answered, "Where would I bring you tears from, you fool? Where from? He's gone, he's gone! My mother went, she went."

I asked the respondent, "Since she covered her eyes, what did she need the saliva for?" She answered with a rhetorical question:

> What would they see when the kerchief slides off? Listen, to this day there are lots of Yemenite women who go around with a cloth kerchief. They open it up; it's like a ritual. They put it on their forehead, hold it with their hand, and that's how they wail. But my aunt could go like this and put saliva so they'd see tears flowing. She was such a politician [whispers]. She had to do it so they'd think she was crying. She'd convince people.

Although the kerchief is used to hide something, there are senses in which it leaves things unmasked. It is a buffer that liberates the wailer from the audience's eyes, directs her gaze inward, and allows a sustained flow to emanate undisturbed from the wellspring of the self. "[The wailer] covered her face with a kerchief so that she'd [wail] and say things with emotion," Mazal explained. The performance episode needs the existence and revelation of emotion-inducing expressions so that it can convey the totality of the maternal, the nostalgia, and the melancholy. This was the essence of the performer's psychological preparations. One respondent called it "intimacy," likening the wailer to "an artist who wants to be by himself." Another respondent said, "She lets herself talk and talk and talk. She sees no one, and no one sees her. They only hear her. It makes her more confident about talking."These explanations suggest that being by herself acquaints the wailer with an inner truth and that being confident encourages her to reveal that truth. It is axiomatic that mindfulness of the presence of an audience is bad for performance (Myers 1988). If the wailer craves for an introversion that will ensure verbal ostentation, the audience may pay a price. "If the artist sees the audience," Tsipora said, invoking metaphors from the theater, "he gets excited in a certain way. But when there are spotlights, he doesn't see the looks on the audience's faces and doesn't relate to them." By implication, the kerchief is not for pretense only. It also allows the performer to face inward, where profound truth resides. One is reminded of the varied and contradictory uses of Muslim women's face coverings. Among the Sohar women of northern Saudi Arabia, for example, the burqa is not just a means of concealment, modesty, or demonstration of kindness and goodwill; it also serves the purpose of stylistic beautification of female faces. The burqa is tantamount to a facial mask (Wikan 1982). Like the wailer's kerchief, the burqa makes an impression on a woman's social surroundings in more than one way.

Being alone, then, is another dimension of the wailer's kerchief custom—a definitive dimension in assessing the play-acting part of wailing. The respondents suggested by allusion that being alone, as a performative necessity, leads the theatrical imagination to the stage on which soul singers perform. On this stage, a shaft of light pierces the surroundings of smoky gloom and emphasizes every feature of the performer's face. People who observe this scene attentively certainly notice the lowering of the eyes, the closing of the eyes, and the chilly and cheery expressions that settle over the singer's face momentarily and then move on. The singer's immersion in being alone packs the message with a constant charge and allows what is bottled up to emerge. The singer articulates the emotions of the song with every wrinkle and contortion of her or his face. The wailer, in her own unique way but certainly not by facial features, creates a path of emotion in text and sound. As she goes through the pretense of her acting devices, her need to be alone appears to lead to a midpoint. It is the diametric opposite of emotional misleading because it belongs to the emotional mechanism that we call deep acting, that is, an attempt to change one's emotions from the inside out (Hochschild 1990, 121). The status of deep acting as a fundamental of performance signals a duality of truth and falsehood in the messages of the lament, between which the wailer migrates. Following Schechner's (2002) distinction, it seems out of order for one to decide whether the wailer's performance is meant to make belief or only to make believe. The wailing performance, unlike that in the theater, is not done on a palpable stage and is not subject to the raising and lowering of a curtain. It is configured as an encounter that does not separate pretense from being, inference from reality. Consequently, perceiving the wailer as a controller of emotions, as if her entire stage existence corresponds to that of a cynical or indifferent actor, is not enough; instead, one should see her as *also* being attentive to her emotions.

WAILING IN ARABS' HOMES

The active motif in Yemenite Jewish women's wailing was taken to a very great extreme in Yemen when the performance exited Jews' homes and entered those of their Arab neighbors. Respondents who described the participation of Jews in Arab death events in Yemen told it in the form of funny anecdotes. Here they had used wailing in a way that had not been intended for it ab initio, seemingly transforming the performance into a manifestation of cynicism and the audience into something more stupid than innocent. Indeed, Jewish women and men were invited and also invited themselves to bewail Arabs' death for reasons that should be described more in terms of reciprocity and power than in terms of respect. By doing this, they turned the demand of respect for living and dead Arabs upside-down—into a gesture that was overdramatized by performers who viewed it as part of their struggle for existence. The story of Jews' wailing in Arabs' homes shows how high the performance stage can be and how eager the audience may be to take in the show.

Importantly, this story may be but one possible narrative in the experience of the Jews of Yemen. In this story the Jews respond to the humiliation applied by the Arabs, while in another potential narrative the Jews are described as enjoying amiable relations with the Arabs. One explanation for this is different life circumstances in different provinces of Yemen,[12] with the Jews' political and juridical status in the cities being worse than in the villages. In the latter locations, they were considered clients worthy of their patrons' protection and respect. The Arab tribespeople in the villages tended to base with them trust, good neighborliness, and even family relations. Arabs and Jews shared a complex and intimate cosmology of beliefs in highly influential magical forces in what pertains, for example, to demons and the Jewish devotional literature (Eraqi-Klorman 2011). Furthermore, there is evidence demonstrating harmonic coexistence to such an extent that Jews and Arabs participated in each others' joy and sorrow, such as weddings and mourning events, and Arabs wanted the Jews to pray for the ascendancy of the souls of deceased Arabs or to fast at times of crisis, believing in their sanctity (Eraqi-Klorman 2004, 2006). Still, the following narrative may be less reflective of experiences in different provinces than of a contrasting and generaltizing perspective that formed among at least some Yemenite Jews long after their immigration to Israel. As I will show, this narrative does not totally rule out relations of respect and understanding between Jews and Arabs and stresses the importance of preserving a status quo. This narrative also alludes to the Jews' performative wisdom. Its uniqueness lies in the revealing of the Jews' confessions about their motives and intentions.

According to my informants, to understand why Jews would attend Arab death events, one has to understand the status that Jews occupied in the Yemeni judicial system, even into the nineteenth and twentieth centuries. They were *dhimmi* (tolerated protégés), subject to discriminatory laws and fenced in by social truism. Such laws, to give only two examples, enjoined Jews against building homes to elevations higher than Muslims' homes and against raising their voices while reading from the Torah (Hollander 2005; Tobi 1999). The prohibitions created a daily reality of inferiority and condescension. Within its framework, Arabs defined eulogizing and bewailing the dead as indignities and added them to the other "occupations" that only Jews were fit to perform (Tzadok 1976). As Chana put it, "The Arabs sort of didn't want to lose face by crying over the dead, while the Jews were experts in eulogies and wailing." Binyamin-Gamliel (1966) dwelled on this phenomenon and described how, in the villages of Yemen, the *dhimma* system made it necessary for Jews to secure the constant protection of sheikhs and tribal chieftains. The result was a relationship of reciprocal guarantees: the Jewish protégé had to assist the sheikh in many ways, including minutiae such as setting up his tools and sewing his clothing, and was entitled to expect full payment for discharging this obligation. Turning to our area of concern, Binyamin-Gamliel (1966, 65) notes that "The ultimate form of protection was the 'eulogy' that Jews had to devote to the sheikh after his death." Research confirms that Jewish men performed such eulogies at Arab death events. My respondents noted that Jewish women also had to attend such events as wailers, although not very often. Rahel, in her memoir about Yemen, related that "They told me, 'You have to go and wail for them.'" It was a difficult event in which two young Arabs had been killed. The Arabs' request that Rahel wail in their home was addressed to relatives of hers and could not be refused.

The Arabs of Yemen considered eulogy and wailing demeaning chores for the Jewish service providers but an important service for themselves. The value that they attributed to this service traces to the significance of lyrical texts for honoring the dead, as their own wailing cultures affirm. Many Arabs in Yemen probably wished to exploit their sociopolitical control of the Jewish minority to emphasize their religious supremacy. By summoning their Jewish subjects, devout Arabs could obey the Islamic injunction against women's wailing by coreligionists (Halevi 2004)[13] and pass on the task of *bka* mainly to Jewish men. As the very devout adherents of an Abrahamic faith, Jewish men were considered half-strangers (Eraqi-Klorman 2011) and as people whose eulogies would surely cause no offense to Muslim religious values. The Arabs also appreciated the Jews' prowess in making tears flow. Their performances were considered ideal and very glorifying. In Yemen as everywhere else, respect for the dead was nothing but respect for the living. "When a Jew came to wail at an Arab['s home]," Leah explained, "it would put the Arab, his neighborhood, and his surroundings on a higher level."

The division of labor in the Yemenite economy made the Arabs dependent on the Jews and enhanced the Jews' ability to survive (Eraqi-Klorman

1993). Consequently, this created symmetric relations in the *dhimmi* consciousness, with supremacy and inferiority figuring on each side. The Arabs, lords of the land who considered it beneath their dignity to lament someone's death, placed their trust in the Jews, who in turn exploited the value of knowledge to derive daily sustenance from it. The value of wailing for the Arabs enhanced the Jews' status. My respondents expressed their awareness of the Jews' supremacy of knowledge in various ways. "The Arabs didn't know how to wail so well," one of them said. "With the Jews, it was huge. They'd come to the [death events of the] Jews to listen in." When I asked why the Jews had an advantage in wailing, Miriam replied that this was "because they know Torah." Tamar likened the economic and value interdependency of Jews and Arabs upon the occurrence of a death to a social security system. This special institution—"wailing for [Arabs]"—could ensure dignity for the Jews. "Arab women would invite Jewish women when they were in mourning and honor them," Tamar related. "It was for society and honor." Even a simple anecdote that Sa'ada told expressed an attitude of respect. Sa'ada described the special chaperone who delivered her to the Arab mourners' house so that she could wail: "This Arab would take me from my father's home. He'd come and go and come and go, waiting for me." That she was chaperoned not only attests to the imperative of maintaining a distance of modesty but also embodies a show of patience on the chaperone's part toward his client: he would do his job only at the pace established by his Jewish woman protégé. The delayed escorting shows how necessary wailing was and demonstrates its status as an expertise that few people possessed; hence, those few should be escorted and appreciated.

Jewish eulogizers and wailers tramped confidently into Arabs' homes in the expectation of receiving some form of material consideration—food for the most part, money on rare occasions. Eulogizers, Binyamin-Gamliel (1966, 65) recounted, "received two to four goats or a cow, all depending on the participants and their status. . . . Every Jewish group that came to give a eulogy would receive a gift separately. Sometimes individual Jews walked along to deliver eulogies . . . and they got their share, too." Zechariah related that "In Yemen, if an Arab died, five or six Jewish men went over to wail for him," adding that "The moment [the Arabs] buried [their dead], the

Jews would come out with two sheep's heads because they'd gone over to wail. I myself experienced this three times. My father took me with him even though I was still a boy." Shlomo noted that "The Jews would walk over as if to wail for a dead Arab. But why?" He then explain that this was "to get a heifer or a sheep." The expectation of a gift of food was explicit and mordant. It resembled the way women in Artas, an Arab village south of Bethlehem, put their wailing to use. Granqvist (1965, 95) describes these women as moving together from one mourners' house to another and conditioning their compassionate lamentations on gastronomic rewards; they were overheard singing "Were it not for the sausages and the (black) bread, we would not have come to shake our heads!"

The Jews realized that the imperative of giving respect might, as one respondent explained, subject "an Arab house that did not reward the wailers with food [to] shame and disgrace." The Arabs mirrored this realization with undisguised pride, saying things such as "Here's your dinner, Jews." The Jews exploited this compulsory respect overtly and made it the topic of demands and bargaining, even within the lamentation text. Many of my respondents knew the story of the poor Jewish widow who was led to wail at the home of Arabs in order to keep her children. One respondent related:

> One widow saw that a funeral was taking place, and she went because the Arabs make food at a funeral and eat there, in the cemetery, after they bury their dead. The woman had to feed her sons and daughters. She came and saw that there was plenty of food, *harish* and *saman* [nourishing Yemenite dishes]. She wanted to go over and eat. But then she had this feeling: how could she eat her fill while her children were starving, starving to death, at home? What would she gain from that?! What kind of pleasure would that be?! She'd gorge herself, and her children would go hungry?! She began to weep [wail] as if she were weeping for the deceased. She wept her pain. She says, "*Samna wasid yesh maspiq.*" If only my children get the enjoyment. If only they'll eat.

Binyamin-Gamliel (1966) described how the imperative of giving respect turned into a vehicle for extortion of the audience by the performers:

> If the gift was satisfactory, the eulogizers turned around and went home. If it was not, they launched into lively and stubborn bargaining and negotiations. The relatives of the deceased would offer two goats, for example, and the eulogizers would demand four goats or a cow. The relatives argued that they had already given something to that particular community [of Jewish eulogizers], but [the eulogizers] replied that this was none of their concern and that the proposed gift was an indignity to the deceased. If he were to rise from his grave and see his son's stinginess, he would pound his hands in rage. Usually, the eulogizers prevailed; they did not budge until they got what they wanted. (Binyamin-Gamliel 1966, 66–67)

The respondents' anecdotes elevated wailing from the status of ordinary merchandise to merchandise that, from the moment it was supplied, obliged its recipients to do a kindness for the suppliers whether they needed the goods or not. Yosef described his family's neighborly relations with one of the Arabs, who visited them daily until the family was sick of him. To rid themselves of the unwanted guest, Yosef conferred with his brother, and together they told the Arab that they would soon visit him at home. The Arab, Yosef continued, invited them gladly, oblivious to the ruse that the Jewish brothers had concocted. When the two Jews arrived, they covered their faces and began to loudly bewail an offspring of the Arab family who had died two months earlier. The Arabs in the house were amazed by the belated gesture. The bewildered Arab asked "Why are you wailing?" as he headed to the kitchen to prepare several dishes for Yosef and his brother, as if for lack of choice.

The discussion thus far may explain why Jewish women wailed and Jewish men eulogized at Arab death events and repeatedly attended them. The motive of deriving something from the performance was an outgrowth of the *dhimmi* relationship, the acknowledgment of value, and the Arabs' need to show respect for their neighbors. This motive is not lacking in Jewish women's wailing within their own communities. However, outside of the communities—among the Arabs—it was amplified to extreme degree. I wish to argue that such was also the case in the matter of disrespect for the audience and the connection between this performative attitude and the tendency to deceive, as the title of the preceding subsection ("Pretense") suggests. The wailer within her Jewish group does not disrespect her audience, although she appreciates the disparity of information and ability between them. Furthermore, I believe that she does not intend to deceive; instead, she has to do so on account of her reputation, which grants her many opportunities to perform. In contrast to the intracommunity context, wailing for Arabs reflects estrangement from the audience and a deliberate intention to deceive. This emotional posture of the Jewish performers was rarely visible to the eye. Behind the scenes, however, it subverted the rhetoric of respect for the Arab kin of the deceased. The performance, as I will show, pushed the audience's trust past the limit at which the wailing strips its fundamentals of truth.

Even though the Jews did manage to parlay their spiritual expertise into a means of livelihood, they still felt insulted by having to wail in the homes of Arab "goyim" and continued to resist it in conceptual and value terms. Wailing for Arabs is a humiliating episode in the story of Yemenite Jewry's survival. At first glance, one may view it as an ancillary occupation like the other occupations that were assigned to Jews, in which they might make a living but not attain true welfare or a sense of long-term economic security. Wailing and eulogy, however, are unique in that the other exchange relations merely entail calculating quantities and methods of delivering implements for an Arab's needs. Jews wailed and eulogized in response to the Arabs' demand for respect—an uncompromising demand that presented its subjects with an impossible emotional challenge. The three-word expression "demand for respect" is an oxymoron in terms of the mechanisms of emotion: it is a self-defeating strategy because *demand* rules out the attainment of *respect.* Those who apply the coercion, which generates resistance and pain, entertain the delusion that the outcome will be a positive emotion. Another uniqueness of these so-called death occupations, one that intensified the challenge that the performers were supposed to withstand, is that wailing and eulogies cannot be accomplished without speech and must be accomplished in public. A Jew can no longer retreat into his or her private domain, strike a hunk of iron with a hammer, or weave thread through a piece of cloth. The Jew has to impress an audience with his or her goodwill and perform the text that he or she has composed. Speaking is a rather committal act in terms of the speaker's experiencing of selfness. Rhetorical coinage is never just ordinary coinage.

Had Jews refused to take part in Arabs' death events, the Arabs might have accused them of schadenfreude. As *dhimmi,* the Jews certainly knew that the Arabs could avenge their insult. This insult was not one felt by neighbors or relatives who asked for a wailing performance and came away empty-handed; it carried a consciousness of political, ethnic, and religious tension that always percolated and occasionally boiled over (Loeb 1999; Hollander 2005). An accusation of schadenfreude could shred the delicate fabric of neighborly relations between Jews and Arabs. For the Jews, who were mere subjects to begin with, its implications were threatening if not fateful. Overshadowed by their *dhimmi* situation and the uncertainty, Jews were loath to put their refusal to the test. Such was the case until the shackles of authority closed in on the tradition of women's wailing as practiced in their Jewish community. From that point on, the end of women's wailing—literally and figuratively—had to be tailored to an intercultural encounter. This denouement was manifested in wailing as opposed to eulogy because male Jewish eulogizers had fashioned an imitation of women's wailing. Importing elements of the women's performance into their own, they distorted its original form.

The fundamentals of women's wailing—from its capacity as a projected form of motherly nostalgia to its painstaking search for the listeners' definition of the truth—could no longer be appropriated crudely. In this sense, they resembled the other fundamentals of this emotion-inducing composite act. Generally speaking, wailing and eulogy are performances that carry clusters of intense meaning. These clusters draw on common sources in the domains of emotion and religion and address themselves to the interior of the community. The Jews' encounter with Arabs set up a confrontation between values and emotional dilemmas. This encounter with these particular "others" portrays women's wailing as an intimate discourse that is limited to those who belong to "us" and is based on mutual guarantee and thorough acquaintance. Not even a trace of this discourse can be sustained by ambassadors who intermingle momentarily with a group of "them," a group that not only does not belong but also presses its emotional claims forcibly, its otherness indelibly confirmed by its "goyishness."

In terms of religious separatism, wailing for Arabs was close to being remembered as one of the symbols of the Jewish exile. Some Jews may have made an associative connection between the emotional demands and public rhetoric with texts involving conversion out of the faith. The original eulogy was read from a holy prayer book; the wailer pronounced "the word of God in her ear," as one wailer expressed it; and everything was geared to heaven and the Jewish redemption. Consequently, the Arab approximates the metaphor of the hobnailed boot that stands in fury between his statues. The statues are metaphorical representations of things that the Jew must glorify unbelievingly and under duress: elements in the image of the goy who boasts of his generosity and his valor on the battlefield. Binyamin-Gamliel (1966, 65), extending his remarks in much the manner in which he began them, stated, "And if one of the Gentiles' dignitaries, be it a sheikh, a rich man, or a powerful official, should die, the Jews would (but not everywhere) go and eulogize him and recount his power, and his heroism, and his generosity, even if he had been neither heroic nor generous while alive." "They wailed even if they hadn't known the deceased at all," Zechariah remarked. Miriam added that the Jews "would say things: he was great, he was special, all sorts of stuff." The Jews' lament, or what was considered a eulogy, did not have to meet the listeners' definition of the truth. On the contrary: the more it was heaped with praise, the more it satisfied the deceased's relatives, who in turn would pay more generously (Tzadok 1976, 157). The Jews, being *dhimmi,* were not inclined to fight the edict and in any case did not know how to. Perhaps for this reason, these motifs do not occur in their songs and laments. Ratzhabi (1987–88, 740) explains: "They were loyal to the reality of life" and "avoided glory that was not rooted in the Jewish reality." Wailing for the Arabs, however, forced them to betray the course of this reality, which concerned itself mainly with the agony of exile, surrender, and acceptance of judgment. As he wailed, the Jew was asked to turn his back on his community's heritage, spiritual identity, and fate, with their multiple hardships. When he mentions great and abiding feats of war and combat, he discourses about something that is not his and embraces a "goyish custom" that was common among Arab women wailers. By implication, the melody of his wailing might echo the woes of his community, but the lyrics are estranged from it. To meet the vain needs of the deceased's relatives and to surmount the humiliation, the Jew had to estrange himself from himself.

Below are lyrics from a lament that Jewish men composed in the memory of an Arab who had died, as found and translated by Binyamin-Gamliel:

The eulogizer said: My heart inside me was bestirred
by the rumor that reached me before dawn
They said that a fortress and a lighthouse had been conquered.
The eulogizer said: My heart inside me was made to tremble
by the report that reached me before I tasted my breakfast bread,
They said a towering mountain had fallen and stumbled.

May his sons and all the women praise him,
May his cousins, straight as snakes, praise him,
May his palace and his bedding praise him—
Badgers' skins
May his courts and his yards praise him,
May his horses and riders praise him.

O he who shoots the mosquito and never misses
and the fish in the water and strikes him,
O hero, he of the red eye
O broad-winged vulture. (Binyamin-Gamliel 1966, 65–66)

The following lament lyrics were transcribed and translated by Rabbi Joseph Kappah:

Woe to the towering fortress whose balustrade has been destroyed
whose ceiling has been demolished and whose stones have been cast aside
a tusk of stone dislodged from its cavity
its fall audible in the clay of the east.

We shall bewail you, king son of king
renowned in all lands;
I shall lament for you, the soil will cry for you,
as will all the provinces.

The crier said, Whose blood is this?
Answer, dead one, scholar of the Quran
The unnamed chivalrous one, cradle of the kingdom.

He left behind hosts of young men
Men of war, of chariot, of horse,
His sons and cousins, clever and brave. (Yeshayahu and Tobi 1976, 416–17)

The Jewish performers masked their denial of the values of the community before which they had to appear and also their resentment of this collective, with its advantage in sociopolitical status. Their lament/eulogy lacked all the meaning that the intra-Jewish communication exhibited. All that remained of the original was a superficial and clumsy similarity in the performance, which satisfied the Arabs' wishes and yielded the derivative: food. To shield themselves from the effects of the coerced pretense and perhaps even to recapture their dignity, the performers adopted two strategies: they flashed their taunts onstage and went out of their way offstage to signal their role-distance (Goffman 1959). They did this to avoid the impression that they were indulging in the surface acting that familiar wailing performances at home required (Hochschild 1983, 1990). In other words, from their standpoint, their performance did not resemble a wailer's conscious effort to pretend in pursuit of the valued goals of honoring the dead and inducing the audience to cry. Instead, it was a deliberately clumsy and sloppy imitation of her actions onstage. Thus, the performers denied themselves any possibility of being caught up in the melancholy that the memory that the words and the melody of women's wailing evoke. To feel sad would signify an intention that the house of the "goy" does not deserve. An example of sloppiness in discharging the wailer's role is visible in the invitation given by Yosef and his brother to the home of their Arab neighbor and in the very performance of a belated lament. When Yosef was confronted with what he had done, he played innocent by staring straight ahead. He also related that he and his brother laughed incessantly behind the backs of the deceased's relatives, who were upset by the puzzling gesture. My respondents described the Arabs as dupes who failed to understand even half, let alone all, of the wailing expertise. Their inability to criticize and control the performance and the state of total dependency that obliged them to respect the performers were translated into creative and unruly acting devices. For example, Eraqi-Klorman tells us that

> Jews sometimes exploited the perception of their "otherness" and mystical knowledge to strengthen their positions against the Muslims by applying cunning and manipulation. They would pretend, for example, that they were forced to do an evil deed, i.e., steal corps, by a demon that had possessed them, and thus they escaped punishment. On other occasions, Jews would pretend to know how to write amulets or master the demons in order to obtain material gains from the tribesman. (Eraqi-Klorman 2011, 136)

Rumia told me about a Jewish man she had known in Yemen who had appeared regularly at Arabs' houses of mourning. To create the impression that he was deeply anguished about the deceased and was telling the truth, he stockpiled a reserve of fake tears in advance. How? A few moments before circulating in the crowd of people, he moistened a sprig full of tiny leaves of a fragrant herb known in Yemenite Arabic as *shugur*. Then he wound the sprig under his hat like a wreath and trusted the moisture to drip down his face. Whenever he wished to amplify the impression of his "tears," he wailed louder and covered his eyes, squeezing the leaves atop his forehead. According to another description, various wailers did something even more audacious. In more than one Arab house of mourning, several men stood, covered their faces with their hands, and intoned, "They're going to go [die] one by one, may none of you remain, may none of you remain" and "May that dead goy never come back." Their lament integrated death wishes into a standard text and sometimes excelled in cursing and taunting the audience. As my respondents told these anecdotes, they laughed at the memory of them. Their stories also described peals of laughter among those present as they went about the practical joke. As for how the performers had dared to do these things, I was told that they switched from Arabic to *leshon ha-qodesh* (Hebrew, the language reserved for religious purposes) when it came time to insert a hostile remark. This language accommodated Hebrew and Aramaic elements that Arabs could not follow. It is well known that Jews used Hebrew as a code whenever they were discomfited by an Arab's presence, not only at death events but also in daily life. Here, the use of Hebrew amounted to a keenly derisive response to the sense of spiritual humiliation that wailing for Arabs imposed.

Wreathing one's head in a crying herb or cursing Arabs to their faces in a tongue foreign to them are acts of mockery from the standpoint of the non-Arab audience. The performers cherished mockery like a clown who does tricks to induce laughter in his home audience, which included the performers themselves and other Jews who attended the event. Using Hebrew was a ruse, like any ruse that accommodates codes of communication to isolate one group from another. The performers used such tricks to isolate themselves from a foreign audience that they could diddle and that had it coming. In the presence of both audiences—the innocent one (the Arab) and the devious one (the Jewish)—the performers created a play-acting situation that resembled one of master and marionette, a symbolic situation that upended the power relations that existed in their daily lives.

The spectacle of Jews wailing for Arabs demonstrates how events associated with hammering the last nail into the coffins of the dead serve the needs of the living. The lamentation lyrics lionize the dead Arab and make exaggerated use of motives of goodness, generosity, and heroism. These values maintained peaceful relations between Jews and their neighbors and sometimes earned the Jews more than one meal at the end of the performance. The Yemenite Jewish wailer's performance stage is revealed from the Arab side in its transposed aspect, which cannot be accurately imitated. Wailing women's performances were presented in the form of parody or farce, as if someone denied the performers the authority to reenact them verbatim. The question is why. As I have shown, in most cases it was the men who appeared at Arabs' death events. Seemingly, their reputation as eulogizers and the latitude that they enjoyed to circulate among and negotiate with the Arabs were the factors that insinuated them into these arenas. Parody, like the use of Hebrew, strengthened the ramparts that separated Jew from goy and appears to have been but a vehicle and a religious mission that the men considered theirs. The uniqueness of these onstage ruses lay in their ability to separate men from women and fence the men off from the image of women's emotionality and spiritual inferiority. The water that dripped from the herb and the forced moaning—two forms of derision—were meant to cement the image of masculine panache; the performers' use of Hebrew clashed frontally with the Jewish women's use of Arabic in their wailing.

Before stepping away from the arena of the performing stage and the emotionality derived from it, we should mention an equally valid proposition: a comprehensive interpretation that defines wailing by Jewish men at a time of crisis with Arabs as a ritual safety valve or a propitious opportunity that frees them to criticize not only the balance of forces and status disparities between them and the Arabs but also the pretense of the women in their wailing. Another explanation for the parody of women's wailing by Jewish men somewhat contradicts what I have said thus far: the distortion that occurred when women's wailing was performed for a non-Jewish audience may have been meant to preserve the value and meanings of wailing in the intracommunity context. An assessment of the true message of the women's acting performance may have made the Jewish men into guardians of the gates of a sociocultural asset—women's wailing—even though they themselves were not in on its secrets.

The making of a wailer—the sole survivor of what once was a highly impressive circle—is a story culled from the domain of motherhood. The complete performance, as I have shown, ultimately needed a voyage into personal memory to inspire melancholy via the images of those near and dear. The wailer includes her dear ones in this beloved circle and, I believe, includes her audience as well. If we add the motif of motherhood to that of play-acting, which implies thorough control and knowledge, we may only conclude that the wailing performance is a symbolic arena for the mother-child relationship. According to Ruddick (1989), the maternal relationship finds expression in contexts of action. To fulfill her emotional goals, about which I shall have more to say in the next chapter, the wailer takes action and induces the audience to do the same. For the most part, the audience is not free to remain apathetic. The wailer is like a life-giving mother who searches for devices that will benefit the subjects of her care even before, and also after, they know their own needs. My belief is that her meticulous motherly attention does not clash with the play-acting and the self-directed stage behavior that she often needs to invoke; the acting originates in a compassion that cannot be disseminated in any way other than play-acting.

The empathetic attitude toward the dramatic unit has long been described in terms of the setting of the theater. In other words, not only in the motion picture era but at all times, individuals seem to shape the context of their emotions and their ways of expressing them by imitating stylized appearances. This is not "artifice" in the pejorative sense of fakery ("forced" behavior) but instead is the use by a culture of the means available to it to define situations (Rapp 1973, 103). A blemish that might adhere to the performance is found in the discussion of wailing for the Arabs. This discussion appears at this late juncture, at the end of the chapter, due to its ethnographic role: it set the limits of acting in women's wailing and determines its value. While it is true that the wailer acts in public and indulges in make-believe, she does not mock her audience. Instead, her performance is intertwined with strands of tradition and bound up with reputation.

·5· Melancholic Power

Wailing strums the strings of melancholia in tones and metaphors of black. It is a gloomy dirge that grips its listeners and generates an inseparable mixture of melancholy and power. This chapter focuses on the audience's response to the performance as though the performance were a stimulus. A simple temporal distinction may demonstrate the preference of the performance-stimulus model over the time-continuum model and establish something resembling a division of roles between performer and audience. This differentiation, as we have seen, aptly describes the relative passivity of an audience as against the activism of a thespian on the stage. Here, however, we will use it for analytical purposes only. It is inconsistent with theoretical outlooks that discuss a performance situation in which performer and audience are equal. According to these outlooks, the audience is not only influenced by the performer's actions but also shapes the performance (Wilce 1998) and therefore should be considered a coperformer possessing a countering kind of power. The ethnography also presents an approach that considers the audience an active participant. The audience's activism, however, will be shown to have been initiated by the wailer and to be expressive of her persuasive power. This approach views the wailer's influence more broadly than in its direct manifestations, that is, the influence that the wailer applies when she addresses friends in the audience (Briggs 1993) and invites them, as well as dead people and other wailers, to take part in the performative process (Feld 1982) or is expected to lavish blessings and felicitations on leading members of the group of mourners (Seremetakis 1991). Burns (1972, 26) expresses exactly the ethnographic sense that I propose in regard to the status of the audience in the performance: "In religious ritual other people are continuously involved in the ceremony although their roles may vary in importance. Everyone has some part to perform even if it is only singing the responses, clapping in time to a dance or weeping at appropriate points in the ceremony. 'Responses,' clapping and weeping are performed as part of the ceremony. They are not the reactions of outsiders." The ethnography treats the audience's weeping as a performed response in the wailing situation.

I used the word "power" in the title of this chapter. For this reason, I should distinguish between the intentions of this chapter and those of the one that follows. Both chapters are divided schematically and imperfectly between describing the emotional power of wailing and the intersubjective dynamic of the performative situation, on the one hand, and discussing the implications of this power for the religious and gender status of wailing. The analysis in both chapters focuses on the interaction of wailer and audience. The combined weight of the analysis in studies on wailing cultures (Holst-Warhaft 1995; Aborampah 1999; Briggs 1992, 1993; Abu-Lughod 1986, 1993) makes it seem that the division forces us into either/or situations that make the ethnographic seem coarse. The question is how to distinguish performative responses that carry emotional meanings that are also social. How can one isolate the weeping of an individual in a group ritual from discussion of the social role of the tears? The challenge in answering these questions, I believe, is worth tackling due to the knowledge that may be attained by maintaining the separation. Slamming the hammer of associative argumentation on the anvil of scholarship in order to separate aspects of a phenomenon is not only a familiar strategy but is also crucial in any effort to make an interpretative contribution. Thus, the mission statement of this chapter is to decode the secret of the psychosocial power of women's wailing—a power that combines psychological healing, unifying affective glue, and erotic temptation. Chapter 6 will describe how the affective power of wailing translates into social concepts about women's grief work in canon mourning rites.

What are the meanings of the power that resides in the episodic excitation that wailing creates? The literature discusses a range of meanings of the concept and the words associated with it. Some of them correspond to the frame of meaning that we will use in this chapter. According to one of the variations on Bertrand Russell's approach, power is a person's ability to influence others deliberately (Russell 1986; Wrong 1988, 2). The wailer's performance fits into this general definition; it is meant to have an emotional influence on others, and its implications are intended and foreseen. According to another approach, the excitation of the audience is a reflection of the wailer's power, which is expressed by means of her action only. This would suggest that the wailer should be viewed as an implementer of power and not as someone who has power of her own. Her power is overt and episodic, as opposed to a latent power that resides in her personal traits (Wrong 1988). The wailer Johara is an exception to this rule; she was shown, within and beyond the confines of the wailing situation, as having the sort of personal authority that could influence others. A third issue of pertinence here is the connection that my interviewees made between wailing and the power of persuasion. Persuasion is presumed to be one form of the power to direct and control others' behavior. People are not equal in their ability to persuade; they can be differentiated in terms of the amount of this resource that they have. To be able to persuade, one must have enough emotional intelligence to translate it into power (Wrong 1988; Myers 1988). Mazal expressed exactly this belief when she said, "Not everyone can be a wailer. Not everyone can persuade. To persuade, it takes someone who's got strong character, a persuasive will." In the previous chapter, we acquainted ourselves with basic elements in the art of persuasion, which directs the wailer to a middle ground, so to speak, between her make-believe and her tendency to commune with herself during the performance.[1] Above, the value of truth was described in respect to the complexity of the performance. This chapter describes the affective implications of the "truth" that emerges from the wailer's throat.

The Reality of Power

My search for the melancholic power of wailing took my participation as a researcher to lengths that surpassed the methodological technique known as observation. To meet the challenge of decoding the picture of collective weeping, I had to do more than just show up at a house of mourning. As a woman of Yemenite Jewish extraction, I helped my cause by being familiar with the manifestations of the wailing phenomenon. My lengthy prior awareness of the wailing performance prepared me to experience its impact in close company with the others in attendance. Even though I was better at following the wailing melody than understanding the lyrics, I found that the performance had its intended effect on me. Indeed, the intensivity of the anguish depends on a formula that is culturally structured (Hertz 1960). My observations, like my interviews, proved to be not only informative but also experiential. In my estimation, assimilation—more so than participation—is characteristic of the subjective (and intersubjective) currents that flowed in the wailing situations that I attended. I will demonstrate this differentiation by describing my experience of melting into anguish, in which anguish was one member of a class of givens that I collected:

> She sat next to me on the open terrace along the street, a beautiful woman in her sixties. As she contemplated me, a light smile crossed her lips, which were smeared with bold rouge. After I asked her to wail, she contemplated me at length with a knowing expression on her face. Then, without covering her eyes and without wiping the smile off her face, still looking me straight in the eye, she made a gesture that told me that she was about to start. The sound exited her mouth, thin and delicate. She recounted how she missed her deceased mother. Her melody poured forth with numerous tight trills.

> Her upper body, held strictly erect, moved slightly in tempo with the coloratura; so did her head. Her eyes, grinning but brimming with tears, examined my face all this time. The coloratura surrounding the words of "Mother, where are you?" continued to emanate like invisible cords that were being wound around me, placing my throat in a painful choke hold. At first I held it in, embarrassed to be seen by passersby as the spiraling melody tormented me like the stubborn itch of a wound that had healed. A few moments later, I knew I had been defeated. The wound bled profusely. Tears flooded my face; I quickly turned my back to the street.

Other encounters of this kind ended the same way. My presence at the wailing performance created a profound inner sense of participation. I admit that often I was swamped with emotions and felt as though I was dispossessed of the means of resistance that people can normally invoke. Through my tears, I found myself talking with the interviewees—the wailer or other women—in a single habitat of weeping. To give this chapter its character, I also wish to add and produce details from the areas where the experience took place. This goal forces me, the researcher, to become an observer of myself and a medium for the description of the power and internal grammar of wailing.

I discovered something about this grammar in one of the interviews. An elderly wailer sat down in front of my camera and chose to wail about herself. Her narrative focused on irksome problems that she was having with her neighbors. Knowing this woman, I realized that the "problems" were figments of her imagination. Her disorder, well known among members of her community, had given her a bad reputation. She imagined the neighbors scheming against her, throwing stones at her house, and perpetrating other imaginary misdeeds. She also bemoaned the disregard in which her self-engrossed children, who lived elsewhere, held her. As her singsong lament continued, I was slowly compelled to seat myself at her side, embrace her from behind, and, between sobs, ask her to calm down. After she stopped singing, she began to repeat the same complaints in ordinary diction, one after another: the loneliness of a mother, the stones, and the vile thoughts. The singsong story that she had delivered a moment earlier was terrifying, very sad, and almost tragic. Now it suddenly sounded monotonous, banal, and anything but tear-jerking. She had demonstrated that wailing can evoke pity and draw clouds across a sunny midafternoon sky even if the text is fictive, hallucinatory, rather predictable or utterly ordinary.

The next account is of an experience that women and men whom I observed as members of a wailer's audience may have undergone. Shortly after the wailing performance ended and its audience dispersed, I wrote down the description in words similar to those appearing below. The metaphors used in the description are typical of the rhetoric of the subjective world. The pace and meter of the text also serve the goal of my reportage. These characteristics, which pertain to the intrinsic essence of wailing, will give way later on:

> A cemetery on a hot summer day. It is twilight. Far away, at the end of the rows of tombstones, a woman has been buried. A crowd of people gathered there. The [death] event had brought them together from all over town. The wailer did not stand with them. She stopped at the tombstone of her son. She placed her hands on the stone and moved them as if caressing it. The voice of her wailing, telling her story, was increasingly audible. As it gathered strength, it filled the burial compound until no room was left; it overshadowed and disrupted the quiet rituality that enveloped the dead woman for whom it had not been meant. The domineering voice overshadowed the facial features of the woman from whose mouth it had erupted. Her other motions vanished as well. All that remain in the memory-picture are sunbeams that illuminate in painful clarity the crowns of the cypress trees that surround the place. The woman with the kerchief distracted with her voice the many eyes that were observing her. Confusedly they drifted left and right, out and up. The blue sky became a yawning abyss. The voice, reverberating powerfully, painted it as the end of the world, as if it were spreading up from below. Knees knocked. No one is allowed to move. They're frozen in terror. An inexplicable anxiety settles over the universe—like a painting in faded colors that should not be trusted. Contemptuously the tears batter every social rule that governs parameters such as when, how much, and where. Sorrow presents itself

> at an unfamiliar depth. The individual is a miserable wretch, gripped in a vise of suffering. She continues to wail. There is no thinking to be put in order, nowhere to hide or set things straight. Everything known is negated by an inertia of childish, vulnerable nakedness in view of a world that has arrayed itself, its whole self, on the opposite side.

My interviewees confirmed the existence of an affective-existential experience of this type. According to their descriptions, told mainly from the vantage point of the crowd of consolers, the emotive dimension in wailing resides somewhere between "tremendous power" and "immeasurable power." To explain what they meant, they used total metaphors and understatements that attested to a verbal gap—an unbridgeable experience. One of them said, "[The wailers] do this trilling thing. . . . What is it?" Another interviewee stated that "There were wailers who could really . . ." A third interviewee said, "It's this thing. You know what it stirs up?!"—leaving her question unanswered. A fourth respondent failed to find words; she merely stammered, "You know . . . it's so . . ." The fifth respondent settled for "What is it, what is it? . . . Going mad." The wailer's powerful words were described as "exciting," "shocking," "penetrating heart and kidneys," "sharp," and "acute." Wailing was also described as able to defeat hard-to-convince types of people. It surmounts the "villain" and the person who carries a "heart of steel" in his chest. It melts the hearts of people who are "cheery" as well as those who are "impenetrable." It breaches people's emotional limits; it jolts the "stones" and, as one of the women said, "even the heavens." It makes "even the dogs, not only the people," weep. The wailer "presses the buttons of sadness," "does this terrible, horrifying action of rending the heart," "gives you goose bumps," "explodes," and "drives sadness into your bones." Several responses to wailing were expressed in total metaphors. One such metaphor spoke of an uncontrollable flow of fluids, for example, "The words make me pour like water." Another pertained to the opposite image: "You're glued to your spot, you're ashamed." A third attested to the perception of the dissociative power of wailing: "You feel like you're suspended in midair. You're not here. You're up there in the sky, you're so worked up, so weeping." In this respect, mourners are allowed one response that distinguishes them from consolers:

fainting. Mourners are more vulnerable to the effect of wailing than anyone else; only they may "faint from the fierce words." Even the most moderate descriptions portray wailing as "stirring up inner emotion" and "giving you no rest" and portray the wailer as "creating the first tear," after which a "deluge" ensues. Another way of substantiating the wailer's power is by describing her as one against many. She not only "leaves everyone in tears" but can also "make a big crowd cry." All people who are subject to her influence, "from little to big," cry. "One woman wails; a thousand people sob."

From here on, we explore the emotional power of wailing by introducing the assortment of participants in the performance who are subject to its influence: mourners, consolers, and wailer. Generally speaking and insofar as I maintain the analytical separation among the types of participants, the first part of the exploration looks into facets of the healing propensity of wailing in the mourning process and describes points of contact between the needs of the mourners and the wailing lyrics and performance. The second part describes the subliminal psychosocial process that the consolers undergo during the performance. Here we discuss a wealth of theoretical concepts that may explain this occurrence, which we define as a response to the performance and place firmly within the bounds of experience. The third part reveals aspects of the power of temptation that wailing has over the wailer and the channeling of this power to the framework of the special relationship between performer and audience. These three sections of the discussion will elucidate the melancholic power of wailing in terms of the mourner's healing and convalescence, the collective convergence that occurs when people link their arms at a time of crisis, and, yes, the erotic relations that can be identified in the wailing performance at large.

Tears That Heal

In his book *Mourning and Melancholy,* Freud writes:

> Now in what consists the work which mourning performs? I do not think there is anything far-fetched in the following representation of it. The

> testing of reality, having shown that the loved object no longer exists, requires forthwith that all the libido shall be withdrawn from its attachments to this object. Against this demand a struggle of course arises—it may be universally observed that man never willingly abandons a libido-position, not even when a substitute is already beckoning to him. This struggle can be so intense that a turning away from reality ensues, the object being clung to through the medium of a hallucinatory wish-psychosis. The normal outcome is that deference for reality gains the day. Nevertheless its behest cannot be at once obeyed. The task is now carried through bit by bit, under great expense of time and cathectic energy, while all the time the existence of the lost object is continued in the mind. Each single one of the memories and hopes which bound the libido to the object is brought up and hyper-cathected, and the detachment of the libido from it accomplished. Why this process of carrying out the behest of reality bit by bit, which is in the nature of a compromise, should be so extraordinarily painful is not at all easy to explain in terms of mental economics. It is worth noting that this pain seems natural to us. The fact is, however, that when the work of mourning is completed the ego becomes free and uninhibited again. . . . Melancholia is in some way related to an unconscious loss of a love-object, in contradistinction to mourning, in which there is nothing unconscious about the loss. (Freud 1953, 154–55)

What has wailing got to do with grief work, and what connects the lyric poetry of the wailing text with melancholia? The first question is related to the fact that wailing is performed in the home of members of the bereaved family and is portrayed by the respondents as aimed also, and mainly, at the mourners' needs. Immediate associations link wailing with emotions of sorrow and woe—a suffering that inundates the relatives of the deceased. However, something about the public and ritual nature of the performance diverts the attention of research away from the mourners. Ethnographies on various aspects of the wailing culture tend to widen their scope from the circle of significant others of the deceased to the circles of the audience and relations with the community. Several ethnographies do mention the possibility of a therapeutic aspect of wailing by noting the importance of externalizing the suffering (Urban 1988; Aborampah 1999; Benedicte 1994), the creation of "communities of pain and healing" (Seremetakis 1990, 482), and the shaping of interpersonal relations that wailing performs (Briggs 1993). However, the analysis of the matter often makes no reference to psychological models for the understanding of emotions and of grief as a special psychological state. An exception is an ethnography titled *Dialogues with the Dead* (Vitebsky 1993). This ethnography, dealing with the death rituals of the Sora in India, is surprising in that it depicts the dialogue with the deceased as a dialogue with the self and applies the Freudian theoretical distinction between grief and melancholy. My respondents also spoke of wailing in the individualistic terms of a suffering self. It is in view of this attitude of theirs, which singles out the individual, that I wish to develop this aspect of the research theme. This section presents theoretical approaches that connect with well-known psychoanalytic distinctions. Our discussion will also relate to the distinction between grief work and pathological mourning (Freud 1961). In this discussion, the word "melancholy," referenced as "melancholic" in the title of the chapter, denotes not a destructive identification by the mourner with the deceased but rather, and in accordance with daily and dictionary usage, sadness, nostalgia, and misery.

EMOTIONAL SUBVERSION

The literature describes grief as a protracted and dynamic response to an initial state of consciousness. Freud describes the death of someone close as a psychoaffective point of departure for grief work. Theoreticians who follow Freud's lead enumerate three to five phases in this work (Bowlby 1981; Gorer 1965a; Parkes 1986). On average, the paradigm is reflected in four distinct responses that occur over a period of a year or more: (1) shock or confusion, (2) protest and nostalgia for the deceased, (3) despair, and (4) overcoming and compensation (Stroebe and Stroebe 1987). Persons in their initial phase of grief are described as mired in shock, confusion, and social seclusion. They tend to be in denial. Their loss is depicted ab initio as a fact that overwhelms their abilities and their conscious resources. Some scholars regard this state of mind as the denial of a reality that is too powerful to accept (Stroebe and Stroebe 1987; Beilin 1981). Referring to the response that people invoke in the first phase, Bowlby (1961) describes a state of psychological imbalance or disorder. In this situation, the bereaved oscillate between inability to believe what has happened, which leads them to behave as if the deceased is really there, and involuntary and unconscious attempts to surmount the loss that resolve in anger and weeping. The griever's weeping is described as an inconsistent response, like the first crying of a baby who awakens in the temporary absence of its mother.

The ritual period allocated for women's wailing, one may argue, overlaps the first phase of the grief work. In the "three days of tears" that follow the burial, the wailer performs for bereaved people who find it difficult to believe what has happened. The lamentation eulogizes the deceased and forcibly reminds the listeners that the death has in fact occurred. The wailer's references to the deceased add up to an unequivocal statement to the bereaved: "Your loved one has left the world of the living for good." The performance seizes the affective pendulum that Bowlby describes, stops its motion, and induces weeping. The question is whether by so doing wailing undermines the etic pace of cognition that helps the bereaved absorb the reality of the loss in small doses or whether it moves ahead of this pace. Defense mechanisms can be likened to gatekeepers of the self that wish to prevent the inundation and disruption of mental working-through processes and, perhaps, madness. Does wailing imperil the natural progression of mental events? Since the pace of working-through is described as a critical factor in healthy grief work, wailing may be considered a disruptive or an antitherapeutic cultural mechanism. Schweid (1984) determines the value of wailing as a therapeutic mechanism:

> What is wailing? First, it is a lachrymose expression of the agony of bereavement, as consciousness of the magnitude of the loss ruptures the curtain of the initial shock. The bereaved recounts what happened again and again. . . . Every reminder elicits a new eruption of weeping, weeping that perhaps could not have erupted as the events occurred. Now, too, [the bereaved] seems unable to "grasp" what has happened. . . . Amidst this

> reluctance, the realness of it penetrates the consciousness and is naturalized there. It is a cruel, painful, but necessary process. It must not be impeded. The bereaved person must grasp reality. If he wishes to return to the way of the living and act within the reality that has taken form after the disaster, he should live through what he has experienced and not hide behind denial. Otherwise, he will remain in a continual delusion-illusion, and a knowingly caused delusion-illusion, prompted by escape, is the onset of madness. From this standpoint, the cruel process of grasping is the process of returning to life. (Schweid 1984, 185–86)

If so, the question is not whether wailing heals but rather how the healing is accomplished. Wailing, like other healing methods, attains its goal when it creates a pain that counteracts a pain—an intensive measure against a strong cognitive aversion. Schweid's remarks suggest that wailing is an active mechanism that reverses the tendencies of the consciousness to deny and to impede. The intensity of the crisis occasioned by the disaster may exacerbate these tendencies so badly as the individual tumbles into a permanent delusional and pathological state. In this sense, wailing takes preemptive action, so to speak, by stimulating the spontaneous paces of the consciousness or forcibly injecting realness into the crisis reality.

Wailing is a painful medication that preempts an irreversible long-term illness: insanity. A Yemenite Jewish dancer and choreographer in an Israeli dancing troupe recounted the motif of insanity in her wailing dance. She describes insanity as a mental ambush of sorts that takes place in a situation where the concrete and realistic manifestations of death are repressed. I tend to accept her remarks:

> The wailer has a psychological dimension. There are people who cannot cry and are terribly sad . . . and we know what happens when people do not let their pain and anger come out. I think the wailer is an ingenious thing. It's just ingenious that the wailer makes someone cry. . . . In wailing, I think, everyone reaches a place of sorts where you become a little mad. You don't let it out, and you don't show it. But if you think about what you think about all the time, about how my brothers died, about my mother,

> about all the feelings that you've gone through, you say, "I really was a little mad." I wasn't realistic, I wasn't sensible. It's hard for someone to accept death. Hard for him to accept that that's how it is, that's our life. We don't make peace with it. It's a kind of insanity. I began to think about where the soul goes, pictured how my mother is lying in the ground; it drove me crazy. All sorts of little things that you usually don't think about, suddenly you think about them. Like rain, suddenly it rained [into the grave]. . . . It's madness . . . ; a person who delves into it and thinks about it for long will definitely go mad.

By injecting the concreteness of death into one's consciousness, wailing articulates the most horrifying manifestations of the reality that afflicts the deceased's body. The realization of the irreversibility of the departure of the person/personality from the world of the living is problematic because mourners find it hard to keep body and soul, the material and the metaphysical, separate. If they could keep the two apart, they would find the parting from the deceased easier. Wailing liturgizes the irreversibility and the absence of either/or in a way that inflicts a shock and echoes the most grotesque and asocial inner thoughts. In other words, the wailer sings about the deceased as a living person who has been buried and is suffering from the darkness and the decomposition. By doing this, she connects with the limitations of the conscious, which cannot put a living thing to death. In this manner, wailing forces insanity out of its ambush and reveals its contents, that is, its tempting power. By addressing the mourner's inner experiential world empathetically, the wailing text imprisons the mourner in melancholic weeping and a sense of profound anxiety. It speaks from the depths of the vise that grips the mourner, from the depths of his or her confusion, in which the mourner can no longer distinguish between the living and the nonliving. This influence of wailing, its cathartic and healing effect, is phrased similarly in the theoretical literature. Cohen (1991) sums up the matter:

> The song reveals the unconscious forces, elevates them to the conscious, and organizes them in comprehensible ways. It is a pronouncedly therapeutic

> process. It imposes order on disorder; it creates harmony out of disharmony and structure out of chaos. The song provides a refuge of sorts, allowing the poet (and the reader) to ventilate unaccepted ideas, unconscious conflicts, and repressed emotions. It allows them to break through the barriers that impede their revelation and to float to the surface. Concurrently, it reveals them to the "I" that observes it and can examine and organize them. (Cohen 1991, 7)

Grief is strongly influenced by cognitive schemes that convey the sense of something that exists and provide a person with the only way of understanding something that appears not to exist. Wailing, with its macabre and nonmacabre lyrics, emulates some of the familiar symptoms of this state: acute yearning for the return of the deceased, searching for the deceased, idealization of the deceased, and preoccupation with his or her memory (Stroebe et al. 1996). For example, the wailer describes a bereaved man standing in misery at the closed door of his dead mother's home; his heartrending plea for the familiar response of her tender, loving voice; and the imaginings of a mother who wishes to become a worm who will tunnel through the soil of her son's grave in order to unite with him. By so doing, the wailer reveals contents that suggest something much more than non-acquiescence with the loss; she reveals the mourners' wishes by acting them out in dramas of the imagination that compete boldly with reality. By so doing, she magnifies the loss and seemingly counteracts the effort to adjust. The mourner's imaginings and fantasies receive full and detailed exposure as well as sanction in the form of many pairs of weeping eyes. The power of wailing lies not only in identification but also in exposing the delusion to the light of day. The wailer signals that she has already encountered loonier ideas than these and that everyone has them; they are discussed in every home. Thus, by making the subliminal liminal, public, and banal, wailing takes the sting out of the madness.

Wailing has banal contents and nonbanal mechanisms that have therapeutic properties. The wailer recounts the good deeds of the deceased, describes the deceased's personal traits as virtues, and mentions his or her limbs that performed religious commandments. Repeatedly the wailer describes the death in full detail, explains that the weeping is justified, and instills a sense of disbelief that the death has occurred. Generally speaking, if death talk is ever welcome and most likely to surface, wailing verbalizes this talk for the relatives of the deceased. Since talking about the deceased and about the death is considered a condition for catharsis and a sense of control, it is important for successful therapy (Weizman and Kamm 1985). If wailing is likened to speech, the argument can be made that just as the bereaved is expected, for his or her own good, to repeat his or her own remarks like a mantra, wailing moves from saying to saying and from one representative category to the next,[2] following a path that encourages the bereaved to identify with it.

Wailing as a mechanism of grief seems to have an advantage over orthodox grief therapy in view of one of the goals of the grief process. The goal, as defined in Weizman and Kamm's professional therapeutic text titled *About Mourning: Support and Guidance for the Bereaved* (1985), is to integrate the loss, which is known to be real, into the external reality so that it becomes an affective reality. *About Mourning* recommends that the bereaved not only talk but also express their emotions freely. In more concrete terms, *About Mourning* urges the bereaved to combine words with tears: "Your feelings must be talked about; words and tears must be shared with other mourners and with family and friends" (Weizman and Kamm 1985, 40). In wailing, as we have seen, the dichotomy of words and tears, the cognitive and the affective, does not exist. The performance leaves the bereaved incapable of expressing themselves dispassionately, as they might otherwise. Wailing is speech set to "music" that causes tears to flow. As an experiential practice, wailing creates a total parallel between the external reality of crisis and the internal reality of the body.

Some parts of wailing are less banal than others. Wailing dramatizes the tragedy and its main actors, who are for the most part the deceased and those who witnessed the deceased's death. Wailing accomplishes this in a way that the deceased's relatives cannot. Within its structure of terse verses, wailing codifies the chain of events, including the actions, beliefs, and hopes related to them. The wailer's expressive methods extract the main parts of the story from the minutiae of daily life. As the story unfolds, the impression is that the wailer treats every episode as a climax in the continuum of circumstances of which the crisis is made. Thus, even expected, nondescript, or common death events become very tragic. For example, a mother bewailed the death of a son from an incurable illness: "You should yet marry and have children. The illness entered you as a drug enters your body. How so? It got stuck in your liver." A mother bewailed the death of a young man who had been murdered, evidently under criminal circumstances: "In the morning you took the girls to school, and by afternoon they said you were already gone." A grandmother lamented the death of a granddaughter in a traffic accident: "You got into the car and could no longer get out. You're a young flower; you just finished your army service." Between the retelling of an event and the experiencing of the event as it actually occurred, "It is well known that people respond emotionally-expressively to events in accordance with how the events are presented and described as dramatic. For example, a death event always evokes less expression of grief (weeping) than the retelling, discussion, and presentation of the event" (Rapp 1973, 162). It stands to reason that the deceased's relatives would weep much less while standing at the death scene than while describing it. My observations, however, reveal that this is not an especially common state of affairs in the first phase of mourning. In this phase, the griever is able to retell the disaster in a laconic tone of voice, as if she or he, so deeply involved in the details, is at a distance from what happened. Consequently, the narrative devices on which wailing may call (along with others) have the power to abolish the distance between the retelling and its meaning. The wailing narrative evokes sobbing, surmounts the moderating effect of the mourners' reiterations of the details to their acquaintances, and even deprives them of the momentary peace of mind that is reserved for storytellers.

A GOOD CRY

The words "crying" and "catharsis" are often linked as if they mean the same thing, in the way that an overt behavior is understood by way of its role. The Freudian theory of catharsis speaks of a hydraulic model in which emotions accumulate within an individual up to a certain level, beyond which internal pressure builds up for release through expression or action (Laird and Apostoleris 1996). Scheff (1977, 485) defines catharsis as "the discharge of one or more of four distressful emotions: grief, fear, embarrassment, or anger." Thus defined, weeping is catharsis; it releases the emotional pressure that has gripped the individual. It is good. This approach is dominant in the accounts of most subjects who relate to the health aspect of wailing. Their references to the experience of sorrow illuminate three phases in the course of tears: accumulation, release, and relief. The penting-up phase is described in expressions such as "a grinding inside all the time," "the trauma of being closed up," and "feeling despondent." The second phase is described in terms such as "release" and "liberation" and metaphors such as "breaking out," "going away," and "opening a door." To stress the therapeutic necessity of wailing, the relief phase is described by affirmation and by negation. By negation, respondents say, for example, "If you don't release yourself you'll have a heart attack," "The moment you're ashamed [to cry] you get something not good here" [the wailer points to her chest], and "If they don't cry, they might blow up." This beneficent weeping is described as leading to "happiness," "calm," "rest," and "cooling off." The respondents' remarks also attest to their realization that the hydraulic path is a recurrent one and that one maximizes its therapeutic effect by applying its cyclical structure. One male interviewee, for example, described wailing as an opportunity "to push everything out of me"; from that point on, "You have to begin to keep everything inside until the next part of the lamentation." Furthermore, a wailer explained, "Wailing lowers the fire in the heart. They're sorry about it and finally it goes down little by little." These remarks reflect an insight expressed by Freud (1961) in "Mourning and Melancholy": that expressed melancholy is an efficient instrument that gradually lowers the affective energy that connects the grieving individual with the deceased object. Thus, wailing serves as a badly needed crucial arena for the gradual coping with loss.

A convention in research about the affective function of death rituals in various cultures depicts wailing as a way of encouraging full expression of melancholy and as a counterweight to inhibition, avoidance, and depression

(Parkes and Weiss 1983; Gorer 1965b). One of the inhibitions to adjustment, in Lindemann's (1979) view, is the tendency of mourners to refrain from expressing their sorrows due to fear of being inundated by them. Wailing persuades mourners to get in touch with their melancholy, submit to it, and accept a long-term sense of pain and discomfort. The interpretative power of the hydraulic metaphor is enhanced by the distinction that wailers make among different kinds of weeping and by their therapeutic approach to the bereaved as people who need their help (Weizman and Kamm 1985). One of the wailers in my study described a bereaved client in the third person and expressed empathy for the emotional distress that his condition might cause. "You know, he wanted to let loose, he wanted to cry, but if there's no wailer, that's that! The [tears] don't come. Maybe he can do it this way: *agggh* . . . [she imitates a mourner's strangled groans], but not like when there's wailing." Another professional wailer went on to explain that "When you begin to wail, it's like you open a door for them [the audience]." Indeed, the weeping that wailing induces among members of the audience, as the metaphors suggest and as my experience confirms, is a different kind of weeping—a kind that surges forth and is replete with tears. The protracted flow of tears is perceived as totally uninhibited and is accompanied by profound, immense pain. The weeping griever, unlike a self-controlled or inhibited weeper, is not allowed to monitor his or her thoughts or inner voices. The griever feels strongly susceptible to influence. The lengthy wailing is experienced as the brutal removal of all levels of defense against the sense of sadness and helplessness that occupy the center of the unconscious core of the self at this time. It brings the participant's self-pity to full expression by making him or her weep like a baby who has just realized that it has lost something (Bowlby 1961). The kind of weeping that wailing evokes is considered cleansing, purging the heart of its burdens of the moment. After it is over, the participant experiences pervasive well-being and genuine relief. Although Sartre (1948) argues to the contrary, the weeping of those who attend the wailing situation is not a refusal to participate but instead is a style of consent and a demonstration of involvement. In this sense, the wailer's power of influence liberates and strengthens her listeners. Some consider this a form of power held only by people in positions such as caregiver, author, and poet—a power that not only does not come at the audience's expense but also can even fulfill empowering mechanisms that the audience possesses (Lips 1991).

The hydraulic model is not the only model or perception of emotion that explains the phenomenon of ritual weeping. One alternative is the self-perception theory of feelings, which is unique in that it turns the *via dolorosa* (path of melancholy) in the opposite direction. According to this theory, people do not weep because they are sad; they are sad because they weep. The emotion of sadness is preceded by appropriate facial expressions, bodily motions, and sounds, demonstrating that when people act as if they feel, ultimately they actually *will* feel (James 1890; Ryle 1949; Stepper and Strack 1993; Siegman and Boyle 1993). By implication, wailing creates an accumulation of melancholy by its own forces, and tears attach themselves to it. This theory stresses the ludic and subversive element of the wailing performance, which generates tears ex nihilo. In my estimation, however, the model elicited by the self-perception theory actually complements the hydraulic theory in that this strategy is more relevant for understanding the performer's behavior than that of the audience. I base this claim on the respondents' perception of the audience as being in agony to begin with. "Everyone's crying, but wailing gives more sadness," one respondent explained. "Everyone has pain in the heart," a wailer reported. "Everyone has troubles at home. There's no one without troubles, and there are no fish without bones." The expert wailer, as we have seen, employs painstaking performative calculus in order to create a show of sadness on her own part. What is interesting, however, is that she herself is also animated by this calculus to some extent. My observations showed that professional wailers are capable of generating a very sad look in their eyes from the moment they sit down in their special place and clutch their kerchiefs. They enter the emotional state of wailing because they are conditioned to regular and predictable bodily motions. Their awareness of what they are supposed to feel generates a melancholic sensation inside them, even though this sensation is somewhat removed from the mourners' melancholia. The fact that the wailer acquires and entertains this sensation blurs the distinction between herself and the audience because the audience, which by its presence supervises the feelings that should be felt, proves to be a performer itself. Against this background, it is no wonder that even though wailers have stated that they do not really indulge in weeping as they perform, sometimes after the fact they address the lamentation to themselves as well, that is, to their own inner burdens. In other words, a process that begins with the external management of emotions may end with a sense of catharsis that places their experience in the category of a good cry.

The wailers' words serve the goal of creating catharsis. One of my respondents demonstrated the advantage of the wailing text in picturesque terms: "The words drape themselves over the pain like clothing." The words are important to the wailer because they help her to manage *her own* melancholic memories, acquired in the course of the losses she endured in the process of becoming a wailer.[3] In her case, it suffices to link the words to a melody that sounds like weeping in order to unburden them of their despondency. Among wailers, the words, more so than the tears, are the elements that sweep the pain away. Dina noted this unique aspect of self-healing: "If there are people at home [her own home], I cry quietly. But it's not enough to cry that way. When you cry, you just sigh. But when you wail, you get the words out into the open." Saida related that "[The wailer] repeats the words again and again, and finally she explodes." Thus, the wailer carries the nexus of words and catharsis to its metaphoric end.

THE TIME SPAN OF HEALING

The healing that a woman needs to achieve by wailing deviates from the time frame discussed thus far, the initial phase of mourning. Wailers perform in mourners' homes for many years during their adulthood. The story of becoming a wailer provides a sketch in which wailing serves as a recurrent motif in the life of the Yemenite Jewish woman.[4] I asked my interviewees, "Does a wailer have to perform only during the three days?" Their responses alluded to an unlimited time of healing. One of them stated, "Poor thing, she cries all her days." Another added, "All her life, because she's nostalgic for everything." Thus, the repetitiveness of the performance attests to a "career" of self-caregiving in which the wailer is the "patient." There is a maximum span of time in which wailing can serve as a healing mechanism. This span is not exclusive to the wailer; it also pertains to anyone whose religious requirement of consoling the bereaved leads her or him to homes. One of my respondents, referring to people in need of a wailer, said, in a manner representative of others, that "Anyone who's outside and whose heart is on fire should go to the home of the deceased and weep." This empathetic rule ensures the availability of the cathartic experience throughout an individual's lifetime even though wailers succeed each other and come and go.

How long does the healing effect of wailing last as a mechanism that is intended for mourners? Is it for them, too, that the range exceeds the first phase, the "three days"? The answer to these questions lies at the textual and intertextual levels of the performance. As I show below, the women's expressions and words by themselves deviate from the official framework of the days of wailing performance. Unlike the custom of women in Papua New Guinea, who wail for the deceased for several weeks (Frankel and Smith 1982), the verbal gestures of Yemenite Jewish women are, so to speak, symbolic extensions of the time-limited wailing; they prolong the mourning trajectory beyond its initial period—to the year following the death event and even beyond. They suffice by themselves to illuminate the perception of mourning as a long-term process. This is illustrated in the circle of wailers that takes shape during the three-day period.[5] In this circle, as we have seen, ritual priority is given to women who are in the midst of their year of mourning. The relative distress of these women is recognized and entitles them to jump the queue and wail before the others. This pattern of comradeship identifies the first year of mourning as a culturally agreed period of time in which the memories of the deceased are especially frequent and painful, making occasional catharsis necessary. A line in one of the lamentation texts expresses this characteristic: "My heart pours blood because of this bleak year."[6] The cultural convention is supported by the claim that the custom of the Jewish year of mourning, like the customs of the phases within this year (shivah and *shloshim*), are consistent with the natural mourning process and respond to the needs of the grieving psyche (Pollock 1972).

The three-day lamentation mentions the mourner's needs during the period following the shivah. The period may be brief or lengthy, confined to the first year or lasting for one's entire lifetime. The wailing as a text and as a performance among women predicts how the events will unfold and offers guidance. This was demonstrated in an interview where two women recalled a death event involving a member of their family. Their retelling of the event, which took place years earlier, revolved around a wailing performance in which they carried out a "division of labor": one as a mourner who "didn't know how to wail" and the other as a nonmourner who wailed. The first of these women reenacted her teary stubbornness during the period of mourning—"But I can't"—whenever women encouraged her to wail. The consolers gave her a therapeutic warning: "Don't be silent; later you'll be sorry that you didn't [wail]." They were troubled by the lack of words in her sobbing. The second woman recalled a different moment in which all the women gathered were chattering, oblivious to the event at hand. She responded with celerity: "I began to wail." Her wailing was presented as an expression of concern, it too totally geared to the future well-being of her grieving relative: "She [the mourner] hears people talking so she doesn't think about [the departure of the deceased]. She forgets about it. She has to know what's going to happen after [the mourning period], 'who's going to come to open the door' [quoting from a lamentation]. It's over, the head of household's gone." The mourning woman in this report was encouraged to fall back on a familiar pattern of ritual mourning, once on her own and then with assistance from the representative voice of a wailing woman. The verbal poverty that enveloped her was considered problematic in closing the gap between the awareness and the reality of the loss. The wailer puts the text to another valuable use by hinting at the turning point in the symptoms of grief that awaits this woman after the house empties out. She wishes to preempt the crisis and prepare the mourner, who is mired in oblivion, for what she should expect do to—to protest the departure of the deceased and entertain acute yearnings for him. The grieving woman will surely respond this way, the wailer promises, as the magnitude of her loss dawns on her.

At the end of the grief work, as discussed earlier, theoreticians presume a situation of detachment from the deceased. The hopeless search for the deceased ultimately gives way to despair. Overcoming and compensation are the final steps, in which the self and the sense of autonomy are reintegrated. According to this outlook, the bereaved are not supposed stay bereaved but need release in order to leave the dead behind (Lindemann 1944; Bowlby 1981; Parkes 1986; Raphael 1984; Freud 1961). The wailing of Yemenite Jewish women, in contrast, sends messages to the bereaved that may support the criticism of detachment, as I show below. The lamentation points to a concept of adjustment to loss that is compatible with the continuing-bond approach. According to the lamentation lyrics, the aspiration to detach from the dead is hopeless; obviously the living will never again be what they had been. The lyrics suggest that the implicit therapeutic quality of the grief work lies not in flowing against the painful memory but rather in flowing with it. From now on, the text advises, the bereaved would do well to integrate the persona of the deceased into the totality of their lives. Notably, this is also the traditional approach of the Sora, in which the cure for the sorrow of grief lies not in obliterating memory but solely in becoming aware of the forms that it has acquired (Vitebsky 1993). Like an extraordinary account in the literature about the integration phase, the lamentation text advises the bereaved that even after they cease to mourn, they will not be able to forget (Weizman and Kamm 1985).

The wailer has her own ways of getting this point across. The most picturesque of them invoke the imagery of the cradle. The cradle is a recurrent symbolic motive in wailing texts and a metaphor that expresses what may be viewed as therapeutic counseling. The wailer advises the bereaved to strengthen their memories of the deceased. She may turn to the deceased's wife, saying "Oh Tami, my mother, my father, all that's left is love, express his love by weeping and place your grief for him grieving in a cradle and keep it fresh always, so it won't wear out."[7] In another lamentation text, the wailer expresses a promise to a dead woman and tells her "Rivka, oh, my eyes, I'll place your grief in a cradle and hang it to the right so that no one will see."[8] A wailer explained the meaning of this special metaphor: "I told Hannah [the bereaved] that there are lots of people [in her house of mourning] now, but her pain will get worse after they [leave], when the house empties out. She should make herself a cradle, like a basket, like a pouch, so that she'll remember [the deceased] all her life. There's nothing like it; [the deceased] will remain in her mind." Madar (2002) explains the origin of the cradle metaphor: a cradle in Yemen was made of sewn-together pieces of leather. After the cradle was put to heavy use, the stitches frayed and had to be resewn. The lamentation alludes to a figurative parallel: just as the cradle is continually kept in good repair, so should the image of the deceased during his or her life be maintained.

Many objects had to be kept in good repair amid the poverty of Yemenite life. Why does wailing choose the cradle as its metaphor? The answer apparently draws a connection between the wailer and her feminine roles. The lyrics liken the cradle to a repository of memory. (Note that the words "memorial" and "mourning" both trace to the word "memory" [Weizman and Kamm 1985].) The cradle is an object of the nostalgic memory of birth and the onset of life (where an infant is placed) and is also an object of remembrance of the dead. Due to this ambivalence, the cradle metaphor may diminish the painful significance of the images of death. The death that the metaphor creates is no longer utter finality. The death or the deceased is "placed" in the cradle, a familiar and incomparably benign place. Thus, the metaphor creates a soothing effect by mediating between the infantile and the terminal. The metaphor of a cradle that holds an infant elicits positive associations of maternal care. This suggests to the bereaved that they may be assured of solace if they themselves give empathetic care, if they make themselves receptive to the possibility of a continual bond with their deceased loved one.

The notion of remaining attached to the deceased at the end of the grief work is also reflected at the level of the wailing performance. The performance aspect may contribute to a continuing bond by means of the overt and interactive dialogues that the wailer maintains about the deceased. This argument is based on the biographical approach, according to which dialogues about the dead are essential in an adjustment process that aims to maintain, not to sever, relations with the deceased (Walter 1996). Walter believes that conversations among acquaintances that center on the persona of the deceased, his or her ways, life story, disposition, and so on, help to construct a common memory. Conversing and talking are tantamount to writing "the last chapter" of the deceased's biography. They may ease the burden on the bereaved by ensuring a consistent image that can be reintegrated and by delivering the deceased to a socially "safe place" (14).

A parallel can be observed between wailing and conversations among acquaintances and relatives of the deceased. Wailing is, after all, a discursive dialogic practice. In the lamentation, as we have seen, I have identified nine categories of addressing, retelling, and speaking on behalf of by means of which the wailer shows that hers is a representative voice. It represents those in the audience—the consolers and the bereaved—and the dead and death. In her performance, the wailer presents diverse points of view and sets up verbal encounters among any number of interlocutors. The wailer, as the subjects relate, speaks "instead of the people." By studying the representative levels of wailing, we find that wailing blends various voices in order to create a consensual biography. The value of the result depends on how well it corresponds to the audience's definition of the truth, as derived from its familiarity with the deceased's personality and life story. Viewed thus, wailing can easily be seen as a parallel of the phenomenon of people's conversations at death events. Let us bear in mind that the postmodern approach to grief (Klass, Silverman, and Nickman 1996) verges on this conclusion by moving quite a way toward traditional mourning rituals.

Extending Walter's (1996) train of thought, I wish to add to the parallel between the two ritual patterns that speak of the deceased (wailing and other conversations) and answer two questions: What does wailing add as a form of speech? What are its advantages over conversation? I believe that if the adjustment entails the construction of a biography for and continuing bonds with the deceased, then wailing acts as a powerful mechanism of social adjustment. In other words, wailing strongly reflects Walter's adjustment terminology in several ways. First and for our purposes foremost, the performer's stage belongs to the wailer and not to ordinary interlocutors. Because they are performed onstage, the represented conversations in wailing are authoritative and public. Thus, every member of the audience receives the wailer's messages without challenging them. The wailer gives everyone in attendance an example of an ideal language in which they may speak about the dead. Briggs (1993, 947) noted such a phenomenon among the women of the Waraos and termed it "collective construction of biographies." Second, the emotive and pithy nature of wailing ensures the firm entrenchment of the wailer's remarks about the deceased in the memory of the collective and, especially, of the bereaved. Thus, the performance may be regarded as a memorial ceremony of sorts. Third, wailing helps to arrange a "safe place" for the deceased, as Walter (1996, 14) claims. One of the women expressed a connection between the safe place and the healing of the bereaved: "[The wailing, which induces weeping,] consoles the bereaved. It consoles them, since after all it hurts people [to lose] their dear one. It's not that someone passed away just so. . . . Wailing elevates the person's soul, good deeds; it reminds [listeners] of the good things the person did in his life. It consoles the bereaved." Her comments suggest that wailing in front of an audience not only determines the place of the deceased in the community but also paves the deceased's way, according to the faith, to the sublime abode of the souls—a belief that is not totally strange to the private bonds of Western people (Walter 1999). Both places—this world and the hereafter—have a positive social significance that consoles and relieves the bereaved. In a nutshell, returning to Walter's proposed new model, we apparently find that memorial conversations among acquaintances play an important role but have a weaker effect than ritual wailing.

In sum, I have shown that during the ritual period of time that is reserved for wailing (the first three days of the shivah, the seven days of mourning), wailing seems to be misaligned with the spontaneous pace of the first phase of the grief work, that of the initial shock. For this reason, one might believe that the performance reflects social time but not psychological time. In her performance, however, the wailer sits next to the bereaved and exerts herself for their psychological needs as well. The intensity and frequency of the weeping elicited by wailing show that wailing is therapeutically efficient while being performed and afterward as well. It weakens the tendency to deny, provides the relief that is needed during these three days, and exposes the bereaved to the mental anguish that will beset them even after the shivah. Additionally, wailing aims its verbal counseling messages at the commemoration and memorialization of the deceased as subsequent elements in the grief work. The protracted therapeutic range of the wailing, prescribed by ritual, places the ritual (social) and the process (psychological) in juxtaposition. In other words, the wailing ritual apparently contains elements that are embodied in a process that far transcends the ritual time. Importantly, the wailing culture overcomes some of the tension that this order of affairs creates, since the performance at issue is repeated at other death events in other homes of other bereaved persons. Yesterday's bereaved become tomorrow's consolers in other people's homes. Thus, they join the represented audience of a ritual performance while still in the midst of a lengthy therapeutic process. At times when the tension is not attenuated in this manner, the memory of the bereaved is equipped with the wailing contents of a representative dialogue and metaphorical advice (the cradle). In several of its psychosocial aspects, as I have shown, women's wailing is therapeutically promising. If we may return to Freud's early terminology, one interviewee was right when she said, "The wailer does an intensive *work.*"

A Collective in Exile

The phrase "a collective in exile" is a figurative metaphor for a group of people united in pain (Seremetakis 1990). As the wailer performs, her audience is in an exile of sorts—a special situation that the literature calls a liminal situation, referring to them being outside the situations that are socially defined (Radcliffe-Brown 1964; Danforth 1982; Holst-Warhaft 1995). They enter the house of mourning, where the inhabitants themselves are suspended from social and religious activities due to their state of grief.[9] Were it not for the wailing performance, many members of the community would treat this home as a place for a social get-together. However, wailing gathers people who may have, as Tzvia said, "no feeling for the deceased and no connection of any kind" and thrusts them into a state in which "they understand why they are there." Wailing reshuffles people's roles in the house of mourning. As wailing is performed, only two roles—performer and audience—exist. All other roles are suspended; the suspension of the mourners' situation applies to the collective as well. I wish to argue that wailing, as a ritual element, not only expands the collective incidence of liminality but also strengthens it. Temporarily, wailing unites everyone in one existential state.

At the risk of using a trivial analogy, one may liken the house of mourning to a waiting room. The house is freely accessible to members of the community; they enter and exit, arrange and rearrange the chairs, during the entire seven-day period. This pattern of consolation deprives the house of its familiar significance as a private domain but does not make it a public house. Perched between the private and the public, the house of mourning lacks a single social meaning; therefore, it can be viewed as a liminal space. The mourners are suspended from their status as equal members of the community. By sitting on the floor, they perform an act of outreach toward the deceased and are the reason for the communal visiting. On their way to the mourners' house, members of the community think of themselves as having been mobilized for the passive support service that their demonstrative presence creates. They go to console, give consolation, or console by their very presence. The special state of presentness may last for a lengthy time. It has an existence of its own, somewhere between prayer, the study of prescribed rabbinical texts, and eating—a pattern that may be likened to a form of waiting. The consolers sit silently with the mourners, ready to serve them at any moment, possibly conversing with each other quietly. Together they share the liminal state in which the mourners are mired. This waiting situation is the wailer's moment. As described in the previous chapter, a wailer decides when to begin her performance "by feel," as one wailer put it. "There are people, it's quiet, and nobody is 'talking Torah.'" Generally speaking, a group in waiting creates a powerful arena of influence for every participant in it. This arena is common in modern daily life. I would hazard that it is not strange to anyone who has been delayed with others for some moments in one public place (in waiting rooms or while queuing for some service or care). The other person in attendance is revealed at these moments as a tyrant: any sound or movement that she or he makes will grab the attention of those present and distract them from whatever had occupied them before. The other person can whisper, laugh, shift his or her body, and even make foolish faces, and those present would not even think of withdrawing. The others will be rewarded by their searching eyes or at least their attentive ears. Thus, times of waiting, which by nature are voids that wish to be filled, seem to accommodate weak matters quite nicely. Ex post, they offer the weak a tall stage that they may mount. This tyranny of the liminal empowers the wailer and contributes much to the construction of the power of wailing.

To illustrate this possibility in full, we should describe two conflicting motions in the liminal space, both of which envelop the crowd of people in attendance. First, wailing has an influence due to the motion of the audience, that is, its presence, which is construed as having socioreligious value. By allusion, this presence induces the consolers to sit there persistently and directs their attention to the performance. The countervailing motion is manifested in the saddening and/or terrifying contents of the wailing text. The wailer speaks of the death that has overtaken the deceased, as it does every human being. She orders everyone present to contemplate the nonfuture-future, the ensured termination of life, with gravitas and tears. "This death makes people tremble. It's scary. In Yemen, there was terrible fear, godly fear," a woman said. When I noted that death is scary for people everywhere, she replied, "Scary everywhere, but not like the wailing that these women make." Another woman remarked that "The wailer makes you remember death. . . . She makes you remember that people don't live forever." A third woman explained that in Yemen, people were scared of neither the wailer nor the deceased's body but instead were scared of the words, which "penetrate hearts and kidneys." Thus, in a place where people are immersed in lengthy waiting, a place where quiet and boredom are liable to prevail, wailing is greeted ex ante as a desired distraction. Ex post, however, this distraction forces the audience to confront something it does not desire and does not allow the audience to be distracted. This characteristic liminal tyranny of the wailing moment traps the audience in grief and fear for itself. The two contrasting motions—the one that brought the audience in and the one that demands its attention—may be likened to the two types of pain (boredom and anxiety) that the mourning situation beggars. The wailer plays a definitive role in this complex pattern of cultural double bind. This inward-striking situation is a pronounced example of the theory that an intensive emotional experience should be expected to breach the limits of time, lock individuals into in a circular present, and create a suspension of reality (James 1890; Sartre 1962).

Death rituals have two functions: crisis and transition (Chidester 1990).[10] The shared liminality and infectious emotionality that envelop everyone are ex ante characteristics of the crisis reality that death rituals evoke. The significance of the crisis lies in the diffuse nature of the death event, that is, the structural situation in which by a person's death, a society loses much more than one unit. Since a society is nothing but a fabric woven of relations among its individual constituents, the death of a familiar member undermines a society's belief in itself. However, faced with their anxiety and grief, the surviving members of the society seem to prepare for a counterreaction that is both conscious and behavioral in order, ex post, to reattach the frayed strands of their relations. At the collective level, crisis and transition are situations that maintain a dialectic relationship. When a community languishes in a conscious or emotional state of crisis, it transforms the crisis into a lever for transition. The transition lifts the society from a state of deficiency (a person's death) into a state of imagined wholeness, each time anew. Even if the crisis situation is not essential for the transition, the reality of community crisis plays a functional role in the transition. The members of the community have gathered together. Their togetherness is fed by the crisis and, at day's end, surmounts it, since a society sanctifies itself by way of its shared emotions. In view of this understanding, theoreticians point to the element of discovery in exile, or, if we wish, the silver lining in the cloud—the emotional warmth that a distressing situation generates.

The reason for this is that a collective crisis is not like a personal one. A collective crisis places those in attendance at what Scheff (1977, 486) calls an "aesthetic distance." In terms of emotions, the aesthetic distance is an in-between distance. It avoids excessive closeness, that is, it deviates from the psychological perception that one may consider a crisis a state in itself, a duration of suffering in which the past has died and the future has not yet been created. If participants in a ritual were to find themselves too close or at a "diminished experiential distance" from the crisis, they would be helpless (486). By the same token, the aesthetic distance is not an excessive distance; that is, it also differs from the perception of reality as being totally devoid of crisis, as though the other's death has no effect on the individual's perception of continuity in his or her own life. In other words, one would not expect to find the participants at an aesthetic over-distance (486). By implication, the most important characterization of a ritual or performance, in Scheff's view, is the participant-observer role of those in attendance. How does the shared emotionality in an aesthetic space relate to the transition from the crisis? The answer lies in the positive experience that an audience has when it undergoes excitation. In an aesthetic space, Scheff claims, the audience is willing to allow repressed contents of its innerness to emerge, that is, to allow itself a cathartic "good cry" (489). Under these affective circumstances, group catharsis is observed as a form of pleasure. The audience experiences emotions without being inundated and carried away by them. Scheff quotes a line from a wailing lamentation—"How good are tears, how sweet are dirges" (Alexiou 1974, 125)—to say that the audience does not allow itself to wallow in pure agony. Scheff's aesthetic distance may hold the key to understanding the sense of pleasure that my respondents experienced when they wept. Several women told me something that I found hard to understand at first. One of them said, "We enjoyed hearing the wailer and cried from the heart. . . . Back then, no one ever interrupted her." Another respondent admitted that "Truth to tell, I really like to hear wailing. If you don't understand the words, their meaning, you can't enjoy wailing." According to the psychological reasoning that Scheff offers, however, the tears—which are unlike manifestations of inhibition and physical discomfort at a time of intense emotional suffering—are symbolic of hope and healing. Collective weeping that connects with individuals' sense of pleasure also seems to symbolize social healing. Ultimately, it promotes the formation of solidarity relations in the community. The distinction by Radcliffe-Brown (1964, 239–40) between spontaneous and ritual weeping provides inspiration for this approach. The latter form is unique in that men and women are required by custom to embrace each other and cry.

In a death crisis, the flow of tears accelerates in other theoretical ways. In all of them, the collective weeping attests to unity and equality among all members. This is the conscious performative purpose of wailing, as women respondents explain. According to Rina, the wailer's intention is especially evident:

> [The wailer] wants to create crying that will make them all cry . . . that will make everyone feel sad. They have to accept the sadness. They accept this sadness together, like with one hand. Everyone there, women, men, brothers, children, even little boys, they all cry. Sometimes [without wailing] they don't all cry: half of the crowd cries, and half of the crowd laughs. She makes everyone, everyone cry. She speaks about [the deceased's] entire life from the day he was born, who raised him, who helped him, how it was, what was, and she does it with weeping and pleadings. Everyone explodes from the weeping.

I ask Rina, "Is it important for everyone to cry?" She replies as if this were self-evident:

> Sure, why not? Why not? You have to make everyone sad and take part in it. Why? Why is it good for one and bad for someone else? It's not written [in the Holy Scriptures]. It's got to be either good for everyone or bad for everyone. [The wailer] treats everyone equally: either they cry together or they laugh together.

From a cultural perspective, tears have special merit because they are fluids of body and soul. They symbolize the unity that exists between the two—an existential form of unity, I believe, that does not allow the weeping participants to disengage from a subjective experience of helplessness. The soul experiences a moment of palpable liquidity and lacks the strength to surmount the actions of the body. At such a moment, inescapably, a submissive state of mind takes shape. In this manner, I believe, wailing mediates between body and soul and, indirectly, between the collective and the deceased. The helplessness attributed to the deceased is primarily physical. The deceased, for whom the collective weeps, is viewed as a person who could not avoid injury or natural extinction. The tears create the intimacy that this understanding entails. The wailer induces weeping in the first days of the crisis, even before the deceased has been "given" a soul and before the collective attains consolation. The tears perform their unifying and symbolic role until these are procured.

The tears are also symbolic in the sense that they unite everyone in a flow. The visual blurring of the immediate surroundings by the veil of tears, coupled with the internal effect of emotion, cause a certain suspension of time and place. The tears prevent the conscience from contemplating itself. In experiential terms, an abstract situation—a flow—seems to take place (Csikszentmihalyi and Csikszentmihalyi 1988). The individuals weep throughout the wailer's performance. The lyrics and the melody shatter their resistance. The individuals are captives of a performer who stands out powerfully in the no-man's-land in which a mass of people has gathered. The flowing tears reflect a state of doom. As long as the tears replace the ability to speak, action and tears converge into an integrated flow in a manner that enriches the dual perception. The individual cannot step outside him or herself in order to absorb what is going on. He or she can focus only on a limited aspect of the reality, a reality that contains nothing but the experience itself. Amid this reality, neither critical or cynical thinking nor any fissure of consciousness that may impair the possibility of believing is conceivable. As Seremetakis (1990, 498) expresses it, the agony "liquefies the self." Referring to the flow at the group level, Turner (1969) called this situation "communitas." Communitas is a temporary state of flow in which all participants believe they are sharing in a common experience and communicate this to each other in ways that include the nonverbal. The tears in everyone's eyes denote not only the power of being infected but also the contents of the infectious experience, without this being interpretable or explainable in words.

The participants' allegiance to a specific cultural way of expressing its grief, according to Urban (1988), denotes the desire for sociability, that is, their aspiration to social acceptance. They attain their goal by displaying the right emotions at times that society determines. In the audience-performer division of roles, this interpretation of the concept of sociability seems better suited to describing the tension behind the performance. From this perspective, the spontaneous and unconscious sociability that the collective experiences is the result of emotion management by the wailer, who imposes the "right emotions." She inserts every member of the audience (the consolers) and the deceased into a unifying equation. One way she does this is by encouraging the consolers to pity the mourners. "The wailer," Miriam said, "talks about how [the deceased] left young children [and] a wife behind and feels sorry for them." She also tries to prevent resentment of and gossip about mourners who do not demonstrate sadness over their loss. "The wailer does this on purpose," Ora said. "She looks for sharp words that will make the people sitting there cry. There are [mourners] who'll sit there like logs, without shedding a tear, unless you say strong words. I know people who are like a wall. Their husband's gone, their son's gone, their daughter, heaven forbid, but their eyes don't even glisten. Then [the consolers] give them a nasty look from the corner of their eye. They say, 'It doesn't hurt them. Do they care at all?!' There's some pretty sharp criticism." By applying this additional method, one may say, the wailer also equalizes all deceased persons, those who were accepted while alive and those who were rejected. Everyone deserves to be wept for. The descriptive contents of the deceased's persona also establish this equality. As one woman said, if a deceased woman was not considered beautiful, the wailer "doesn't make her out to be ugly. . . . She doesn't set her apart; she uses the same word [for all women]." All the living in attendance cry for all the dead who are gone. No one is made to feel inferior; no one is allowed to feel superior.

Temptation

Temptation contains power: the power to divert behavior from its ordinary course. The potential reward for accepting the temptation interferes with the weak resistance mechanisms that the recipient of the tempting message applies. By resisting the temptation at first, the recipient of the message demonstrates that she or he is moral, conservative, socially assimilated, and habitually guided by the truth. Temptation is the enemy of a social constraint that has become a habit and stresses the value difference between the ex ante and the ex post levels of an action. Temptation causes the individual's self to vacillate about its "sinful" identity as the properties of what is "proper" are constantly defined and redefined. I believe that one may find a temptation, albeit a sin-free one, in the arena of death: in the covert workings of women's wailing. Amid a collective of people and a death crisis, my respondents offered some reflections about what a woman in the public domain should be. Beyond the proposals that the literature provides, the temptation that was patched together by the respondents' remarks, my observations, and my participation seems sketchy in the greater web of relations between wailer and audience. "Temptation" is too explicit an expression. I use it here only to elucidate the characteristic of power that the performer and the audience have vis-à-vis each other, albeit perhaps unintentionally and even unwittingly.

When a group is placed in a waiting situation, it faces more than tyranny against its members, as described above. The other side of this coin is the temptation that the group confronts. When a group waits quietly, its members' heads bowed, this suggests the existence of a social no-man's-land that begs to be occupied. The silence encourages one wailer to raise her melancholy female voice when her turn comes. Hers is a bittersweet voice that is ordinarily suppressed between the walls of her home and is sounded with symbolic fragility at the grinding millstones in her kitchen.[11] The group of women is separate from the men but not far away. In my observations, I sensed that the nodding and whispering among those in attendance generated suspense. I inserted myself into the world of the elderly women around me—most of whom were swathed in kerchiefs and long flower-patterned dresses—and became somewhat aware of their consciousness of submissiveness. As I murmured together with them, stooped and motionless, my imagination began to cook up amusing pictures of actions that would command the attention of everyone present. I felt how tempting it was to stand out from the crowd, to weep loudly, to say something about the deceased that everyone would agree with, or to blurt a familiar adage of existential significance in the Yemenite Arabic dialect. This tyranny was within my grasp or, as perhaps one should say, within the grasp of verbal expression. It clashed with any manifestation of weakness that I had known in these women and made me think that the wailer accumulates this silence, to which she is sensitive, in order to exploit an elusive opportunity to express herself. For the group, the crisis-like emptiness of the situation is a weakness in the state of mind. For her, it constitutes a temptation that is hard to resist. The wailer knows that the persona of the deceased, suspended in the void, provides sufficient if not emphatic justification for the raising of her voice and may attach to this conspicuous voice words that are not only handy but also culturally sanctioned. In my participant-observations, the silence was always interrupted, and so were the movements of the imaginary beings. Eventually, one of the women in attendance emitted a real voice. The silent presence of waiting people has a tempting power of its own. The situation offers the possibility of empowering oneself, and this seemingly may weaken the resistance of a woman who imagines herself to be weak. This part of the discussion, focusing on the temptations of the dramatic unit, describes the dependency relations that exist between performer and audience. These relations originate in the power of temptation that the stage exerts on the actors, without which their acting would be devoid of charm.

The term "temptation," which alludes to a deviation in behavioral values, would be totally invalid if we accepted at face value an argument that my respondents often expressed: that the wailer's performance is meant only to make the audience cry and should be viewed only as a form of honoring the dead. The temptation sets the wailer apart from the audience in that it directs its attention to her inclinations, her needs, and perhaps also her capriciousness. This term also separates the few wailers from the nonwailing women, since the latter can encourage a performance merely by means of eyes and words; they are not caught up in the situational opportunity for self-expression. In the performance, the wailer deviates from the image of woman that is familiar in daily life in Yemen. As described in chapter 4, she has reached her period of maturity/senescence, and as the respondents said, she "courageously" overcomes the "shame" that ordinarily adheres to women. In this matter, Saida stated, "A death event is not a disgrace! I'm not ashamed of such an event, no." There is something about the characteristics of the postfertility age that liberates women from the threat of contamination or ritually defilement and prepares a few of them to be ritual leaders. The wailer, in my estimation, exploits the implicit sanction that the death event creates to overstep the contours of the image of her modesty—an image that exists until the moment of the performance and reestablishes itself afterward.

NOT LIKE AN "OLD WOMAN"

Rosaldo (1974) views the roles of elderly women in traditional rituals as the building of honor and authority. The story of the wailing of Yemenite Jewish women confirms and demonstrates this but, in contrast to Rosaldo's approach, does not credit women's presiding over "authority rituals" to them having been liberated from roles of motherhood and sexuality (28). Even though the meaning of "authority rituals" is the replacement of one set of roles with another—leadership in lieu of child care—I find it hard to see how a woman in a traditional society, despite her advanced age, can be liberated from the very female roles that define the core of her identity. Perhaps we should be more precise in interpreting the expression "liberation from roles," which easily may confirm our stereotyped perceptions of the social state of elderly men and women. Let us bear in mind that "liberation from roles" represents the outside observer's point of view, which may be foreign and painful to the subject who experiences it. The observer perceives the appreciable change and gives it a name; the subject, in contrast, of whom it is said that "She isn't what she used to be," establishes paths of continuity for herself (Turner 1990; Covey 1981). By implication, the wailer only seems to have been liberated from her maternal-feminine roles; her liberation is valid from the cataloging social perspective but not from the standpoint of her innerness (Chodorow 1978). As I have shown, the process of becoming a wailer is rich in symbols, emotions, and memory that originate in the creativity cycles of females/mothers.[12] The phenomenon of menopause does lower people's expectations of her and alleviates the social supervision that has been monitoring her actions. However, a normative liberation of this kind is unlikely to be devoid of a subjective sense of loss. Furthermore, it would probably encourage elderly women to take a counteraction by retaining, maintaining, or reexperiencing roles that had always lay at the core of their power (Rosaldo 1974; Gilad 1989).

Two Yemenite Jewish women.

Scholars agree that in traditional societies, wailing provides women with a stage for the articulation of their unique voice (Holst-Warhaft 1995). The focal point of the interest or cultural discovery that surfaces in many of their accounts centers on social inequality and class hierarchy between men and women. This is not the place to use our research case to add to the existing debate; we will do this in the next chapter. Here I wish to argue that a different kind of social inequality, that observed in the wailing arena, has not been privileged with similar development. I refer to the age status of wailers who perform as dramatic units or what may be viewed as a class relationship that relates the wailing performance to the stage in the life cycle that the woman has attained. As stated, Yemenite Jewish wailing is reserved not only for women qua women but also, and mainly, for elderly women. The normative significance of assigning wailing to people of a specific gender and age cannot be ignored. It should elicit several questions that relate to the case at hand: Might this designation point to a hierarchy that differentiates young women from elderly ones? If so, who benefits from this hierarchy? What is its psychosocial significance? Such questions, it seems, are not being asked in the broader social circles in which Yemenite Jewish wailers participate today. This is due to the existence of age stratification in Israeli society, like many modern societies. Since age stratification basically reflects values that sanctify the body, beauty, and youth, it places these elderly women at a disadvantage. Its manifestations are so firmly entrenched that they dispose of the perception of womanhood in favor of one of the genderless elderly (Browne 1998; Arber and Ginn 1991). Thus, Israeli society probably considers these wailing women old, members of the category of old, and therefore doomed to rolelessness, labeling, and social exclusion. The proper place to ask these questions is in the original context of the performance—the Jewish culture as it had existed in Yemen—and especially in the context of a comparison, in value terms, of the patterns of a traditional society with those of a modern one.

What we have said thus far suggests the following: in contrast to the circular continuum of the life of mother/woman that the Yemenite Jewish wailing structures, modern culture creates a fractured structure. Traditional wailing for the dead is an expression of the fabric of a woman's life. The wailer pours her entire life cycle into her wailing: childhood, mother-figure, the suffering that she experiences when she gets married and leaves her parents' home, and motherhood, which begins with the suffering of pregnancy and birth giving. This is the story of her becoming. To attain the excitational depth of the story, an elderly woman must be preferred over a young one. Although the wailer is no longer fecund, she delivers a performance that speaks on behalf of young birthing mothers—a performance that the latter, for the most part, lack the maturity to carry out. The continuum of the wailer's entire life cycle can seemingly be constructed against the background of the real and symbolic circle of the women in attendance, who are at various stages of their lives. The wailer's representative voice inseparably integrates her own past ordeals with the present-day experiences of the women in attendance and links both sides in a single female-maternal fate—not a fate of pride or advantage but rather one of suffering. Her lyrics suggest that just as death is present in everything, so are the experiences of woman in that women tend to be contemplative of themselves and their lives. Thus, the performance establishes authority among women without having overt hierarchy or status. The wailer is the young women's equal in value terms, neither inferior nor superior. By sketching suffering at two levels of time—the long extant and the suffering that awaits her and others in the future—the wailer seemingly compensates for her "old age" after the fact and by means of her performance. This compensation is attained paradoxically; the tendency of the performance to dwell on the loss, equalize it, and distribute its meanings among other women renders the wailer into a timeless mother-woman.

In Israel, as stated, the wailing circle resides in the midst of a society that does not give its elderly women any valuable role to play, let alone accepted paths of womanly-motherly behavior. As long as the wailing culture continues to exist in distinct Yemenite Jewish communities, the tension between the value systems will probably prompt wailers to persist in their roles. For them, wailing is a tempting stage. The wailer may consider it a last bastion, where she may challenge the loss that the escalating cultural assimilation represents. Leaning on her cane, she shuffles down the street toward the house of mourning. Her presence in the street, in the public domain that extends to the edge of the courtyard or the door, is undistinguished and blighted by the anonymity of old age. The moment the rules of her ritual situation are established, however, the masks that the "weakness" of her appearance has created are torn aside in one stroke. This transformation of image traces to three sources. First, as described above, the performing wailer reclaims something of the semisweet level of suffering that she finds desirable because it is bound up with the mysteries of her being a daughter, a wife, and a mother of children. Second, her performance is a display of emotional control and physical power that drives a wedge between her and her advanced age. This impression is confirmed by a remark that one of my interviewees made about Johara: "She never wailed again to her dying day," he said, because sometimes "she didn't have the mental strength to wail." Hedva, Johara's daughter, said, "She had a weakness: she didn't have the strength to play [her role]." Johara stopped wailing at around the age of eighty. One of her acquaintances explained the matter with imagery from the modern world of work and retirement: "It's like a soccer player who quits while he's still great." Saida, who had already passed the age of eighty, expressed the same idea when she turned down my request to wail in a house of mourning. Sitting at ease in front of the mourners, she whispered to me that the imperative of wailing has been overtaken by the imperative of taking care of her health, because "Wailing takes strength and a big effort." In another episode at a house of mourning, an expert wailer told me not to expect the woman next to us to wail because "She's old. She hasn't got a voice any more." The wailer is aware of the audience's judgmental gaze, which defines her as old not in terms of years but rather in terms of her ability to perform. When she performs, she shows that the "old age" label does not fit her. Therefore, her wailing should be considered synonymous with a public functioning that has nothing to do with age. When the wailer stops performing, she may join the so-called belated old-age club, a club that a growing number of people in our culture are joining (Disney 1996; Friedrich 2001). Third, however contrary the example may be to the modern labels of old age, the wailer retains something of the positive image that traditional societies attribute to the elderly (Simmons 1970): she is someone whose advice should be sought, who knows what to say and how to take care of things. Her ritual knowledge is transmitted from the very heart of the event. She is not the "old woman" whom we observed a few moments ago shuffling down the street.

What we have said thus far distinguishes the wailer from the "old woman" as a familiar social label that abounds with negative connotations. The wailer, immersed in community life, is something other than an old-woman figure not only because she plays an active public role but also for two additional reasons: the functional demands of the role in mental and physical terms and the requirement of demonstrating strong affiliation with the group of women and the articulation of motherly emotions. As we show below, everyone looks upon the wailer as a woman and mother. She is distinguished from the others by her expertise, her rich life experience (suffering), and the freedom of expression that she allows herself. We would do best, it seems, to relate to her image only as it is established by her cultural partners. Our reference should object to points of view that are foreign to the sort of cultural context that sees nothing in the human body except its external manifestations of wear and tear. Where should we begin to wrap our minds around the matter? I propose that our discussions of the wailer's image from here on should follow the symbolism of one of her pieces of clothing. The most noteworthy thing in this regard perhaps is her strictness in swathing her head in a kerchief. In the Yemenite Jewish community (and in other Jewish ethnic groups), even elderly women customarily wear kerchiefs. The kerchief covers women's hair from the onset of adulthood to old age. In accordance with the impression that one gets, the self-inhibition that the kerchief creates may be viewed as symbolic of the potential immodesty that the manifestations of the female body augur. In our research case, this potential exists at all points along the life cycle. The requirement of keeping one's head covered establishes equality among women, does it not? Does it not suggest that woman qua woman carries temptation within?

JUST LIKE A WOMAN

In contrast to the lack of age differentiation among women, excitation and sad facial expressions represent a dramatic division of labor between men and women among Yemenite Jews and in other cultures (Sarris 1995; Alexiou 1974; Lutz 1988). Even though we identified the perception of expertise in the wailing performance and even though it embodies some extent of authority, a wailer is nothing but a woman who has been placed in charge of tears by women and is expected to act like a woman. Expertise and authority—both relating to weeping—cannot bridge the worlds of women and men. Furthermore, the way these are consolidated in the consciousness of members of their community creates a fence between women and men in that if weeping is a feminine mode of expression, then the experts in weeping are conspicuous in their femininity. In my fieldwork, I conducted two group interviews with about forty men at the time of their *tazqina* (khat chewing) get-together. They were asked to express their opinion about the image, role, and performance of the wailer as they had known them in their community. Remarkably, they said nothing whatsoever about the wailer in terms of her age or old age; their only terms of reference concerned her femininity. Before they relate to her in any role, they view the wailer as a woman.[13] Since their attitude in this matter is so clear, I believe that the wailing performance should be regarded as more than an expression of the wailer's nostalgia for something that has dried up and blown away. In her adulthood and old age, her lament is a refined way to demonstrate femininity.

We now observe another "feminine trait" that the wailer possesses: ambivalence. The mourning aligns the wailer with her audience, but her expertise separates her from it. These types of contrasts between the crisis of bereavement and the control of expertise reside at the structural level of the cultural phenomenon and make the performance ambivalent. Two additional manifestations of ambivalence, which we have encountered saliently thus far, are the wailer's ability to generate strong emotion without shedding any tears of her own and her assumption of a funny role at the end of the dolorous performance.[14] This ambivalence, or as we call it this duality, is a doubling of the value of the self-performance, a double entendre in the domain of emotion and will. It is a psychological act of distribution into contents that are mutually exclusive, one canceling out or replacing the other and being reincarnated as its total opposite. The wailer's performance is rich in a duality that brings together contrasts at several levels of reference. For this duality to become femininity, I wish to argue, it is in dire need of an audience of men. If we return to the element of ambivalence in the performance, we must admit that while the wailer's expertise distinguishes her from the audience, the differentiation does not exist the same way in regard to men and women. When the wailer separates herself from the other women due to their silence and in view of what one may attribute to them—their relative familiarity with ambivalent psychological states (Douglas 1966; Lutz 1988)—she separates herself from the men, who, being unfamiliar with the secret of her performance, cup their ears in order to hear. Amid the crowd of women, the wailer raises her voice until it can be heard as far as the courtyard and the street, spreading from the feminine space into the adjacent space, that of the men. She may even intend to project her voice into the men's space (Feld 1995), although it is also possible that they simply overhear her (Urban 1988). Either way, her voice carries to quite a radius. It attracts a crowd of onlookers who, as they peer at her from their place among the seated women, assimilate the implicit duality experience of the performance.

I also find duality in the ritual encounter that the wailer establishes between herself and death. "Your days were not filled," she may thunder into her listeners' ears as though she were talking to the deceased, and she may express bewilderment about cruelty that she has witnessed. The depth of the grief in her melody makes it clear that she has already experienced her share of death. She likens a man who has been snatched away in his youth to an "infant in the cradle," who needs the food that she will place in his mouth and the motherly caress that her arms will provide. As the lamentation proceeds stanza by stanza, the wailer's compassion turns away from the deceased and returns to her. And if it fails to return at her allusive bidding, she has more vehement words to call on. "My heart is burned," she sometimes says in a banal turn of phrase. Sometimes she says things like "Alas, my luck, your arrival is a bolt of lightning"; "I am ill and in care, dejected from head to toe, because my luck is black and my eyes know no rest"; "God will make me suffer"; "I have no one in the world"; or "I call your name, and no one answers." Repeatedly she describes herself as standing in front of a common metaphor for loss—a closed door—and as walking about while shrouded in a void that gnaws at her psyche in her many days. By relating to her mental agonies in these ways, she makes it easy for her listeners to regard her performance as the depiction of herself as a victim. The emphasis on suffering in this context is typical of wailers in other wailing cultures. The Inner Mani women, for example, wail about the "burning of the pain," a pain so intense that it consumes wide swaths of the self and cleanses and refines the entire self. The pain creates a subjective experience of victimhood, and on this basis these women liken it to an inner holocaust (Seremetakis 1990). Briggs (1993) also describes the victim experience that is particular to the wailer, who, he says, unburdens herself of thoughts during the performance in a process that creates a multidimensional alignment between her subjectivity and death. One of the manifestations of victimhood that I found among my women respondents, an especially extreme one, shows how strongly suffering manages the wailer's psyche. The suffering distorts her will so badly that she wishes to reduce her entire humanness to the lowliness of a minuscule body that creeps along the ground. It is this that will let her get her way. "If only I were a worm that would enter his grave and I'd think that he would come back to life," one woman wailer said. Thus, the wailer expresses her suffering in words. Since these are her words, she says nothing else, let alone anything contradictory. The overall meaning of her performance, I believe, is based on the duality that exists in a mother's encounter with death. At a certain moment in my observations, I wondered how the victim appears on a stage. The intensity of the pain that nestles within the words is not imagined as auguring anything other than paralysis and muteness; it is a pain that leaves the victim no room to seek anything for herself. After all, the crowd that congregates around a wailer cannot be likened to people who gather randomly on a street corner. The wailer's victimhood rhetoric is uttered in the course of a systematic performance, and it is the nature of this performance to contradict the impression of being doomed. The phenomenon resembles the impression of duality that one gains by formulating the role of suffering in evaluating the performances and determining the prestige of Pakistani wailers (Benedicte 1994); indeed, the accepted saying in their community is "The saddest stories are the loveliest ones" (86). Woman's dignity and suffering are intertwined. In the Pakistani case, this is traced to the influence of Islamic ideology. As the Yemenite Jewish wailer faces her audience, she seems to oscillate between the image of a victim who pours out words, or her heart's blood, and one whose hope lies in the very act of expressing herself. She reveals her weaknesses without anyone believing that they are only weaknesses.

This duality is reinforced by the goals of the performance for the human beings involved: honoring and healing. The value of honoring the dead and the importance of allowing tears to flow give the wailer authority. They place the reins of the performance in her hands from the very start. As they rest in her hands, however, she elects to dwell on her sufferings—among the other messages—until the whole message becomes depressing. The wailer, having come to honor the dead, seems to be dishonoring herself for some moments, insofar as self-respect conceals need, and the would-be healer proves unable to heal her own inner agony. Nuanced impressions of superiority and inferiority, advantage and disadvantage, and kindness and misery are tools in her performance. Now that she has thrown herself so fully into remembering the agonies of her motherhood, whether or not she has forgotten the reason for her willingness to wail—that is, the needs of the deceased, the mourners, and those in attendance—cannot be known. A man named Shlomo, one of the participants in my group interview, described it in such terms and confirmed what we know from other Muslim wailing cultures (Abu-Lughod 1986; Wilce 1998): "The moment someone dies, they seize the opportunity and come to wail over their own bitter fate. It's like they turn things upside down. How do they say it? 'Send a message to this guy who died a year ago . . .' and then they begin to make up all kinds of essays about their problems and other problems. They wail, but it's not for the person who died any more; it's for someone who died before him, and they mix the two together." The expressions "upside down" and "mixing together" express the audience's sense of ambivalence. The contradiction between honor and need refuses to resolve. For those who wipe away their tears and reflect, the wailer always enunciates a dualistic intention: willingness to sacrifice or, perhaps, opportunism and management of the audience's mood. "The enchantment of agony captures [women's] hearts," and "The masochistic goal blends and intermingles with woman's various ambitions," says Deutsch (1961, 223) in an attempt to get to the root of the complexity of the female psyche. As Deutsch describes it, a self-writhing in pain and pleasure occurs even before the externalized and demonstrative performance is observed. This "masochism," possibly the wailer's main possession, "wraps itself around her in a smokescreen of heroism," says Deutsch. "And her ego gains many advantages from this, foremost the gratification of her self-love" (222).

Duality creates a disturbing sense of disquiet as a tactic in interpersonal relations. It encourages people to ignore each other's allusive play-acting, to escape from the rashness that has gripped the others at the place where clashing desires intersect. Dualism demands a second-order solution that will remove it totally from the gnarled web that it has created. The wailer, with open arms, tempts those in attendance to enjoy an experience, and they respond by burying their eyes in their palms. They weep, they encourage others to weep, and they may forgo the tantalizing issue itself, the very asking of the well-known Freudian question "What does [this] woman want?" Men interviewees revealed another style of reaction when they described how they cope with a woman's tears. As spouses send each other various messages in daily life, the men cope with duality by denying it. My group interviewees instructed me that they, as men, know "women's tears." This familiarity taught them to protect themselves against their common "nature." One interviewee said, for example, that "When I was young my late father would quote an Arabic saying that meant, 'Women's weeping counts for nothing.' . . . Even if she cries, it's like play-acting. It doesn't mean [anything] to anyone. . . . There's a folk saying: for a man, woman's crying is a game, he knows woman's crying in his daily life because he's bossy. He knows woman's crying inside and out, in all sorts of situations, when she gives birth. . . . He's not sensitive to this crying." Another "off-the-cuff saying," which the subject almost certainly had in mind, suggests the meaning, according to Ratzhabi (1953, 321), of "Women can make even the eyes of mules water." "Sometimes," another participant added, "she uses her wiles even in court: when she begins to cry, the judge is considerate toward her." Here Ratzhabi quotes another saying from the collection "Woman in the Parables of Yemen": "If a woman cries for help, she's saved her husband" (321); that is, a woman's play-acting excitability sometimes serves a man's interests as well. These sayings do more than center on the spontaneity of women's tears; they allude to the play-acting and manipulative dimension of womanhood. Male interviewees spoke in this manner when answering my questions about the wailing performance. To their minds, the clashing dimensions of "woman's weeping"—the duality of weakness and strength—come to their full development in the wailer's role. Weeping and denial are two response strategies that men use to cope with duality as a "female trait." Unlike the response of weeping, denial is evident but falls within the framework of interpersonal relations and is not typical of the wailer's audience, men and women alike. One rarely finds members of the audience who do not bow their heads or look about sadly. Even the most hardened cynicism cannot withstand the power of wailing, which urges it to squelch itself. The effect of wailing overwhelms the faults of its creator and rivets the audience to its seats.

Duality contradicts the thinking that underlies social organization and accepted behavior in community institutions. It is considered unmanly. When it is demonstrated in the public domain, some may view it as an instrument of power that lies in women's hands (Rosaldo 1974). By means of the duality, women stress the anomaly: their aspiration to disrupt the order of things. "When women lament and wail," Abu-Lughod (1993, 202) explains, and "they suggest to those around them that death is so terrible that it prevents them from maintaining faith."

When the wailer in her role as mother-victim uncovers her eyes, they reveal no weakness or any traces of weakness. They are dry. Her voice is already gliding into speech, reverting to the utterly mundane. How? How does she find herself in view of the trauma? What is her "being"? her attitude toward herself? toward people? toward the situation? She confuses everyone. This may be one of the cultural configurations that a woman uses to signal her inclination toward unfamiliar logic, cognitive chaos, her stubborn insistence on remaining where she is, on the bridge. She tends to disturb the illusion of security that separate and parallel conceptual embankments create, that is, the familiar meaning of either-or that they carry. The death event also disrupts systematic thinking, but for her it creates a no-man's-land that needs to be delimited by her domestic inclinations, which offer her innumerable possibilities of *both*. In this sense, we second Briggs's (1993) view that wailing, as interpreted in the Warao culture, derives its power from its ability to disrupt conventional meanings. This power, which illustrates woman's latent potential, has no place in ritual practices of death that aspire to create a secure world of meaning (Das 1986).

WAILING AS AN EROTIC PERFORMANCE

I now wish to revisit the wailer as an erotic figure, that is, one who embeds erotic messages and symbols in her performance. I admit that the claim about the existence of an erotic dimension in the wailing performance may be perceived as problematic because the ethnographic literature does not seem to offer it much support and, in the main, because my subjects made relatively few direct references to it in their responses. The relative paucity of discussion in the literature and in the findings of my research may originate mainly in the conceptual weakness of the term "erotic," the vagueness that shrouds its definition, and the value resistance that the pairing of "erotic" and wailing for the dead evokes. Consequently, my argument about the erotic characteristic of the performance is based less on a collection of facts that may be edited and sorted with interpretative rigor than on a possible alignment of concepts and ideas that one may glean. With these drawbacks in mind, I attempt below to demonstrate the erotic as a symbolic characteristic of the wailing performance and to gather it under the spotlight of theoretical attention. After all, at the deepest core of the wailing culture resides the wailer, a woman who lends her feminine voice and bodily motions to the needs of her female and male observers. As a picture viewed through a keyhole, this may evoke theoretical suspicion. The meaning of the "erotic" will be interpreted and will branch out from this picture. By calling the wailer an erotic figure, the implication is that she is a performer whose monologue may resemble a dialogue between herself and the audience. This kind of misleading monologue, in which we recognize levels and symbols, will establish the bounds of the continuum of interpretations that this chapter lends to the expression "the power of melancholy."

What does the word "erotic" mean? It originates in Eros, the Greek god of love. The word "eros" is attributed to one of two human instincts: survival of the species and love. Mirroring the set of mythological imageries, people routinely attribute to the word "erotic" various and sometimes clashing meanings that span an existential continuum of matters that lie between body and soul. In this context, Jung (1984) termed as a common mistake the tendency to limit the meaning of the erotic to the sexual. To his mind, "erotic" denotes attachment. The conceptual fog seems to originate in the combination of both dimensions, the physical and the emotional, that the term carries. If I may cull two expressions from the corpus of definitions that exist in the literature, I would say that the erotic is manifested as spiritual sexuality and as sexual spirituality. What I mean by "spiritual sexuality" is that sexuality or sexual bonding between man and woman embodies a spiritual experience (e.g., love and profound feelings of happiness, hope, and excitement). Sexual spirituality, in contrast, denotes the conscious domination of a spiritual activity—artistic, religious, or other—in which the participants/observers may find symbols of sexuality. Mor (1998) seems to refer to the first combination—spiritual sexuality—in the following way:

> [The erotic] is the meaningful bond, formed by sex, that lovers sense and understand. This [quality of the] erotic that we sense in sex and romance is also a broader attraction that preserves the integrity of the universe, the mediating spirit that should watch over the movement of the stars in their orbits and the timely advent of the seasons. We ask sex not only to provide physical gratification but also to respond to the soul's need for everything that the erotic has to offer, for a whole world and whole creative lives that are powered by love. (Mor 1998, 9)

Sexual spirituality, as I define it, is an extension of the more conventional meaning, the one cited above (spiritual sexuality), to the word "erotic." To be more precise, the latter sense (sexual spirituality) better befits the declensions of the word "erotic" than the declensions themselves (e.g., "erotica") do. People may attribute erotic meaning to a painting, a poem, or the petals of a flower. They use expressions such as "an erotic picture," "an erotic statue," "an erotic motion," and "an erotic flower" whenever associations of the vitality, goodness, and beauty of bodies in sexual union are epitomized in an aesthetic experience.

A good example of the difference in meaning between spiritual sexuality and sexual spirituality is the biblical Song of Songs. The commentators disagree about the nature of this work and what its author had in mind (Ben-Gershom 2001). The prevailing approach favors the sexual spirituality outlook, construing the erotic contents of the Song of Songs as but symbols of exalted religious ideas. In the remarks below by Ben-Gershom (2001), spiritual sexuality is represented in the word "parable," and the word that represents "sexual spirituality" is "object." The parable in Song of Songs is an erotic dialogue between lovers, abounding in expressions of sexual yearning, and the object is a relationship of exalted spiritual love between God and the Jewish people (Cassuto 1967). Here is what Ben-Gershom says:

> Song of Songs was not inspired by an intention to write a paean to physical love. No one disputes this; after all, it is self-evident that the scroll has a hidden meaning, an object, that transcends the implication of the literal text. This is not to say, however, that the object should be concealed from the masses. Evidence of this is the fact that the Sages, too, did not consider [the Song of Songs] the retelling of a love affair between a man and a young woman. They discerned the level of meaning that transcends the implication of the literal text and did everything they could to call this exalted level to the attention of the masses. (Ben-Gershom 2001, 24)

The wailing performance, I believe, is not a form of erotica in the sense of spiritual sexuality but is an erotic performance because it embodies—among its other meanings—sexual spirituality. I propose that wailing, being captive to moralistic religious rhetoric, be viewed as a performance that does not exclude symbols and messages of sexual love. The poet Tuvia Sulami supports this by noting that Jewish girls in Yemen grew up listening to recitations of the Song of Songs and understood, loved, and were influenced by the contents and spirit of this biblical book. We may also test this interpretative possibility by means of an Eastern approach that looks upon the human body as one of many reliable instruments of the aspiration to spiritual exaltation (Gonzalez-Crussi 1989).

"Modesty" is one of two expressions that clarify my subjects' perception of the erotic. The term "modesty," and not the terms "erotica" or "sexuality," was invoked in the give-and-take of questions and answers because it is well known in the religious-moralistic discourse that typified all the subjects. Another reason for talking about modesty is that this word carries an inner meaning; it is a device that speakers can invoke to mask crude words and thoughts and impress others with their lofty morals. The subjects inserted such a stricture in their emic rhetoric in order to uphold their dignity. The word also protected them from the guilt that they may have felt due the questions that I asked; that is, they considered the term "sexuality" a verbal abomination that has no place in a death event. However, they caused no loss of understanding or interpretation by speaking of modesty, because the thing that they rendered modest by speaking this way was sexuality.

Thus, modesty and sexuality are complementary concepts. By describing a performance as "modest," a respondent is also admitting that a menace hovers over the performance: the menace of a display of sexuality. If so, the evaluation of something as being modest alludes to the existence of an associative range on which the evaluator may call, within which images of sexuality reside. By implication, the word "modesty" may serve the sexual spirituality perception of the erotic but not the opposite perception. Another expression that recurred time and again in my talks with the subjects was the saying "Woman's voice is incestuous."[15] Whenever I invoked this familiar saying, I established a special rapport with my subjects: Look, we said, so to speak, we're talking about the wailer's sexual behavior in modest language that is fit to be spoken.

Wailing is the performative incarnation of a flirtation between the spiritual and the sexual. In its concrete form, this flirtation exists primarily between the woman who honors the dead by wailing and many attendees who do not share the sorrow. By speaking of flirtation, I mean to say that the performance arouses erotic thoughts from a great distance, in that there is a message of consent in a message of refusal, and even refusal is woven into the cloth of consent. As Simmel (1984, 135–36) puts it, "Flirtation must make the person for whom it is intended feel the variable interplay between consent and refusal; the unwillingness to submit oneself that could be an indirect way to self surrender; the surrender of the self behind which the withdrawal of the self stands as a background, a possibility, and a threat." The nature of woman does not clash with the duality of the act of flirtation, Simmel claims, and her flirtatious relationship with the man represents a distinct synthesis of the definitive aspects of this relationship. In other words, in this relationship one may find consent and denial, friendship and rancor, and an assortment of interests that conflate into an action on behalf of moral solidarity. As I suggested above, the duality of the erotic message that the wailer may send her audience lies in the structuring of her power to tempt.

Amid her melancholy words, the wailer entices her listeners to step into the schemata of life. Her performance signals the potential of creation of life that rests in the ongoing reality of mourning that women and men share. This assertion about the intention of the performance is extracted from a much broader interpretation that relates to mourning practices in the ancient Hebrew culture and in many other cultures, such as the Turkish, Indian, Polynesian, and Tonga. According to this interpretation, the expressions of mourning, orchestrated mainly by woman, attest to women's adherence to life symbols that reside in the body insofar as the intensity of the pain requires this (Frazer 1923). They can be found in customs of bloodletting, facial or abdominal laceration, the infliction of physical injury, the growing or ripping out of hair, and the growing of fingernails (Pollock 1972). Obviously, the nature of the wailing performance of Yemenite Jewish women is more delicate than these. It also differs from the conventions in other wailing cultures. The difference, however, is not only relative to conventions that prescribe savage or immodest behavior such as the rending of clothes and parading in front of the men (Abu-Lughod 1993; Halevi 2004), exposing the breasts, tugging the hair, drinking blood, and sending sexual messages (Bourke 1993). The Jewish Yemenite wailing culture also differs from conventions that create arenas in which participants enter frightening states of trance (Aborampah 1999) and from those that encourage wailing women to shout loudly (Seremetakis 1990). The Yemenite Jewish wailer transmits messages of sexuality and life with pious delicacy. She's just flirting. She fills her lyric poetry with verbal metaphors. She also uses her body in ways that, although cautiously measured, are not devoid of symbolism.

Let us begin with the metaphor that wailer's bodily motions suggest. Her motions during the performance are not only motions of melancholy. To make this clear, it is worth rereading the detailed description above.[16] The wailer presents motions that denote undressing and deployment. Her hands open up in circles that move away from her torso and then return. The position of her legs does not contradict the presentation of a wish to draw closer. Her back and head move in a rhythmic way that has nothing in common with the intellectual strictness or the motherly responsibility that dominate the perception of women in daily life. Although above I describe the movements as restrained and express the belief that they could expand,[17] I believe that the overall effect of motions in wailing deviates somewhat from the daily monotony that the modesty imperative imposes on the female body from head to toe. I refer to the modesty that was practiced in

Yemen in routine physical conduct in all domains: the private, the public, and even in happy patterns of dancing among women as individuals, in pairs, or in groups. The following description of the dancing of Yemenite Jewish women bears this out:

> The most conspicuous traits of [Yemenite Jewish women's] dancing are submission to authority, restraint, and modesty, in the sense of [the rabbinical saying], "The dignity of the King's daughter is totally inner." These traits dictate the language of motion and the entire structure of the dance. . . . When they go over to the couples dance, after a change in the drumbeat, the legs move somewhat more energetically and their motion is sometimes accompanied by leaping, spinning, etc. Here, too, however, the rest of the limbs maintain restraint and the women allow themselves only a severely limited amount of extra freedom in moving their legs. One cannot relate to the dancing without noting an immensely important component in the motion and the steps: the clothing. A Yemenite [Jewish] girl was covered from toe to head. Only her face, hands, and feet were revealed. Accordingly, the bodily motion was alluded to and shaped by the cut of the cloth. (Avraham and Bahat-Ratzon 1994, 189–91)

Limited motion, as described above,[18] is a typical trait of both dancing and wailing. Just the same, there is a performative difference that may shift the latter into the domain of the erotic. First, a sole performer amid circles of a large audience is typical of wailing and not of dancing. In dancing, there was no solo performance. Thus, performative courage, or immodesty, is attributed to a woman in her role as wailer and not as a dancing partner. "The woman had modesty. We, they always taught us modesty," said Mazal about herself, adding, "A woman shouldn't advertise herself, to say she's like . . . to speak out and all . . . no. We're modest." I asked, "Are you saying that the wailer is actually less modest?" "That's right," Mazal replied. "She's in the middle of everyone. Everyone's looking at her. She wails aloud. She makes it as though everyone wants her." Another respondent remarked about this characteristic: "A wailer has more impudence. She's got more confidence, more boldness, more pride." Second, wailing motions are different in nature from dancing motions. Wailing is typified by opening horizontal movements of the limbs and back; in dancing, the limbs are typically held together, and a vertical posture is maintained. The wailer's movements, which have an opening-up appearance, are accompanied by an additional departure from normative feminine behavior and verbal and nonverbal messages of helplessness: a slight raising of the voice. This symbolic combination of motion, voice, and weakness is a form of flirtation; if it may attest ab initio to the channeling of the melancholy onto bodily channels, it is also a sublimational metaphor for female sexuality.

Metaphors are tools of temptation. They obtain their potency by intensifying the duality in interpersonal relations and fashioning a replica of reality. To understand this possibility, we need to probe the meanings of metaphor and other examples. A metaphor is a word that has the unique ability to enrich language by means of transference or task swapping. The word changes meaning from case to case, but an associative relationship is maintained between the new object of reference—the symbolized one—and the word that performs the symbolization. "The candle of the house has gone out," the wailer says in an independent-clause metaphor that is transferred to the domain of grief over the loss of someone beloved. In contrast, the formal mission is reflected in an adjective when the deceased is called a "white flower" or in a verb when the wailer's heart is described as "thirsting." Metaphoric forms intertwine with and augment images culled from nature. "You didn't reach youth, and you didn't grow old," the wailer may address the deceased. Such a form of address creates an opening through which a metaphoric flow ensues. For example: "The house craves you and the step awaits you. Avraham is a fresh sprig. A scholar who learned to read early. The books are sad. Oh, you flower of scholars. Avraham's gone and won't come again." The metaphors populate many lines of the lyric expression. Metaphors are descriptive doors that open onto the inner chambers of the emotional world. "The words, the images, are but a springboard to the listener's spirit" (Breton 1969, 43). This is because figurative language draws its inspiration from the primeval; it is said to be infused with creative spirit (Neumann 1974). The wailer's metaphor is unique in that it is not summoned from nature, whose concrete creation is death, but instead is paired with compassion, birth, and childhood. The metaphor expresses as directly as language can the twinning of rupture and healing with their emotional varieties, allowing verbal orders of the mind to progress immensely. A metaphor is a cultural-symbol bridge to the depths of the soul. The "craving" of the house for the deceased and the "thirsting" of the heart for his presence are among the innermost descriptions of yearning. The melancholy gaze fills itself like a house, and the grieving heart bleeds and is drained of vitality. One of the wailers offered another example: "My heart, why are you burnt? Alas, my luck, your arrival is a bolt of lightning or you will drown in a wave." Psychological pain has no cosmological limits. The phenomenological way of looking at the world, a gaze exclusive in its all-embracingness, is determined by means of metaphors. The metaphor is an outgrowth of the limitations of the logical words, which cannot transcend the object. It is created at that very moment, before the individual's wish to create an experiential transmission between it and its counterpart is frustrated by despair over words. One almost has to choose between it and silence. The metaphoric form, if one falls into its tempting embrace, grabs and reverberates inside the person; that is, it applies power. The wailer's metaphor contains psychological truth that it delivers at a very high level of persuasiveness, induces the person being addressed to recognize things by their figurative names, and gives the object of the address aesthetic satisfaction and catharsis.

The wailer's metaphors rupture every dam that the tears may use to restrain themselves. Seemingly, however, the significance of metaphoric power is not limited to persuading people to be sad. The metaphor, like an oil painting, a sculpture, a photograph, and any other product of inspiration, is an artistic form of the erotic. This is not to say that wailing metaphors embed sexual contents in messages of melancholy. I found no such examples. I am saying that metaphors, as forms of displacement of meaning, carry some of the allusions of erotic communication. By transferring and carrying the listener from one realm of meaning to another, the metaphor has an element of invitation. The metaphor is a weapon that is aimed at reality and invites the addressee to leave behind the drab symbolic space of the familiar and the trite language used to describe it and join the charmed world of the poet. The same can be said about wailing: its metaphors serve its lyrics, the intensities of the melancholy, by urging the listener to step away from the here and now and its implications, such as "He's gone," "He was," "How could this have happened? It's a pity," "He won't come back," and "It can't be helped." Wailing metaphors do the work of the imagination in places where things talk and feel, eagles cry, and flowers on rooftops exude wisdom. They surpass the death story, which itself may elicit weeping (Rapp 1973). They are also stories of transcendent beauty (Harries 1978). As such, they do more than invite people to enter; they may also snare the addressee in closed forms of conceptualization. The aesthetic gift allows the wailer to deprive the audience of its own metaphorical ability and impose her own control over the relevant interpretation of the death event. Its lovely figurativeness is exciting. It establishes a verbal momentum that instructs everyone, indisputably, on how precious the deceased really was and how badly he or she will be missed as well as on the intensity of the pain, which feels as if it burns, sickens, and drowns you in the sea. Some scholars consider this a performative form of emotional colonialism that disturbs the audience's ability to phrase its inner world for itself (Fiumara 1995). In greater part, however, the audience shows by its behavior that it is under the wailer's thrall. Its emotions are engaged, and it has joined the world of images that she offers.[19] The audience appears to be willingly controlled. As I have shown, the audience invites the wailer to place its emotions under metaphoric control and praises her linguistic formulations as a gift of words. Thus, the metaphor also has the trait of duality: its implicit imprisonment of the mind has a beneficent side that resembles an intimate embrace.

The metaphor generates a special intimacy between the wailer and her audience. In terms of its situational and cultural context, it is an intimacy that excludes strangers who are not in on the secret of the symbolic displacement. Shoshana, from her seat on the tour bus, sings in Yemenite Arabic: "My heart is full, Mother; to whom will I recount [the pain]?" Thus, she wishes to show me how she bemoans the absence of her mother. Shoshana's sentence is very familiar: one encounters it in women's wailing texts and wedding songs. It may, with one verbal thrust of the sword, bring to immediacy the sense of abysmal loneliness that the absence of one's mother creates. The heart can accommodate a great deal of suffering but now is filled to overflowing, and only Mother, among all people in the world, can offer compassion. The accommodation metaphor portrays the absence of mother as an infinite concretization of the sadness that resides in everything that the abandoned child's heart may conceive. When Yemenite Jewish men and women hear this lyrical expression in public—after all, they are fluent in the Arabic dialect used—their faces become masks of sorrow, irrespective of whether their mothers are alive or not. This evocative metaphor is outside the target range of anything that can conceivably happen. It reverberates from the depths of the dictate of separation that life imposes. Eyes begin to moisten; heads slump a little. The audience's motions slow down and converge in self-surrender for the receipt of more "true words" of the same kind. The metaphor mocks the denial that pervades people's mundane activities—an outing, a trip, the summer, leisure. It is transcendent—it lifts the audience out of the caprice of the here and now and plunges them into tears. It is indeed a form of interpretive tyranny. Nevertheless, it is heartwarming. It serves as a narrative code that presses emotional buttons. When I asked Haviva, a widowed wailer, to give me a demonstration of wailing, she slipped into familiar metaphors: "My husband left the house; he went out in the light and returned in darkness," she pronounced. Afterward, she explained the lyrical custom: "So they gave a parable. Lots of times they talked in parables." Then she added, "They say, like, for example, 'The eagle that cries and wails for me from the great mountain, how he cries for me when I'm sad.'" Since the people at issue want to weep, even if only to themselves and far from the wailing audience, it suffices for them to utter the consensual metaphor to themselves. "If you get this sentence," Naomi said, "then when you're in pain you pull it out [say it to yourself]. [Whenever] you want to cry, you pull it out." Hannah likened her deceased mother to a birthing mother and a flower at home, quoting the Yemenite Arabic folk, and said, "My mother, giver of birth, what a pity for you, what a pity." Immediately her eyes watered, and her voice turned hoarse. The response to the shared code in the course of the wailing performance reflects the profound relations of solidarity that exist among those present. The tightening sense of "us" is obtained by the specific metaphoric form to which everyone responds. The symbolic meaning of the metaphor is universally agreed and culturally unequivocal. The metaphor is an instrument for the creation of intimate relations.

The literature describes the nexus of metaphor and intimacy in its occurrence outside the traditional performance arena, that is, where people meet, converse, and wish to send messages. As soon as the metaphor escapes the speaker's lips, one may view it as an invitation to a verbal dance of sorts in which one participant takes steps and the other responds with countersteps. The result is a formula for relations of intimacy—what (Cooper 1986) calls "special intimacy."[20] This kind of intimacy depends on the metaphorical use that speakers make of the set of images available to them; it is based on specific metaphors, such as those that are not "ordinary" or "basic": "'Special' intimacy . . . [is] the intimacy presupposed by an utterance which is both 'extra-ordinary' and 'justified.' It is the bond which unites those who are reasonably deemed capable of hearing it—and, indeed, uttering it—with understanding" (158).

Special intimacy is created from the deep meaning of the metaphor. This meaning, concurrently emotional and intellectual, does not dissipate when the metaphoric speech stops; it is invasive, leaving its imprints on the future thoughts and emotions of the participants in the conversation, who, from the outset, appreciate each other's ability to interpret it in a similar and specific way. Their rhetoric, which began with the metaphor, develops and centers on its objects and expresses a symbolic metaphoric exchange in which aesthetic pleasure is implied. Its very existence isolates the participants from reality—although they do not eschew reality totally—and from other social partners in discourse. The metaphor draws together those who utter it and excludes those who are oblivious to its symbolic secret. It is something like an interactive code, a joke that only some people laugh upon hearing, and the laughter of those who get it creates a tie that binds them in some way. The metaphoric dialogue also resembles whispered speech that grabs the people who intend it to be only for each other. The whisper, like the joke, riddle, and metaphor, contains a hint or a secret. Each of these media has the ability to transfer its participants from foreignness to intimacy and sharing. In the view of Cohen (1978, 7), the sense of intimacy rests on the awareness that not everyone can present the metaphor and not everyone can relate to it. The wailer's monologue imitates this type of dialogue. The audience, which by listening is defined as part of the performance, expresses the notion that not every wailing woman can generate the same metaphors for it. The definite article preceding the word "wailer"—the fact that she is held in special esteem—indicates among other things the audience's performative judgments and its appreciation of her words and her ability to turn a metaphoric phrase.[21] The audience is invited to listen to a monologue that is representative of it. In the course of what the audience imagines to be a dialogue, the wailer assumes roles, speaks in the name of "X," turns to "Y," and tells the story in metaphorical coinages.[22] The most picturesque metaphors, those that strike deep into the audience's spirit, seem to be the most appreciated. It is those metaphors that establish the exclusivity of the wailing arena and bar all but the cultural cognoscenti from entry (Cooper 1986). This intimacy is one of the domains of the emotional event that takes place among a public and exists among the public as a collective in exile. It also exists between audience and performer as an it-her relationship.

The metaphors in wailing do not belong to the types of imageries that relate to "something," that is, the mundane concerns of people's daily reality. Instead, they reflect on a crisis that has occurred in this reality and probe its meanings. They concern themselves with matters that are very existential. Their purpose is to transform "groundedness," in which people are overwhelmingly mired, into "ground" and then "ground" into "soil." Thus too, the coloration of "materialism" is reduced to a colorless "material" of the sort that is doomed to dissolution. The metaphors steer the imagination to the brink of an abyss and instill anxiety about the existential emptiness that lies just ahead. The nonexistence of someone a familiar and beloved person demonstrates the arbitrary power of death and the human being's utter inability to counter it. "He who has taken the step down, he who goes down will never again return." The wailer refers to "he who goes down" in order to explain that this fate awaits all living beings. The "step" is the oh-so-palpable step into the grave, taken by the body en route to its final rest. An audience may feel love for a performer, a storyteller, a singer, or a pianist if that person's work makes this kind of appeal to the emotions. The audience senses the performative hand that is extended in its direction from the stage, grasping its heart, sensitive to every spasm that the thought creates. In the intimate reality that I have described, the wailer's metaphors and words are a form of deep empathy. The audience imagines the wailer as a person who loves them. The empathy that she projects in the direction of the audience has the mystical power of crossing a boundary, invading the audience's hidden domains and revealing the audience to itself (Reed 1984). The wailer offers herself as a sacrifice for the death of a certain person. Her reference in so doing is the universal victimhood that always exists in regard to the fact of death. The wailer expresses herself in the most deeply buried words of a terrified, anxious soul that, in its anxieties, is very beautiful, childish, innocent, and remote from any form of evil. She says, as it were, "I know what's deep inside you, my friends. The roots of your fears are intertwined in yourselves and in me. I'm just like you. You'll let me press your most fear-provoking buttons because you trust me. For a few moments, I'll be like a loving mother to you if you get something from my act of 'undressing,' because I strongly express that pain." Thus, the audience may sense the meaning of itself as being a victim of death and may also sense the wailer's sacrificial surrender of self, which is meant to impart this emotional understanding.

Far from the performative picture—not to mention the experience—let us imagine one last thing. The wailer sits in the middle of the house or the tent, surrounded by people and the silence that her performance has imposed. With one hand she places a small kerchief over her eyes. Her voice undulates, her head rolls from side to side, and her upper body sways as if in prayer. Her other hand makes gestures like a storyteller—striking her head, resting itself over her heart. Thus, she sends a message stripping herself of every garment that alludes to power, control, or the intention of outsmarting her viewers. She takes her life in her hands, as it were, and submits it to the audience's judgments. She invites those present to regard her as one who strips herself of the pride and the faux grandeur that the masks of the personality grant. She surrenders herself at all levels of her performance in order to create a spectacle of helplessness and total submission to death. She offers no consolation, does not deny the magnitude of the disaster, and holds all systematic forms of speech in contempt. Only she heaves and surges;

the audience is riveted. The rhythm that invests her body is channeled to her limbs and liberates them from ordinary language. Thus, she creates the impression of verging on madness. A stranger might ask, "What's come over this exhibitionist woman? Can't she restrain herself at all?" How can it be that right there, in the middle of an audience of people, she is so natural in her helplessness, writhing and falling to the ground? When the wailer peddles grief and existential dread in a wrapping of performance, she looks as though she is alienated from herself. At these moments, she sacrifices her daily image and makes souls out of the very fact of her strangeness. Some scholars would say that she reveals her feminine masochism as a narcissistic temptation for every shred of the audience's attention (Deutsch 1961). By so doing, she presents itself as an unfathomable and uncompromising mirror of the existential wretchedness that everyone in attendance shares.

This aspect of the performance—the sacrifice—is connected with the erotic. The unconditional surrender to death, a synonym for the forces of nature, itself lies at the hidden focal point of the creation of life. George Bataille, in his *Erotism: Death and Sensuality* (1986), champions this argument. The erotic act, Bataille says, connects people with death in a way that parallels the offering of a sacrifice. The wailer strips away her social identity during the moments of her performance, does the bidding of the audience, and induces it to weep and to feel respect and solidarity. She is a social agent who, as a wailer attested, "gives all the love that she has." As Bataille would say, she demonstrates one side of the erotic relationship between lovers, which seeks to satisfy, to merge totally, to unite with the other until self-abnegation is achieved. Lovers offer themselves to each other. The offering is their self-identity. They are so addicted to being good to each other that they commit acts of madness and pursuit. As they do so, they half-shed, half-lose what they had recognized in themselves as distinct personalities. "Love is the undoing of normality," the Jewish saying has it.[23] Wherever it exists, it demands sacrifices and ritual. Bataille (1986) takes his argument one step further: the altar of love on which people offer sacrifice is the sexual union. He describes the moments of sexual release as the climactic moments of the sacrificial act. At such moments, people are poised at the brink, glimpsing something higher than them before falling back into the state of separateness. This glimpse is described as a direct contact with death. It is attained by virtue of people's willingness to sacrifice all assets of their selves for a transcendent sense of oneness. People may even surrender their ultimate assets—their souls—in service of the goal of unity. The significance of their sacrifice lies in the ritual integration of life and death. For example, the decisive moment in the death rituals of the inhabitants of Banaras, India, simulates the crucial moment between lovers. At this moment, the neck of the (actual) dead person is broken, and his or her soul (vital breath) is released in a symbolic act of sacrifice (Parry 1994). At this moment, the deceased's face resembles the exhausted but contented face of the lover who has attained release. The release that takes place in the wailer arena is weeping. I would argue that the entire performance is a metaphor, a faint parable of sorts on erotic love relations. Both the wailer and her audience sacrifice something of themselves—she by the very fact of her performance and they in their lachrymose response. Wailer and audience, the two sides of one performative coin, respond to each other's needs. Both occupy an erotic space in the sense that their anxieties and existential desiderata cross the threshold of the consciousness and coexist with fierce emotions. In this erotic manner, the wailer seems to be a bridge between life and death. This is a very abstract road to travel, paved with symbols from the corporeal and psychic domains that suggest the positive outcomes that a crisis may bring forth. Bataille's (1996, 91) remarks about the sacrificial urge are not far from this: "It is the common business of sacrifice to bring life and death into harmony, to give death the upsurge of life, life the momentousness and the vertigo of death opening on to the unknown. Here life is mingled with death, but simultaneously death is a sign of life, a way into the infinite."

I admit to some interpretative conceit in offering this analysis. My argument favors the theoretical outlook that views a performance as a nonreflexive occurrence, a cultural instrument that narrows the representation and coding abilities of those involved in it. The components of a performative occurrence are difficult to decode within systematic and familiar frameworks of understanding only. A performance is also an arena of flow and permeation of experience and craving (Feral 1982).

The melancholic power of women's wailing has three forms. First, we discussed it in the context of the medicine of tears that has to be administered in the course of grief work. Afterward, we described emotional processes that take place among people who together establish a collective presence. Finally, we decoded the power as a form of temptation that establishes the wailer as a social presence and creates symbolic erotic contact between herself and the audience. What is the singular nature of the melancholic power? A tie that binds exists here. It connects what begins with a performative statement about the mourning event that is about to take place and concludes with a hidden erotic facet. This tie connects the pungency of crisis at the beginning with the sweetness of an intent to heal at the end. The tie connects the consciousness and death with the semiconsciousness of love and life. What is the nature of this thread? The answer lies in the domain that is thought of as the psychology of feminine power. In mythological traditions, a goddess is an entity that confers forms, forms that originate in the ancient, primeval mystery that transcends all categories of thinking (Bolen 2002). The title of this chapter, "Melancholic Power," reflects this outlook in the sense that it surmounts the barriers that separate familiar categories. The two words—"melancholic" and "power"—exist in internal tension, as if the one had the ability to nullify the implications of the other. They suggest that the dimensions of this power are dual. In its direct dimension, the power may reside in the intention of the indirect; in its control dimension, it sometimes takes on the form of helplessness (Lips 1991). The melancholy of mourning does not stay within itself. It overcomes itself and transforms itself totally by means of the lyrics and the fullness of the performance. The words wrap themselves around the anxiety like a garment; the production of the words, systematically and with descriptive wealth, creates an antibody to the pain. It resembles a properly performed act of psychotherapy in which the words know how to enter and exit the forms of pain and strip it of its power. Thus, the performance is allowed to reshape the affective understandings of people whose culture, as we have seen, establishes ex ante a topical intimacy between weeping and laughter. The story of power in this chapter circumvented the woman-wins/man-loses approach that underlies the traditional concept of power. Melancholic power is one of the assets that the subject possesses;

it is primed within the framework of intersubjective relations and may be conferred by a performance. Melancholic power constitutes the ability to grow, to expand, to be fruitful, to create, and to put suffering to good use. The wailer, in her performance, points to the path that leads from death to the creation of life.

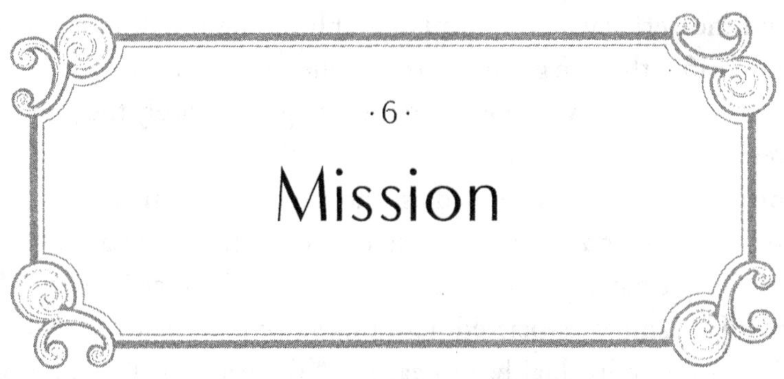

·6· Mission

Women's wailing is a maker of reputation. The wailer is sought after due to the sheer respect that she commands, and it is on behalf of this respect that she captures people's hearts. Authorized by the force of a mitzvah (a religious imperative), her performance is privileged with rapt attention. Were it not for the mitzvah of honoring the dead, there would be no story to tell. The wailing appearance would lack all social justification; it would not fall into the domain of a culture. In his "Laws of Mourning," Maimonides teaches that "The dead are honored by eulogy. Accordingly, survivors are required to pay [male and female] wailers to eulogize them."[1] The self-induced weeping, under dramatic circumstances that I probed in chapter 4 and those who trigger it (see chapter 5), now resemble the gesture of tipping one's hat; the audience's sobbing is an expression of respect for itself and for those among its members whom it has singled out as central in the event. One of the beneficiaries of this gesture is the woman wailer, who places her every movement in the service of a worthy value and the performance of a mission. Honoring the dead is the source of the honorifics that are granted to everyone: consolers, mourners, and the wailer. It is connected with honoring the living at precisely the point where the bereaved come together.

Honoring the dead is defined as "the nature of the treatment that the deceased receives, and the prestige associated with this treatment, in appreciation of his having lived in accordance with the social norms" (Rubin 1997, 116). The lament associated with this value is an instrument of social control, and the individual has to earn it. "The wailer is like a reward for the deceased," my respondents explained. In the Greek wailing culture, this conventional belief is expressed in the form of an adage: A person dies without a woman wailing for him is unlucky (Holst-Warhaft 1995). An unlamented person is likened to someone who has "died naked," in the sense of the nakedness of a tree in autumn. It is a shameful, unwitnessed, quiet death, far from the glory of a "good death"—a form of social "poverty" (Seremetakis 1990, 492). The common expression among the respondents that "The groom is honored with singing and the dead is honored with weeping" alludes to the perception of wailing as a form of caregiving that carries social prestige. Among the various terms of honor, honoring the dead is included in the sense of glory—an exalted and metaphysical glory, inseparable from the absolute, perfect, immutable essence of God. Honoring the dead is bestowed on a person like a congenital trait and is absolute due to man having been created "in the image of God." Jewish sources warn against any impairment of this metaphysical trait, especially at the time of a person's death. According to the *Abridged Code of Jewish Law,* failure to observe the rules meticulously is judged and perceived as "mocking the wretched" and "disgraceful" (Deblitzky 1979, "Rules for the Removal of the Dead, the Funeral, and Justifying [God's] Verdict" and "Rules of the Burial and the Cemetery," 198–99). Echoes of this warning—the imperative of honoring this image of God in miniature—are audible in the wailer's explanations: "It's a mitzvah to wail, *banti* [Arabic for 'my daughter']; even for the Arabs it's a mitzvah." To bestow this honor, one is allowed to make others cry and dramatize the loss of a human being who is gone, never to return. The melodramatic intent is expressed in phrasings such as "Because for the dead you have to cry. Do you take [the deceased] to a wedding?! No, you take him to the grave. You have to cry for him"; "If you don't cry, it's like it doesn't matter. If they don't cry, they're inconsiderate of the dead. A person who concentrates and understands the value of life, he watches"; "How will people feel when someone has departed from them? If they take him away like the simplest of objects to throw into the trash, when everyone is quiet and everything is calm, isn't it like nothing happened?"; and "A dead cat you bury. You don't say a word for him. But we're people. Someone has gone, someone you knew, after all. He did good things and you're in such pain. You cry." When I asked what the keening ambit of wailing has to do with honoring the dead, Ora replied that being vocal "makes them feel that somebody great has gone away. I give [the deceased] weight." A person who dies unlamented is like the simplest of objects, like a cat. The connection between wailing and honoring traces to the prophet Jeremiah: "They shall not lament for [the moral transgressor], saying, Ah my brother! or, Ah sister! They shall not lament for him, saying, Ah lord! or, Ah his glory! He shall be given the burial of a donkey, drawn and hurled beyond the gates of Jerusalem" (Jeremiah 22:18–19). The melodramatic importance of wailing was expressed ironically in one of the wailers' stories. The son of a deceased woman pleaded with the wailer in tears to wail for his mother. This order of events—crying in order to persuade someone to induce crying—may seem odd. By weeping, however, the son acknowledged the intrinsic drama of wailing, the thing that would transform his tears into others' tears, that would thrust the audience into melancholy and thereby honor his mother's memory.

"Mission"—not "honor"—is the word that I choose to represent the matters discussed in this chapter. I select it to suggest the existence of a connection between the value of honoring, shared by all death rituals, and the female practice and the order of things that it creates. The term "mission" is defined by *Merriam-Webster's Unabridged Dictionary* as "a continuing task or responsibility that one is destined or fitted to do or specially called upon to undertake: a lifework, a vocation." According to this definition, the wailer's expertise acquires almost the religious meaning that the German word *Bernf* or the English word "calling" impart to the concept of profession in accordance with Weber's (1958) analysis; that is, the wailer's mission is not much different from holy missions that aim to carry out God's will. As a task and a responsibility, the concept of mission may capture the definition of the feminine: the task, in essence, subordinates the self and is not easily reconciled with a lust for power. The task is always undertaken on behalf of something or someone—a person, an idea, or a spiritual entity. When the task is a public mission, it implies a social duty stemming from a perception of what is good, an object of choice and devotion, and comes with an element of admiration of an idea that transcends any conflict (Miller 1976; Lips 1991).

In this chapter, I take the further step of elucidating wailing in the sense of it being a destiny. The destination in this definition of the term "mission" alludes to movement from a place of origin toward a goal. Such is the case with wailing as a mission: although anchored in its divine origins, it takes a social turn. Its lyrics are far from any intention of creating a god (Blackburn 1988). This mission moves in the opposite direction of men's worship—it descends from heaven to earth.

The first pages of this chapter dictate the nature of what will follow. The remarks in the first part of the group interview, discussed in chapter 5 above, carry a similar meaning. The interview was conducted in a circle of men who attended a *takhsina* and sat around a number of hookahs. Sa'id, one of the elders of the group, sat at the doorway of the spacious terrace as an observer. He took the floor and held it for quite some time. No one interrupted him, and no one embellished his lecture by taking measured tokes on the hookah, as is customary. What he gave me was a special introduction to the matter at hand:

> First of all, we're pleased to say "welcome" to you. Second, today is the sixth of the Jewish month of Tevet [December 21, 2001]. Third, maybe I'll be able to answer some of your questions.
>
> The wailing women are a subject unto themselves, and the eulogy [that men say] is related to the wailing of the wailing women. On that subject, I'll tell you what went on in northern Yemen, around [the town of] Sa'ada,

sixty years ago and more. We [men] didn't eulogize the dead; instead, we wrote a letter forty centimeters by thirty centimeters. Here's what they wrote in the letter: "It's a pity to have lost him and his religious learning, it's a pity to have lost him and his crafts, it's a pity to have lost him and his ways, it's a pity to have lost him and all his good deeds." What does this mean? It means, it's a pity that such a man has parted from society, family, and relatives; the most important study that he did [his religious study]; and the craft that he'd learned. In northern Yemen, especially, they did crafts for a living. Not trade or anything else, as in southern Yemen. "It's a pity to have lost him and his ways." The soul isn't ours; it belongs to the Creator of the Universe. He deposited it in the human body, but if [the deceased] escorted it with good deeds and good behavior, then everyone weeps and laments the parting of the soul from such a body. . . . Even [the soul] itself ascends to the Creator of the Universe and says, "It's hard for me to part with this person's body." But it's decreed in Scripture. No one in the world can prevent it. "The living shall pay heed," it says in Ecclesiastes [7:2]. What does "shall pay heed" mean? Today you see people who are no more. Tomorrow will follow today, and you'll see that people and personalities will vanish from what you've seen today and from what you saw yesterday. They'll follow in the footsteps of the ones who are no more. It's as though you had a dream at night: this person was here, walking, laughing, and joking here.

People say all sorts of things. They praise [the deceased] after he's gone. If he was a bad person, they say it isn't good to mention him at all. Don't bother to mention him, since he was bad all his life. He behaved very badly all his life, so there's nothing to mention him for. They'd say, "May his bones rot in hell," in so many words. Everyone whom he'd hurt would say it: "May his bones rot and [may he] not be mentioned for [God's] mercy." It's all written for us in the [holy] books. I didn't make up anything new.

If he'd been important, they'd say all kinds of good and important things about him in the eulogy. Why? To calm the relatives and family members about their loss and to speak well about his soul. If it is pure [they say],

> then may it merit the status of an immaculate soul and may it find its place in the heavenly Garden of Eden.
>
> Now, the women have nothing to do with this. What they have to do with is inspiring the listeners to weep. Not every woman can say these things, only trained women who've learned over time what to sing and what to say in order to make [the people] weep. The song [the women's lamentation], that's something else altogether. This is what you've heard from me; anyone who wants to add to it is free to do so and you can write it down.

The respondent's introductory remarks say almost nothing about women's wailing. They mention wailing at the beginning and at the end to demarcate the boundaries of the parallel ritual, the men's eulogy, about which he had not been asked. He may have first mentioned the eulogy—the "men's lament" for the dead—to suggest that it is more important and central than the women's creative genre or to deal with it by negation. His remarks imply that eulogy is unique because it is rooted in Scripture, derived from the sanctified sources, and circulated among the deceased's relatives in the form of a letter. This portrays men as literate people whose actions are informed by God's commands. Another topic embedded in the respondent's opening remarks is the essence of eulogy as a vindication of God's judgment. The men, by means of their eulogy, seem to think of God as a father figure of sorts who may subject the deceased's soul to the afflictions of hell or the delights of Eden. Returning to the topic of women's wailing, the respondent described it as "something else altogether" and noted that the women themselves "have nothing to do with" what he had described thus far. He also depicted women's wailing not as a phenomenon of intrinsic value but instead as a mere instrumentality that "inspires the listeners to weep." By so doing, he created a taxonomy that recurs in another wailing culture in which differentiations between men's eulogies and women's wailing are central (Kaeppler 1993).

I believe that when an informant speaks in a knowledgeable and unhesitant tone—and specifically in such a tone—a thread can be drawn between his or her opinion and the set of beliefs and shoulds in the hegemonic discourse of the person's culture. Before I came around to this view and after I committed it to writing, I collected points and counterpoints from the respondents. They revealed contrasts within one sentence, that is, the informant's opening sentence, which captures this chapter better than anything else: "Wailers are a separate matter, and eulogy is linked to the lament of the wailing women." The ethnography from here on engages in the constructions of gender differentiation and similarities that exist in the Yemenite Jewish wailing culture. These constructions establish a dualistic stance toward women's wailing. In the discussion that follows, the essence of the wailers' mission is revealed against the background of the depreciation that social recognition/nonrecognition creates in regard to women's creative endeavor and role.

Segregation

The Jerusalem Talmud comments on gender segregation as follows:

> "And the land shall mourn, every family apart, the family of the House of David apart; and their wives apart" [Zechariah 12:12]. Two sages [expounded on this verse in public. One interpreted the verse as referring to] a eulogy for the Messiah; the other said it is a eulogy for the evil inclination. He who says it is a eulogy for the Messiah [who, according to tradition, will be killed in the first stages of the future Jewish redemption]—if men and women are apart when they are mourning, *a fortiori* when they are rejoicing! He who says it is a eulogy for the evil inclination [God will kill Satan when the end of days comes]—if men and women are apart after the evil inclination has departed, *a fortiori* [should they be apart] when the evil inclination exists![2]

Spatial gender segregation at joyous and sad occasions originates in a separation that cultural intelligence creates concerning the question of what men and women will have on their minds, in their mouths, and in their imagination. Community events in Yemen were typified by segregation of men from women. The ubiquitous phrase "for reasons of modesty" evolved into formal segregation that was implemented to satisfy various transient needs in crisis events. Although it is impossible to determine how to contend with the moral gender boundary in terms of cause or effect, at some point the boundary also became an authorization for self-segregation and the creation of autonomy. "Women apart and men apart," the respondents stated in order to place wailing in women's circles only. I should preface my remarks by saying that the respondents assigned similar meanings to the terms "wailing," "eulogizing," and "singing." Although they differentiated between women's wailing and men's eulogy, sometimes they called a eulogy a "lament" (Hebrew *qina,* as opposed to *hesped*) and explained that men's eulogies are written in a book called "*Lamentations.*" They used the word "singing" to denote a woman's performance at her wedding as against her performance at a time of mourning, but sometimes this term was replaced by "lament"—women's singing—and was presented as something distinct from men's singing. To follow the mental-cultural representation that Yemenite Jewish women's wailing creates, I will contemplate it as contemplated by the respondents and by researchers who consider it a genre within the totality of women's singing (Tzadok 1967; Dahoah Halevi 1995; Binyamin-Gamliel 1975).

SINGING

Yemenite Jewish women's singing differs from men's in two essential respects: content and language. This distinction can be understood only against the background of the Muslim intellectual and artistic life that surrounded the Jews of Yemen. The research literature on the singing of Jewish and Muslim women shows that the two forms have so much in common as to constitute identity and "plagiarism" (Binyamin-Gamliel 1994, 152). The singing of Jewish men, in contrast, is so dissimilar from that of Muslim men that the two forms sit at culturally opposite poles. Jewish women's singing was done in Arabic; that of men was saturated with the Jewish holy tongue. Accordingly, men's singing was called *shira,* Hebrew for "singing," whereas women's singing was called *ghuna,* Arabic for "singing" (Tzadok 1967). The distinction between the types corresponds to the distinction between the sacred and the profane, a dichotomy amazingly similar to that drawn by members of other cultures between the artistic endeavors of men and women (Chernela 1993). Women's singing is considered folklorish, utilitarian, and equally performable by all. Its contents relate to many areas of life: home and family, work, the obligations and burdens of women's lives, childbirth, and death. Women's singing abounds with emotions and metaphors from nature and is constantly self-renewing and impromptu and never permanently committed to writing. Some consider it "a subtle articulation of daily life" (Binyamin-Gamliel 1994, 148). Men's singing, in contrast, shares its quarters with prayer and supplication. The rabbis of Yemen considered men's singing a moment of psychological exaltation with which God Almighty might be influenced to bring forward the end of the exile (Tzadok 1967). These songs are written in a *diwan,* a book that contains a repertoire for use in celebrations and religious observances. Many of the songs are attributed to Shalom Shabazi, the national poet of Yemenite Jewry. His works have been described as faithfully expressing the Yemenite Jews' emotions and ardent yearnings for redemption and are said to be embellished with kabbalistic symbols and allegorical phrasings that convey deep meaning and linguistic richness (Tobi and Serri 2000). Amir's (1993) remarks in his introduction to one of the *diwan*s underscore the singularity of Jewish men's singing in comparison with that of women and that of Arabs. Songs included in the *diwan* met the value and moral standards of the Jewish spirit and faith in the sages. That is, special literary qualities in themselves did not make a song fit for public performance. The singing of the Jews of Yemen conveyed something of the gravitas of the synagogue and the song of prayer, because for these Jews singing *was* praying. As evidence, the letters of both words have the same tally in Hebrew numerology.

Study of songs on one theme—love—accents the differences between men's and women's singing in intent and content. In this matter, as I have already shown, women's singing was a refined but unfettered instrument with which to express the poignancy of love and erotic yearnings.[3] Its turns of phrase were directed at real or imagined people whom women truly, literally loved. They might fit into a stanza titled "In the shackled snare" and report that "The beloved captures the lover's heart with his beauty." Here is an example:

The tormented one said: Deliberately did I go away today
because there is sadness in my heart.
I met my blue-eyed beloved, the lord of the female beauties[4]
that resides in my heart.
And behold, a young boy adorned in golden jewels . . .
peered at me from the window and blinked
and took my breath away. (Ratzhabi 1975, 113)

Love in men's singing is not like this. Tzadok (1967) notes that even when a dialogue between a lover and a beloved does appear in a song, it is but an allegorical expression of the dialogue between God and the Jewish people (as in the Song of Songs). An example follows:

My only one, be unique in the secret of your thoughts and your words
and return to your abode; in your glow does my face glow
May the life of my soul and my melody and my praise be pledged to my Rock, my Master.
May the merit of the Patriarchs and He in whom I trust one accompany me in Yemen
and may I hear the song of the sons of Heyman and the sound of the flute and my bells. (Tzadok 1967, 163)

Below I quote Ratzhabi (1968) on the Jewish nature of the song of Yemen. He suggests that the "fence" behind which the Jewish men secluded themselves from women's art was erected for self-defense against non-Jewish religious influence:

> When we try to assess the Jewishness of Yemenite song, we may state with near certainty that it is the least influenced by foreign melodies of all Jewish song. This was caused by the national and religious singularity of Jews and Muslims. The cultures of both peoples that inhabited the country

> were religious in nature. . . . For this reason, a barrier between Jews and Muslims arose by itself. Each people went out of its way to preserve its national and religious singularity and avoided all cultural rapprochement with its counterpart. The two peoples' songs were also songs of religion and nationhood. Among Jews, they were songs of exile and redemption, yearning for the return to Zion and the ingathering of the exiles. Among the Muslims, they praised the Prophet and the wonders of the adherents of Islam. A Muslim melody was tantamount to a foreign invader of the sanctuary, something that a Jew must not even raise to his lips. A Muslim would definitely not hum a tune composed by a Jew, whom he regarded as subhuman, contemptuous, and lowly. The singing of Yemenite Jewish women, in contrast, which is active in its content, is extremely close to the song of Muslim women. It has more in common with Arab folk song than with Jewish song. In Yemen, women, both Jewish and Muslim, were illiterate. Jewish women did not have the same Jewish wellspring that the men, who labored over Torah in cheder, synagogue, and home, had. The [women's] culture was mainly an oral one—songs, parables—drawn from those of their gender, including Muslim women, especially in the villages. The Jewish men, too, did not treat the women as strictly as they treated themselves, since women were free of the yoke of Torah and exempt from many of its obligations. Therefore, the non-Jewish influence is also reflected in [women's] lyrics and melodies. (Ratzhabi 1968, 20)

LAMENTS

The categorical and hierarchical distinction between the sacred and the profane in Yemenite Jewish men's and women's singing also applies to death singing: laments. We adduce this by studying the origins of men's and women's laments in this community and the intercultural circumstances that relate to them. Generally speaking, the source of influence on men's laments came from far away—Spain—whereas that of women's was immediate and proximate: the singing of Yemenite Muslim women. This difference in terms of geocultural distance also carries class significance. This is always the case in cross-border and cross-language works and in intraborder works as well. Studies by Ratzhabi and others address the influence of the Sephardi school of singing on the singing of Yemenite Jewish men and their eulogies that began before the thirteenth century (Ratzhabi 1988). Their picture of Yemenite Jewish men's lamentation is after the fact, presented by way of negation. The festival prayer book of the Jews of Yemen is based on the *piyyutim*—liturgical songs—of Spain, Babylonia, and Palestine. Some of these works are familiar, authored by Solomon ibn Gabirol, Yehuda-Halevi, and Abraham ibn Ezra. Sephardic song had a definitive influence on song in Yemen. Importantly, however, the sages of Yemen did not adopt this corpus en bloc; they excluded its solo opuses and secular ideas. Thus, the singing of the Jews of Yemen, in the distinct form that it acquired from the seventeenth century onward, tended toward religious ideas and collective events. The community's devotional song, shaped and transcribed into writing, dealt with the agony of exile and expectations of redemption, God, the transmigration of the soul, and the kabbalistic doctrine of the occult. Due to this singularity, it did not develop wine and tavern songs, nature and garden songs, and companionship songs, as Sephardic song did. Furthermore, in our context, it did not develop laments. The Jews of Yemen appear ab initio to have delegitimized these themes, including personal laments, and to have relegated them to the women's circle, if anywhere.

The question is how to explain the rejection of the laments that were performed by the Sephardi liturgical poets. The answer may stem from the stance of the Jews of Yemen, who tended toward separatism, on the influence of Arab motifs on Sephardi Hebrew song (Ratzhabi 1987–88). It may also trace to the difference in the Jews' political status in the two countries. Ratzhabi (1968) notes that the Jews of Yemen, excluded from government posts, could not establish the kind of courtier class that flourished in Spain and nurtured poetry and poets. This caused a scarcity of solo songs in Yemenite singing and songs of praise for community benefactors (Ratzhabi 1968). Notably, however, personal song was typical of the work of the Yemenite Arab poet known as "Dushan,"[5] a court bard whose expertise included the management of public ceremonies and events (Caton 1990). A contributing factor in explaining this status is Padva's (1987–88) distinction between two types of Sephardic laments: classical secular lament and strophic lament that follows the pattern of devotional song. Padva hypothesized that laments in the category of secular song were meant to be performed in court settings. Moreover, these laments underscored the poet's status as a private individual. However, the Jews of Yemen also eschewed the model of strophic lament due to the powerful influence of the classical lament genre on the laments of the Jewish liturgical poets. The laments that one finds in the repertoire of Yemenite Jewish men today are versions that revolve around public and transcendental matters of the sacred; they never speak in the lamenter's personal voice or in the "voice" of the deceased (Ratzhabi 1987–88; Padva 1987–88); that is, they never originate in the Arab model or the tenor of women's wailing. The men's laments are more similar in their general characteristics to Sephardic sacred song in that they convert the pattern and motifs of Sephardic song into songs of melancholy, anguish, and acceptance of God's verdict. One exception is that the main characteristic of men's singing is "neither a grooms' song in honor of a particular groom nor a lament for the deceased about a particular deceased. Wedding songs and eulogies are worded in general terms and are said for every groom and everyone who dies" (Ratzhabi 1988, 13–14).

What does the psychocultural segregation that took hold among the Yemenite Jewish communities have in common with the teachings of biblical sources about men's and women's laments? Rubin (1997, 307n11) cites biblical expressions that treat the "eulogizer" as parallel to a "wailer," that is, in Genesis 23:2: "Avraham came to mourn for [*lispod*-eulogize] Sara and weep for her [*ve-livkota*]." Following up on this attempt, I will mention three additional common examples: Jeremiah's call for wailing women, the Book of Lamentations, and the Lamentation of David. They acquire their value, I believe, by blurring the aforementioned distinction between the male devotional collective and the female earthly-personal collective.

Male respondents cited Jeremiah's urging in their attempts to specify the role of women's wailing:

> Thus says the Lord of Hosts: contemplate and call for the wailing women, that they may come, and send for the skillful women, that they may come,

> and let them make haste and take up a wailing for us, that our eyes may run down with tears and our eyelids gush out with water. For a voice of wailing is heard out of Zion: How we are ruined! We are greatly confounded, because we have forsaken the land, because our dwellings have cast us out. Yet hear the word of the Lord, you women, and let your ear receive the word of His mouth, and teach your daughters wailing, and every one her neighbor lamentation. For death has come up into our windows and has entered our palaces, to cut off the children from the streets and the young men from the broad places. (Jeremiah 9:16–21)

Commenting on these verses, which belong to the prophecy of the destruction of the First Temple, David Altshuler in the *Metsudat Tsiyyon Commentary on Jeremiah* explains the following:

> *Contemplate:* give thought so you may understand the impending decline, and consequently, *call the wailing women,* women who know how to eulogize and wail for the dead, *that they should come:* to you, to inspire lamenting and wailing, *and to the skillful women,* women skilled in quickly composing sayings of sorrow and melancholy to sadden the listeners' minds. *Let them make haste:* they should hurry to wail for us so that our hearts may awaken and our eyes may shed tears. (Altshuler 1999, n.p.)

The verses and their interpretation imply that women's wailing is a mission ordained by God in that it is He who places the words in the women's mouths.

The emotional skill of the wailers, as wise women, entrusts them with an important public mission: to help the beleaguered prophet of rage to overcome the stiff-necked members of his community and plant God's message in his listeners' ears. Women's wailing, a unique performance known for its melancholic power, is expected to help people understand and internalize the dire prophecy.

The second example is the Book of Lamentations, also known in Hebrew as *Qinot* ("Wailings"). Its contents concern the destruction of the Kingdom of Judah, the burning of the First Temple, and the exiling of the population by Babylonia. Jewish men recite this text on the eve and the morning of the Ninth of Av, the day on which the destruction of the two temples is mourned. I wish to call attention to the wording and metaphors that this text invokes. Jerusalem is personified in the form of a woman. The account of her personal losses and horrific tragedies is intertwined with an account of the atrocities that the nation has sustained. The scroll blends the personal and the collective, the symbol of the Jewish people's sanctity and symbol of femininity, body, and vulnerability. An example follows:

> How does the city that was full of people sit solitary! How has she become like a widow! She that was great among the nations and a princess among the provinces, how has she become a vassal! Verily she weeps in the night, her tears on her cheeks: among all her lovers she has none to comfort her; all her friends have betrayed her and have become her enemies. . . . Jerusalem remembers in the days of her affliction and her miseries all the delights that she had had in the days of old, when her people fell into the enemy's hand and none helped her: the adversaries saw her and gloated at her destruction. Jerusalem has grievously sinned; therefore has she become loathsome: all who had honored her despise her because they have seen her nakedness: she herself also sighs and turns backward. Her filthiness was in her skirts; she took no thought of her last end; therefore, she declined astonishingly and has no comforter. (Lamentations 1:1–2, 7–9)

David's lamentation, in contrast, is personal in complexion. David laments the deaths of Saul and Jonathan, members of the leadership caste with whom he had been intimate:

> Saul and Jonathan were loved and dear in their lives and were not divided in their death: they were swifter than eagles, stronger than lions. Daughters of Israel, weep over Saul, who clothed you in scarlet and with other delights, who placed ornaments of gold upon your apparel. How are the mighty fallen in the midst of battle! Oh Jonathan, slain on your high places. I am distressed for you, my brother Jonathan: you were very dear to me:

> your love of me was wonderful, more than the love of women. How are the mighty fallen and the weapons of war cast away. (II Samuel 1:23–27)

It is not only the personal facet—the loss of male leadership—that sorts itself into the categories laid down in the sources of eulogy in the Yemenite Jewish wailing culture; the motif of heroism in war sorts itself this way as well. This motif of physical strength is totally absent in the Yemenite Jewish art form due to the Jews' *dhimmi* way of life in Yemenite exile (Ratzhabi 1987–88, 740; Nicholson 1942).[6]

The absence of the heroism motif in the works of Yemenite Jewish men and women might have united the genders against the songs and laments of the Muslims. This, however, did not happen: the pattern of Yemenite Jewish separatism is inimical to such in-between, neither-here-nor-there meanings. The Yemenite Jewish male discourse suggests that the in-between meanings represented by the biblical examples may have been correct for their own time only, in the historical and political contexts in which they were created and presented. This discourse reflects the fear that such meanings might threaten the foundations of the religious order, to which the Yemenite Jews adhered with particular stringency. Relating to the warranted separation of men's laments and women's wailing and the connection between this separation and the sources, Netanel said, "Of all the Jewish communities, the one that kept the true tradition best is the Jews of Yemen. In Jeremiah it's written, 'Call for the wailing women, that they may come . . . and take up a wailing for us.' So they'd invite mainly women to stir up the emotions. The men in Yemen couldn't weep and make others weep the way the women could. The men said eulogies that had permanent words. They didn't make them up. With the women, it was usually put together then and there. Now, they were based on something. There was an initial basis, a format, a structure. But they filled in the contents according to the situation. When it was someone important, they mentioned his importance. If he'd been devout from childhood, they mentioned that. A woman who did acts of kindness—they mentioned her acts of kindness and they also mentioned her by name. That's how the wailers did it, and that's how it was at the time of our first Patriarchs."

THE CEMETERY

The spiritual gender segregation among the Jews of Yemen was manifest in a practical way: spatial segregation. When applied in a death event, this segregation crimped women's steps and reserved the religious obligation of escorting the deceased and attending his burial for men only. The *Abridged Code of Jewish Law* explains the rule: "One must take great care that women not be seen with men in the procession to the cemetery and all the more upon their return, because it is dangerous, heaven forbid" (Deblitzky 1979, "Rules for the Removal of the Dead, the Funeral, and Justifying [God's] Verdict," 198). Standard rabbinical law warns men and women not to look at and think about each other but does not deprive women of the mitzvah of escorting the dead to their graves. The Yemenite Jews, however, applied the extra stringency of totally excluding women "in front of the litter" and "behind it" (Rubin 1997, 132). In the book *Halikhot Teiman,* the injunction is worded unequivocally and explicitly: "Women do not follow the 'litter' at all, be it the litter of a man or the litter of a woman" (Kappah 2002, 249). My respondents—both women and men—justified this moralistic prohibition, which typified the way of life in Yemen and no longer prevails in Israel. The justifications revolved around two interrelated outlooks: the danger in women's sexuality and their nonparticipation in the ritual. Perhaps due to modesty on the part of male respondents in addressing a woman researcher, women interviewees spoke of sexuality, whereas men spoke about nonbelonging. "Wailers," Tamar said, "when they bring out the dead person, whether it's woman, a man, a child . . . , they sit in the dead person's own courtyard. No woman walks behind the litter. Women are not allowed to walk behind the dead. Woman is called the evil inclination, and I'm not the one who says it; the great rabbis of our generation say it: a woman must not mingle with men even if she's modest a thousand times over. Man is made of fire and water. It's not that he wishes [to transgress]; the evil inclination controls him. At just the time when Satan stands up, when a man or woman has died, then the Angel of Death looks for a job, looks for any transgression. Trouble happens." Mazal explained that "It's because every woman has a woman's way [menstruates], and she mustn't enter the cemetery." Women whom I encountered at a golden-age club spoke with each other, in fragments, in the same way. In their remarks, they alluded to a fit and proper injunction that is breached today but had helped to strengthen the underpinnings of the faith in bygone days:

ESTHER: They say women shouldn't go to funerals at all.

SARAH: I say that if bereaved [women] don't enter the cemetery, none of them should enter. The rabbi already tells them not to enter: "Be careful not to enter." They're not careful. The rabbi says that the dead speak against them. There are wrongdoers.

ESTHER: The evil inclination enters together with the women.

SARAH: The women who are still young, they enter while they're menstruating.

TAMAR: But in Yemen, dearie [turning to me], everything had its own place. If there's a wedding, it's two weeks. Today, it's that very evening. Half of the [people in the wedding] hall are naked women. Her skin is like a mouse. . . . What's she showing at all? Should *this* go to the cemetery?! . . . Now there are young guys. This young guy. . . . Nothing can protect them from illicit relations! I've sinned to God. Today [women] follow the dead just so and say they're doing a "mitzvah"!

Tamar continued by recounting something that had happened a year or two earlier and combined the story with her own symbolic interpretation about what should be prohibited even if others consider it permissible:

> You should know that when my cousin died, I walked right next to the family, really close, where they were taking the litter. Then, all of a sudden, a snake stood there. . . . He went like this [waves her hand]. . . . The litter of the deceased was [on the ground]; he [the snake] showed that he didn't want to see women at funerals. Now listen up. . . . I was behind the litter. The snake went like this [used her forearm and palm to demonstrate the snake standing over the litter, shaking his head]. The pallbearers put him down and ran away, they were so scared of the snake. The people behind the litter, the ones escorting him, ran away because they thought the dead man had stood up. I saw the whole scene. I'm not afraid. I stood there and saw first of all how the snake said "Shalom" to us from over the litter.

> They [the pallbearers who had fled] put the litter down, the snake folded himself up and went down to Yehezkel's plot [Yehezkel being a familiar person in the community]. Moshe [another participant in the funeral] picked up a stick to kill the snake. The snake disappeared from view. He just went down and disappeared. An angel. An angel declaring that he didn't want women to enter the cemetery.

The dispensation that Tamar gave herself to join the funeral did not result in a total breach of the injunction, as would have happened had she entered the cemetery. Furthermore, even if the snake had been sent there on a mission, I found no sign of a breach having been committed against the rules relating to menstruation, which require a woman to avoid only the synagogue and only on her special days (Deblitzky 1979, "Rules Concerning a Menstruating Woman," 153). The "snake" made only one more appearance, in sundry remarks by a wailing woman about singing at a wedding: "The snake all around and the girls up above. The snake is the boy." A snake such as the one that inhabited in this story symbolizes the temptation to misbehave in places where people gather. At a time of revelry or mourning, the women's remarks hearkened to the myth of the famous primeval sin in which the snake tempts Eve and the temptation defiles her and Adam with loss of the flesh. Ultimately, it decrees perpetual segregation on both genders' offspring to prevent their mingling.

The respondents consider Kabbalah[7] a valid source for the injunction against women's presence in the cemetery and the interpretation of the mythical narrative. Given the status of this important source, women's presence in the cemetery is forbidden altogether. Men's religious work at this venue was privileged with similar expressions that denoted something self-evident and upheld women's inequality in the ritual. Netanel said, "No woman went to the cemetery. She has no business being there. First of all, there was respect—women don't mingle with men. Also, she has no business being there. She doesn't give eulogies, she doesn't say *kaddish,* nothing. So they shouldn't leave home."

Meleney (1996, 132) describes the injunction against Arab women's presence at funerals and cemeteries in Yemen as being relatively moderate:

"Women do not attend the graveyard on the day of burial, but they may visit the grave, just before sundown, on the third and thirtieth days. They hand out food (dates and sorghum bread) to the poor or the neighbourhood children." The explanation for the Jewish exceptional stringency about women's presence in the cemetery may lie elsewhere, that is, in the theoretical identification that is made between women and the body of the deceased. I found a veiled reference to this in men's remarks about the desuetude of this injunction in Israel in recent years, which has given women the "status" of nuisances. The men explained: "The women start wailing once the deceased has already been buried, so as not to bother the men. The whole *ritual,* the men do." "Now, what they [men and women] do here in Israel, they go up to the cemetery and they have to learn [the men read from prayer books]. Then they say, give the women a role in it that'll be their own, let them go put on a little show at the grave, let them cry a little. We'll stand aside. They won't bother us with our learning, and we won't bother them with their crying. We stand aside. Afterward, when [men] approach the grave, they say what they're supposed to say at the grave. If [the women] don't cry, they talk. Then it's a nuisance. The same thing [happens] on the thirtieth [day after the death] and on the anniversary."

Theory has it that the feminine, like the decomposing body, is unstable, liminal, and disruptive. Mourning rituals and representations of death are practices that strive to stabilize the body, that is, to take the body away from women's care and transform it into a stable memorial object—a real or symbolic tombstone (Goodwin and Bronfen 1993). My respondents expressed an attitude of self-defense in regard to the uncontrolled presence of women. This presence, for them, symbolizes difference and disorder, like death. The cemetery is not a nice place for women because women are expected to wail there, and wailing has an implicit element of confusion. They are also expected to chatter there, that is, to do two things that intrinsically strip the ritual of its holy intent.

The religious ritual derives its meaning from the theoretical nexus of women and corpse: the ritual is perceived as something that renders the body of the deceased literally and symbolically permanent. This construction of the matter is consistent with the attitude of egalitarian segregation of men and women that follows in the house of mourning. The sealing of the grave gives the corpse a secure place, as it were; thus, the implicit threat of women's presence and wailing wanes. When men and women coexist in the house of mourning, they maintain a segregation that is more a division of space and patterns of activity than an exclusion or the avoidance of interaction, as had occurred at the cemetery. The structural urgency of the funeral and the burial in the sequence of events is replaced by an unstructured, protracted stay with the mourners. Against this background, we should not find it hard to see in wailing what the respondents see in it—a nonritual custom or, in professional terms, a performance (Brown 2003; Schieffelin 1985). In one of its accepted definitions, a religious ritual is a formal and stylized pattern of behavior, a recurrent pattern accompanied by lyrics or song, sometimes also by bodily motions, and occasionally by the presentation of sacramental objects. This activity is aimed at a deity or a supernatural beings (Rubin 1997, 47). Below I discuss the transcendental object of the ritual activity. Here, I note that the difference between the wailing performance and the death ritual stands out in view of the perception of the ritual as being transitional. The wailing performance should not be attributed to the stage that has disengagement from a previous status or integration into a new one as its permanence-inducing significance. Both stages are typified by emphasized and structured rituals (Van Gennep 1960); both are more identifiable at the funeral, the burial, and the memorial rituals for the dead than during the shivah. This has been pointed out by those researching other wailing cultures, who note the transitional element in wailing (Feld 1995) and its nature as a death-ritual element that reinforces the concept of liminality (Radcliffe-Brown 1964; Danforth 1982).

In the previous chapter, I dwelled on the significance of the house of mourning as a liminal arena and the wailing performance as a configuration that intensifies a situation that is vague in terms of symbolism and role expectations. A wailing performance is fundamentally different from death rituals because it constructs a symbolic reality not by putting forward a claim, a description, or an interpretation—in the manner practiced by men—but instead by setting up a social situation in which the participants experience symbolic meanings as part of the process of what they already doing (Schieffelin 1985; Bloch 1974). The wailing performance belongs to an in-between stage of the canonic religious ritual, a space that is shallow in cognitive symbolization and wide open to experiential symbolization.

THE HOUSE OF MOURNING

The wailing performance fits into the sequence of the ritual by accommodation, not only in terms of the tertiary structure of the transitional ritual but also in the allocation of time and space. Women's wailing was originally meant to be performed in a house—a house of mourning. This venue, which the Bara culture calls "the house of many tears" (Huntington 1973, 67), accommodates the wailer in its interior. My respondents defined this as a respectful accommodation that originates in the aphorism "The entire glory of a king's daughter is inward" (Psalms 45:14). They—men and women—would certainly reject a hypothesis that terms this a Yemenite Jewish version of a situation of women's lack of control over their public image, lack of privacy in their lives, and perpetual subordination to the requirements of the immediate situation (Rosaldo 1974). The limitation of wailing in time—times of mourning—is also a form of accommodation. Male interviewees repeatedly stressed the trio of Hebrew letters: *gimmel,* the third letter in the alphabet, representing three days for weeping; *zayin,* the seventh letter, representing seven days for eulogy; and *lamed* (30 in Hebrew numerology), representing ironing and hair cutting (from which mourners must desist for thirty days) (Deblitzky 1979, "Rules Concerning Avoidance of Excessive Imposition on the Dead," 115). The three days of wailing are included in the seven days of eulogy. The expression "men's eulogies" generally represents the program of ritual in the house of mourning; eulogies are said at fixed and specific times.[8] In the first three days of mourning, women's wailing is performed in between the study of Mishna, prayer services for the elevation of the person's soul, and requiems, all delivered by men.

More than they spoke about the "ritual," the respondents equated women's wailing to men's eulogy—one creative genre balancing the other—thus giving evidence of a genderic division of labor. The question is whether this division of labor has a hierarchical meaning. That is, does the subordination of women's wailing to the rest of the ritual mean that the respondents consider wailing less important, or do they think of it in some other way? Netanel, who as stated introduced himself as a eulogizer "following the Yemenite custom"—the son of a woman who had been a renowned wailer—answered by stressing difference: "The difference is that for men, [eulogy] is a religious obligation that's performed by rote. You say what's written in the book and dress it up a bit. With the women [when they wail], she says what she remembers about the deceased. And if she doesn't remember a lot about him, she remembers about herself. Then she tells about her brother who was this or that kind of person, or about her husband who was this or that kind of person. By getting it wrong, she gets it right." This respondent also demonstrated the importance of melody in eulogy, as in wailing. He did so via a play on words, placing the prayer book [*siddur*] at the focal point of the men's genre and the narrative [*sippur*] at the center of that of the women. In Netanel's opinion, the possibility of forgetting to carry out the religious obligation is intrinsic to wailing, of all things, because wailing is improvised and needs emotional aids to be steered toward "getting it right." The difference that the eulogizer expressed—not in judgmental language—explains Meir's estimation of women's wailing as, at the most, "a custom that's not illegitimate" and another exceptionally negative assessment of wailing as "shallow words."

When Yitzhak was asked to comment about one participant's remark that "The language of women's wailing is probably higher than daily language," he said, "I don't think so. Maybe it's the other way around. The wailer plays with words." This aside, the respondents taught me that the less important place of wailing is manifest not in words but instead in the right-of-way that eulogy, prayers, and other ritual elements receive—itself evidence of a scale of priorities. An expression of this scale, as I have shown, is given in the methods of situational consideration that the wailer uses to show that her performance has begun, that is, the approximate time of the permission that she "receives" from the men's area (not during prayer services, blessings, sermons, etc.).[9]

This, however, is only one side of the coin of the value of wailing.

The reverse is imprinted with appreciative attributions that transcend the accommodation of women's wailing and have the effect of elevating the practice. Thus, respondents likened wailing to a "eulogy" delivered in Arabic, "prayer," "women's psalms," a "blessing" that should be uttered only in its correct way, and "service of God." They compared a wailing woman who carries out her mission to "a Torah scroll" and a "rabbi" whose words are holy. Hearing these appreciations, again I found myself extracting from the heart of the discourse the expression "The groom is respected with singing, the dead are respected with wailing." This adage confirms the impression of dualism that I have described thus far. Among imaginary onlookers who take its measure, the lenient-minded are pleased to claim a religious victory; to reinforce their view, they would say that women's wailing, alone among all practices, has the merit of representing a definitive event in the life cycle. The more stringent would note that fewer days are allotted for wailing (three days) than for extended wedding celebrations (seven days). Furthermore, they would identify with the melancholy element of the status of wailing, which earns its place of honor not on its own laurels but rather from the deceased and his death—events that are as far from weddings and celebrations of life as one can go.

A Feminine Religion

I consider Yemenite Jewish women's wailing a feminine religion that is reserved for women and that functions alongside the canon faith.

In many societies, death rituals express the dictates of a male-led canonic faith. Sered (1994) proposes that women's religiosity be viewed as a unique alternative to men's religion. Sered believes that motherhood allows women to sense spiritual truths and attain higher levels of moral understanding; this justifies their tendency to create their own religion and invest it with contents. Women in antiquity, from a feminist perspective, were able to develop religious beliefs, mystery, and rituals due to their supreme role as creators of culture, as mothers, and as main bonders with the spiritual world. The mystery of creation, transformation, and recurrence originates in the unmediated psychic and physical experiences of women: bleeding, child raising, caregiving, working with fire, cooking, and seeding (77). Women adopted dualistic symbols from nature—purity and primevalness on the one hand and savagery and pollution on the other (Lutz 1988)—and developed a religion that corresponds to their sagacity and emotionality. Their contact with others, their tenderness, and their emotional vulnerability explain why various cultures characterize them as susceptible to possession by demons and as media of unique potency who occupy a position that men cannot access (Sered 1994).

One of the men attempted to describe this mysterious dichotomy as I went about my research, saying "The men in Yemen couldn't weep and make others weep the way the women could." The position of the women in this in-between zone—between the world of the living and the world of the dead—and their ability to speak in more than one voice correspond to the metaphors of the magic ritual and religion that they create (Holst-Warhaft 1995; Beit-Hallahmi and Argyle 1997).

FROM TEARS TO IDEAS

"From tears to ideas" is a quasi-metaphorical turn of phrase that establishes a difference between men and women in the psychological transition that they make when a death occurs. The phrase conveys a sense of mission and may clarify the uniqueness of Yemenite Jewish women's wailing as a feminine religion. According to Holst-Warhaft (1995, 22), stereotype has it that women, ab initio, are the ones who take care of bodies and corpses. By wailing, they transition from experience to art—from tears to ideas. Men, by and large, are absolved of the physical experience, that of touching, that women undergo. To experience death, men must revisit it by means of art. Consequently, their transition seems to go in the opposite direction of women's wailing, from ideas to tears. This way of expressing the matter, I would say, alludes to the possibility of wailing as an instrument for use in crossing the psychological divide. Women cross from tears to ideas, and ideas, in turn, perform a service in men's fields of meaning.

Wailing is not just an evocative melancholic force that glues people together. It should also be viewed as a style of dialogue. Ethnographies have noted the social power of wailing, identifying it with communication (Tiwary 1978), a unique adjoining of ideas, or a discourse (Abu-Lughod 1993). Irrespective of the kind of discourse it is—alternative, critical, or subversive—it is delivered in a woman's voice that pounds on the gates of the men's circle and gains admission. Yemenite Jewish women's wailing is like a conduit that terminates with the emission of a woman's voice from the very midst of a canon ritual. The lamentation lyrics present a unique commentary on something that happened without materially undermining the hegemonic foundations of faith and morals. The wailers' religious mission is embodied in her conceptual translation of the divine into the corporeal, filling in gaps in the men's labors. Wailing is the maximum form, or perhaps I should say a hesitant form, of the allocation strategy in women's discourses. This strategy is known for its ability to inject women's interpretations into ideologies that are not theirs and to redefine what is considered to be legitimate (Jones 1986; Kristeva 1982). The wailing culture is not a religion of segregation based on a quest for segregation on women's part. Instead, it verges on something that might be called a domestic religion, given the awareness that the women's contribution merits even if it does not overstep its assigned place (Sered 1988). Among all things that a mission may be, the expression "from tears to ideas" reflects women's yearning for Jewish sanctity without surrendering their own point of view. I found an allusion to this outlook in the attitude of Sulami (1995), who produced a profile of women's wailing and considered it a song of faith and Judaism:

> Women's singing abounds with a religious atmosphere of fear of God, which gives expression to faith in God the Creator, from Whom everything emanates. He determines people's fate and is willing to hear and requite the prayers of the individual and the collective. Although it is true that women are absolved of having to attend services in the synagogue, their spontaneous prayers are also accepted, just as God accepted the prayers of our ancient Matriarchs and prophets. (Sulami 1995, 31)

The significance of yearning for sanctity lies in the definition of sanctity, that is, its abstract meanings that acquire tangible expression. Sanctity is a theme that conveys images of splendor and purity; it cannot be deciphered at the moment of the ritual. In settings of action and ritual, sanctity is not connected with a performance in the manner by which it typically connects with a ritual. This package of traits makes sanctity a rarity—the powerful source of a mission that bridges the material and the spiritual. It is against this background that we should regard sanctity as an underlying theme in the gender relationship as this relationship translates into attributive levels in men's and women's religious work. As for indications of yearning for sanctity among Yemenite Jewish women, we find them in their attitude toward three things: Torah study, the destiny of the soul, and sin. Between sanctifying Torah study (as this emerges in their attitudes) and specifying the act of repentance as a fundamental in their wailing, they also interpret the connection between the destiny of the soul and the three days of lamenting for the deceased.

Torah Study

"The [Jewish] woman in Yemen was God-fearing," Shmuel said. "If she learned [Torah] anyway, it was something important. [The rabbis of Yemen] followed [the teachings of] Rabbi Yehoshua and Rabbi Eliezer [of the Talmud]. Rabbi Eliezer said, 'As long as you raise your daughter, let her go so she will get married.' Rabbi Yehoshua said, 'Anyone who teaches his daughter Torah is like someone who taught her folly.' Those women had an excellent sense of how to behave right." The association of "folly" with women, a linkage that many women know well, outraged some of my respondents. Some presented themselves as "severe" and the men as being at fault for this, because they "hadn't learned Torah, hadn't learned Bible, nothing." What impressed me most of all, however, was their acquiescent attitude toward what might be viewed as religious exclusion and their attempts to cope with it. Rumia explained that "There were women whose husbands explained to them and they got it. She'd pray and know Torah law like a man. There are some who do good deeds as the Torah intended: customs, everything. Then she'd get it. They were considered learned, yes." Two respondents told me about the oral compensation: "The women didn't learn to read," one of them said. "They'd pull out the words letter by letter. In Yemen they said women mustn't learn Torah." In reference to wailing, one of these respondents told me that "Wailing is like when you read [the Book of] Lamentations about the destruction of the Temple. They read and weep. This wailing is the same thing: reading and weeping. The wailer is like a reader. She talks from her heart. . . . The words are like writing a book."

Tamar shared with me a piece of exegesis that men say about women when in a magnanimous mood: "A woman is *mitzvot* through and through. On Mt. Sinai, the Holy One said, 'Tell it to the house of Jacob and say it to the sons of Israel.'" She added, "*Woman* received the Torah first." My women respondents made abundant use of the expression "It's written in the Torah" to invest their wailing with the status of mitzvah or "a very great mitzvah." I do not know what they meant by "Torah"—the Pentateuch or the entire corpus of Scripture and rabbinical law. Either way, the anchoring of wailing in Scripture gave Yemenite Jews justification for appreciating wailers and perceiving them as "righteous," "wise," and/or "holy" women whose wailing was materially different from that of Muslim women. Mazel stressed the difference: "Arab women wail, too. But Jews do it more. The emotion of the Jewish woman's heart is a deep emotion, holy mothers." The scriptural anchor totally rules out any challenge to the correctness of God's verdict. At an early stage of my research I once asked, "Did wailers ever address God angrily for having taken someone?" Ora angrily replied, "Anyone who says that is a boor and a jerk. Someone who doesn't know the meaning of Torah and Judaism."

On the Destiny of the Soul

According to Sa'id, who spoke at the entrance of the men's circle, eulogy is meant to "advocate for the soul" and facilitate its transmigration to "the celestial Garden of Eden." However, "Women have nothing to do with

A woman reading Psalms.

this business. What they have to do with is to make the listeners cry." My question is: Is it so? Do the women really have nothing to do with this discourse on the transmigration of the soul? Basing myself on the totality of their remarks, I infer that they indeed have something to do with such sublime matters of the spirit. This "something," however, does not transport the individual's soul all the way out of this world. A similar distinction exists, for example, in the Indian wailing culture in Banaras: women are described as prone to being occupied with the fate of the deceased whereas the men are creators of a new world, one of denial (Parry 1994). The "something to do with" that my women respondents described about the passages between the worlds belongs mainly to the volatility of the soul as it hovers close to this world, exiting and entering. The soul on which they remarked is an object that they can influence with their wailing so long as it remains within the liminal time interval that precedes its entrance to the upper realm.

The women's "soul stories" do not contradict the afterworld narrative; instead, they establish the importance of their wailing and justify its limits.

"You have to encourage the deceased," the wailer Miriam said. "To encourage him means saying how he was when he was alive, how he was happy and raised children and was a fantastic family man, and in the end he left everything and went away empty-handed. Wailing encourages the deceased [whose soul still hears the words], sure. A great mitzvah." The wailer Sa'ida, who washes the bodies of the dead in her community, stressed that she wails in the cleansing room "before the body is immersed. Before it's immersed." Why? "Because after it's immersed the deceased can't hear anything anymore." Continuing, she explained, "They say *ma'aze* [wailing] is good. Especially if the deceased is still on the floor [before being taken to burial]. They say he hears what they say about him until he goes." The women believe that the deceased's soul "consumes" wailing before it vanishes or is concealed in the interred body. The women offered me an interpretation of a clause in the *Abridged Code of Jewish Law.* The clause states: "Do not overly impose on the dead, as is written, Do not bewail the dead and do not move him about. The Sages asked, can this possibly be taken literally? Instead, do not bewail the dead too much and do not move him more than is necessary. How so? Three days for weeping" (Deblitzky 1979, "Rules Concerning Avoiding Excessive Imposition on the Dead," 115). "They say one shouldn't bewail the dead an awful lot. He doesn't rest in his grave," the wailer Haviva said. "In some cases, the deceased appears in a dream sometime later and tells whoever's weeping, 'You're not letting me sleep. You're burning me up with your tears.'" The women's stories also gave me an example of belief in a dream that defines the transmigration of the dead as nothing more than becoming invisible:

> They say that if you wail for the dead more than three days, every tear that falls lands on the his skin and burns it. Afterwards they weep quietly, noiselessly, without bothering the neighbors, because the melodies of this dirge arouse the emotions, penetrate the bones. It's forbidden, and they say it bothers the dead, too. For example, I had an aunt, may she rest in peace. Her daughter had a stroke at age twenty-eight. So my aunt would go to the cemetery, sprawl on the grave, and cry and wail and wail. One day, her daughter came to her in a dream and said, "Mommy, are you awake?" She

> said, "Yes." [The daughter] said, "Why are you crying for me?" She said, "I ache for you." They talked like that in the dream—the daughter said, "You cry all day long from the window of your room and you also visit the cemetery and cry for me. You should know that you're burning my body with your tears, your weeping. I feel every tear that you shed like a burn. So please stop it." My aunt came and told me. I said, "Stop! You know, you're the daughter of Torah Jews, so stop. You mustn't."

The men, unlike the women, construed the three-day limit for weeping as a "deposit," showing that the permanent abode of the soul is not in this world. The human soul, in this simile, is a deposit that God places with the individual, whose death means the return of the deposit to its owner. This notion originates in a Talmudic story about Rabbi Yohanan, who was mourning for his dead son. His students wished to console him with words, but he refused to accept until Rabbi Elazar visited him and used the deposit simile. The grieving father was touched by the simile and expressed his approval of it: "My son, you have consoled me as only a man knows how to console" (Kashani 1996, 27). Yosef, my respondent, likened the soul to a book that he deposits with me and expects to come back and reclaim at some future time. By putting it this way, he implied that the deposit simile makes anguish [the response that I would expect] irrational. A deposit is an essentially temporary arrangement; it justifies neither the addressing of questions to Heaven nor exaggeratedly weeping.

One of the wailers told another tale, this one about a voyage. It includes themes of belief in the afterworld, mourning procedures, and the kabbalistic doctrine of reincarnation. However, it construes the religious idea of the throne of glory as a stopover on the transmigration of the soul before it returns to the world of familiar terms.

> For three days you should wail for the deceased so that his soul will stand next to his grave and not ascend to heaven. It should ascend, but only to migrate around the world. We cry for him so his soul will be sad and stay near him, circling over the grave. It flies around for three days, until the end of the fourth evening, until the shivah is over. Until the end of the

month, it stays around the grave. When they finish the tombstone at the end of the month, its ascends to its throne of glory.

Wailing saddens the soul, too. The soul is sad about the deceased who has gone. It circles over the grave because it wants to return to the deceased and God doesn't let it do so. God allows it to be sad and allows people to cry so that it should remain around the grave in sadness. God won't accept it with sadness; He accepts it with contentment. The soul remains suspended, as it were. God doesn't accept it in order to place it in another body for a whole year, until the first-year memorial ceremony. Then God makes an opening for the soul, gives it a task to carry out, and reincarnates it somewhere, as a dove, as all sorts [of animals]. In the Garden of Eden, God gives man a spiritual body and another soul. Not a soul of this world; the soul of this world returns to this world in reincarnation. Once a year, once every two years, once every ten years. It sustains the previous body's life. God has an unlimited number of souls for this world.

On Sin

The women's discourse about sin centered on the confirmation and adoption of moral values that regulate interpersonal relations in daily life. They described wailing and its inherent mission as they described eulogy: as a correctional device. Netanel explained: "The words in the prayer book are the kind that cause people to reflect on their deeds." Sa'id too, speaking at the entrance to the circle of men, alluded to this when he interpreted Ecclesiastes 7:2: "And the living shall lay [the end of all men] to his heart." The book of prayers for the ascent of the deceased's soul counsels that "Anyone who does not mourn as the Sages commanded is cruel. Rather, he should be fearful and apprehensive and should probe his actions and repent."[10] Below is a question-and-answer session about the correction of one's deeds, combined with remarks by Mazal, a woman who did a great deal of listening to wailers:

AUTHOR: You say the wailer sometimes creates suspense.

MAZAL: Sure. Sometimes she can say things about what she sees and they're true, but the other side [a relative of the deceased] doesn't want her to say true things, doesn't want them to find him out. Sometimes she also drops hints with what she says. Now, no one really pays attention, but if someone's offended he pays attention. Whomever knows [the family secret] knows. Whomever doesn't know says she's just talking. Whomever knows says that she dropped this hint because he's like that.

AUTHOR: According to what you've said, people should have walked away from the wailers.

MAZAL: You couldn't. It was accepted that there'd be a wailer for the first three days. Everyone in Yemen expected it. Some were ill at ease, but that's natural. You couldn't tell the wailer to go away. I remember once when a relative died, they wanted to invite a wailer but one person objected. He said he didn't want to hear. They told him that she'd speak in order to honor the deceased. He said the deceased couldn't hear anymore and he didn't want to hear either. He'd let the others cry in order to soften up anyone who had a hard heart. There were cases like these. Lots of people don't want to hear. That's because it hurts; not everyone's an angel. There's no life without mistakes. Sometimes there are people who make up with their friends after hearing the wailer. They see there are mistakes in life. Sometimes she explains by means of her weeping, her words. Whoever understands them, then they understand. Whoever's a riffraff, a bumpkin, he doesn't understand. The wailers know exactly what to say.

AUTHOR: Do the wailers also threaten? Do they say, "If you don't do such and such, then such and such thing will happen to you"?

MAZAL: No, that they don't say. They get it across in some other style . . . with hints that shatter the hearts. Shatter. It's not easy to shatter. It's hard to break the heart of someone who's bad. I've already seen such cases. There are types who go their own way. God gave the best gift, which is to forgive and forget; those are the two things. Rabbi Akiva said to love your neighbor like yourself. Before there was Torah, there was being a regular person.

The wailers says words that break your heart, that hurt. If someone has a guilty conscience toward the deceased, it hurts him. He feels uncomfortable.

> The wailer lets the other regret what he did. She gives him [a chance] to correct his ways. We're living in a generation that has a lot more to correct. When someone's alive, he doesn't think he'll die tomorrow. He always lives on illusions.

The wailer is an emissary who takes actions that will ensure the success of her mission. She transforms interpersonal hostility and alienation into conciliation. When she has something true to allege, she expresses it by way of allusion and addresses it, respectfully, only to the cognoscenti. By expressing the lament in the form of a riddle, she protects sinners from the others. Her message pounds on their cupped ears without triggering altercations. At first, the vocality of wailing evokes emotions of regret, dread, and profound sorrow. It does not breed anger. Furthermore, as Na'ama explained, until she drops those hints about the sin and the need to correct it, the wailer is alone in her wailing. She lets no one make her the target of resistance: "She doesn't have to say the hard words face-to-face. She goes into her trance. She's alone with herself. She takes a stance. She has no stage fright. She accepts no criticism and doesn't look around to see how people are reacting." In this sense, wailing resembles women's singing in daily life. It is how women maintain domestic tranquility while criticizing their husbands' actions; by lodging her grievances obliquely, a woman calls her husband's attention to her issues with him. She sings melancholy songs as she scrubs the house and grinds the flour. Even when he is very close to her, she expresses herself in third person and behaves as if talking to herself. Thus, amid the unstoppable warbling torrent, her husband realizes that she is in distress. Because her singing is a work of respect, it voids his anger and replaces it with other—worthy—emotions. It is a corrective instrument that employs sorrow, empathy, and compassion—bright emotions that stimulate contemplation.

THE DIVISION OF LABOR: PRAYER BOOK LAMENT VERSUS NARRATIVE LAMENT

The analysis that follows pertains to the gender division of labor. There is nothing novel about this division; it mirrors gender categorizations in other wailing cultures and recurs in feminist approaches that connect the feminine with the maternal (Miller 1976; Chodorow 1978; Gilligan 1983; Jordan 1991). In comparing women's wailing with men's eulogy, I call again on the model presented in chapter 3, "Giving Words."

By separating these works into textual representations of death and of life, I intend to illustrate the dissimilarity and similarity of wailing and eulogy and clarify their significance. This sorting reflects what we know as members of a culture and what the feminist critiques oppose. Even though the analysis progresses hand in hand with stereotypical knowledge, it subjects the contents of the gender categories to deep contemplation. The use of an equally proportioned nonhierarchical model has important value: it aims to gauge the complementary or compensatory role of women in death rituals and challenge the status of wailing as a pseudoritual. I wish to show that what is perceived ex ante as confirming the marginal and problematic status of women's wailing is challenged ex post.

In women's wailing, "giving words"—the essence of the lament, cast into textual form—is a narrative, a generalized and polyvocal narrative about the dead and about death. Two identified categories in wailing are termed "story about the deceased" and "personal story." I contend that the attitude expressed by Sa'id, a male respondent, that "Women have nothing to do with this business [eulogy]" is directed specifically at the textual dimension of these narratives, which represent the thing that makes wailing singularly feminine. I have already shown that the opinions of women connect wailing with eulogy as a moralistic discourse of faith and definitely do not posit wailing as something that clashes with such a discourse. If so, we need to return to the lyrics and to the whole that the women create from them; we should also juxtapose the women's words to the men's words. The former emerge in an outcry from the wailer's heart; the latter have "earned" the right to be written across the systematic pages of a prayer book.

Live-Live: Recounting the Deceased

The narrative about the deceased in women's wailing fits into the live-live arena. The narrator and the audience have live selves, and the other, the deceased, is given the honor of being a living selfness.[11] The lament rewards the deceased, the object of the story, with the honorifics of a biography and an aesthetic topography of his or her body and its organs. The descriptions shape the impression of the deceased's righteousness and convey the spiritual messages of the lament. In expressions such as "Oh for her son," "an inspiring forehead," "the candle of the house," "a sapling that had just grown," "wise in Torah," and "mother of righteous acts and *mitzvot*," death is managed for the cause of remembering the deceased, who becomes the hero of the community of the living, that is, the mourners and the consolers. Men's lament also occupies itself with the positive aspects of the deceased in his life and fits into the live-live arena. Most of the *text,* however, concerns acceptance of man's existential fate as a universal being and divine reward and punishment. By emphasizing the soul's migration to the afterworld, men's lament turns the death event into a parable that forces members of the "community of living" to ponder moral lessons. For example, the prayer book contains a "eulogy for women" that follows a regular wording:

> Pleasant among women, O guileless and pious one. May the God of her life have compassion on her and remember her righteousness and inscribe her merit. For her separation of the challah [tithing the dough]. And lighting candles. And maintaining her purity. And may You set her portion with the four Matriarchs. With all of the righteous and pious women. The Rock, Whose actions are pure.

> Pleasant among women, O esteemed and modest one. May the God of her life have compassion on her and grant her deliverance. May her lineage have mercy on her. May He Who remembers [His] covenant and vow forgive her sins and be mindful of momentary pressure. May she be

> taken to the Garden of Eden. With all the esteemed women, the wives of imposing men. The Rock, Whose deeds are perfect. (Hozeh 1973, 164)[12]

Both types—canonic eulogies and feminine wailing—that are performed in honor of the deceased reflect the life needs of a religious community. However, if we juxtapose the two as expressions of divine justice, we will notice the emphasis of the former on the worshipper's assertion of the correctness of God's judgment (e.g., "The Rock, Whose deeds are perfect") and the emphasis of the latter on expressions of grief pertaining to the unique persona of the departed (e.g., "His hands were full of good deeds"). The feminine expressions of sorrow over the loss of a worthy person exacerbate the human sense of helplessness against God's decree. Since none of the wailing texts challenges God, it stands to reason that these expressions of weakness also affirm the correctness of God's judgment but do so indirectly. Thus, whereas the women's exoneration of God's judgment is based on emotions of love and respect for the human uniqueness that has been lost, the masculine version reflects fear—in the sense of awe or of fright—of the cosmic God.

Another difference has to do with the time orientation reflected in the women's narrative wailing and the men's prayer book wailing. Women's wailing is built on material from the past; it expresses in gossamer strands what once was and is no more, whereas men's wailing sets the details of the events in the present, immediately after the death event, and extends the setting to the future that awaits the deceased's soul. Women's wailing deals with individuals whose corporeal nature has been revealed, whereas men's wailing almost totally disregards this aspect of being and transforms the uniqueness of the individual into an abstract soul that lacks identity. In other words, the official male-controlled death ritual routes the collective consciousness along linear lines of transitivity that lead to a future or to timelessness. The wailing of women, in contrast, tunnels through the events of the past cyclically and amplifies the crisis that the present has generated due to familiarity with a specific person. The more the contents of the wailing texts are arrayed around the metaphysical and the physical, the more the male bonds with the transitional function of death rituals and the female bonds with the crisis function.

Here I digress slightly from text to weeping. The men describe their weeping as something other than that of the women. Men's remarks imply that theirs is a weeping prayer, or a weeping of prayer, that has nothing in common with the contents of women's wailing. Unlike women, who progress from tears to ideas, the men put the ideas first, moving from the printed text to general weeping. The relationship of contrast between the transcendent (the sacred) and the crisis on the ground (the profane) is also preserved in this division, which pertains to emotion and the body's response to it. The men's weeping, however similar it may be to women's wailing in much of its phrasing, is a form of worship. "The more one succeeds in arousing emotion, the better. The mitzvah is to arouse the heart," Netanel explained. He proceeded to the connection between emotion and the sacred: "Try to go to the Great Synagogue. Try to go to *selihot* [a penitential service]. Parts of it are truly moving. If a man who says them understands what he's saying, he's got to cry. So they cry. It depends on the prayer leader. Psalms are recited; a plea for mercy is recited." Yitzhak linked this sobbing with the Jewish exile, which not only reveals itself in the earthly dimension but also reflects the spiritual situation of a collective: "In Yemen, there was a problem of exile and poverty. There was this one unique man, the talk of the town. Whenever services took place, they wanted to hear him. Not only was he sensitive, he also had this kind of voice. I remember him. To this day I'm moved. When he'd open his mouth, you got so emotional, cried so much that you felt you were up in heaven. You'd hear the whole synagogue go *hhhhhhhh* [imitates sobbing]. He'd cry and he'd make you cry."

Men's chanting at the cemetery elevates the paternal image of God, an uplifting that elicits tears of limitless yearning for existence beyond the present world. Their prayer, pleading for everyone in the same words, transforms the grave and its contents into the redemption of all souls: "O King, King of kings, may You in Your mercy shelter him in the recesses of Your abode and under the shade of Your wings. May he have the merit of witnessing the pleasantness of God and visiting His sanctuary. Make him stand erect in the end of days and invite him to life in the afterworld. Allow him to drink from the stream of Your gardens. Let him bask in the glow of Your presence. May his soul be bound up with the host of the living. May his repose and shelter be so honorable that it may be said that God is his portion. Escort him safely. May he reach his resting place safely."[13] The prayer sets up a rapprochement between the deceased and God. It too is recited in tears and, similar to the wailing culture of the Tamil in southern India, may symbolize victory over death (Blackburn 1988).

Dead-Dead: A Personal Story

The wailer-person who tells her "personal story" in the dead-dead category is fully personified in the reality of her suffering and femininity. Her messages, which equate her symbolic death with the death of the deceased, are expressed in the words "My heart, why are you burned / burned from long ago, too, and from long, long ago / O my fortune, a bolt of lightning has come upon you / or you will drown in a flood / Be my heaven-bird / please have pity and mercy on me / I am ill and burdened / totally shattered / my fortune is bleak, my eyes know no rest." We should regard the dead-dead category as the most indicative arena of women's wailing and consider the alive-alive category the only arena that may be indicative of men's wailing. The equating of these categories underscores the crisis basis of women's wailing much more intensively because the main objects of attention now are the identities of the self and the other in the encounter—that is, dead-dead versus living-living—and not the contents of the narrative per se. Accordingly, the contents of men's wailing are directed toward a transitional task. The task begins with disengagement from the status of social death that members of the collective have adopted by identifying with the deceased and the mourners and ends by merging with the status of people who lead ordinary lives. The living-living identities in the collective encounter represent the aims of the men's text and ritual—a daily reality of denial. In view of this task, the feminine agenda has the opposite goal. The woman wailer reinforces ramparts that surround a consciousness of delay and creates an inhibition against the response of doomedness—dead-dead—that she has established among the members of the group. This may explain why women's wailing is not given the autonomous status that other feminine rituals have attained.[14] The purpose of this practice, it turns out, is to amplify the crisis experience, and this, from the standpoint of the life of the collectivity, means that the past is over and the future has not yet been created. Insofar as this pertains to gender relations, we may believe, as theoreticians (Lutz 1988; Durkheim 1952, 1964) and ethnographers (Abu-Lughod 1986, 1993; Alexiou 1974) have stated, that women's wailing is devoid of social responsibility. In other words, it seems convincing, ab initio, that the female voice clashes with the tone of the canon text wherever it is allotted time and space in the overall order.

Why does women's wailing prefer crisis over transition? My answer is that if women's wailing were not implanted in the mourning culture, the experience of the death of a member of the community would boil down to a struggle for the readoption of the metaphors of life. This kind of coping would lack the difficult transition between the world of the living and that of the dead. Coping of this type would lack the bridge that, when crossed in bold strides to its dark edge, gives life its meaning. The wailer must have enough power of temptation to counter another powerful temptation that exists at the time of a death: the lust for life. This instinctive lust, whose schemes are monodimensional by nature (Freud 1918; Bauman 1992), inhibits all contrasting consciousnesses. Confronting the wish to forget, disregard, deny, and console, the wailer has to marshal all her resources to build "underground" paths and break into the unconscious. She can accomplish this only by assuming responsibility for the outcome of her mission and performing her abstract "striptease." In her "personal story," the wailer violates powerful codes of modesty and rationalism by offering to take her life in her hands. In her performance, she raises her voice to a pitch that lies somewhere between talking and shouting. In one moment she invokes convincing metaphors to demonstrate the bitterness of her fate, enunciates her chaos in perfect rhyme and timed breaths, and spreads her fingers and waves her arms in movements that are coordinated with her message and the pace of its delivery. Thus, she announces the immeasurability of the existential despondency. She pledges much time to this. Her feminine voice cracks, but she holds it in line, jolting her audience with intense weeping without shedding tears of her own. By invoking this power of hers, which is attributed to woman's experience in suffering, her proximity of consciousness with nature, and her being a mother (Ruddick 1989; Chodorow 1978), the wailer leads the audience's capacity for empathy into an abyss represented by the persona of the deceased.

CONTRAST AND NONRESISTANCE

In a collective dead-dead reality, those in attendance identify with the deceased via the wailer's total identification with him or her. The lyrics push toward a cul-de-sac. The state of melancholy created in this manner imitates the state of the deceased's body, whereas the male ascent to a cosmic world order combines with metaphors of the transmigration of the soul. The object of producing the story in the live-live and dead-dead arenas has a similar effect: the wailer's own physical appearance directs the focus of attention to the "personal story," whereas for men the letters in the prayer book create abstract ideas and timeless scenes. Thus, by combining the symbols, the women's and men's discourse splits the image of the deceased in half by appealing to diametrically opposed consciousnesses—body and soul, transience and eternity, nonexistence and existence, nature and nurture. This fundamental binary relation may have done good service to a fashionable approach that attributes oppositional/subversive aspirations to publicly expressive women (Abu-Lughod 1990; Seremetakis 1991; Raheja and Gold 1994; Bourke 1993)—the approach that turns the emotionalism of oppressed groups into a symbol of their antistructural tendencies (Lutz 1988, 62). I believe, like Fegan (1986), that absent proof of conscious intent, women's self-expression cannot be interpreted as opposition, let alone subversion. According to Kielmann (1998, 136), we can begin to attribute meaning to opposition only when women themselves observe and express clashing possibilities within the orthodox frameworks of meaning.

My respondents expressed something that might be construed as a clash reflecting an intent of some kind to oppose the canon order. Their remarks weaken the temptation, inherent in the feminist paradigm, to attribute Western-created desires to Eastern women. As stated, the respondents repeatedly defined the wailer's appearance as a religious imperative originating in Scripture. Hasan-Rokem's (1996) interpretation of the exegesis of Jeremiah 9:16—"Contemplate and call for the wailing women, that they may come"—sets their perception on a solid basis; it presents women's wailing as a cultural manifestation of mourning in biblical times. More than this, it expresses a spiritual force that captures the nexus of women and culture, whereas the men epitomize uninhibited natural craving. According to my respondent Miriam, the justification for the women's discourse rests on ideas borrowed from the men's discourse: "It's an honor for the dead to be cried over. [It's done] so that even the angels on high should watch and say that the deceased was righteous. The angels say that even those who dwell in this world can't part with him." The thesis of opposition is surely incompatible with another woman respondent's puzzlement about how Binyamin-Gamliel, in his various writings, "makes all this effort over women's singing and not over a Torah scroll." Neither can it be reconciled with explicit statements by women, such as the following:

AUTHOR: Why don't men know how to wail like women?

ZAHARA: Men are readers. They read Psalms. They're in the room, and the women are in the *diwan*.

AUTHOR: What's more important, men's reading or women's wailing?

ZAHARA: [in a "that's obvious" tone of voice] Men's reading. Sure, that's more important.

AUTHOR: Why is it more important?

ZAHARA: The women cry for the deceased but he won't come back. It's prayer that elevates the soul. Prayer is more important for sure.

AUTHOR: But wailing arouses emotion.

ZAHARA: The deceased goes to the cemetery. He doesn't get up, he doesn't walk, and he doesn't eat.

Similarly, women respondents emphasized the importance of strict compliance with the "three days of weeping" constraint to women's wailing within the shivah. Their acceptance of the time limit suggests a complementary relation between the live-live and the dead-dead arenas. Arguably, the latent melancholic power of wailing is so great that women only need to demonstrate it part of the time—three days—to establish gender equality. This power, by its nature, amplifies the sense of suffering to a level that cannot be withstood for long. According to theory, grieving is abbreviated or limited in time to avert the development of pathological grief and fear of the spirits of the dead (Miller and Schoenfeld 1973; Steele 1977; Blackburn 1988). "The three days," in contrast, is an expression representing a ritual authorization that is accepted by men and women alike. Associating it with coercion is foreign to the respondents; it is this that triggers their resistance. Does the contrast between the contents of the two arenas reflect power relations in a patriarchal arena shared by two voices? Probably not. Instead, although it looks like a conceptual binary structure between the sexes, it appears to have earned social recognition and created a social space for the women's creative genre.

In my opinion, the nature of Yemenite Jewish women's wailing as a voice of mission and not of opposition is related to the Jews' political status in Yemen. As described in chapter 4, "The Performance Stage," the Yemenite Jews had a protected status and were considered tolerated subjects. The extension of protected status to members of a wailing culture is unique to Yemenite Jews; it makes them an unusual example in any survey of the characteristics of other ethnic communities in which tendencies of resistance and subversion among wailing women have been detected. I have shown that Jewish men's singing in Yemen was essentially devotional, replete with yearning for Zion. The other side of the craving-for-redemption coin is a shared consciousness of exile. Accordingly, this singing reflected the Jews' state of inferiority and political impotence. The following lines of poetry demonstrate this:

I hope for Your kindness, You Who dwells in heaven
Send your salvation to the nation sanctified in wandering
Return us to Mount Zion in desire
Ingather the dispersed [exiles] to the sound of the shofar. (Tzadok 1967, 162)

It would be no overstatement to say that men's singing was a practice meant to inculcate the reality of national devastation and remind the practitioners, continually, that the Jews were in a place not theirs. This drove the singers to tears even on the Sabbath and during festivals and is clearly a discourse of victimhood against the decree of God and His emissaries. One may conjecture that when women listened to the men singing, they absorbed something of the powerlessness of their men relative to other men, the Arab lords of the land. The men's singing suggested in a very oblique way that the craving for redemption and the urge to cast aside the yoke of the "goyim" warrants the unification of the ranks. The unpleasant necessity of forcing Jewish men to wail like women in Arabs' homes presumably carried a similar message.[15] The men's singing generated collective self-pity amid the very lengthy era of woe. This state of consciousness appears to have been strong enough to rule out the possibility of rivaling gender camps. By resisting the idea of resistance, the women respondents taught me that when a collective lives in existential insecurity, resistance is only a short distance from subversion and betrayal of the group. This kind of insecurity may also foster relations of mutual respect between the sexes. Whenever the structure of gender relations and particularly of marital relations at home surfaced in the respondents' distant recollections, respect and powerful yearning for respect were intertwined in their remarks. One woman said, "Family was family. Men treated their wives as men should treat their wives, and here in Israel everything has gone dark." Another woman said, "In Yemen, there was respect for a man and respect for a woman. Not like here, like dogs, in offices and at court [in divorce proceedings]." Contemplating the disrespect that, in their eyes, typifies the pattern of relations in Israel, some emitted the familiar sigh: "*'abni 'al a-teymoun,*" meaning a pity for (the respect that had existed in) Yemen.

Further Remarks on the Collective in Exile: The Latent Social Power of Wailing

Women's wailing carries an implicit secret relating to the social order. I mentioned this claim, expressed by Urban (1988), in the section "A Collective in Exile" of the previous chapter. I return to it now to dwell on the aspect of mission in the unconscious impact of wailing. The "secret" with which Urban deals concerns the question of how a culture imposes control on emotional processes. In Urban's opinion, the secret lies in the "alchemy" that transforms an effect into a metaeffect, that is, the coexistence of one emotion (sadness) with another (the desire for social acceptance) (386). In Radcliffe-Brown's (1964, 239–40) distinction between spontaneous crying and ritual crying, the latter is defined as a situation in which men and women are urged, as if by custom, to hug each other and cry. This distinction inspires discussion of the sociability aspects of wailing. To Urban, wailing is a symbolic, complex, and powerful response to the violation of the social solidarity that a death symbolizes:

> Ritual wailing represents not simply the feeling of loss but, in a more complex way, the desire for sociability that is the inverse side of loss. Loss occasions the wish to overcome loss through sociability, and it is this sociability that is signaled through adherence to a culturally specific form of expression of grief. One wishes to signal to others that one has the socially correct feelings at the socially prescribed times. (Urban 1988, 393)

Putting forward this argument acknowledges the aspect of social responsibility that women's wailing possesses. By inference, wailing encourages the coordinated demonstration of emotions and for this reason, indirectly, focuses attention on the community's future collective conduct. Urban's (1988) point of view places the wailing cultures that he investigated in the live-live quadrant. Notably, however, his analysis fails to distinguish between sociability and solidarity. Consequently, it views wailing as the performer of a unidimensional social function, contributing only to reconnecting and establishing sound relations among members of the community. I do not dispute this point of view, but I wish to add an interpretation that distinguishes between the wailing situation and the collective mourning rituals that Durkheim (1965) regarded as mechanisms of solidarity. The mourning rituals that Durkheim described were typified by considerable emotional agitation. In his descriptions, the purpose of inflicting physical suffering and discomfort in tribal rituals was to down barriers between mourners and nonmourners. Sociability, in contrast, is a special and quiet state of shared consciousness that fits into the dead-dead quadrant.

The Yemenite Jewish wailing situation, I believe, expresses the idea of sociability. It does so not only due to the display of the right emotions in a melancholy situation but also, and mainly, due to the gist of the experience. The original meaning of sociability in Simmel's (1950) theory may continue to help us to articulate the reality of the audience, the collective in exile; it corresponds more accurately to the reality of unity and the mystery that exists in it. Simmel describes sociability as a reality that surpasses and transcends individuals—a pleasant and quiet form of social togetherness that leaves no room among those present for friction, egoistic interests, and status symbols that drive wedges among people. The reality of oneness settles in so firmly that no member of the collective cries out or puts on a show of any kind to set him or herself apart from the others or challenges the wailer's vocal authority. The sociability situation in full blossom links classless people in a democracy of equals—a democracy of total consideration and delicacy. I call this form of sociability a "solidarity of respect," a concept that I developed in an earlier work on the near-death experience (Gamliel 2001). Solidarity of respect has an ontological meaning: a reality of social fraternity amid nothingness, of equality in being doomed to death. In this reality, people find solace in unity and are willing to shower each other with acts of respect.

In my opinion, attributing crisis to women's performance in mourning rituals is much an at-first-glance interpretation or one that belongs to the conscious level only. The metaeffect of the performance, following Urban's (1988) nomenclature, resides in the deep levels of the experience of the need for human togetherness. This experience is unlikely to be attained by having the person in charge of the ritual prod the community members to make an experiential transition; instead, it should happen via the delay that a marginal but normative leadership imposes. In other words, my argument is that wailing is perceived only at first glance as a situation that imposes a consciousness of crisis on those in attendance. A second glance reveals that the crisis consciousness is a condition for the consolidation of a deeper consciousness that is fundamentally socioexistential. In a departure from Urban's approach, I propose that the participants in the contemplation are social players who, at the sound of wailing, are not only interested in signaling to others that they have the right feelings at the time the society determines but are also participants in the present, some attaining the special awareness that they are undergoing an internal transformation of consciousness. Thus, if we observe women's wailing from a superficial point of view only, we may find it either devoid of social responsibility or unnecessary. Its importance, it should be stated, flows from the regulating necessity of the liminal, from the illusory but constructive power of emptiness and dread (Koestenbaum 1971), from the end to the beginning.

Narghiles: Women's Wailing in a Men's Circle

In chapter 4, "The Performance Stage," I showed that the links that join to form the circle ex ante are the wailing women. As performers, they are well versed in the secrets, movements, and social gestures of shared weeping. In the group interviews that accompany this chapter, however, male participants took their place. From here on, the ethnography assesses the feminine mission of wailing as it was reflected in the circle of men. The agents in this assessment are the hookah smokers at the *takhsina* session with whom I conversed after Sa'id, the first interviewee, made his opening remarks. As the reader will recall, the men in the group interview sat in a circle on the terrace of the home where they were being hosted. They were about forty in number and ranged from forty to seventy years of age. An integral part of this group picture is the set of colorful hookahs that was stationed in a small circle in the middle of the terrace, next to their owners. On several small stools stood cups and decanters of hot tea and water. Leaves of khat were strewn everywhere.[16]

This custom, preserved from Yemenite ways, is called *yeshivat ha-takhsina* ("sitting together"), an arena of male fraternity. Among Yemenite Arabs, these khat parties fall into two main categories: everyday khat parties and hosted khat parties. The research group seemed to be organized in a manner that was closer to the latter category. According to Weir (1985, 109), "These do not usually mark any special event. They take place relatively spontaneously at the initiative of those who want to 'chew khat together' and with the co-operation of the owner of the room or house in which they are held." In contrast to some of Weir's findings, the characterization of this gathering as an arena of male fraternity is tenable because Yemenite Jews in Israel usually exclude women and children from the custom of smoking and chewing khat. The men sit together for several hours until shortly before the beginning of the Sabbath. During this time, the group serves as an information clearinghouse. Its members discuss various matters related to work, family, and current events, but they do so in a distant style that transcends daily concerns. According to Weir, folk publications, and my personal observations—as best as I could interpret them—the chewing of khat has a positive affective and cognitive effect. It generates feelings of tranquility and calm and induces profound thinking about the realities of the world. Since the group is made up of men only and is susceptible to the calming influence of the khat leaves, the gathering gives the participants a special opportunity to create and cement social relations. The group typically displays a tolerant attitude toward behavioral manifestations of separatism and, in its conversations, tends to mingle individual and collective affairs. Under these psychosocial circumstances, the group is a mechanism that helps strangers to assimilate into the community (Weir 1985). As an Israeli Jewish woman of Yemenite extraction and a scholar who approached the group of men as an outsider, I was amazed by the warm reception that I was given and the assimilative potential of the circumstances of the encounter, which eased my subsequent visits to the community. Tolerance and cooperation were widely evident in both interviews, even though the interviews distracted the men from their regular agenda. Notably, an informant had given the participants prior notice about my wish to conduct a group interview on the topic of Yemenite women's wailing. Even though women's wailing had never been a topic of discussion in their circles, the men expressed their unmitigated consent.

In presenting men's opinions and thoughts about women's wailing, I have two main goals. First, I wish to present an interpretive approach that centers on the study of men's perspectives. Such a presentation makes it possible to test the interpretation and its potential contribution to research literature on the topic. Second, I wish to explain the meaning of male perspectives within the broad framework of wailing culture and death rituals. To attain these goals, it is important to analyze the subjects' attitudes and the structure within which they are arrayed. By paying attention to the structure within which the contents elicited during the two unstructured group interviews may be arranged, we may come away with a better understanding. During the time interval between the two interviews and as more and more participants joined the conversation, the attitudes toward the women's wailing changed. Two participants, each at a different time, undertook to make statements that would mark the beginning and the end of the interviews.

The first of them was Sa'id. His remarks, with which I began this chapter, portrayed the hierarchic relations between man's eulogy and women's wailing and alluded to the inferior status of the latter. Yekutiel's remarks, with which I conclude, make a diametrically opposite point. Between these brackets, other participants expressed a range of views that reflected attitudes of exclusion and inclusion of women's wailing. The range of views and the gap between the introductory and the concluding remarks created a sequence that can be viewed as circular. The circle metaphor seems to symbolize the holistic style with which women relate to the world and excludes the linear and binary structure that is typical of the male perspective (Ruddick 1989). Below I probe this immediate association again and again in regard to what began as a very palpable act of sitting together.

"THEIR" TEARS

Some respondents linked women's emotionality during wailing with their very nature and portrayed women as excitable creatures. These respondents' remarks reflected lay theories that assume contrasting types of emotionality between the sexes (Zammuner 2000). The participants adhered to the attitude unequivocally, and several of them expressed it by contrasting strong men to weak women. Dan said, "Women, we know, are more prone to tears than men." Another participant claimed a woman is "more sensitive. She makes you feel pity for her. She's more sensitive and weaker by nature. You're more concerned about her. She needs more caressing, help, and compassion than men do." Gideon said, "I'll explain it to you. The woman has the traits, she's got emotion, she can say things differently. She expresses pain differently, too. Not like a man. Men are stronger. It's natural; it's been that way ever since woman was created." Sometimes woman's special emotiveness was described as a code that might prompt men to take action due to the weakness being signaled. David supplied a historical explanation of sorts: "Since women also had emotion, of course they let women do the wailing. It's because, well, imagine that I'd hear Shlomo [one of those present] crying, and then I'd hear a woman. Of course I'd get more agitated when I'd hear the woman." Gabriel said, "A man loves to hear a woman wailing because she's more exciting, and it's deeper than man-to-man. Woman-to-man is different; she stirs up his emotions, and he cries." Hannanel added his own example: "Sometimes she can be manipulative even in a court of law. When she starts to cry, the judge treats her considerately. A woman's tears are a whole different world. The emotion is built in a totally different way. A man can cry in court or anywhere else, but they don't relate to him as they do when a woman cries. Women are pitied."

The participants lectured to me about the "fact" that, as men, they are familiar with "women's tears." This familiarity taught them how to protect themselves against this "natural" trait. Their attitude centered not only on the spontaneity of the women's tears but also, by allusion, on the dimension of play-acting and manipulation that they embodied.

A PRACTICE OF THE PRESENT WORLD

The men in the group related to the verbal contents and lyric performance of the lamentation in an attempt to gauge its characteristics as a form of expertise. Their description was ultimately segregational and marked the wailing women as somewhat unique. "No matter how often I hear the words and no matter how well I understand this Yemenite Arabic that they use, it's hard to follow them," David stated. "The [wailers] relate mainly to the dead person," he explained. "They put together rhyming stanzas and, amazingly, they make them up right then. They finish the rhyme so that every word ends the same way, and then they flip the word around so that it has the same poetic meter. The wailer flips it even if it doesn't have the same meter as the song. She doesn't exactly repeat the previous word, but the sound of her '*eeyah*' or '*oyah*' flips it around somehow, no matter how it ends." Ezra expressed astonishment about the wailers' performance: "I've had opportunities to talk with poetic women who put together amazing rhymes on the spot. Ask her to repeat it an hour or a week later; she'll repeat it. It's been imprinted in her mind, you might say. It's a unique kind of memory." The lamentation, like women's ordinary singing, is enunciated in Arabic (Binyamin-Gamliel 1994). Thus, wailing is foreign and inferior to men's eulogies, which are delivered in Hebrew, the holy tongue. The lamentation is described as an improvisation and as having linguistic and musical mechanisms that facilitate the spontaneous creation of an accepted text. The flipping of words to make them rhyme is described as an "open door" for words that have an aesthetic target—that is, the listener's ear—and are not meant to be recited from a written text.

The participants emphasized this separateness by describing the extent to which women's wailing, which ostensibly deals with death, actually relates to material affairs. Their remarks, validated in ethnographic findings (Briggs 1993; Seremetakis 1990; Urban 1988), portrayed wailing as a practice that is deeply involved with social relationships and matters of power and status. First, someone described the wailer as a dominant personality who functioned as a repository of social information in her community: "The wailer was like a 'wailing wall' for all the women. That's why she could produce texts about someone who'd died. In Yemen, women would sit in a group and talk about cooking, food, and how husbands treated their wives. Who did they talk with? With the important woman, so that she'd use her power and make her husband behave well. So the wailer knew the woman and her husband from up close, and when the time came she had what to say in her lamentation. She did the wailing simply because she had all the information." Evidently, then, the performance and contents were determined on the basis of social information that the wailer possessed.

"Wailing women had their preferences and priorities," Dan said. "If the deceased was just anyone, the women usually didn't wail for him. Nothing. They visited [the bereaved] to console them, like everyone else, and that was that. It all depended on the person's level and whether he had or didn't have friends. If it was a man who'd died and his wife was important and well liked, then the women usually came and wailed and wanted to show how concerned they were for her and how they commiserated with her." This led the participant to a generalized conclusion that wailing is a political instrument: "Everything has always depended on a man's connections and status in the community. They wail for the man's status. That's how it's always been." Women's wailing was also described as a means of social discrimination and therefore as something separate from the men's custom. "Men say eulogies and give short divrei Torah *in any event*," the participant stated. "But the wailing woman you spoke with"—he turned to me—"wouldn't be happy to come and wail for some wretch whose wife had nothing to do with the community." Social parameters also determined the volume of the wailing and the impression that it made on those assembled. "In cases that I encountered, I saw that the women really wailed, especially when the event was very tragic. Say that a young guy or a young woman died or was killed. Then the wailing bursts from the heart much more powerfully. You also notice the wailer's voice, her melody, the way she moves her hands, how she weeps, and how the people around her weep. . . . You feel much more emotion, much deeper emotion. Everyone's crying. When an old man who lived a full life dies, there's less."

Wailing served the cause of social relations in cases where it became an arena for the voicing of women's personal problems. "Women often blend totally different subjects into their lamentations," Yosef stated, explaining that "The moment someone dies, they seize the moment and bemoan their [own] bitter fate. They turn things around, you might say. How do the women say it? [They turn to the deceased and say,] 'Tell the man who died a year ago . . .' and they begin to make up all kinds of lyrics about their problems and other problems. They wail, but it's not for the same dead person anymore. It's about someone who died before him, and they mingle the two. Most of them bewail their own bitter fate." In this case, as among

Muslim women (Abu-Lughod 1986; Wilce 1998), the wailing event allows wailers to tell someone in the audience about their vulnerability, their actual situation, and how they relate to it. It is an act of impression management and an implicit call for help or consideration.

Haim, relating to the need to be conspicuous, said, "Usually when outside guests arrive, [the wailers] want to make an impression that will be etched into the memory of the guests or the mourners. So they stir up this noise. It comes out in the wailing; it's a matter of being too conspicuous. It's like saying, 'I'm here, listen up.' Either they cry too much or they wail too much. Those who come from [out of town] want to stand out; they make an effort to call attention to their presence. I assume that they go to the funeral and they know they're not going to come again [during the shivah], so they want to leave a mark of some kind. She cried a lot and wailed a lot." This information corresponded to something that the informant Tzviya told me about the importance of approval of the wailer's conspicuity. It was customary, Tzviya said, to thank the wailer by saying things such as "Thank you very much, be well, may God watch over you." Consolers and mourners swamped her with these expressions of gratitude lest she take offense and disappear.

The expression "They turn things around, you might say" gives a good illustration of the personal and social uses of women's wailing. Other participants used similar expressions, as noted above, such as "It's hard to follow them" and "They flip the word around." These expressions also allude to the men's assessment of their lack of control over these women. Women's preference of telling a coherent and singular narrative about the dead and of pointing to the social aspect and lasting relevance of the event were manifested in their choice of words and in the volume of their voices. By the same token, the participants themselves noticed the written, impersonal aspect of their form of lamentation, citing the permanent text that they use. Some repeatedly stressed such sentiments as "Men didn't wail that way. They said divrei Torah." One participant, tracing the origins of the mental differentiation to the spatial segregation that was strictly observed in Yemen, said, "Women wailed to themselves. Why? Because they didn't sit with the men. The men would say divrei Torah. Since women had nothing to do with that subject, of divrei Torah and argumentation with God, but had more to do with tears, only women, never men, expressed themselves [in tears]. It's also inappropriate and unbecoming [for men], only for women."

Basing ourselves on the participants' presentation of women's wailing as an expression of the earthly and the social, we have seen that men's eulogy distinguishes itself by the afterworld, whereas women's wailing concerns itself with the deceased and death in terms of the present world. Given this clear difference—as I showed above—one might lend some support to ethnographic and theoretical conclusions about the clashing relation between the canon religion and women's wailing (Sered 1994; Abu-Lughod 1993). In the circle of men, however, another voice became increasingly audible, especially in the second encounter as the interview progressed. It was a less segregated and less separatist voice; it centered on the factor that unites and bridges the genders upon a death event. This voice positioned women's wailing somewhere between the social profane and the transcendental sacred and privileged women's wailing with an accommodative response in addition to the nonaccommodative one. The more the men spoke about the women's wailing, the more they expressed respect for and familiarity with its spiritual virtue. They did so, however, without sanctifying it totally, that is, by terming it as being unrelated to the afterworld.

MEN CRYING

One way in which the men regarded women's wailing inclusively was the equalization of the trait of emotionality. The men spoke of the cathartic importance of wailing and admitted that they resorted to ludic restraint in death events. This was an acknowledgment of the value of women's wailing. Some of the men expressed this in a special way, and one participant traced the women's role to Scripture: "We men are rigid by nature and we need someone to make us emotional. Why is it said, 'Summon the dirge-singers; let them come' [Jeremiah 9:16]? Because of the way the verse continues: 'That our eyes may run with tears, our pupils flow with water.' We want to cry." Some participants, like men in the Greek wailing culture, have learned that women are different from them in the outward expression of emotions but not in their intensity (Sarris 1995; Danforth 1982; Caraveli 1986).

Benjamin, as if divulging a secret, said, "You ought to know that those who say they don't want to hear the wailers are just pretending. It's make-believe. A man who's just lost a parent wants to erupt and let his emotions out. He'll go and listen because he wants to cry. Then he'll pretend to repress his feelings and say 'I'm tough, I'm not crying.' That's not good. That's not a real man. That's all there is to it." Yosef illustrated this need from his personal experience. "I'll tell you," he began. "My mother died on the Sabbath. We stayed with her until Sunday afternoon; only then was she buried. I held it all inside because people, friends, and family members were coming. I controlled myself so as not to burst into tears, and I sealed myself up. When we got to what they call the end of the road and the wailers came and began to wail, I felt that I'd come to the juncture where I could let loose, to let out everything I'd been holding in at the time. . . . I think part of the wailers' role is to bring out what's really inside you. Even though you're trying to overcome it, to be high-minded, and not to let people notice that you're crying, there's a moment when the wailers begin where you say, 'OK, this is the moment when I'm allowed to blow up, let it all out, and from then on to let it begin to build up inside until the next [lamentation].' It's something personal that I wanted to say about the wailers." Zion recounted an emotional experience that he had undergone during the period between the group interviews. His remarks, expressed in a humorous tone of voice, indicated to us that he had never considered women's wailing an element in the circle of men and that the interview had placed it there after the fact. "You took us off our regular track," he said, turning to me. "You made us think about [wailing]. Last week I was at an *azkara* [memorial ceremony] for my wife's uncle, and there were wailing women there. Because of you I went up close and listened, and because of you I cried, too. [The deceased] had been old and ill. Because of you, the wailing made me break down and cry. You're making us think, thinking, who paid attention to it at all?! So what do we care if they wail? But when people talk about it, they notice it."

Sometimes the participants associated the emotiveness of the lamentation with a religious act, commandment, or prayer. When they did so, they spoke of it as an act of almost equal status and as something not exclusive to women. "Wailing is a good thing that's disappearing and ought to be revived," Shlomo maintained. "Your research topic has to do with emotion. In Yemenite Jewry, emotion stands out strongly all over. Being hospitable . . . yes, it's a Divine commandment but it's an emotion. Sometimes when they talk [wail] they lift a man out of the trauma of being withdrawn into himself. It's an emotionally important issue for us; it makes us yearn again. There aren't lots of sources about wailing. It gets around only by word of mouth. As they say, 'I gain insight from my elders' [Psalms 119:100]." Another participant took this reasoning further: "[Women's wailing] is like praying. Praying stimulates emotion. It's like a prayer leader who has a really pleasant voice and melody; he stirs up your emotions and makes you want to pray. The opposite example is someone who gets up to lead the service but hasn't got a nice melody or voice. He recites the prayers as though he were walking down the street."

Some participants took issue with the remarks about the social significance and possible manipulation of women's wailing. "I don't think wailing depends on the person's social status. I think the wailers in history . . . we also know this from Scripture, where the prophet Jeremiah said, 'Summon the dirge-singers; let them come.' It means that wailers had the status of wailers; it was like a profession. If you called them, they came; if you didn't, they didn't. It was that way in all generations, more or less. Everywhere, in every generation, every [Jewish ethnic] community has had wailing women who've treated it as their profession." This was David's way of claiming that wailers are unbiased in their work. Several participants mentioned well-known women in their community by name, distinguished between an expert wailer and a professional wailer, and agreed that "the expert is influenced by the social surroundings" and that "the professional wails in any situation." Associatively, Said, one of the older participants, stood up and demonstrated in body language the typical motions of the wailer and the eulogizer, absolving the former of any intention pertaining to social relations and besmirching the latter: "The woman wails with her eyes closed. She does up her kerchief [as a covering] so she won't see the men and get embarrassed and mix up her words. A man who comes to give a eulogy behaves differently: he glances left and right to see who's looking and staring at him with his eyes open." Later on, David reinforced his remarks by drawing a connection between the emotionality of the lamentation and its religious purpose: "The prophet also had this in mind when he said 'Summon the dirge-singers.' The idea was to arouse them and stir up their emotions so that they'd appreciate the wretchedness of their [spiritual] situation." In this verse from the prophecy of Jeremiah, women's wailing turns out to be a very important religious task even though Jeremiah's words express a clear gender differentiation in the articulation of emotions. Interestingly, Hasan-Rokem (1996) offers a similar perspective, noting the importance—and superiority—of the role in her analysis of the rabbinical exegesis (*Eikha Rabba*) of this verse. The exegetic parable describes a king (God) who murders (exiles) His two children (the twelve tribes of Israel) and wishes to call on the dirge-singers because He lacks the power to bemoan His children. This call for their assistance, according to Hasan-Rokem, confirms the immensity of the women wailers' psychological and spiritual ability to endure bereavement. Even more, it attests to the *reversal* of the formal equation that places women in the realm of nature and men in that of culture. After all, according to Hasan-Rokem's analysis, "The object of the parable associates wailing women with the traditional cultural expression of the mourning situation in the form of a lamentation, whereas the male (the father-murderer) appears as the embodiment of an uninhibited natural urge" (127).

Some interviewees even elevated women's wailing to *tsidqut* (righteousness) and likened the lamentation to *shira* (spiritual song) in the sense of this term in the Torah portion *Be-shalah,* in which the "Song of the Sea" appears. Shlomo referred to two verses in the portion (Exodus 15:20–21)—"Then Miriam the prophetess, Aaron's sister, took a timbrel in her hand, and all the women went out after in dance with timbrels. And Miriam chanted for them [Hebrew *lahem,* the third-person masculine form] 'Sing to the Lord, for He has triumphed gloriously; horse and driver He has hurled into the sea.'" His remarks attributed to the woman's voice, which applies masculine language to itself, powers of spiritual influence in her personal and collective relations. "One of the theories," he said, interpreting the Torah, "is that in the very act of picking up the timbrel . . . the woman provokes the man a little, in order to lead him onto a good path. It's written that she chanted *for them—lahem,* in the masculine and not in the feminine. Once she gives the order, woman is capable of leading men in whatever way she intends. So with the wailer. . . . Women are believers. It was by the virtue of righteous women that the Israelites were delivered from Egypt, and so will they be delivered in the future" (Exodus 15:21, portion *Be-shalah,* Tractate *Nashim*).

Yekutiel, one of the rabbis of the community, wishing to share his knowledge and thoughts, spoke in the concluding part of the group interview. Like Said who spoke at the start of the interview and was quoted at the beginning of the ethnography, the rabbi began the concluding remarks in a personal tone that related to the place and time at issue. From that point on, his arguments turned the two dichotomizations—sacred and profane, men and women—upside down. By citing rabbinical motifs that are extraneous to the tradition and stated only implicitly, he helped to elevate women's wailing to a plane very close to that of men's eulogies. I do not know whether the rabbi did this by chance or whether he had been influenced by the few moderate arguments that had been expressed in his presence. Be this as it may, Yekutiel's remarks closed the circle in terms of timing and approach:

> First of all, these matters are Heaven-sent [i.e., no coincidence]. Today at this time, I normally sit with a man whom I strongly respect. We study [Torah] together every Friday. Today he isn't here. So I told myself on the way back that I'll stop and visit this fine group.
>
> Singing is divided into women's singing and men's singing. When you speak about the singing in Yemen, you have to make a distinction between that of men and that of women. In my opinion, it is usually claimed, inaccurately, that men's singing is sacred and the women's singing is totally nonsacred. In Yemen, there was no such thing as nonsacred; everything was sacred. But the nature of men's singing pertains to the synagogue and

prayers, and it's the nature of women's singing to deal with life. You might say that women's singing is a song of life, not of the nonsacred. Men's singing is in Hebrew [the language reserved for sacred use], and some songs have Aramaic in them. Women's singing is almost entirely in Arabic.

Women aren't subordinate to men. Men keep to themselves and have a leader. So do women. In the Yemenite household, it was the wife who determined how life would be lived and how the children would be educated. The father took care of the formal side of reading the Torah and the [Aramaic] translation and [the commentary] *'Ein Ya'akov.* The wife decided what kind of education the children would receive. The wife ran the house. One of the rabbis called her *'iqar ha-bayit* ["the essence of the household," instead of the customary term, *'aqeret ha-bayit,* "housewife"].

For men, the eulogies had a permanent wording; it's not something they made up. For women, it was usually a local thing that they made up on the spot, although they already had a basis for it. The initial basis, the format, the structure, existed. They filled the structure with contents in accordance with the situation that they found. When it was an important person, they mentioned his importance. If he was a religious man, they mentioned that. If she was a woman who did acts of kindness, they mentioned her acts of kindness and they mentioned her by name, too. That was the style of the wailers in Yemen, and that's how it was in the time of our earliest forefathers. The whole idea is as it's written in the Mishna. Just as you say a blessing for something good, so do you say a blessing for the bad. . . . If a man receives bad news or if something bad befalls him, he has to bless [God] anyway. Now, what blessing does he say? "Blessed be You, the Lord our God, Judge of the truth." And you have to say it with as much focus and intent as you would if something good had happened. It's the same thing with the wailing women. They're part of the same idea: that you have to thank God and bless Him even for this event, which doesn't seem to be good. But there's no such thing as something bad in Judaism. Everything that God does is good. It's written [in Aramaic]. So what do the wailing women do? They tell the blessed Creator that people deserve everything that He's done, that's how it ought to be for people, and so on. This is why they start the lamentation by praising the blessed Creator.

> Every lamentation begins with praise. I asked, "Aren't they questioning God's actions by doing this?" The rabbi answered, "No . . . Heaven forbid." I persisted: "But doesn't she wail, bemoan the loss?" "For sure," the rabbi replied. "She says that we're very sad but also that we accept what blessed God has done. As we [men] say, 'The Rock—His deeds are perfect, all His ways are just; a faithful God, never false, true and upright is He'" [Deuteronomy 32.4].

The rabbi associated the women's creative genre with life and that of the men with sanctity. This reflects the perception of women as having a circular psychosocial consciousness that is all-encompassing and that fuses dissimilar elements. Women represent life, that is, everything "from the beginning of the world to its end" or perhaps from cradle to grave. This is reflected in the local improvised texts that they create on the spur of the moment. Theirs is a creative art form that loses none of its value by being mindful of the temporality and changing needs of life. The rabbi's remarks, which substitute the word "life" for "nonsacred," extricate the imagery of women from the binary categorization of sacred and nonsacred, a categorization that fits the imagery of men. The women fit into a scheme that one may liken to a canopy that is drawn over and transcends all categories. Although the rabbi's comments promoted this message, it is noteworthy that he ultimately overstated his claims so badly as to totally refute the other participants' views. His arguments returned women's wailing to the category of sacred by likening the lamentation to a blessing of God and to the message of acceptance of judgment that appears in the men's text, the eulogy.

The Value of Absence: Method and Theory

The circle of men is a metaphorical event. The circle exists not only in the documented gathering of some forty men for the *takhsina* ritual, an event of sitting together, but also in the practice of a separate assembly for death rituals. The participants were mindful of two circles from which women were absent: the momentary and the ritual. The group interview on the topic of women's wailing proved to be a special situation that encouraged the participants to be aware concurrently of the representer and of the object being represented. Although the encounter was defined in time and place, it was sometimes translated into other circles—of eulogy, prayer, and study of Mishna (a tradition in gatherings of and for the bereaved)—from which the men pondered my research questions. The men spoke about women's wailing as if expressing an opinion about a practice that was either desirable or undesirable in their circles. As they did so, they also offered an opinion about proximity to and distance from the feminine and the masculine. The absence of women left its imprint on the interview; its contribution to our theoretical perspective became clear after the fact.

It was my research strategy to gather information on a topic that was foreign to the research arena. The topic was foreign not only in the sense that men excluded themselves from wailing as a practice and left it to women but also in respect of the collision between the atmosphere of bereavement, which the lamentation is designed to encourage, and the serenity of the khat party. The foreignness, which is cultural in origin, was also manifested in my very appearance as a woman in an all-male gathering and in the act of research as such. Although the group had expressed its collective willingness to be interviewed, these aspects of foreignness caused several individuals to resist. "I don't think you ought to look into these matters," Issachar said. "I think it's unnecessary. There's nothing at all to gain from it." Yihye grumbled, "You never ask about anything happy, only about wailing and mourning. There are good things to say! There should be a time for everything. . . . You ought to be happy, not sad." The rabbi interpreted these remarks for me: "Here you've got an example of the typical Yemenite, who loves ordinary natural life. He's not interested in research studies." Dan believed that the interview bumped those present from their "regular agenda" and that "Anything that doesn't belong upsets the equilibrium." Someone else noticed a reversal of traditional roles and likened the group to a lion's den into which a woman researcher had stumbled. The resistance, more than any form of cooperation, revealed the state of confrontation into which the situation had thrust the participants in the metaphorical and literal circle—an acute confrontation between the participants' consciousness and something that was culturally taken for granted.

For many of the men, it was the first experience in speaking out on any unifying theme. As Mordechai expressed it, "I'm getting a great deal of pleasure from the conversation for the simple reason that we're all taking part in it. . . . What's good about it is the culture of talking these matters over and expressing ourselves about them." When an opinion was expressed in the circle of participants, the speaker pronounced it to himself and to the others in a reflective way. Amid the give-and-take of point and counterpoint, the distance from the traditional experience grew in geometric progression. Under these conditions, the participants improved their ability to contemplate and generated metaperspectives on the research theme.

The value of the process that the participant noted lies in its challenge to the linear structure that typifies immobile outlooks. Such outlooks, by their nature, may corroborate initial premises and prejudices. The process also challenges linearity as a metaphor for men's thinking. The interview proved to be an opportunity for a circular experience in which all participants contemplated one topic from all angles. In terms of ethnography, the interview gave its participants a singular opportunity to reflect about women's wailing in its ritual definition and about femininity. The interview also served as a way to illuminate the complexity of the research topic for the reader.

As the participants' references to women's wailing moved toward their end, the ethnography illuminated the changing status of the practice. On an axis of "otherness" to "familiarness," the perception of wailing solidified during the interview as "otherness." In other words, although unique components of wailing have survived, wailing as such has become structured and has moved closer to the world of men. Ultimately, wailing has become a creative form that uses the men's holy language. The first part of the ethnography described the women's tears as objects that patriarchal circumstances and nature have made commonplace and invested with manipulative power. As a practice performed within the earshot of everyone, including men, wailing was portrayed as an instrumentality in the service of relations among members of the community of wailers. In respect to listeners, it was described as an arena, a stage, an instrument not devoid of ulterior motives that puts to derision the Jewish imperative of *hesed shel emet*—the performance of favors for the dead with no intention of practical reward. The verbal and vocal virtuosity of women's wailing was described as amazing, more colorful than the canon text, and the genre most able to respond to the needs of the moment. In contrast, the second part of the ethnography showed that the participants were able to cope with women's wailing from a religious point of view and to station it within the boundaries of the sacred. The inclusionary intent also took on implicit and explicit form in the men's references to their emotions. My conclusion is that this discourse of attitudes and thoughts gave rise to nuanced differentiations that clashed with a stereotypical attitude. At day's end, the difference between women and men nearly came down to forms of expression that, as stated, can remove women's wailing from the domain of otherness. We should emphasize that the meaning of the difference between them is that from the affective standpoint, women display a *sense of pain that they share with men,* and in religious terms, women translate the belief in the parting of the soul, *a belief that they share with men,* into a loss that should be rued. It is women who dare to delay in the zones where the parting occurs.

In view of the different attitudes expressed in the men's circle, the ritual itself seems to be regulated by its intrinsic potential of differentiation. For it to take place in the manner described, the special ritual situation creates a forced emphasis of differentiating views and the silencing of bridging ones. This is one way in which collective behavior patterns of men and women become polar. It may be part of the normative process of self-differentiation to which Bateson's (1980) theoretical concept of schismogenesis refers. In this process, as Sarris (1995) observes, women overperform in their weeping, and their exaggeration proves to be lasting in view of the men's emotional self-restraint. The result is a circular chain reaction in which women cry more and men restrain themselves more. The final outcome is the preservation of the male and female ethos.

The challenge in preserving the emotional-sexual ethos lies in the tendency to homogeneity that a death event in the community sets in motion in terms of crisis experience and the intensity of its anguish. Emotional homogeneity, in which everyone responds the same way, is especially dangerous to the male ethos because it forces men to maintain their composure instead of displaying the appropriate response to weeping, that is, the release of emotion. The male interviewees in our study reinforced this hypothesis by describing women's wailing as *an instrument designed to actualize their emotions.* As I have shown, some respondents believed that "What [the women] have to do with is inspiring the listeners to weep" since the wailer "stirs up [the male listener's] emotions and he cries," and that "part of the wailers' role is to bring out what's really inside you." Someone also explained that "We need someone to make us emotional." It is in this light that one may interpret expressions that denote indifference, contempt, and religious condescension toward women's wailing as a means of erecting ramparts. Those who view wailing in this manner use these expressions to defend themselves against the propensity of wailing to "turn things around," to "flip," and to be "inconsistent," that is, against the emotional impact of wailing. Like in other cultures, if the weeping of Yemenite Jewish men resembles that of women in the course of a ritual, it might breach a taboo and diminish the men's reputation. Therefore, in contrast to the other differentiated attributes of wailing, one may regard the three-days dispensation in the traditional death rites as a strategy that serves the male ethos in two ways: the divisibility of time creates a hierarchy in men's favor and gives them a defined legitimate time for some manner of visible emotional release.

Why is the conspicuous differentiation of the sexes in death events important? More specifically, why does this differentiation gather strength in the transition from the *takhsina* ritual, sitting in front of the narghiles, to the circle of rituals? Sarris's (1995) answer concerns itself with the structuring of complementary roles and claims that every cluster of roles, male and female, abets the resolution of a crisis. The emotional hyperbole in wailing and its escalating demand for a response other than restraint may, according to Sarris, underscore the relative roles of each group in a ritual that itself constitutes a social challenge. This argument does not seem to differentiate between death events and other social crises, nor does it explain the relatively high level of men's and women's compliance with segregative norms in these events and the relatively strong perseverance of rigid taboo proscriptions (Freud 1952; Douglas 1966). The hypothesis that I wish to offer represents an extension of the ideation implicit in the concept of schismogenesis and is based on the view that unconscious knowledge may be reflected in the behavior patterns of a social collective and in death rituals (Geertz 1975; Durkheim 1965).

This is the erotic hypothesis discussed in the previous chapter. As stated, the hypothesis about the erotic nature of the performance was inspired by several sources, including attitudes expressed here and there by men in the circle.

I believe that the phenomenon of extreme differentiation at the boundaries of the death ritual, as practiced in various wailing cultures, attests to an inversion—a so-called Freudian reaction formation—in the response of a collective to crisis. As against the destructability, dispensability, and finiteness of the human being, which are represented by death, members of both sexes construct themselves in accordance with the symbolic tension; they separate from each other in a binary, stereotyped way that corresponds to many of their characteristics. The result is the crystallization of images. Thus, women wallow in their wailing and by so doing give onlookers the impression of vulnerability and weakness—traits that make them "more feminine." The men, in contrast, plunge into silence or prayer, slipping into a nonparticipatory posture of observation that attests to their strength and to their being "more masculine." The emphasis of different sex roles culminates with the insinuation of femininity and masculinity into the very innards of the ritual. Thus, after reading the participants' remarks between the lines, I wish to argue that the ritual does not rule out erotic messages and to some extent may even be viewed as encouraging them. The ritual is a focal point of attraction, literally and figuratively, for both sexes.

This interpretation is related to the argument that the differentiation tendencies of men and women, from their very inception, carry a subtle and complex set of symbols of coupling and fertility. Notably, relations of sexual differentiation and integration are noted for an ambivalence that is not alien to the Jewish tradition. For example, it is the *tuma* ("ritual impurity") of woman's menstrual cycle that regulates difference and hierarchic sex images that culminate with procreation. This is the sort of "impurity" that results in the banishing of women from the cemetery. Consequently, the argument can be made that the response of survivors in death rituals is consciously related to the creation and continuation of life, although the degree of consciousness is indeterminate.

An interpretation that relates to manifestations of bereavement in ancient Hebrew culture and in many other cultures, such as the Turkish, Indian, Polynesian, and Tonga cultures, may support this claim. The expressions of bereavement in these cultures include customs of bloodletting, laceration of the face and chest, maiming, the growing or plucking of hair, and the growing of fingernails (Pollock 1972). Frazer defines blood and hair as symbols of life and strength that are sometimes brought into contact with the body of the deceased in order to invigorate it (Frazer 1923). Women often are considered special agents of various blood customs. In the course of the rituals and the sounding of their lamentations, they rend their clothing in demonstration of their weakness and vulnerability. In this fashion, in which symbols of life are implanted in the arena of death and in which the sexual role of women may be demonstrated before men's eyes, a consciousness of sexual differentiation-integration takes root. These are examples of the claim that sexuality is a ramified theme in the acknowledgment of loss and death and is able to replace the finite (death) with the infinite (continuity) (Bataille 1986; Brown 1985; Lifton 1979). I propose that the differentiation of the sexes in death rituals, with its implicit erotic allusion, be viewed as a necessary social mechanism that is meant to blur the boundaries of consciousness that separate life from death.

Notably, studies on wailing cultures have thus far attributed the characteristic of bridging between life and death, in a combination of sexuality, fertility, maternity, and death, to women and women's wailing. Madar (2006) showed that this basic attribution is also reflected in the study of texts translated into Arabic in the Yemenite Jewish tradition, including the Exodus account and the story of Hannah and her seven sons.

Wholly immersed in concrete life experiences, women are credited with the attributes of spanning both worlds and incorporating contrasts. They are expert in bodily contact at the time of birth and ahead of burial and are placed in a conscious position of mediating between worlds (Rosaldo 1974; Chodorow 1974, 1978; Deutsch 1961). The absence of women in the men's circle, in our case study, neither validates nor invalidates these images. Its value lies in revealing the possibility of a relatively abstract contribution by men to a community's efforts to cope with death. One theoretical manifestation of this realization, in the differentiation-integration spiral, is the insight that the bridging function in existential situations does not belong to women alone and that a consciousness of social continuity cannot serve the glory of men only.

Before I proceed to the Epilogue, I wish to claim that study of the mission, that is, of gender relations within the framework of the feminine wailing culture and its gender division of labor, has been deferred thus far because most of the women I interviewed did not describe wailing in contrast to eulogy. Furthermore, wailers were not juxtaposed to worshippers, and performance was not depreciated relative to ritual. The numerous descriptions that I obtained yielded a picture of wailing as a legitimate and important cultural practice that stands on its own, one not defined in comparison with the worldview of members of the other sex, let alone in opposition to them. The women's disregard for what the men want and how they accept wailing clearly suggests that wailing should be recognized and discussed as an autonomous practice. This practice expresses an autonomy that is geared to gender activity and reflects a feminine point of view. Given the women's self-importance and the priority that they gave their practice, I inferred that the wailing story should first be told from the perspective of the absence of men in the women's circle, as if women were the first sex. It is this perspective that placed the detection of the full essence of this feminine practice in this part of the ethnography, the concluding part, which treated it from the standpoint of gender partnership and more so of the absence of women in the circle of men.

·EPILOGUE·

The Lament of the Printed Words

BY USING THE EXPRESSION "THE WAILING CULTURE OF YEMENITE JEWISH women," one reveals one's attitude toward something that is foreign, inscrutable, different, archaic, and so on—adjectives that erect permanent barriers between cultural realities. A women's culture that was lifted out of exile, from the collective memory of a community that no longer exists, seems totally enveloped in a fixation over the tradition that death invokes and the loss that it inflicts. The femininity in this culture is estimated only from afar. From there, it gives the appearance of self-flagellation, flagrant crudity, or the high-mindedness that is offered in response. If so, one may liken the characteristics of the wailing culture to those of a stranger in a strange land whose glimmering exotic exterior other phenomena cannot match. What is the value of an ethnography that has such a culture as its object? What can it teach us? The ethnography thus far twines the assets of the wailing culture chapter by chapter. Until this Epilogue, it presented things from the perspective of the respondents' nostalgia, a tracing stratagem that allows today's research to bring yesterday's vestiges to life. Chapter 6, "Mission," concluded the voyage that had gone in that direction. From here on, we describe the wailing culture from the standpoint of willingness to let it go because its present-day signals are too weak to portend a continuation. The Epilogue, befitting a concluding chapter, will judge the assets of this culture by assessing its losses, that is, by discussing the possible implications of wailing's decline. As it draws to a close, I will dwell on these characteristics as singled out by the ethnography. On this basis, I will note elements of the culture that merit expansion, commentary, description, and conjecture and others that are best served by brevity. Here I also present ways of parting with a cultural phenomenon that no longer has the strength to keep itself alive. I will show that as the wailing culture edges toward its grave, it is being accompanied by feelings of sorrow, statements denoting willingness to relinquish it, and also censure. Thus, we will find different audiences congregating there, in the mourners' house.

Community: A Crumbling Structure of Emotion

The ethnography did not introduce us to a community in the traditional sense, least of all as it had existed in Yemen or even in the sense of a structure of emotion (Appadurai 1996, 199) or a community of emotion. I encountered Yemenite Jewry in a state of disintegration. The respondents adroitly gauged the emotional gap that lay between here and there. The erosion of the quality of their solidarity, they said, made them feel emotionally defective. This surfaced in their anecdotes about having organized "doing good deeds" and "helping each other," initiatives that allowed community life to flow under the circumstances of their lives in the distant past. These attitudes, expressed associatively, link by link, demonstrate how emphatically women's wailing has lost its place for good in the social reality that we inhabit. An example that I find especially apt concerns the social treatment in Yemen of someone who was deathly ill. Tamara recounted:

> The people in Yemen were doers of good deeds. They helped each other. I'll give you an example: when someone in some house becomes bedridden . . . from the first day, if the patient really doesn't feel good, all the neighbors help. They don't let him lie there. That's how it's done here [in Israel]. Everyone takes turns helping. They put the patient on cushions and rugs, and [the neighbors and relatives] who come in all take turns. . . . They even take turns all night long so that the patient won't be left alone. They're not afraid that he'll be contagious. The one who nurses the patient, he puts him on his body just so, on his body, they put the patient on their bodies [the respondent makes a hugging motion]. They hug the patient until God takes his soul. The family and the neighbors always surround [the patient]. The bodies of the patient and the caregiver might sweat . . . but they aren't afraid that he'd be contagious. . . . Those are lovely things. We [Yemenite Jews] would nurse the patient's very soul with all his suffering. The patient says to himself, "There's still someone who wants me, there's still someone who's taking care of my soul," even in the last moments. There's a closeness and warmth between people. Here in modern life [in Israel] humanity has gone downhill.

When I asked questions about wailing, I received in return generalizations about states of illness, dying, and birth giving. This is because wailing is considered a practice of solidarity per se, one linked with acts of kindness and welfare. Wailing, originally performed in a circle and by taking turns, included an inherent element of solace for the mourners and community; its emotional contagion embraced everyone. This is why even though death is death—a crisis event—the respondents distinguish between "over here" and "back there" in its context, too.

"People died in Yemen," one of my respondents recalled, "but everyone was anguished, the family and others. They hurt and they wailed to high heaven. Here in Israel, it doesn't happen anymore." Another woman phrased this alternatively: "Really, in Yemen there was very, very great sadness when we went to the home of someone in mourning. Today, it's not like that. Today, it's less." "Emotion, emotion," a third respondent said passionately.

"The wailers had emotion; even little children cried terribly when they heard the wailing. Just terrible. From kids to grownups. Now we're in another era."

It was the Israeli media that breached the boundaries of the community of emotion that had formed after having immigrated to Israel. The respondents discovered the connection between this powerful conduit of information and their community's relations of solidarity. They described, among other differences and values between here and there, the absence of any way to connect the small, isolated, and far-flung Jewish communities in Yemen. "In Yemen there was no television," one respondent said, "and even in each city [the wailing] was different. If someone died in another city, you'd never hear about it." Another respondent said, "In Yemen, all you had was your city. There you had to give the mourners food: morning, afternoon, evening. There weren't lots of people." The limits of compassion in Yemen corresponded to the geographical limits of the community. The community was a dense social network in which death events united the ranks. Ora's remarks, quoted below, illustrate the connection between the density or sparseness of people's social networks and their experiencing of the human and social crisis that death causes (Rubin 1990). "There's so much pain in Israel," Ora said, "so many problems, that these laments are unneeded. Besides, with so much killing, so much murder, people don't cry anymore. Crying has become an embarrassment. In Yemen, when someone died, people were stunned and cried all year long." Bad news reportage on Israeli radio and television competes for the feelings of solidarity that members of a small community of emotion maintain. It makes people aware of much higher death rates than those underlying a culture that empowers an individual who has died, especially since most individuals described in media reports are strangers. My respondents taught me that solidarity—the object of their nostalgia—is fractured by the very ability to be aware of objects of identification outside the "us" that inhabit one place. This paradoxical nexus illuminates an additional aspect of the wailing culture, a quantitative one: the more the respondents can describe Israel as beleaguered by wars, terror attacks, murders, and traffic accidents—the more such scenes are shown again and again from one end of the country to the other—the less room remains for collective weeping in which all hearts blend into one. An example from the Waraos of Venezuela gives the same lesson. Among the Waraos, an increase in the death rate does amplify the importance of the wailer's roles but only when it happens in the community setting (Briggs 1992). This may explain why wailing appears only once in Binyamin-Gamliel's (1975) book, and there in the context of a national event. That sole lament—surprisingly—was for the murder of the Israeli athletes at the 1972 Olympic Games in Munich. It begins with the words "Why did you [in the singular] go to the land of Germany to play? / Now who will capture the murderers / and keep them away?" (240).

In addition to external information about the circumstances and frequencies of deaths, the Yemenite Jewish community of emotion in Israel has been infiltrated by the influence of external values. Transmitted in various ways in addition to the mass media, they ultimately find expression in patterns of individual and group communication. Secularization, permissiveness, weakening of parental authority, materialism, and individualism are all effects that the older respondents judge as being the results of their community's encounter with Israeli society. These respondents do not see the decline of women's wailing as a freely standing event; instead, it represents a religious, moral, and cultural decline that merits classic Jewish expressions of regret: "decline of the generations," "a generation that does not recognize its God," "The air is full of impurity," "We are bringing darkness on ourselves," and "In Yemen there was respect, respect. Here it's different." These remarks arose in intense discussion over the Yemenite Jewish immigrants' assimilation into modern Israeli society. Below I discuss aspects of the connection between these processes and women's wailing; here I wish to say that the toehold of women's wailing in the Yemenite Jewish community of emotion matches that of their community of emotion in the social reality of Israel. They are interdependent, and both are toppling.

Interpretation: Open and Closed Paths

Had my research been done in Yemen, I could have discovered the mechanisms that allowed wailing to weave itself into community life. Back there, community life was circumscribed geographically, psychologically (in the sense of individuals' membership in a social whole), and historically under the unique circumstances of Jewish exile in a Muslim religious state. Researching in Yemen would have been a privilege of sorts—an epistemological privilege as well—that typifies several ethnographies about women's wailing in other countries. The cultural snapshots that such ethnographies yield are rarely taken amid the complex reality of an immigration country or among the manifestations of dilution that the encounter with modern ways of life instigates. Wailing cultures have been investigated among the women of the Awlad 'Ali tribe in Egypt (Abu-Lughod 1986), Brazilian women in Brazil (Urban 1988), Indian women in India (Tiwary 1978; Parry 1994), and Greek women in Greek villages (Alexiou 1974; Danforth 1982). Alone among them, the latter group has been graced with abundant ethnographic documentation; the most recent studies about the Greek women analyze the effects of modernization on women's traditional death rituals and roles (Sarris 1995; Holst-Warhaft 1995). When a wailing culture is researched in a community in its country of origin, one finds a relatively undisrupted spread of wailers' voices from the locus (the middle of the wailing circles) outward and extensive structuring processes that are controlled by the wailer's voice. The results of these structuring processes are evident in community relations that transcend the event that the women address in their performance. The wailing of Inner Mani women, for example, proved to be a mechanism for the challenging of male political interests. It became a medium for women who wished to apply their concepts to the socioeconomic order (Seremetakis 1990). Similarly, the investigation of Venezuelan women's wailing reveals that it structures identity, tests and creates social relations, and offers new points of view on community events. Another ethnography implies that when women engage in polyphonic wailing and are not pressed to silence themselves or put some design into their performance, wailing also signals the hierarchic structures of the country and the colonial regime that something of social value is about to be said (Briggs 1993).

Ab initio, the Yemenite Jewish wailing culture in Israel is subject to constant comparison of what it is and what it does not belong to, that is, the inner and outer circles of the community. In this respect, it is no different from any other tradition—and there are many—that is transported from exile. By saying this, I am not suggesting that Jewish women's wailing in Yemen was isolated from itself. Instead, like the other components of Jewish community life, it was in exile, in the throes of an intercultural encounter. As I have shown, its internal language and motives adopted something of the Arabic vernacular. Chapter 6, "Mission," also recounts the reflection of Jewish women's wailing in one of the bleakest moments that the Yemenite exile held in store: Jews having to wail in Arabs' homes. Given the sociopolitical-socioreligious state of affairs in Yemen, the Jews transformed women's wailing into a medium by which they could negotiate over the uniqueness of their religious heritage and maintain the requisite separation of the sexes. For this reason, the intercultural encounter among communities in Yemen and, a fortiori, among virtual postcommunities in Israel entails a dialogic approach in cultural research, an ex gratia stance relative to the ideal known as cultural relativism. This essentially reflective stance reflects the vacillation of respondents who belong to the culture in the sense of what is theirs and what is not, heritage versus assimilation, the original versus the nonoriginal, truth versus falsehood. According to one of the most recent approaches, this position fits into the frame of the discussion of authenticity. It is an authenticity grounded in dialogue and is expressed as follows: "Authenticity, unlike 'primitive society,' is generated not from the bounded classification of an Other but from the probing comparison between self and Other, as well as between external and internal states of being" (Ferrara 1998, 17).

Theoreticians in the field of symbolic interactions tell us that the awareness of self-authenticity is the outgrowth of a conflict between one's own values and the value sets of others (Hewitt 1989; Goffman 1963; Mead 1964). In my opinion, this principle may reflect not only the individual's aspiration to authenticity—a topic that I take up below—but also the aspiration of members of a cultural community. A community, like an individual, is an entity that depends existentially on the definition of its boundaries and the differentiation of its identity. The value conflict that typified Yemenite Jewry's encounter with its surroundings, both in Yemen and Israel, did not translate into a dialogue of power versus power. The sociopolitical experiences of life in both countries relegated this community to a position of social inferiority[1] and possibly for this reason armed itself with tools for the contemplation of its past and present. These tools helped members of the community in Yemen by allowing them to defend their originalities from non-Jews by deliberately distorting the assets of their heritage. As I described, women's wailing was performed in the manner of a parody in Arabs' houses of mourning, as though the men who performed were not authorized to replicate it accurately.[2] When Jewish men "wailed," they inserted imprecations in Hebrew, obsolete words, and emphatically fake tears, all to show that their performance was a distortion of women's wailing in their own eyes, a stunt that they used to mock the Arabs and finagle a day's food from them. I expressed the conjecture that this pretense, which only the Jews knew in its crudest forms, made it possible to maintain the value and significance of women's wailing in the intracommunity context, that is, to maintain its authenticity. Acknowledging the women's wailing as a sociocultural asset, the Jewish men behaved like its gatekeepers—a role they could keep up because only they were well versed in its authentic form.

In Israel, the immigrants from Yemen faced no challenge of this kind, to their delight. Thus, their consciousness of authenticity took on other forms. My respondents expressed matters such as cultural belonging (which is still not taken for granted), originality, and a folklore that is losing its place, in an en passant manner in the course of encounters where wailing takes place or should take place—in death events, during the shivah, and at the grave. By articulating these topics with emphasis, the ethnography constitutes a text in which dialogic authenticity (Handler and Saxton 1988) rises to the surface.

The ethnography offers various paths of interpretation, some open and others closed. The decline of the wailing tradition that followed immigration to Israel, the comparisons that the respondents offered to explain their culture in the present and the past, and the sense of relinquishing something that can no longer be revived sorted themselves into two integrated blocs: granting or obstructing access to cultural information. Furthermore, as noted, the snapshots in this ethnography are black and white; they have not yellowed with age, their edges crumbling at the touch of our fingers. In other words, the tableaux of the imagination that the ethnography creates do not stay fixated on the narrow roads of Yemen, where Jews trembled at the sound of bad news, cried in anguish from the windows of their dried-mud homes, or quaked at the sight of the baskets of food that were rushed to the house of mourning once the word of the death spread. Most of the pictures are crisp color photos, set against the background of Israeli houses and streets and the cypress trees that surround the cemeteries.

If so, the detailed color footage in the ethnography tells less about what was and more about what is by describing what remains of the wailing culture and contemplating the vestiges. The outcome, I would say, is clear: the ethnographic concern with what remains or has been preserved has evolved into occupation with the most material, by which I mean the most substantive, characteristics of the wailing culture. In regard to performance, for example, the original form of women's wailing—in a circle in the *diwan*—is reported on the pages of the field journal of memory, whereas the wailer's appearance as a dramatic unit that even I could observe is privileged with an amplitude of documentation. In another example, the social aspects of the value of honoring the dead attract relatively scanty discussion, while wailing as a practice of consolation and healing is described extensively. The data are such, in terms of their content, that while my respondents did not always offer rhetorical compensation for what could not be observed or shared, sometimes in their remarks they made up things that their real experience had not included. Their reflectivity created an open path that allowed points of view to affect the description of their culture. The foreignness of the context in which the wailing culture was investigated, in contrast, paved a closed path. This truncated type of access to information narrowed the road to knowledge in one place, widened it elsewhere, and also abetted the ethnographic emphasis on the psychosocial aspects of the culture and the description of the performance in terms that confine it to the exact boundaries of the house of mourning.

In chapter 2, I introduced Johara, the "mother of the wailers." The stories recounted by respondents who had known her and celebrated her posthumously merged into a web that captured the image of a mythical woman, hyperidealized in her wailing. Chapter 2 stresses the telling-about element to say that "Johara" is but the product of an audience that has extracted her from its memory. Like a monument into which words have been engraved, the raconteurs stand like a buffer between us and the real Johara, their anecdotes reinforcing the words etched into the monument and their various adjectives glorifying the "mother of the wailers." "Johara" is the title of a special narrative of the wailing culture. She stands out from the culture in a dualism that can include or exclude her at one and the same time, justifying those who question her ability to represent the cultural whole. The chapter demonstrates the potential width of the gap between an authentic cultural reality, embodied in one woman, and the manifestations of the reality that the intercultural encounter in Israel has created. The more representative "Johara" is of authenticity, the wider the gap becomes and the more able the stories are to demonstrate the significance of the loss of the women's wailing tradition, a tradition whose characteristics are spread throughout the ethnography. Possibly, however, the Johara image fails to represent. A discriminating reading of chapter 2 may emphasize Johara's singularity in the context of the community in Yemen as well. Those who read it this way may find that in contrast to the stereotyped view of tradition, a traditional society cannot homogenize all its members by fiat. In other words, a tradition should not be viewed solely as a plowed furrow down which everyone walks from generation to generation. Johara was unique because she embodied wailing as a matter of personality. Arguably, she lent the wailing culture a highly idiosyncratic interpretation. Her persona contained socially significant contrasts and opposites because it was a symbolic type that is always separate from its audience. Furthermore, her wailing branched to the additional services of washing the dead and healing the ill, her dreams presaged death and engaged the dead in dialogue, and her general appearance honored the dead but also signaled the power and impetus of life. Accordingly, it is hard to see, for example, how this woman would have fit into the original egalitarian circle of wailers. If one may judge by the respondents' anecdotes, Johara's wailing was and remains unsurpassed; it was almost a positive mutation. Accordingly, for them, she deserves the status of a solo performer whose voice causes other women to fall silent or, at the most, to mirror it like a chorus.

Chapter 3, "Giving Words," documents the laments—the wailing lyrics—and debates the meanings of the gift that they convey. The laments that appear in this chapter were provided in the course of interviews. The interview, an artificial situation for the collection of words, is a difficult medium for wailers. As they attempted to accede to my request, the wailers among my respondents had trouble remembering, trouble translating (from Yemenite Arabic into Hebrew), emotional trouble in producing words, and, once the words were produced, trouble in being aware that they were symbols of decline. The ethnographic account demonstrates the data loss that occurred in the intercultural encounter that I had created between a tradition and Western rules of conduct—that is, the research situation—and suggests that almost certainly, important information was lost when the women respondents switched from one language to the other, as they had to, and amid their emotional responses. This can be considered an asset: a narrowing of focus that comes with the possibility of expansion. In other words, it is precisely the interview, a form of encounter that symbolizes the death of the tradition, that allows us to gauge the element of giving in the giving of words in the wailing culture. The women valued these words dearly, more than the refreshments that they placed on the table as we sat down for our question-and-answer sessions. For them, wailing words are not only vocalizations or means of communication—they are a gratuity. It is not just the words that express metaphors; what the wailers invest in the words is also metaphorical. That is, the words must be given and must allow the listener to be satiated. In addition, there are words—the wailers spoke about them—that not only denote something but also place an aesthetic, empathetic grip on the listener's ear. They reflect an emotional investment, a quasi love for their audience. I doubt that any other research method could have extracted this meaning that the women imparted to their words.

Because the context of the research was foreign in both location and language, the interview created a symbolic disruption. The way the words were given indicated the importance of the context of the cultural act (a death event) and the Yemenite Arabic dialect as credible limits of authentic wailing, insofar as "authentic" also means an exact replica of the performance (Rubidge 1996). I found that the wailing performance and the event that induces it are interdependent: wailing needs a dead person, that is, the entire contingent of elements that belong to its proper context, no less than a dead person needs wailing. Chapter 3 showed how both the wailers and the researcher coped verbally with the disintegration of the wailing culture. More than other chapters, chapter 3 illustrates the complexity of an ethnography that deals with a process of cultural decline.

The impression of women's wailing as an act of giving prompted me to continue searching for other hidden treasures in this practice, to detect categories within it, and to station the wailer at the intersection of identities of life and death. This analysis broadened the meanings of the gift and the objects of the wailing performance, apart from the deceased, in the direction of the living people around him and the God Who determines human beings' fate. I showed that the wailer's words migrate among categories of identity in a way that blurs the distinction between life and death and links the wailer and her listeners to the deceased's ultimate destiny. Furthermore, by nature, the lyrics announce, so to speak, that the limits of logic are being approached. They "acknowledge" the menace of insanity that nestles in anguish by expressing the wish to become a worm in the ground, a creature that is buried alive and continues to live. I will not revisit the functions and inner messages of wailing, but I should ask whether any existing form of eulogy goes as far as this one, women's wailing, to conflate those standing over the grave with those buried in it that proclaims our profound and unconscious existence without maintaining a perceptible professional distance. There is none, I would say. The eulogies familiar to us are uttered or recited from a printed text until the eulogizer chokes on tears, if she or he does so at all. It is beyond the ability of this kind of speech and tears to transform the living into the dead and vice versa. Furthermore, this kind of eulogy lacks the protective armor of a melody. The eulogy deals with the sadness of the deceased's parting from the living in a manner that suggests one side that has suffered a bad break (the deceased) and another that holds an absolute advantage (his or her kin). A respondent of Ashkenazi origin with whom I spoke in the final days of my research expressed something of this impression:

> I think the wailers' goal with the texts is something else. Their goal is to connect the person with himself, to connect the person with his weeping,

> his emotion, his sadness, his pain. That's how I see it. And these [modern] texts and speeches, their goal is also to glorify the individual [eulogizer] and to elevate him and also to request something for himself for those who are still alive. To me, [the speeches] are a defense mechanism of some kind that protects people and keeps them away from the most basic situation.

Following this thinking, I believe the greatest giving in the words of the lament lies in empowering the dead so emphatically as to indicate the inferiority of the living. Some wailing words do this in a manner that exceeds the imperative captured by the Jewish religious adage *Aharei mot qedoshim emor* ("speak only well of the dead"),[3] indications of which are evident in the oral eulogies. In wailing, with its melodic accompaniment, we found metaphors/similes such as "His eyes glowed like sunbeams with light and sanctity" and "The candle of the home has gone out." Metaphors and similes, as I have shown, are powerful mechanisms that wailers use when they wish to give.[4] This giving bridges the gaping abyss between a person's social identity, which is limited to a place, a time, and a community, and his or her soul, which Jewish mysticism identifies as "a portion of God on High."

The title of chapter 4, "The Performance Stage," signals the intent to focus more on the wailer's performance than on the audience's responses even though the traditional performative forms of wailing did not allow this separation and did not appear on an identifiable stage. This chapter likens wailing to a stage performance. A postcolonial argument about the foreignness of the theater in comparison with the performative world has it that one should not view Eastern cultures as irrational relative to Western ones; instead, one should contemplate these cultures' performative practices as surpassing the parameters of the Western theatrical tradition (Fortier 1997). Chapter 4 took this premise another step forward by showing first that the sole remnant of the original wailing circle and the solo-chorus paradigm is a dramatic unit and second that the positioning of this unit on the stage and the use of theatrical terms to describe it are important for the reaping of an ethnographic harvest. Indeed, they yielded abundant information about wailing on matters such as different types of wailers and performative styles. This step was surely not prompted by doubt about the ritual or expressive rationality of wailing; instead, it was my intent to expand—to pluck interpretive fruit in terms that are no longer foreign to the respondents, who not only attend an occasional wailing performance but also watch films and plays, at least on television. It may have been on the basis of such a theatrical encounter that Meir chose to describe the extent of exaggeration that may be employed in describing the wailer's persona: "Woman is one big theater to begin with. I'd say a woman and a chameleon are one and the same. . . . A woman is sly, conniving, a chameleon, she changes her mind, changes color." By placing the wailer on a theatrical stage in this chapter and especially by describing her "performative sequences," her "pretense," and her "switching of images," I show after the fact that Meir's impression has a dollop of truth.

In terms of structure, chapter 4 transitions from emotional authenticity to performance, theater, and finally a parody that represents fakery. Thus, the chapter first describes the making of a wailer in her family roles—a daughter, a sister, a wife, and a mother who carries the suffering that is inherent in woman qua woman. The description of tomorrow's wailers defers to the definition of her expertise and an account of the performative sequence of her wailing. Finally, the chapter dwells on wailing performances by Jewish men and women in Arabs' houses of mourning. Although it is surprising to find manifestations of play-acting in death events, the onlookers, it seems, will always find themselves weeping whether the home they occupy is Jewish or Arab. As in the theater, even if the actors are too tired to appear and they burst into a crescendo of mockery offstage, the loyal audience wishes with all its heart to see only what the stage lights illuminate.

The "Performance Stage" chapter, like the "Giving Words" chapter, recounts the last link in the chain of transmission. The wailers, it turns out, were determined to pass the baton one last time. They accomplished this by dispersing the fog that blanketed the secrets of their performance and tearing off the mask, or the kerchief, that covered their faces as they wailed. They gave me inside information on how to make an impression, how everyone accepts their anguish as the real thing and heaves with sobbing even as the wailers' own eyes remain dry. They described their practices with the audience in the initial, middle, and final stages of the performance and how they avoid failed performances (Goffman 1959). By stripping the performance of its ritual and religious mantles, the ethnography exposes the tension between the making of a wailer and the play-acting that she invokes as she performs. I showed that a woman becomes a wailer by receiving the tradition from her mother and from older women, by experiencing personal losses, and by facing the mortal danger that visits every birthing mother. Nevertheless, she play-acts. In her performed weeping she plays both sides of the game, communing with her personal baggage of anguish but stage-directing herself in ways meant to enhance her audience's trust. The ethnography emphasizes this tension between sincerity and pretense. By comparing the contents of the "Performance Stage" chapter with those of the "Melancholic Power" chapter, we add meaning to this tension and render it irresolvable.

The form of wailing that endured for years after the immigration of Yemenite Jewry to Israel, as stated, is the appearance of the dramatic unit. It is of course much easier to put on a solo performance than to organize a group of women into a circle and obey the stringent rules of pouring coffee and vocal synchronization that accompanied this form. However, the disintegration of the circle, more than indicating laziness on the part of women who know how to participate in it, reflects the effect of an attitude of disapproval, hesitancy, and doubt among elderly women whose daughters have not appropriated their performative wisdom and even mock them and among would-be listeners who silence them. The elderly women's active maintenance of the dramatic unit form, which serves their mission and demonstrates their courage, excuses them from having to preserve the circle paradigm; in fact, much time has passed since they considered this a real requirement. I would say the full ethnographic value of the dramatic unit cannot be captured by analyzing its motives and its theatrical motifs. The fact that it has survived as a performative form for some fifty years under the circumstances of Israeli cultural assimilation and that it was the form that the community in Yemen chose to imitate under hostile circumstances in Arabs' houses of mourning shows that this is a basic wailing paradigm. An anthropological analysis that includes historical information of the kind presented in this book suggests that cultural performances may include basic elements and accompanying elements, some material and others marginal.

The question that remains unanswered here is whether, theoretically, a distinction should be made between them.

Chapter 5, "Melancholic Power," revisits the riddle with which the book began: From whence does wailing derive its phenomenal influence over its audience? My goal in this chapter was to decode the performance beyond the dramatic credibility that the wailer wishes to establish for herself and to focus on the innate verbal and motoric characteristics that justify the attribution of primordialness to women's wailing. Explaining such attributions, Talya said:

> The wailer brings you back to the roots. I don't know how to explain it. It takes you back to the earliest feelings, to originality, to rootedness. It takes you back, back in time, back in childhood, back to my parents' childhood. They told about Yemen as though it were a land . . . there's this nostalgia for wonderful things that existed there, for authenticity, honesty, fraternity. I love those stories. Wailing brings me back to . . . When I go somewhere where there are wailers, they help me understand the feeling that I'm temporary in my world. That all the vanity around is just an external wrapper and we should take it off and relate to what's real.

Chapter 5 is the third and last in a succession of chapters that concern the integral components of the performance—words, melody, bodily motions and gestures, the wailer's dramatic skills, time and place, and the listeners' reactions. In this sense, it forms a chain with the "Giving Words" and "Performance Stage" chapters. Each of these ethnographic segments is abetted by the methodological and theoretical use of elements that are foreign to cultural performance. As I have shown, I derived the giving-words insight from the interview encounter, and the "Performance Stage" discussion reflects the modus operandi of the theater. In the "Melancholic Power" chapter, in contrast, my main metaphor is theoretical in a comparison-and-similarity sense. The craft of decoding the subjective and intersubjective experience that one undergoes at the sound of a wailer's voice was based not only on the respondents' reportage and my assimilation of the audience's experiences but also on an analogy between the house of mourning and what happens there as well as on vast domains of theory and meaning. For example, theoretical sources have associated wailing with psychotherapy in the field of mourning and bereavement and performance with love, temptation, and erotic messages. The sequence of topics presented in chapter 5 is indicative of the many levels of meaning in wailing, a circumstance that in itself forces the researcher to marshal the strength to analytically penetrate the recesses of this melancholic power. Chapter 5—here I note its main themes only—illuminates the transition that takes place from the reality of the emotional power of wailing to the curative propensity of tears and then to the liminal situation of a collective in exile. The characteristics of temptation and erotica in the wailing performance are discussed at the end of the chapter. In this transition, the information that the respondents provided directly loses some of its potency, and the need for theoretical imagination gathers strength. Although the structure of the ethnographic presentation that gives the respondents' reflectivity primacy over theoretical models stands out in chapter 5, it recurs in other chapters and reflects a theoretical approach that is well grounded in the field (Corbin and Strauss 1990).

Wailing, I found, is a form of mental mourning work. I inferred this from the respondents' examination of the contents of the lament and from the difference in the experience before and after participating in it. Neither the early psychotherapy literature (from the 1960s and 1970s) nor the later literature (the 1990s) even hints at this insight about the efficacy of wailing, although perceptions of healing in wailing cultures correspond strongly with dominant models that the professional literature developed in its early and later periods. Until recently, Western psychotherapy was too ethnocentric to see past its intellectual nose, let alone to understand the value of information that the picturesque cultures of people other than white upper-middle-class Anglo-Saxons could offer. Had it understood this, the debate over the validity and content of concepts and models of mourning cited in this chapter, such as catharsis, the hydraulic model, and the continuing bonds model, would have been immeasurably richer than it is.

To substantiate this claim, I should dwell briefly on the last-mentioned model and the theoretical criticism that it has drawn. In researchers' estimation, the model of mourning that originates in Freudian theory is based on a perception that emphasizes people's separateness from each other. In their opinion, the ideal of parting with the dead at the end of the stages of grief—shock, protest, despair, reorganization—should be considered solely the product of modern Western thinking, since it is unparalleled in other societies and eras (Stroebe et al. 1996). A model that lauds the act of relinquishing—letting go—indicates that it raises the values of independence, autonomy, and individuation to dominance, as against the states of dependency or interdependency that typify traditional societies. Modernity has cultivated an instrumental I-you relationship, which requires severance and distancing from the dead on the assumption that the very commitment to their memory overlooks the individual's needs and impairs his or her ability to reconnect with society. Today, the validity of these assumptions in an intercultural comparison and within an intracultural framework is doubted. Against this background, a model of grieving called "ongoing relationship" has been developed (Klass, Silverman, and Nickman 1996; Silverman and Nickman 1996) as an alternative anchored in interdisciplinary thinking. In its essence, this model encourages verbal and other forms of expression that signify nostalgia for the deceased, spiritual dialogue, and creative memorialization in daily life. The more I studied the logic of the ongoing relationship, the more convinced I became that its theoretical sophistication is entirely embodied in the cradle metaphor[5] and in the giving of words that wailers knew to offer their audience in an undeclared healing encounter. Obviously, if scholars of the human psyche made it their custom to cull information from the ethnographic inventory that anthropologists labored to produce, neither this model nor the one that constructs a continuing biography for the dead would have anything novel to say, let alone be presented as a revolution (Walter 1999)—both about mourning and about other fields of knowledge in which Western thinking has been dominant.

Chapter 5 also broaches an erotica hypothesis that is central in the melancholic power. The hypothesis consists of ideas such as the property of dualism in human behavior, the craving for a return to the womb, and a possible dichotomy of spiritual sexuality and actual spirituality. The hypothesis centers on the discussion of the wailer's and the listeners' psychological needs and proposes the existence an intersubjective process that is both profound and hidden from view. The basic argument is that the wailing performance for the dead does not revolve around loss and death only. As it stimulates weeping, the performance is an act of temptation that targets the audience and sends a set of allusions in its direction. The unconscious purpose of the performance is to uncouple the listeners from their sense of impotence and thrust them into a sense of sexuality and life. The far-reaching ethnographic account that is needed to substantiate this hypothesis is a reworked story about wailing as a solution invented by a collective consciousness in crisis to stand up to death. I supported the erotica hypothesis by conducting an ethnographic experiment, described in chapter 6, "Mission." Analyzing the findings of the group interview in the men's hookah circle, I found that the erotica hypothesis expands from the performer-audience context to the gender-group level. My argument is that the psychological and spatial segregation of men and women that is stringently maintained in death events has existential significance: it underlies a sense of sexual tension between men and women that alludes to future union and fertility as a solution, of equal weight, to the death crisis.

Two additional points in the "Melancholic Power" chapter are noteworthy. The chapter proposes a powerful indicator with which to draw the limits of cultural authenticity: the metaphor implicit in the wailing lyrics. The ethnography describes several aspects of metaphor as an instrument of emotional influence. Here, however, I wish to revisit the metaphor as something that creates a special intimacy.[6] Wailing abounds with metaphors that derive their meanings from the closeness to nature that had existed in Yemen, singular meanings of things in Arabic, and the exilic past that the Jews shared. These metaphors, with these origins, envelop those who invoke them from every direction with mutual understanding, isolating them from all others. Only quintessential members of the culture respond to them by shedding tears. Therefore, one should not trade in these metaphors or use them to set up a cultural exchange. Metaphors are much more than words; they carry immeasurably heavier symbolic baggage. It is hard to imagine how they could service an intercultural dialogue without surrendering their magic and meaning. Metaphors are like jargon, like an accent, like a folk saying, like a joke, like culture-bound physical gestures. They are the superstructure of cultural authenticity. People who do not respond to certain metaphors spontaneously and profoundly do not belong. The metaphor test leaves no room for limited partnership. Here then is another subtle implication of the decline of the wailing culture: not only relinquishing of the formal aesthetics that the metaphors represent but also, and rather, the loss of what the metaphors contribute at the level of consciousness to the sense of "us" and a unique way of understanding the world.

Chapter 5 also deals with the internal minutiae of solidarity at the time of death. The emotions of solidarity that the audience evinces when it hears the lament are presented as something based more on the childhood bond with mother than on any other social partnership. This argument, which I repeat in the "Mission" chapter, offers a possible feminine explanation of the sociological fact to which theoreticians, including Durkheim (1965) and Simmel (1950), resorted. Theoretical landmarks that lead to this claim originate in psychoanalytic theory and ideas from the field of existential philosophy; therefore, their explanatory power should not be seen as necessarily limited to contexts in which the female voice dominates. Women's wailing proves to be a medium for the radicalization of two emotional states—one negative and one positive—and amplifies the isolating sense of existential angst, a matter of much concern to theoreticians (Becker 1973; Rank 1958; Heidegger 1962). Conversely, women's wailing preannounces the profound solace that will prevail once the sense of social togetherness—the sense alluded to in what Freud (1961, 11–12) calls an "oceanic feeling"—is released. Thus, wailing concretizes extreme situations and invites those present to spend time in them and shift from one such situation to another. This property of wailing reveals in a unique way an emotional work by women that may create a situation that transcends the pattern of ordinary emotional life. Some people see in this a reason to justify pejorative images that have clung to wailing, such as associations of wailing with chaos, loss of control, and madness. This would seem, however, to be a rather simplistic understanding of wailing and its raisons d'être.

The ethnography sought to reveal the possibilities that the melancholic power offers for psychological structuring—that is, the claim that, yes, wailing has the ability to lead its listeners to a nadir where neither language and logic is present, but the listeners' contact with their existential angst with all defenses down serves as an essential superstructure for emotional healing and the formation of social cohesion. This, I believe, is what the respondents had in mind when they described the socioemotional impact of wailing: ex ante, wailing showed their lives to be a vanity of vanities; ex post, however, it made them think about what they had done and intended to do in their interpersonal relations. The performance culminates with the realization that women's emotionality is not chaotic, as at first might have seemed to be the case. Furthermore, wailing creates emotions in social and predictable ways. Urban's (1988) analysis of the covert social power of wailing and his distinction between effect and metaeffect is compatible with his description of the transformation that wailing creates.[7] I have shown that performance is a process that anchors the individual's subjective situation in a social reality. If this explanation of solidarity relations is serpentine and complex and if it challenges the tool kit of sociological language, this is only because a woman's wailing in a house of mourning is a voice that encrypts its intentions well. Schieffelin (1985) dwelled on this when he defined performance as a form that structures a situation and not symbols and gave greater emphasis to the drama in the concept than to the rational thought. A performance acquires objective social validity when it has participants who participate intensively, irrespective of any individual's opinion or the ethnographer's interpretation strategy.

Chapter 6, the final chapter, is titled "Mission." The wailers' mission is described in terms of the religious value of honoring the dead. Why does the connection between women and canon faith merit development only in an ethnographic collection? This manner of presentation reflects the notion that wailing is primarily a women's culture. The women in my study told me about themselves, their practice, the circle, their missions in life, and so on. Their ways as women were paramount among their concerns; they showed no inclination to mention or concern themselves with men. Thus, they invested the insularity of their circle with meaning, demonstrating the kind of gender authenticity that has only one more conspicuous example: the support circle for a birthing mother as had been set up in Yemen. Wailing has changed direction so much that even the men's weekly fraternal circle, devoted to smoking and hookahs, lavished attention on the women and their customs. In this circle, as I have shown, the men wished to reserve death rituals and eulogy for themselves but only by comparing these practices with wailing and the "excitable nature" of women. In my estimation, it should be possible by studying the Yemenite Jewish communities to trace the extent of autonomy in women's circles and the elements of which women organized it. Such research would also establish a basis for a gender point of view that does not fixate on protest, as in the dominant perspective in other ethnographies (Abu-Lughod 1986, 1990; Seremetakis 1990; Briggs 1993; Holst-Warhaft 1995). In accordance with the point of view proposed, which I have presented before, the expression "gender authenticity" represents feminine characteristics that propel women's social actions, states of mind unique to mothers and daughters that are embodied in ritual or other forms of organization. I adduce this from Sered (1994) and Chodorow (1974, 1978) among other examples. Women may perform the roles of their culture—even if not only for themselves—for the underlying purpose of reinforcing their gender solidarity. That their culture isolates women is important to them. This argument emanates from another feminist reading of women in the Muslim world (Rouse 1998) that allows one to differentiate between the practices of the two genders without necessarily inferring any deficiency in the women's culture. In my opinion, the wailing of Yemenite Jewish women falls into this cultural category. This is why the previous chapters first oriented the reader in the wailing culture per se, in its specific components, and only then described its spiritual meaning and religious standing relative to men's devotional labors.

Positioning the "Mission" chapter at the end also attests to a critical approach that aims for a different social order, albeit one that is limited to a text printed in a book. In the Introduction, I dealt with manifestations of disregard of women's wailing in the research literature and the special discrimination against this creative form relative to Yemenite Jewish song. The discrimination in the literature has hardly been described from a gender perspective, an entrenched perspective that seems to defeat attempts to bring wailing to general representation. To gauge the validity of my contention, I wish to study Ratzhabi (1988) about folk songs in Yemen, which have several characteristics in common with wailing:

> Of all types of song, the least known is the *qasid*. . . . While other types stand out for their national and religious complexion and the use of Hebrew as the preeminent language of creative endeavor, the *qasid* has different features. It is a refreshing secular folk song that has light, entertaining, and amusing themes. *It is produced in spoken Arabic and is meant mainly for women and the masses, who are insufficiently fluent in Hebrew. . . . Due to the general nature of the* qasid, *its folk* [register] *and its language, the copyists of the* diwans *tended to hold it in contempt and have not included it in the collections of song as they had the other types.* (Ratzhabi 1988, 30, my emphasis)

The literature review that I produced for this book casts doubt on the claim expressed by Ratzhabi at the beginning of his remarks. No Yemenite Jewish art form, I would say, competes with women's wailing for the least-representation prize. Therefore, a more appropriate way of putting it is that wailing is less known than any type of songs, including *qasid*. A blatant example of this is Binyamin-Gamliel's book *Ahavat Teiman* (1975), which omits wailing even though it documents and translates women's songs.[8] As I related, Binyamin-Gamliel said in an interview that "I didn't want to touch this field [of women's wailing] at all" because the words caused him such emotional pain that he could not deal with them professionally, as was his habit. In Binyamin-Gamliel, a person who focused his efforts on women's creative art and held it in appreciation, I found the opposite of contempt. The tears in his eyes demonstrated that wailing has melancholic power. However, neither the mention of this interview nor the devotions of a few researchers can dispel the impression of wailing as being inferior and generally something that the *diwan* copyists distinguished from works of value.

The sequence of themes in this ethnography corrects the injustice that has been done to a magnificent example of mourning work by women. This ethnography should be considered a feminist gesture of sorts that tries to explain manifestations of power relations—in the field, in the arena, and in text. This gesture does not hesitate to approach things differently and has no objection to the sorrow and tears that the study of this form of women's creative art elicits. Furthermore, the ethnography relates to sadness as one of the most fascinating forms of women's encounter with the world. By choosing to conclude the ethnography with a chapter on what is essentially a religious mission served devotedly by women, I expressed the way that I found to pay homage to their culture.

These are last respects not only in terms of the location of the chapter in this book but also in the conventional sense of honoring the dead. Women's wailing is the subject of imminent death, and the title of the Epilogue, "The Lament of the Printed Words," aims at it alone. In the "Mission" chapter, I compared women's wailing with men's eulogy but not in regard to the preservation or decline of each form. They should be compared in this sense, however, because death rituals among Yemenite Jews in Israel have retained their religious complexion (Deshen 1970; Rubin 1986; Levi, Levinson, and Katz 2002) and because some of the immigrants' children and grandchildren have been making a large-scale return to the faith that has proved to be a return to sources, if a rather selective one. The ethnographic information presented thus far, along with information gleaned from several subsequent interviews, may explain the tendency of most of my respondents to let go of women's wailing and the difficulty in reviving it. Women's lament is a storytelling lament that commands less religious validity than the prayer book lament, the eulogy. The contents of women's lament are perceived as more physical than spiritual, bemoaning a loss more than acquiescing in it. From a metaphorical perspective, as I have shown, the contents center more on the gloom of the tomb than on the transmigration of the soul. For members of the culture, the text does not represent religious devotion or spiritual probity of the highest order. The wailer's voice makes its impression by being geared predominantly to relations in the community as it represents the dead, the mourners, the consolers, and the wailer herself. Given its rather earthy symbolization, it is reasonable to expect wailing, and not eulogy, to become irrelevant and doomed to early death as its community of emotion disintegrates.

The Arabic vernacular of the lament also argues against its persistence. It is a foreign, "Gentile," exilic, and non-Jewish element that consigns it to inferiority relative to Hebrew, which, as the holy tongue, can sanctify the men's creative form and it alone. Consequently, when we contemplate texts that unite Diaspora Jews with those in Israel, we find that women's wailing reflects a salient cultural difference relative to eulogy. Women's laments in Israel are expressed in the languages of various countries of origin (Yemenite, Iraqi, Moroccan, Ethiopian, etc.); therefore, they sound very foreign vis-à-vis each other. Jewish men in every ethnic community, in contrast, deliver eulogies in Hebrew. The eulogies may be worded differently, but while differences in wording do signify each community's cultural distinctiveness, this is a relatively narrow cultural gap that the Hebrew language bridges. In view of the religious ideology of ingathering of the exiles, the difference between wording and language abets the preservation of eulogy and the extinction of wailing.

In addition to these content and linguistic differences between women's wailing and men's eulogy, eulogy is anchored in rabbinical writings that strictly regulate death rituals, making it a material part of the ritual process. Wailing, in contrast, is a performance, a level of custom that appears in a ritual void governed by rules that are neither specified in rabbinical law nor binding. Furthermore, wailing is transmitted orally from one generation of women to the next. Its performance, the only medium in which this intergenerational transmission takes place, is heavily context-dependent and sensitive to changing circumstances. Unlike eulogy, wailing is not set forth in a prayer book, a text accessible to all that appears in print and is always available, irrespective of the Zeitgeist and artistic expertise. The unanimity among Yemenite Jewish men and women about the metaphysical superiority of eulogy over wailing magnifies these differences. Unsurprisingly, Yemenite Jews of both genders believe that wailing cannot match eulogy in its effect on the eternal celestial fate of a person's soul. The conclusion to draw from all this is that wailing is assigned to the domain of tradition and eulogy is assigned to that of religious in an imbalance of forces. An allusion to these power relations is expressed in the statement that in a traditional society, religion dominates all aspects of life, whereas tradition is valid insofar as it conforms to religious principles (Katz 1984).

These arguments, however, do not suffice to explain the decline of the Yemenite Jewish wailing culture, let alone to doom it to absolute demise, an unusual fate among traditional rituals in Israel. The fact remains that the death rituals of Yemenite Jews in Israel have retained their religious complexion (Deshen 1970; Rubin 1986) and women's wailing, unlike the *hina* (wedding) rite and the singing and dancing of Yemenite Jewish origin, has not lent itself to syncretism in Israel. In other words, it has not been privileged with a synthesis of elements from different traditions, has not undergone adaptive transformation, and has not spawned traditional-modern variations (Sharaby 2002).

Thus far, I have offered a particularistic explanation for the decline of Yemenite Jewish women's wailing, one that should probably be extended to women's wailing among other ethnic groups in Israel. Its essence is that even if the laments were committed to writing, wailing would be rejected because it deviates from the faith and the community-in-exile reality that it represents. This reality has become irrelevant in the social life that has evolved in Israel and is even considered undesired. In the next section, I approach Yemenite Jewish women's wailing from a more inclusive standpoint that links it to other wailing cultures in the West. Many wailing cultures in Europe and America can be described as declining and vanishing (Holst-Warhaft 1995). None of them has really avoided this fate, and many of them can be studied only in the literature. If so, might the reason for the cultural decline be sought somewhere else?

Research on patterns of change in Western mourning rituals since the mid-twentieth century (Wouters 2002) attest to the establishment of a regime of silence (Bauman 1992; Aries 1981; Gorer 1976), the personalization of death rituals (Walter 1994; Wouters 2002), and generally stronger appreciation of emotional authenticity and understanding of inner feelings (Bellah 1985; Lofland 1985). The regime-of-silence paradigm reflects values of emotional restraint as well as a tendency to deny and suppress the fact of the death. This paradigm is gradually giving way to individualized rituals of separation, funeral, and burial that reflect the "emancipation of emotions," as Wouters (2002, 6) puts it, and the percolation of different values: spontaneity, informality, and sincerity.

The definitions of the ends and means of the wailing performance reinforce its stereotypical perception. On the ends side, the performance is regarded as a way to elicit a collective demonstration of emotions. The means side includes rules of expression that dictate the time, place, and intensity of the emotions elicited (Holst-Warhaft 1995). Wouters (2002) believes that the more strongly people in Western societies demand the expression of personal identity and individual sincerity in innovative death rituals, the more they experience traditional death rituals as rigid, inauthentic, and governed by rules of emotion that encourage fraud and falsehood.

A salient example of this is the changing status of village women's wailing in modern Greek society. Young Greek women mock the exaggerated mourning of the traditional elderly women and describe it as *theatrinismous,* or play-acting. The emphatic rejection of the traditional wailing practice by modern women is also explained in their perception of wailing as an embarrassing and anachronistic expression of superstition, backwardness, and ignorance (Sarris 1995; Danforth 1982; Caraveli 1986). Contemplating this, my questions are: Does Yemenite Jewish wailing share similar social characteristics or attributions with women's wailing elsewhere that place it on the same plane with them? If so, what are the characteristics or attributions that seal its fate or, at least, relegate its presence to the bookshelf? To answer these questions, we need to acquaint ourselves with another group of consolers in the crowd that surrounds the wailer, one that I have not introduced thus far.

The Wailer's Sincerity and the Authenticity of Her Weeping

The ethnographic story, chapter by diverse chapter, was told almost in its entirety by veteran members of the wailing culture. These respondents, known in Israel as Yemenite immigrants, are steeped in the tradition, and many of them regret its decline. The study encountered them in their adulthood and old age. For the sake of the discussion that follows, I will define them as members of a culture who belong to the first circle that surrounds the wailer as she performs. It is an intimate circle in its attitudes, an inward-facing one, and possibly an exclusive group because only from it could I extract the codes and manifestations of the culture and obtain a picture of its past. Their children and grandchildren also participate in the death rituals; some of them can describe a performance, cite an acquaintance with this or that wailer, and mention their experiences. However, they cannot be lumped with their parents and grandparents in one circle. They are a younger Israel-born crowd, and the metaphor that best captures the extent of their cultural familiarity and value orientation is "second circle." The second circle surrounds the first circle by coming into less contact with manifestations of the wailing culture than cultural patterns that are considered extraneous to it. It sits between tradition and a modern Israeli way of life, wavering between contrasting values. So, at least, it seems at first. The elderly consolers recognize, and may have internalized somewhat, values different from those of their culture. The young, however, define themselves by these values and contemplate the world through them. Some members of the second circle feel as though having stumbled, for no personal benefit, into death events where women happen to be wailing. Some gaze at the wailer, reflect on her appearance, wipe away a tear, and shake their heads. Despite the tears, this audience is of two minds about and is critical of the traditional wailing pattern.

Thus far I have focused on the collective meaning of the word "authenticity." From here on, it is worth dealing with the word as a modern ideal attributed to the individual. The main target of criticism among those in the second circle is the value of self-authenticity. Let me pause briefly. An easy way to characterize the authenticity ideal is via a metaphor from archaeology: the authentic self lies under layers of pliable external selfness that conforms with social norms. The nuclear self is considered deep, true, subjective, original, and spiritual. Some construe it as a highly refined version of the id following the stratified Freudian model or as an archaic product of repression as in Jung's psychology of depths (Guignon 2004). In whatever garb, it is perceived as sublimely private, asocial, encrypted, precious, and transcendent relative to many standards of cultural performance. Our society protects the authentic self by granting the right to autonomy and nurtures it by encouraging mental exercises such as introspection, reflection, and meditation. Taylor (1995) captures the gist of this attitude. His description, drawing on the philosophical approach of thinkers such as Kierkegaard,

Rousseau, Mill, and Nietzsche, notes the ideal of authenticity and links it to the notion of human dignity. It is powerful moral idea, Taylor says, that is included in our heritage. It lends moral importance to an individual's relation with himself or herself, with one's natural innerness. It is endangered in part by pressure on the individual not to deviate from the collective and also in part by the individual's tendency to perceive him or herself instrumentally, which menaces a person's ability to heed his or her inner voice. Being true to oneself, Taylor continues, means being true to one's originality, that is, to something that only the individual can discover and put into words. By putting it into words, one also defines oneself and fulfills a potential that is altogether one's own.

To put oneself into words, one must know the manifestations of one's uniqueness as a person distinct from others, of the language that divides the inner from the outer, the individual from society, the public from the private, artifice from nature, falsehood from truth, and so on, such as the inventions that modern binary thinking introduced to keep the world in order.

I return to the wailer's listeners, foremost those in the second circle, whose gestures showed me something of the spirit that I had previously cited from the literature. These listeners' attitude toward the wailing performance splits into four objections concerning the place of wailing in the Israeli reality. This attitude, as I will show, judges the logic and status of the traditional practice by the standards of lifestyles and values associated with individual control and emotional expression. Befitting a discussion that makes room for attention to Western influence, I think it apt to use the lyrics of the well-known song "No Woman, No Cry" to distinguish among the respondents' objections and to invest them with meaning. "No Woman, No Cry" is a reggae piece by Bob Marley and the Wailers, first performed in 1974, widely known in 1975, and performed many times since then. The four famous words are appropriate for a discussion about wailing due to the focus of wailing on *women* and *crying*, the lyric tenor of the lament and the entire song, and the way others invested the words with new meanings and interpretations by punctuating them as they wish. The title "No Woman, No Cry" expresses pathos in the culture of Jamaica, Marley's place of birth; it means "No, woman, don't cry." The words, however, are often construed otherwise, such as "If there are no women, there won't be crying" or "Don't cry if you haven't got a woman."[9] The categorization I present below is based on the possible meanings of the word "no" (no, don't, aren't, none) and reflect the tendency to free interpretation of the riddle posed by those four so-contiguous words.

"NO WOMAN, NO CRY": NEGATION OF EMOTIONALITY

"No woman, no cry." If women do not bring their tears to a given social situation, obviously there will be no crying. Some participants in the first circle, women and men alike, subscribe to this belief, that is, that a woman can produce tears at will and stimulate weeping in others. The men in this circle, who define the tears as "belonging" to the wailers, described this adroitly. For these respondents, however, the meaning of "no woman, no cry" is not limited to an ostensible gender dependency of the weeping on the wailer; it also announces a stance that rejects the melancholy per se and regrets that it came up at all. The remarks of some elderly women respondents implied the same by appreciating the wailer and her wailing but delegitimizing the sadness. "Wailing is upsetting; it spreads depression," Chana said, speaking for others as well. "I think," Meir said, "she creates a depressive, sad situation just so. It's unnecessary." Ora expressed a preference for the joy of her life over the continued existence of wailing in her culture. I asked her, "Would you encourage your granddaughters to learn how to wail?" "No," she replied. I countered, "Why not?" She replied, "Because it's sad." I continued, puzzled, "Don't you want wailing to pass on to the next generation?" "No," she stated vehemently. "I don't want it to pass on in my family. If another family is willing, be my guest." I persisted, "Why not your family?" "Look," she said, "I don't like sad at home. I like happy at home. I go to sleep with a 100-watt lamp on. I like happy. I'm a happy person by nature."

Even one expert wailer spoke in favor of eradicating the "sad." One day, she related, she wailed for her son while doing housework. As she performed, her daughter turned on a recording device to produce a record for posterity, that is, to preserve the sadness. Discovering this, the wailer objected at once. "I turned around and told her, 'I'm erasing it! I don't want to leave these songs behind for you. Isn't it painful enough that you need to be reminded of it?!" Other wailers, however, described the aversion to melancholy not as theirs but as the response of second-circle offspring who tried to gag them. Rumia related that "My daughter didn't want me to go places to cry in homes. She says it's depressing, it's depressing. It isn't depressing, she's wrong." "You sing and it rattles people's hearts," I said, trying to re-create her daughter's argument. "All right, but it isn't depressing, just for someone whose heart is weak. If he's weak, so it hurts his heart. But anyone else who's in pain, it's okay for him, it's better that he unburden himself, that he shed tears and not collect them inside." I asked Haviva, "How does your son relate to your wailing?" "Oh," she replied, "he gets angry. When he comes home and doesn't see me there, he says, 'I bet someone died in town. [That's why] Mother isn't at home.' No, he doesn't meddle with my life. He just says, 'Mother, I'm afraid for you. I don't want you to get upset [due to the wailing] and come home so sad.' I told him, 'It's the other way around, Abba' [a nickname for her son].' And that's right. Look, when you're sad or if someone hurts you, crying lets it out. You don't let it grind inside you all the time."

These remarks show that the wailers are expected to silence themselves, to desist from their wailing. After all, sadness is undesirable; the cathartic value of crying does not matter. In recent times, members of both circles of listeners evince the wish to move on, to visit mourners' homes without disengaging from the ordinary flow of life, to deny the fact of the death and the anguish of the loss as it taps elegantly on the shutters of the conscious mind. After all, "It can't be helped no matter what," they recite. "Life must go on." The wailer is ordered to keep her mouth shut. "Don't give a speech," as one of the young women put it, about the loss and the sorrow. Her silence is the only way of insuring those in attendance against her emotions. Bauman (1992, 1) terms this typically modern defense strategy a "conspiracy of silence"—a state of expressive impotence, the absence of an emotional event that signifies the listeners' contact with their pain and the extrication of their grief from its loneliness (Aries 1974, 1981; Gorer 1965b). This emotional wariness, typical of both circles of the wailer's audience,

The empty chair: The death of the Yemenite Jewish wailing culture.

plays a role in the symbolic dilution of death rituals (Jung 1959). It is one of the quiet manifestations of the "pornography of death" in Western societies (Gorer 1976).

"NO WOMAN, NO CRY": NEGATION OF EXTERNAL CONTROL OF EMOTIONS AND THEIR PUBLIC EXPRESSION

"No, woman, no cry." Approaching a woman in this manner applies the negation of weeping with redoubled intensity. The wailer is asked demonstratively to stop crying—"demonstratively" because her wailing threatens the individual's sense of autonomy. Wailing's lachrymose outcomes are perceived as being several levels graver than those described from the point of view presented above, and it is these that explain the behavior of a young man in a mourners' tent who silenced a wailer by grumbling, "Enough, enough, don't wail any more. You're making us faint; he [the mourner] might die." Only first-circle participants admire the power of the voice to mold them into a collective in exile; only they reflect in amazement on the emotional potency of the lament. True, they describe the lyrics as "shocking" and the wailer as "doing this terrible, heartrending thing" and "putting sadness into the bones." Were it not so, however, they would judge the performance negatively. They admit that wailing infects its listeners with melancholy and briefly imprisons them in collective weeping, but this is the crux of its role. This is how it allows each and every one of them to perform the mitzvah of honoring the dead. Second-circle participants have a totally different attitude, even if they also have the imperative of honoring the dead in mind. What they want is to settle for honoring the dead in ways that are practiced in any case, without the wailer's mediation. "I honor the dead by going to the funeral. I honor him until the burial," Simone said. "How do you honor the dead? I'll tell you how," said Galit. "By going to the funeral, during the shivah, when people come and give consolation and sit and talk about him. And telling stories about him and giving the weekly portion and all sorts of sermons by rabbis."

These women belong to the second circle, those who are scandalized by the sound of the wailing and the sight of the wailer's movements. Their remarks attest to a stereotyped attitude that saddles Yemenite Jewish wailing with a burden of qualities that it does not have, making it seem like an altogether exaggerated and warped form of expression. Their ethnocentric view of their heritage transforms wailing into "madness," "an outburst," "hysteria," and an "irrational," "vulgar" act, a perverted "mentality" that Jews had received from the Muslims. The wailer in her performance is described as forgetting herself and thereby endangering her social image. "It might get to such a level that people can make fun of that woman, make fun," Tali said with the strength of inner conviction. From this standpoint, the listeners are quite right to respond to her performance with ridicule and cynicism because they show adequately that the wailer cannot break through the listeners' protective shield and that the listeners can disarm her. I inferred this from the respondents' remarks. This situation, however, is not common. Those in the second circle described wailing as an assault on their emotions, an ulterior design on the wailer's part. Ultimately, the audience "pulsates," is "swept away," and "erupts" in emotion and bitter weeping. The perception is that the wailer embarrasses, challenges, and thereby dishonors those in attendance on behalf of the duty of honoring the dead. Those in the second circle, much like the first-circle listeners, consider wailing an instrument that undermines control and shatters emotional barriers. The second-circle audience, however, accuses the wailer of having taken the floor on her own authority and wishes to condemn what it experiences as emotional colonialism (Fiumara 1995). In the eyes of these listeners, the wailer defiles the inherent sanctity of the sense of "self-sovereignty" (Dunne 1996). The aspiration to self-autonomy—a value that has become entrenched in modern life—inspires Ronit's resistance to wailing: "I wouldn't want to run into a wailer. I think it would really embarrass me. I'd feel that maybe my crying didn't come from somewhere natural; it's not from the real inner place of my personal sadness."

The second-circle participants illustrated the existence of a hierarchy that clashes with the one that we are accustomed to contemplating in the modern order, one in which the private domain prevails over the public domain (Guignon 2004). The ideal of authenticity prompts us to view the individual's natural inner emotion as pure, true, spontaneous, uncalculated, and beautiful—a cherished subjective essence that should be protected from outside interference (Bellah 1985; Riesman, Glazer, and Denney 1950). Such a self-autonomy seems possible or at least easily attainable, but only in the private domain. All the more is this the case when one is confronted by the aggressive emotional intervention of wailing, which, in the respondents' opinion, justifies gagging the wailer or at least denying her the public weeping that she desires. Attempting to fathom the origin of the attitude that rules out public weeping in mourners' homes, I asked Sigalit, "Why do you think this weeping isn't nice? Why isn't it legitimate? Look, everyone's mourning; they're not doing it outdoors or in the street." "It's because the pain is personal," she replied. "I don't have to show everyone what I'm feeling. When my father died I cried by myself, not in front of everyone." I asked Simone, "What's wrong about the things the wailer does to make people cry in the house of mourning?" Her answer alluded to values of individualism, autonomy, and privacy that had solidified in the consciousness and took up a self-evident place: "The wailer draws out the emotions in a terrible way. You don't need a wailer to cry. What do I need a wailer for?!"

For those in the first circle, the public nature of the weeping signifies something else. Elderly women in this circle perceive the separation of the personal and the public domains in a different way, a way that took shape in their community of emotion over many years. I cite it here to build a bridge between the two circles' attitudes and to argue that had the young respondents been familiar with the wailing culture, they would not have taken vehement exception to it. Miriam expressed the essence of this point: "*La'azi* [Arabic for 'wailing'] and talking about the pain is okay at the moment of the death. Not at some other time. It's [okay] at the [right] time. It's okay. No one's going to say 'What, she's gone mad!' when she *ma'aziye* [Arabic for 'wails'] at that time. She's in pain." I asked, "And what if a woman cries on an ordinary day?" "That's just wrong," Miriam replied. "You can tell her, 'You're crying now, you shouldn't, don't hurt your eyes.' They try to soothe her, but when someone dies they say, 'Let her cry, let her vent.'" This perception corresponds to research findings showing how emotions repressed in certain discursive contexts may be celebrated in others (Abu-Lughod 1986; Brenneis 1990). In my findings among Yemenite Jewish immigrants in Israel, individuals do not consider a houseful of relatives their private domain and do not regard a house of mourning as a public place like any other. Such was the case at least at a time when privacy was not celebrated as it is today, before mansions were separated by towering stone walls and when fences were lower than the height of a child.

In Yemen, privacy in daily life was not identified with the physical space of the home. One who sought it isolated him or herself away from home and far from others' company. Elderly women told me that they are reluctant to weep in the presence of children and husbands; they do so only when these kin are away. Their custom in Yemen was to cry in hiding, up in the hills, alone, while drawing water, chopping wood, or taking a walk. At other times, they imposed maximal self-restraint on themselves, striving to satisfy norms of respect that governed relations between spouses and between a mother and her children. Under these circumstances, they view the house of mourning as a special place sublimely suited to the shedding of tears.

Naomi asked rhetorically about woman and wailer "Where should she let go?" and then answered "Only in a place like [a house of mourning]." "She [one of the wailers] once came to the synagogue in the month of Elul," Banya recounted about an acquaintance. "Her children were abroad, and this weeping overcame her and she wailed this lament in the synagogue. I told her, 'That's not how it should be, it's not nice for you to do, it's not nice to do in the synagogue.'" For these women, a house of mourning is a legitimate place to cry, an opportunity for emotional release in terms of time and place. The validity of this approach to the proper time and place for emotions is strengthened by the attribution to wailing of magical properties and the danger that a lament may inflict if it oversteps its intended context. The belief, as I showed, is that deviant wailing of this kind can cause grave harm indeed. This conviction is held so strongly that it leaves no room for the emotion of shame or for doubt about whether it is or is not proper to cry in others' presence. In my estimation, however, the concept of the house of mourning as a collective opportunity for emotional expression does not totally clash with the emotional values that our society cultivates. Weeping in public cannot serve as evidence that a first-circle audience has no grasp of the separation of public and private domains or that it rejects self-autonomy as a value to be fulfilled. Paradoxically, the reality of collective life in a community of emotion emphasizes the sovereignty of the self in the very fact of the active and continual search for an isolated, out-of-eyeshot place. It also requires long-term emotional control during the interval between two death events. An example that supports the importance of the emotional boundaries of the self in traditional society is the concept of *obonona* among the Waraos in Venezuela:

> One mode of perceiving emotions locates them in the obonona, a locus of personal identity cognition and affect. Warao feel that this phenomenon (obonona) affords a strong sense of self and a means of earning respect. However, when powerful emotions come to dominate one's obonono, disrupting personal relations and giving rise to sudden, uncontrolled outbursts, these internalized emotions are viewed as a dangerous threat to the individual and her or his community. (Briggs 1992, 348)

Notwithstanding the attitude of the second circle, it deserves emphasis that the wailing performance per se entails self-control if not second-order control, an immeasurably more complex and strenuous level of control than the options of remaining silent, denying the fact of the loss, and refraining from wailing. This control is implicit in the sequence of the performance and the interaction between wailer and audience.[10] The very fact of it challenges the cultural evolution theory that asserts, according to Elias (1978), that the evolution of a culture reaches its peak in the form of modern individuals endowed with a system of inner control and self-restraint that aims to conceal physical and emotional acts from public view. In terms of the intensity of self-expression, uncontrolled hysterical weeping is considered contemptible. In the Yemenite Jewish wailing situation, as in other cultures, wailers view their craft not only as a vehicle of catharsis but also as a way to channel emotions away from the loss of composure or the insanity that the encounter with death may create (Danforth 1982; Holst-Warhaft 1995). The very commitment to a text (the lament) is itself a restraining factor because it induces the shift "from tears to ideas" (Holst-Warhaft 1995, 22); after all, the enunciation of words and the surrender to tears are mutually exclusive.

In its essence, wailing represents two coexisting opposites: self-restraint and encouraging emotional release in the form of weeping. An important reason for this, in my judgment, is the sense of religious mission that accompanies the wailing performance. The wailers, who also serve as inspectors of each other's performance, associate their role with the God-given imperative of honoring the dead. To carry out this socioreligious mission, the text to be wailed must be clear and flowing, something that cannot be enunciated in a state of emotional turmoil. Furthermore, the Yemenite Jewish wailer is supposed to appear aristocratic.

The aesthetic element of the Yemenite Jewish wailers' performance was appreciated by the male respondents and some of the wailers. This appreciation was reflected in familiarity with other forms of performance among Israel's Jewish ethnic communities. Although the basis for the acquaintance—encounter and involvement or stereotype—cannot be determined, their derogatory comparisons indicate that they consider a worthy performance one that is measured and restrained. Netanel said, "With other ethnic groups here [in Israel], it's just screaming [mentions a wailer from another ethnic group] and you don't know what she's saying. With us, there were words, there were words—there was rich content." Badra noted the components of movement and posture. "When someone [from another ethnic group] dies," she said, "they lacerate themselves, kill themselves, go out of their minds." I asked her, "What's your opinion about that?" "It creates madness," she ruled. "But not the Yemenites. They wail and it hurts them, but they don't go mad." An expert wailer recounted a group wailing performance that she had witnessed. "If you see [members of another ethnic community], you'll laugh yourself to death," she began, smiling. "They sit, twenty of them, in a circle on the floor, with the grieving family in the middle. The wailer came in on the side, and I laughed. Even if you want to cry, you'll laugh. They sit and yelp boo-hoo-hoo like animals. I saw them and got out of there." If so, the Yemenite Jewish wailing performance is perceived as different from the accepted practice in other wailing cultures, not only those that allow savage and immodest behaviors such as revealing breasts, pulling hair, drinking blood, and voicing sexual messages (Bourke 1993) but also those that usher participants into states of trance that frighten those present (Aborampah 1999) and even cultures that encourage wailing women to shout and cry out (Seremetakis 1990).

And what about the behavior that is expected of the listeners? The lament lyrics, which express profound empathy with the sense of loss, present the listeners with a challenge that, as stated, they resolve by being silent (Bauman 1992; Gorer 1976). The words force the bereaved and their relatives to gaze directly into an emptiness that will steadily overtake them as time ticks by. The words speak graphically of the condition of the corpse, snared in nature's cruel grip. As I have shown, wailing aims at an existential melancholy and helplessness that a death event amplifies immeasurably. Its words focus on the individual death, the fate of a person who had a name and exhibited singular characteristics. By doing this, wailing forces those who have gathered to reflect on why they have done so, draws the fate of a familiar person who has died closer to that of the living, and stirs self-pity and fear. The gist of it, however, is that the consolers and the mourners are expected to heed the words and emote without disturbing the wailer with

The empty chair: The death of the Yemenite Jewish wailing culture.

vocal weeping. The interaction resembles that between a caregiver and a patient or between an audience and an actor in which everyone is expected to obey an authority who knows what to say and bases its power on expertise (Giddens 1991). In this analysis, which touches on privacy, self-restraint, and respect of expertise, a bridge needs to be built for those in the first circle between the reality of traditional immigrants and that of their modern offspring—a bridge that may disconnect modernity from the dimension of time and contemplate it as a symbol of worthy values at different times and in different societies.

"NO WOMAN, NO CRY": NEGATION OF EMOTIONAL ACTING

"No, woman no cry." The wailer, whose performance embodies the emotional dualism that is inherent in every woman, does not really cry. It is a pretense; it isn't real. A first-circle listener elevated this approach to the status of a folk belief by uttering an Arabic saying to the effect that a woman's weeping is totally unimportant; even if she cries, it is like an act. A man needn't be moved by it. It's axiomatic: "For a man, a woman's crying is a game; he knows this game from his daily life because he's been a tyrant. He knows woman's crying before and after, in all kinds of situations; when she gives birth, he isn't sensitive to this crying at all." These mordant remarks, however, were countered by opposite remarks that found their way into the field journal. I asked Leah, "What you think about the declining numbers of wailing women? What you feel about it?" She said, "My feeling is that the whole real generation has gone." I asked, "Really?" "Yes," she replied, "the elders' generation." "Why do you call that generation 'real'?" "Because they loved the real words, they told the truth, they didn't fake it. They were innocuous people. You get it? Innocuous. When they said a word, it was a real word." When I asked whether she included the wailing woman in this assessment, she said, "Yes, the wailer, too. She didn't wail for 'Listen to me, look at me.' She wailed because the pain of the [grieving] parents hurt her." The contrasting approaches to the truthfulness of the performance fall nicely into two of the four categories that I presented in chapter 4, "Performance Stage," that include the extent to which the wailer's narrative relates to herself or to the deceased and the extent to which wailing uses standard or original expressions. Interestingly, despite the implicit protest against the first of these stances and even though only members of the first circle provided information about the wailer's complex play-acting strategies, this circle's criticism does not match the ferocity of that expressed by members of the second circle. The criticism I heard from the second circle attained the level of genuine wariness, the setting of an ambush, as it were, to halt any effort a wailer might make to pose in mourning for the deceased. The young express this criticism without being aware of the constraints of the performance, its limits, and its important role in creating the mourning community. They are also oblivious to the counterweight function of the wailer's socioreligious mission, a worthy justification for the need to play-act.

The lengthiness of the interview situation prompted some members of the second circle to reflect on the details of the performance. It was then that these respondents replaced their general judgments, mentioned above, with references to the wailer's acting or faking. By speaking this way, they revealed their opinion of what a worthy performance should involve. "I know the wailer's tears aren't real," Shlomi stated. "Until I was sixteen, I was sure that those old women were really crying, that they were really torn in pain about someone's having died, but later I realized that it isn't real. Once at a soldier's funeral, I saw a wailing woman who cried and swept people into it, and they all cried. Suddenly she lifted the kerchief from her eyes, stood up, and walked around, and she didn't have any tears at all. She ate something, drank something, and began to laugh with her friends. I asked myself, 'Oh my God, what is this?!' I was floored." Amir expressed himself similarly: "Right [after the wailing performance], she shouldn't make a quick transition. Also, she should get up and go home after wailing." Thus, in the respondents' opinion, to create the impression of a sincere performance, the wailer must make a moderate transition from her special emotional state and ordinary life.

The wailer's credibility among members of the second circle, I found, depends on how much they know about her intimacy with the deceased or her personal anguish. These respondents lack the diffuse kind of information that always seeps through a small community of emotion. "When I see a wailer, I always look for the family connection," Dikla said, explaining that "It's inconceivable to see a total stranger wailing for someone he doesn't know." Tsahi added, "If I know the wailer or if I'm aware of her pain, [the wailing] hurts. You know her and her life and what she went through; you cry. It's real, it's not an act. My pain connects with the wailer's pain. It all comes together. It depends on who the wailer is. If she has no residues of her own, nothing that happened to her, if you don't know what she has in mind, if it's a show or what, it doesn't affect you like a woman who's hurting." The purpose of both kinds of information—the wailer's closeness to the deceased and the circumstances of her life—is to assure the audience that the wailer is sad. Her sincerity is described as one aspect of a worthy performance that aims to kindle emotional empathy in people. Tsahi demonstrated this: "The most important characteristic is that the wailer should be real. Otherwise, there's nothing." If so, the listeners tell the wailer something else: No, woman, no—cry! Shelve the act that you know how to play and wail for real.

The respondents admitted that they could not always gauge the wailer's sincerity up front. Here they demonstrated how highly they value total identification with the contents of the lament. Ruhama said, "It hurts when I know it's a little artificial. I don't know if it's artificial, but if there's no strong connection between the dead person and the wailer, it hurts; [a sense of disbelief] crops up here and there. Even so, wailing does have an effect." Amir related that "If I know the wailer's for real, it creates a totally different empathy inside me, totally real." He described a wailer who delivers the same performance in different houses of mourning: "She does something, but it's not on the same scale as if she knows [the deceased]." Sincerity is so strongly valued that some respondents made it a categorical imperative. It should be a constant, an indicator of a way of life, they said: the wailer should be a "woman of melancholy" or, alternatively, "righteous in her ways." "Sadness should accompany her all her life, in her daily conduct," Shlomi advised. "She should be withdrawn; she should represent sadness. She should be better in terms of her ways, too. Quieter. It's a role she's got to play. She mustn't joke around—a wailer should always be stern."

Despite these attitudes, the respondents claimed paradoxically that wailing, in its ability to evoke empathy, is like a stage performance or a movie. Wailing, some of them said, "is like watching a film"; it "helps me connect with my pain." This comparison of wailing to other types of performances does not square with the respondents' demand for performative sincerity on the wailer's part only, that is, their singling her out from actors in other kinds of performances. One of the respondents expressed this: "Her crying has to be real. It shouldn't define her as a wailer in quotation marks." When I brought this problem to the respondents' attention, their reactions showed me that their comparison of wailing with the rules of the theater is far from total; all they mean by it is to demonstrate the declared purpose of the performance: emotional persuasion. Here is how Daniel explained it:

> [Wailing] is like someone who wants to be an actor and is asked to show what he knows. He starts to act. Right away they can tell whether he's doing it from the heart or to impress the audience. If he wants to make an impression, he'll look at them and grin and it'll be fake. But [the wailers] do it not to be looked at but to be listened to. In fact, they put their heads down and they can't see if they're being looked at. Even if people aren't crying, they'll continue until the wailing is over.

The wailer can achieve emotional persuasion, make herself "listened to," in two ways—by displaying *sincere devotion* to the performance or by putting on *a convincing display of sincerity*. Do second-circle respondents assess the wailer as merely an actress who is adept at expressing emotions? Evidently not. As stated, they limit the similarity between wailing and acting to the goal of arousing empathy; they expect much more sincerity from a wailer than they do of a stage actor. Daniel's explanation above, which distinguishes wailers from other stage actors by likening wailers to actors in an audition, indicates as much. The wailer submits to the stringent, tense, and unforgiving tests of the second-circle audience. She is perpetually on audition because, as I have shown, the audience wishes to challenge the boundaries of her affective world, to know where she has come from (i.e., if she has anguish of her own), and to know where she is heading (how strongly her words are directed at the deceased).

It is this foundation of beliefs, patterns, and rules in the wailing culture that gave the wailer an important role to play in the situational performance arena for so long. On long-term reckoning, however, her advantage does not seem to endure. It dissipates as the generations and eras succeed each other, as the first circle contracts and the second circle expands. The difference between the circles originates in a cultural gap of which one aspect is the young respondents' deficiencies in knowledge and symbolic experience. They are distinct from the elder members of the wailing culture in that they do not know the wailer, do not acknowledge wailing as an expertise, are oblivious to its dramatic assets, and treat it with neither appreciation nor importance. Their main concern is given to their innerness (Goffman 1959); they do not wish to be defrauded. Their attitude is poor in information and depth; they strip the wailing appearance of its linguistic, vocal, and physical characteristics. By doing this, they hint at their cultural foreignness. Since few members of this circle have any command of Yemenite Arabic, they cannot use a wailing performance to judge the wailer's acquaintance with the deceased and the correspondence of her words to his or her persona. Their oft-repeated remark "I don't understand what the wailer says" demonstrates their unfamiliarity with the linguistic metaphors that the wailer has implanted in the lament and, accordingly, their deafness to the emotional grammar that is coded into them. This is also true of the vocal and motional characteristics of the performance, even though these are not necessarily specific to the Yemenite Jewish culture. When the wailer raises her voice in "weeping" and contorts her body, everyone in the house of mourning senses sadness. However, those in the second circle do not grasp the full complexity of the crystalline symbolism of these elements, which therefore have less of an effect on them than on first-circle participants.

The interjection "*Allah yustur*" ("God protect") repeatedly uttered by wailers during the interview and their refusal to wail in this context demonstrate that the act comes with an ab initio charge of magical attributions of danger and misfortune if performed away from the house of mourning. The young listeners are unacquainted with the taboo that the culture imposes on the vocalized weeping and physical gestures of the wailing woman in daily life; consequently, they cannot gauge the devotion that the performance entails. Those in the second circle are also oblivious to, or at least do not fully understand, the cultural meanings that surround the performance. It was not from them, for example, that I learned about the great extent to which the female performance deviates from the Yemenite Jewish rules of modesty, about the overarching importance that the wailers attach to their religious mission, and a fortiori about how these two outlooks are reconciled. If so, the meaning of the cultural gap between the circles is that the wailer's acting in front of the young audience is anchored in nothing, almost an act for acting's sake. Accordingly, it cannot be translated into an attitude of trust toward her.

Another aspect of cultural gap relates to the ethic of our era and the value conflict that it embodies, both of which related to the expectations of participants in rituals in Western societies. In accordance with one of the sociological narratives that I mentioned above, the ethic at issue is one of self-segregation and self-isolation in view of multiple choices among possible identities and the commercialization of metaphors, lifestyles, services, and experiences (Boorstin 1987). Our social world is managed by metaphors and images in a wide variety of fields, something that forces most people, most of the time, to package, market, and manage themselves efficiently (Hochschild 1983; Jackall 1988). This reality raises no few problems, because the packaging relates not only to the individual's appearance but also to more integral parts of the self such as attitudes, morals, and emotions. Some scholars believe that this background can be cited to explain the interest that has arisen in recent decades in questions pertaining to the truthfulness of things. The consciousness and multifacetedness of today's commercialization of the self generates continual suspicion of what it is masking and of false images. Consequently, the current ethic itself gives rise to a craving for sincerity and authenticity (Erickson 1995). We should, I believe, expect to see an upsurge of manifestations of this craving in crisis and death arenas due to the stress, or the value conflict, that is inherent in them (Mead 1964; Goffman 1963). The perception that such things exist at an occasion that rules out any form of play-acting clashes with the appearance of individuals in the packaging of role players. A quintessential role player in this sense, of course, is the wailer.

The case of the Yemenite Jewish wailing culture demonstrates an essential link between sincerity and authenticity. To assess this matter, I return to the insistent demand for sincerity that second-circle listeners express. This audience immediately and painstakingly assesses the wailer's *sincerity* and, in accordance with it, the *authenticity* of the weeping that the performer elicits from the audience in each and every case. As stated, wailing suspected of diminished sincerity does not play on the same emotional scale, that is, it "doesn't affect you like a woman who's hurting." By implication, while the first circle emphasizes the importance of the collective effect of the performance and describes it in the plural, those in the second circle respond to a performance in accordance with their requirement of authenticity on the part of a separate, individual self. This audience's commitment to the ideal of authenticity sheds light not only on a possible reason for the relinquishing of wailing as a ritual practice but also on the existence of different levels of conscious identification with the performance and its affective implications. This differentiation may contribute to the theoretical discussion in the field of the anthropology of emotions; it signals the need to bridge between the inner experience and its outer manifestations, proposes conditions for the experiential realization of this bridge, and suggests that one of these conditions ultimately is the intersubjective dependency of the individual (in one's role as the member of an audience) and his or her counterpart (as a performer).

"NO WOMAN, NO CRY": NEGATION OF EMOTIONAL ALIENATION

"No woman, no cry." If there's a woman, there will be crying. Crying is good and may be experienced through the medium of a woman. In this fourth construction we revert to the punctuation that we used in the first one, except that here the wailer's weeping takes on a positive value. The reflective process that the interview allowed prompted some second-circle participants to reassess the importance of wailing in social life. In their attitudes, they portrayed the wailer less as an excitable woman and more in the favorable role of the manager of motions. Few respondents thought this way at first. Most of those who adopted this approach did so as a corollary of their responses to my questions. For them, the interview was the first time they had given thought to the social meanings and implications of this traditional practice and above all to what will prevail once it disappears.

I asked Shai, a newly Orthodox Jew, "What ritual do you think there will be after the wailers are totally gone?" "Look," he replied, "when the wailers [don't perform] anymore, it suggests something. It suggests apathy, indifference. People get used to things. There's an indifference." As Shai continued to speak, his attitude changed strikingly. First, he defined wailing as "a public role. People raise their eyes to a wailer. She stands in the center for several minutes. Like a rabbi. When do you believe a rabbi? When he gives a class and you know he stands behind what he says in the way he lives. That's how he gets his following. His 'flock' follows him through fire and water. Why? People expect someone who teaches them, especially a rabbi, a counselor, a teacher, and so on, to practice what he preaches. With the wailer, there's this sharp transition. First, they believe her that she's on the brink [of an abyss]. She sounds broken, shattered. But then there's a sudden transition [from sorrow to ordinary speech]." However, Shai added that "If you're sensible and you think about it and realize that it's a role, it's okay; somehow you understand." The change in attitude represented in his remarks is reflected in the wailer's transition from one role category to another. This transition signifies the abandonment of the emotional demands of the performance (the wailer's sincerity) for the sake of its emotional outcomes for the listeners. Oded made a similar transition, from emotional denunciation of the wailer's play-acting to intellectual appreciation of her social influence:

> At my grandmother's funeral, a wailer suddenly came over and I realized that what she did was actually an act. It really got me angry, and I shouted at her, like, "Stop that, it's preposterous for you to shout just so." Hey, isn't she embarrassed?! I know this old woman. Hey, can't she cry for real?! I wanted to tell her, "Get out of here!" I really didn't accept that it had anything to do with me. But when I think about it now, [wailing] is important because the wailer drew in people who hadn't known my grandmother, who came to the funeral because they knew my mother, because they know me, because they know my father, and they know my grandmother's relatives, and she made them cry and remember things about themselves and about Grandma.

This positive view of the wailer is evident in the respondents' attitude toward the weeping that they did in her presence. Unlike the third construction that I offered, they did not consider themselves victims of a melancholic power that was inherent in the wailer's play-acting. Their remarks imply that they had managed to mobilize the wailer's lachrymose voice for the cause of emotional catharsis, of their need to make their participation in death rituals meaningful. In the situation of having to console the bereaved, some preferred the management that her words provided over whatever they might say on their own. Her outer voice draws out their inner voice and is considered a praiseworthy form of assistance. Her wailing forces them to look into themselves and evidently does not diminish their sense of self-authenticity. Ruthi said, "I really connected with this thing [wailing]. Yes, I did. Because you always find yourself really embarrassed because you don't know when's the right time [to express emotions] and you want to connect with the pain to unburden yourself. The wailer makes crying legitimate. I think she puts on this show for a good purpose. It's not to pull a fraud on us but to make us grieve." Yael said, "At first you cry as though it's a game but afterwards the crying comes from you. It's like when you hear a song. You hear what it refers to, and you get into your pain." Orit added, "I think people who sit and cry because of the wailer's show shouldn't get upset about the fact that it's a show. A sad movie makes me cry because I automatically project it onto my personal life. It's what stirs the crying inside me, not that [the wailer] sits down and puts on a fake act. Wailing makes me think all sorts of things about myself, and it brings out the tears. [The listeners'] tears are real tears."

In the respondents' opinion, the estrangement that has become prevalent in mourners' homes and cemeteries makes it a good idea for people to stop checking the credentials of the wailer's role. That is, they should stop reflecting on the performer's lack of tears and her failure to set a personal example. What matters to them is that the listeners do their thing, that is, that they cry. In this sense, the second-circle respondents feel exactly as those in the first circle do. The latter repeatedly expressed this by saying, as one respondent put it, that "You have to wail and cry because, after all, we didn't bury a cat." In both quotations that follow, the speakers, members of the second circle, appear to have seen through the wailer's professional play-acting but felt differently about the mourners and the listeners; they took a dim view of both groups, whose responses are restrained and whose social obligations translate today into an unconvincing performance of emotions. Their remarks suggest that only real tears in the eyes of the listeners—the purpose of the wailer's expertise—may dispel the impression of the management of impression on the listeners' part and make their response authentic. The remarks of Oded, a grandson of Yemenite Jewish immigrants in Israel, follow:

> Wailing is an act, but it's extremely important. Without wailers, I don't believe that the importance of the person who died would make people cry that way. I think people would take it for granted and as the nature of life that you have to come to grips with. The wailers create real emotion even if it's an act, and no matter how unacceptable I think it is, I'd rather have the act than no wailing at all. When people cry, even if they didn't really know the person who died and they come from the outside, their participation also contributes a lot to themselves because they feel they didn't come just to stand like statues at the funeral and wait for the funeral to end so they could go home—they saw them and "see you around"—but they truly identify. Wailing gives them a sense of identification. The crying actually reminds them of relatives who've died, so I think, and that makes the funeral a unique event.

The next remarks belong to a woman respondent, a psychologist of Ashkenazic extraction. They should be construed against the background of recent changes in traditional mourning rituals in Israel and other societies (Wouters 2002).[11] The trend in these changes is an extent of secularization in rituals that rules out the need for burial officials and legitimizes personal expression by the grieving relatives—a matter reflected, for example, in prepared eulogies and parting remarks, the use of musical instruments, and the recitation of poetry at the graveside.[12] That people prefer to secularize traditional death rituals rather than abandon them is a social fact that attests to the unchallenged status of death as an event that induces emotional, mental, and social mourning work. This may explain the following respondent's more positive view of the wailer's play-acting than of the listeners' real weeping; her remarks, citing the funeral of the assassinated Israeli prime minister Yitzhak Rabin as a formative event, show that she wishes to turn the hands of the tradition clock back:

HAVA: I can see some substitution [of the wailing performance] in what happens today at funerals. I see a performance. Today, I think, we may have reached a stage of some kind in the process of crystallizing the performance. But I find, at least at certain funerals, microphones, the poems they recite, people coming with prepared notes, people even feeling that they should perform. I know I had guilt feelings after my mother died, and I carried them for many years. I unloaded it with this terrible crying, but I didn't perform; I didn't appear there as someone who's talking, communicating something, appearing before the crowd. Today, at least at the last few funerals that I attended, a performance is expected. By someone from the family. It's already happening, and I'm beginning to identify the various parts of the appearance. I think one of the turning points was Noa Rabin's appearance, a very public one and a very documented and global one, because it went out to the whole world, [where she said] "Watch over us from up there." I think there's hardly been a funeral that I went to recently where they didn't ask the person who died to watch over us from up there. It means that this show is also starting to receive its own texts. . . .

AUTHOR: You know that wailers sometimes don't know the deceased; all they're given is someone's name and a brief résumé.

HAVA: But [the wailer] represents something. The wailer herself is of no interest to me; what interests me is what she represents. She represents pain, she represents grief, she gives the stimulus. From my standpoint, she's not a specific person. She's this voice of a Greek chorus, she has a voice that comes from deep, deep down, a voice that says you can cry, you should cry, it's good to cry. We are saddened, we cry, it's hard for us! And that seems to me, somewhere, more authentic. I see the bereaved people [reciting eulogies] and I feel that it comes from the bottom of their heart, but I hear this clicking from behind that forces them to appear just then because that's what's accepted today at funerals, to make an appearance. I have this feeling that it's very much expected today, at least in my social circles, that the granddaughter will come with the—and the son will say what he should say, and if it's the wife, so what the wife would say, and something like "Watch over us from up there." It's a social clock that's ticking. The wailer's professional and symbolic acting is better because she represents a symbol for me. And this symbol, I don't care if it's not sincere.

AUTHOR: Even though she goes to great lengths to impress people with her sincerity?

HAVA: Yes, because she wants to be the best in her profession. She's professional.

AUTHOR: How would you sum up your attitude?

HAVA: My attitude is that it's a shame that women's wailing is dying out.

The four constructions described above split the second-circle audience four ways: into defenders and accepters of the wailer's act and into those who are deterred by the forced tears and those who appreciate their demonstration. My question is this: Is it possible to bridge between *the negation of the wailer's performative act* and *the negation of the estrangement* that the silencing of her lament is bringing about? One method that the respondents devised was to demand that the wailer, too, mask herself in tears, thereby signaling in her performance the profundity of her empathy with the loss. As I have shown, this demand punctuates the words of the famous song as "No, woman, no—cry!" Since tears are the main medium of exchange in the socioemotional economy of a wailing culture (Clark 1997), the weeping of the woman leader of a temporary mourning community is also considered an ideal form of participation in an emotional exchange.

The word "ideal" deserves emphasis due to the material contrast between visible torrential weeping and the aesthetic and harmonic performance of words, movement, and melody. In other words, if the wailer cries, she will become a member of the audience, driven by her emotions; in this sense, her performance will fail. Any symmetry between performer and audience is unimaginable because the performer must retain enough control and awareness to avoid losing herself totally in the performance (Myerhoff 1990). The performer's self-control resembles an attitude toward the distress of a stage actor or of the poet of whom Diderot wrote: you say you're crying, Diderot (1957) remarked, but you're not crying when you grope for some snappy metaphor that eludes you or when you reach out for some harmonic rhyme. If the tears flow, Diderot continued, it means that the pen has slipped from the poet's hand; the poet is addicted to his or her emotions and is not writing. If so, what does the wailer do in her effort to turn "tears into ideas" (Holst-Warhaft 1995, 22)? She redoubles her self-control and then triples it. She is an actress who instructs herself, as if she is her own stage director, to settle for the creation of verisimilitude in her emotional sincerity. Thus, she seeks to bridge between those who laud the audience's weeping and those who decry her play-acting. And more important still, a real similarity comes about between this actress of a tradition and modern stage and screen actors, whose uniqueness lies in authentic acting (Bandelj 2003). Here I merely relate to several similarities between the two types of acting, because the very reference to the topic may challenge the justification for the total negation of the acting element of the wailer's performance and clarify the limits of her ability to appear in authentic emotions. Also, given the performative similarity, why do modern listeners allow actors artistic license but do not allow this for wailers?

Method acting, also known as the Method (as we will call it from here on)—the brainchild of the Russian director and actor Konstantin Stanislavsky[13]—is a theatrical and cinematic genre that emphasizes the authentic presentation of an emotional reality. As such, the Method can be viewed as part of a more general trend in late twentieth-century art (Orvell 1989). This genre, in my judgment, represents a close approximation of the wailing performance in terms of the definition of the goal of the stage direction, the paths to its attainment, and the importance of cultural knowledge on the actors' part (Bandelj 2003). First is the goal. The wailer's goal is the same as the legitimate goal of stage and film actors who practice the Method: to convince via emotion, that is, to create such verisimilitude as to leave the audience no room for error. The attainment of this goal defines the success of the performance among members of the wailing culture and the excellence of an acting performance among exponents of the Method. Wailers and actors also follow the same path to the attainment of the goal: both are expected to think of themselves as a mine that needs to be plumbed and excavated for psychological truth. The wailer mines her losses and the entirety of the process of her becoming. The kerchief over her face, as I have shown, allows her not only to make believe but also to be alone with herself. She wails because she is affected by her suffering; therefore, like Method

The empty chair: The death of the Yemenite Jewish wailing culture.

actors, she does internal work of the deep-acting type (Hochschild 1979). If she lacks internal sources with which to guide the performance, she will not perform and accordingly will not have to resort to external strategies of impression management (Goffman 1959, 1961).

According to another precept of the Method, stage and film actors should invest quasi-religious self-devotion in their emotional work, an investment based on the power of truth in acting. Importantly, I found an amazingly similar demand for self-devotion in the case of the wailer. It becomes evident when the value of honoring the dead is translated into the persuasive efforts of a wailer who herself wallows in melancholy. As for the importance of cultural knowledge, the wailer, like a Method actor, is a performer who adjusts her acting to cultural typifications that she and her audience share. Her creative materials and those of the actors, as well as the emotional effects of their performance, mirror a local rationality and depend on the logic that equates truth to the contents that rest within the framework of the culture (Schudson 1989, 169). The rule is that the wailer and the actor stand out for being members of a culture. If this principled comparison were taken to greater detail, I believe that women's wailing could be declared part of the Method genre. In fact, in a variation appropriate to the stage, wailing might even be a preeminent example of this genre.

The question now is this: Having found a modern artistic home for women's wailing, is there any positive message to report? Can wailing acquire new-old forms in connection with the original performance and be accepted sympathetically in our environs? Such a hope is probably naive and unrealistic. This is also true due to the difference between performance and theater. A performance is considered a community event, something that happens in a community's life. In cultural typifications, wailing is neither like an art nor like a theatrical presentation; that is, wailing is not considered to be an arena of representation (Feral 1982) that is privileged with the audience's patience. On the spectrum of performances, wailing is not perceived as an informal act that approximates many other rules of daily social life. The following quotation from Sartre (1956, 59) about a grocer, a tailor, and an auctioneer may clarify how wailing, like these roles, is susceptible to a performative failure that may offend the audience: "The public demands of them that they realize their occupations as a ceremony: there is the dance of the grocer, of the tailor, of the auctioneer, by which they endeavor to persuade their clientele that they are nothing but a grocer, an auctioneer, a tailor. A grocer who dreams is offensive to the buyer, because such a grocer is not wholly a grocer."

A death event makes the difference between a wailing performance and a stage performance all the more material. The crux of the difference is that if the theater or the cinema suspend ordinary life in favor of an act or something that isn't serious to induce the audience to contemplate them again, wailing has the opposite intent: its performance grabs the audience in a state of existential seriousness, gloom, and dread from which ordinary life represents the state of suspension. The respondents' attitude also shows that wailing is an appearance that mirrors the craving for self-authenticity amid a childish, primordial, primeval sense of reality. Consequently and paradoxically, the wailer uses dramatic play-acting to express a very deep, authentic reality. This is indeed a paradox. If we add the essence of the event that brings the performer and the audience together—a real death—we would expect the audience to find it hard to apply theatrical conventions to the wailer, that is, to forgive her acting as easily as the audience can forgive an actress for removing her facial makeup offstage. If so, a wailer's smile is not like that of an actress who has to cry only because the role requires it: the wailer's smile is a stinging offense that only an audience in a house of mourning absorbs.

The second circle of listeners resides in the space that separates the wailing culture from the reader—a distance that plays a mediating role in the question of the decline of women's wailing today. The respondents' reactions suggest that they reflect on the tears in their eyes in view of a performance that elicits a value confrontation. The rules of the performance challenge inherent values of the commitment to authenticity: sincerity, autonomy, emotional control, and positive self-presentation. From this standpoint, women's wailing became and has been what Goffman (1959, 208–37) called a "failed performance." Young listeners respond to it with forced tears, aversion, and protest, deeming it an embarrassing, manipulative phenomenon that pushes them into a corner. "Failed performance" is the profile of women's wailing on which today's descendants of the Yemenite immigrants in Israel agree the most. This itself is a clear indicator of the Yemenite Jews' social assimilation in Israel. I sorted the respondents' remarks into four constructions: three against wailing and one in favor. The latter embodies the lament of the printed words; it must be remembered that this construction was attained by dint of the reflective dynamic that the interview created in favor of the deconstruction and contemplation of the three previous attitudes. In ordinary life, people are not interviewed and do not take the time to contemplate, especially in regard to a topic such as wailing, which has always been abandoned territory. Otherwise, one male respondent would not have stated that "I've never thought about it, I have no strong opinion about it. I don't know"; another would have stated that "I don't really know so much, no, I have no firm attitude"; and a third would have stated that "I haven't made up my mind." All of this illuminates the ultimate fate of women's wailing: stereotyped attitudes are the ones that count in regard to it; raw public opinions are the ones that matter in social life. Furthermore, wailing is losing the cultural legitimacy that it had enjoyed for centuries because it has failed to adjust to new normative expectations. Only its emotional line of credit remains, and even this will dwindle until it is all used up.

Notes

INTRODUCTION

1. The following chapters of this ethnography mention and quote from Madar's work. By and large, I do this not redundantly but rather to augment my presentation in what I consider a unique way.
2. Operation MAGIC CARPET is the best known of the waves of Jewish immigration to Israel from Yemen. The first wave was in 1882. Notably, some 30,000 people, one-third of Yemenite Jewry, reached the country before statehood (1882–1947) and were dominant among Jews from Islamic countries who immigrated to prestatehood Israel. This fact has associations with the nature of this group's intercultural encounter in Israel, the nature of its social assimilation, and its positive image. In this matter, see Nini (1988) and Gilad (1989).
3. Quoted from the prayer book *'Iluy neshamot,* following the Yemenite Jewish rite.

4. Following Shokeid (1984), one would expect the religious tradition of Yemenite Jewry, like that of Oriental Jewry at large, to outlive the immigrant generation. This prediction is reinforced by subsequent findings about a high proportion of religiously observant individuals among the Oriental communities (Levi, Levinson, and Katz) and data on the phenomenon of returning to the faith in Israel (Sheleg 2000).
5. This postulate is based on Wikan (1988), where comparison is between wailing cultures in two Muslim communities, one in Egypt and the other in Bali.
6. Miller (2002) implies that the same applies in the matter of *balah*'s performance at weddings.
7. My research took place during the Second (Al-Aqsa) Intifada (2000–2005), a time of rampant terrorism in Israel.
8. Exceptions to this rule are two ethnographies that present an acute constructivist perspective that weakens the claim of dissonance between the affective and the social. Kaeppler (1993) draws a gender comparison between women's wailing and men's eulogies among the Tongas of Polynesia. Kaeppler describes women's wailing (*tongi*) as (a) wept thoughts, (b) performed because of emotion, and (c) conveyors of a sense of loss. In contrast, men's eulogizing (*laulau)* is described respectively as (a) thoughts that induce weeping, (b) triggers of emotion that demand contemplation and knowledge of the sociocultural system, and (c) conveyors of a sense of honor. This distinction suggests that women's wailing constitutes grief and that men's eulogizing constitutes mourning. A different strategy is adopted in Aborampah's (1999) interpretation of women's wailing among the Akans of Ghana. Aborampah describes the laments as institutionalized and predictable opportunities to express deferred grief. Grief, in turn, is portrayed as an emotion that typifies not only the deceased's relatives but also the wailing women, whose performance, in body and textual language, articulates symptoms of grief. Accordingly, the articulation of the grief emotion in this ethnic group depends more on a social formula than on an inner state.

CHAPTER 1

1. Most of the respondents' names are fictitious.
2. The mezuza (literally meaning "doorpost") is a parchment scroll bearing words of Scripture. Kept in a small container and mounted on a doorpost at the entrance to a Jewish home as the Torah instructs, the mezuza is credited by tradition with protective powers.
3. Nissim Binyamin-Gamliel died on July 7, 2004, during my research and about a year after my interview with him.
4. The yearlong period of mourning for a parent.

CHAPTER 2

1. Johara was her real name.
2. Researchers describe childhood in Yemen as a very brief period. By age three, boys already cringed under the yoke of religious study, and girls were mobilized for housework (Tzadok 1976).
3. Pre-Islam (fifth century CE).
4. I discuss this at length in chapter 4, "The Performance Stage."
5. In using the word "husband" to denote the woman's spouse, I do not mean to ignore the recent disapproval among women of the traditional concept of a woman becoming her spouse's property upon marriage.
6. For additional songs on this topic, see Dahoah Halevi (1995) and Binyamin-Gamliel (1975).
7. Notably, the pain of separation is a familiar cultural and literary motif among Yemenite Jews and is significantly attributed to women. Serri (1994, 165–74) devotes a special chapter in her book to this.
8. See Ganzfried-Goldin (1961, 4:98, para. 2) and Rubin (1997).
9. Tzadok (1967, 158–59) describes the *naqas* ritual in detail and terms it "one of the accepted remedies among the women."

CHAPTER 3

1. Few studies address the musical aspects of wailing. For two of them, see Feld (1982) and Seremetakis (1990).
2. Indeed, the Hebrew word *devarim,* used by the respondents, denotes both words and things.
3. Hasan-Rokem (1993) described a unique division of labor in her study on the sayings of the Georgian Jews in Israel. While not proficient in Georgian, she had expertise in the theory and practice of folk-literature research, and on this basis she conducted a two-level dialogue about the translation process and the interpretation of the source language. She accomplished this with the assistance of the researcher Antalov, who speaks Georgian and carries the Georgian cultural tradition.
4. For discussion of the respondents' inhibitions, see chapter 1, "Wailing: A Topic That Defies Research."
5. Madar's work, performed under the auspices of the Department of Jewish and Comparative Folklore at the Hebrew University of Jerusalem, presents a different working method for the recording and translation of Yemenite Jewish women's lamentations. Madar availed herself of an interpreter, an academician fluent in Yemenite Arabic. The process of jointly listening to the recordings and attempting to decipher them yielded a list of twenty complete lamentation texts, translated and transcribed (Madar 2002).
6. The wailer related that in Yemen, it was the practice to send letters announcing the death of family members. A piece of paper slightly burned at its edge signified bad news.
7. Gazel, an Arabic cognate of the English "gazelle," was the deceased's name.
8. The deceased's first name.
9. In Jewish practice, public worship requires the presence of at least ten men.
10. The Yemenite wick lamp, the wailer explained, was a vessel filled with oil. She used it as a metaphor for the deceased's premature passing.
11. Binyamin-Gamliel possesses additional unpublished lament texts that he translated into Hebrew several years ago.
12. Binyamin-Gamliel explains: "a strong-smelling flower, an excellent perfume."
13. A Yemenite delicacy.

14. A Yemenite delicacy.
15. Binyamin-Gamliel explains: "Whiteness in women is considered beautiful."
16. The cemetery.
17. Binyamin-Gamliel explains: "The *mehaneh* is God, who wishes to take the finest portion, i.e., life."
18. *Mehil* denotes forgiveness in Yemenite Arabic. The wailer forgives the deceased for whatever the deceased may have done to her. Binyamin-Gamliel explains this as "a way of saying 'the end.'"
19. The source of this incomplete text is Ben-David (1999, n.p.).
20. That is, the woman is likened to a fine flower that has been placed on a rooftop to please onlookers with its appearance and fragrance.
21. The metaphor invoked is a bell of pure gleaming silver in description of an aristocratic woman.
22. The deceased is complaining, as it were, that maggots are consuming her flesh.
23. That is, the breast, the seat of emotions.
24. Culled from Ben-David (1999, n.p.).
25. The ten-man prayer quorum.
26. The model was composed of arenas or fields, each representing a category of reality constructed from the discursive and practical whole of the members of a death culture. The fields reflect theoretical points of view that connect an identity with an encounter so as to position the other in the center of the definition of the self. Accordingly, the individual acquires self-identity from his or her response to reflections provided by others. The individual reflectively contemplates his or her self, which seems to be split between subject and object (James 1890; Cooley 1902; Mead 1934). By following an approach rooted mainly in social phenomenology, we can confirm the perception of the encounter as a place where social entities in formation engage in negotiating processes. The participants in the encounter are considered, above all, members who take part in the elucidation of its meanings; this projects onto the way the identity of each is perceived (Gubrium and Buckholdt 1977). Thus, self-identity is solely a discursive process typified by a dialectic between the self and the other concerning the perception of the imagination and of the differences between them (Mead 1934).

27. This issue is discussed in chapter 5, "Melancholic Power," and in the Epilogue.

CHAPTER 4

1. The discussion that follows distinguishes between appearance, which denotes only what the wailer does, and performance, which includes interaction with the audience.
2. Two of them were noted in chapter 3, "Giving Words."
3. The word *diwan* denotes both a guest room, as in the usage above, and a book of sacramental poetry that men use when they gather on Sabbaths and festivals.
4. Here we should present an example that appears to deviate from this rule. In the wailing culture of the Mani, women in the circle are liable to descend into arguments. As they vie for the right to be the first to wail, they boast about their shared history with the deceased and recount how they had been one with him materially and emotionally. The priority ultimately determined, however, does not attest to any status or importance that would transcend the demonstration of offering service in honor of the dead (Seremetakis 1990).
5. See *'Illuy Neshamot;* Maimonides, *Rules of Mourning* (11:5, Yemenite version).
6. On separation at the wedding see chapter 2, "Johara: Mother of the Wailers."
7. In the course of my research, I found one woman who was infertile. For her, the main purpose of wailing was to lament this fate.
8. In Yemen, the symbolic significance of menstruation led to the exclusion of even older and aged women from the cemetery.
9. This discussion is a composite derived from several similar observations.
10. For more on this point, see chapter 2, "Johara: Mother of the Wailers."
11. For more, see ibid.
12. See chapter 1, "Wailing: A Topic That Defies Research."
13. This also appears in Wilce (2009, 90). Islam forbids women's wailing due to beliefs related to challenging God's will, obstructing the transmigration of the soul to the hereafter, and performative modesty (El-Cheikh 2003).

CHAPTER 5

1. See chapter 4, "The Performance Stage."
2. As described in the section "Categorizing the Wailers' Discourse" in chapter 3, "Giving Words."
3. See chapter 4, "The Performance Stage."
4. Ibid.
5. Ibid.
6. Quoted from the collection of wailing lamentations in Madar (2002, 99).
7. Ibid., 52.
8. Ibid., 71.
9. During the shivah, the bereaved assume a wide assortment of restrictions that carry the significance of social death (Rubin 1997).
10. The next section of our discussion expands on these functions by relating to the gender division of labor.
11. In regard to women's singing while performing housework and in daily life, see Binyamin-Gamliel (1994).
12. See chapter 4, "The Performance Stage."
13. See also the "'Their' Tears" section in chapter 6, "Mission," 323–24.
14. See in chapter 4, "The Performance Stage."
15. The expression comes from the Talmud, Tractate Berakhot 24a: "Shmuel said, 'The voice of a woman is incestuous,' as is stated, 'For sweet is your voice and your countenance is comely'" (Song of Songs 2:14).
16. See chapter 4, "The Performance Stage."
17. Ibid.
18. Ibid.
19. Except for metaphors that, in the eyes of the deceased's acquaintances, overstate the worthiness of the deceased or the intensity of the survivors' pain. As we have seen, the audience is able to judge the performance in view of the truthfulness criterion. See chapter 4, "The Performance Stage."
20. Cooper (1986) draws a comparison between this type of intimacy and "general intimacy."
21. As demonstrated in chapter 4, "The Performance Stage."
22. The representation of the audience in wailing is analyzed in chapter 3,

"Giving Words."

23. So says the medieval commentator Shlomo Yitzhaki (Rashi) in his commentary on Abraham's compliance with the commandment to sacrifice Isaac (Genesis 23:3).

CHAPTER 6

1. Cited from the *'Illuy Nishmat ha-Met* prayer book, chap. 11, following the Yemenite rite.
2. Palestinian Talmud, quoted in Ellinson (1997, 19).
3. See chapter 5, "Melancholic Power."
4. The use of masculine and feminine gender is not clear; the source also remarks about it.
5. The word *dushan* also denotes a crier.
6. This matter is discussed in chapter 4, "The Performance Stage."
7. Kabbalah is a system of Jewish mysticism.
8. In the *'Illuy Neshamot* prayer book (Yemenite rite), there are brief paragraphs of eulogy under the heading "And These Are for Eulogy" along with a rabbinical ordinance: "Eulogies are delivered during all seven days at the house of mourning."
9. In this matter, see chapter 4, "The Performance Stage."
10. Maimonides, "Laws of Mourning," 13:12.
11. For an explanation, see chapter 3, "Giving Words."
12. The text is presented here only in part.
13. *'Illuy Neshamot* prayer book, p. 40, following the Yemenite rite.
14. Such as birth rituals.
15. In this matter, see chapter 4, "The Performance Stage."
16. See chapter 1, "Wailing: A Topic That Defies Research."

EPILOGUE

1. In this regard, see the Introduction and chapter 4, "The Performance Stage."
2. See chapter 4, "The Performance Stage."
3. To wit: make sure to maintain a positive attitude toward someone after his death. The Jewish sages adduced this from the titles of three weekly portions in Leviticus.
4. On the effect of metaphors/similes, see chapter 5, "Melancholic Power," particularly the section "Wailing as an Erotic Performance," 256–73.
5. See chapter 5, "Melancholic Power," the section titled "The Time Span of Healing."
6. In this matter, see also chapter 5, "Melancholic Power," particularly the section "Wailing as an Erotic Performance," 228–35.
7. For an analysis of Urban (1988), see chapter 6, "Mission."
8. See the Introduction and chapter 1, "Wailing: A Topic That Defies Research."
9. For more about the song, see "No Woman, No Cry," Wikipedia, http://en.wikipedia.org/wiki/No_Woman,_No_Cry.
10. In this matter, see chapter 4, "The Performance Stage."
11. An example is the secularization and modernization of rituals that led to change in the wailing culture of the Akans in Ghana. There, a popular culture has developed that replaces women's wailing with media notices about the deceased's deeds and accomplishments (Aborampah 1999).
12. I base this statement on my observations of rituals among Yemenite Jews and members of other ethnic groups. For more on this matter, see, for example, the site of Tekes Yisraeli, an institute that promotes and conducts secular rituals (www.tekes.co.il/English-index.html).
13. For background on the Method and how it took root in America, see Stanislavsky (1961), Vineberg (1991), and Easty (1994).

References

Aborampah, O. M. 1999. "Women's Role in the Mourning Rituals of the Akan of Ghana." *Ethnology* 38, no. 3: 257–71.

Abu-Lughod, L. 1986. *Veiled Sentiments: Honor and Poetry in a Bedouin Society.* Berkeley: University of California Press.

———. 1990. "The Romance of Resistance: Tracing Transformations of Power through Bedouin Women." *American Ethnologist* 17: 41–55.

———. 1993. "Islam and the Gendered Discourses of Death." *International Journal of Middle East Studies* 25: 187–205.

Alexiou, M. 1974. *The Ritual Lament in Greek Tradition.* Cambridge: Cambridge University Press.

Altshuler, David. 1996. *Metsudat Tsiyyon Commentary on Jeremiah.* Jerusalem: Machon Meirav.

Amir, Y. 1993. *Diwan shabbi el hai* [Selection of Yemenite Songs]. Kiryat Ono: MSA Institute.

Appadurai, A. 1996. *Modernity at Large: Cultural Dimensions of Globalisation.*

Minneapolis: University of Minnesota Press.

Arber, S., and J. Ginn. 1991. *Gender and Later Life: A Sociological Analysis of Resources and Constraints.* London: Sage.

———. 1995. *Connecting Gender and Ageing: A Sociological Approach.* Buckingham, UK: Open University Press.

Aries, P. 1974. *Western Attitudes toward Death from the Middle Ages to the Present.* Baltimore: Johns Hopkins University Press.

———. 1981. *The Hour of Our Death.* Oxford: Oxford University Press.

Aslan, M., and R. Nissim. 1982. *Mi-minhageihem ve-orah hayehem shel yehudei Iraq* [The Customs and Way of Life of the Jews of Iraq]. Tel Aviv: Ofer Library.

Averill, J. R. 1982. *Anger and Aggression.* New York: Springer.

Avraham, L., and L. Bahat-Ratzon. 1994. "Ha-shira ve-ha-mahol ke-emtsa'i le-'olama ha-penimi shek ha-yehudiya be-Teiman" [Song and Dance as Means of Expression for the Inner World of the Jewish Woman in Yemen]. In *Bat Teiman: 'Olama shel ha-isha ha-yehudiya* [Daughter of Yemen: The World of the Jewish Woman], edited by S. Serri, 175–94. Tel Aviv: A'aleh be-Tamar Association.

Baddeley, A. 1990. *Human Memory: Theory and Practice.* Boston: Allyn & Bacon.

Bandelj, N. 2003. "How Method Actors Create Character Roles." *Sociological Forum* 18, no. 3: 387–416.

Bar-Yosef, R. 1968. "Desocialization and Resocialization: The Adjustment Process of Immigrants." *International Migration Review* 2: 27–43.

Bataille, G. 1986. *Erotism: Death and Sensuality.* 2nd ed. Translated by M. Dalwood. San Francisco: City Lights Books.

Bateson, G. 1972. *Steps to an Ecology of Mind.* New York: Ballantine Books.

———. 1980. *Naven: A Survey of the Problems Suggested by a Composite Picture of the Culture of a New Guinea Tribe Drawn from Three Points of View.* London: Wildwood House.

Bauman, R. 1977. *Verbal Art as Performance.* Prospect Heights, IL: Waveland.

Bauman, Z. 1992. *Mortality, Immortality and Other Life Strategies.* Stanford, CA: Stanford University Press.

Becker, E. 1973. *The Denial of Death.* New York: Free Press.

Becker, H. S. 1986. *Doing Things Together: Selected Papers.* Evanston, IL:

Northwestern University Press.

Beilin, R. 1981. "Social Functions of Denial of Death." *Omega* 12: 25–35.

Beit-Hallahmi, B., and M. Argyle. 1997. *The Psychology of Religious Behaviour, Belief, and Experience.* London: Routledge.

Bellah, N. R. 1985. *Habits of the Heart: Individualism and Commitment in American Life.* Berkeley: University of California Press.

Ben-Amos, D. 1973. "Hagdarat ha-folklore be-heqsher ha-tarbut" [Definition of Folklore in the Context of the Culture]. *Hasifrut* 3: 416–26.

———. 1984. "The Seven Strands of Tradition: Varieties in Its Meaning in American Folklore Studies." *Journal of Folklore Research* 21: 97–131.

Ben-David, A., ed. 1999. *Hod* [Grandeur]. N.p.: Self-published.

Benedicte, G. 1994. "The Role of Suffering in Women's Performance of Paxto." In *Gender, Genre, and Power in South Asian Expressive Traditions,* edited by A. Appadurai, F. J. Korom, and M. A. Mills, 81–101. Delhi: Motilal Banarsidass Publishers.

Ben-Gershom, L. 2001. *Perush le-shir ha-shirim* [Commentary on the Song of Songs]. Ramat Gan: Bar-Ilan University.

Ben-Rafael, E., and S. Sharot. 1991. *Ethnicity, Religion and Class in Israeli Society.* Cambridge: Cambridge University Press.

Ben-Zvi, I. 1976. *The Exiled and the Redeemed.* Jerusalem: Yad Izhak Ben-Zvi Publications.

Bernard, M., P. Chambers, and G. Granville. 2000. "Women Ageing: Changing Identities, Challenging Myths." In *Women Ageing: Changing Identities, Challenging Myths,* edited by M. Bernard, J. Phillips, L. Machin, and H. David, 1–22. New York: Routledge.

Bilu, Y. 1993. *Le-lo meitsarim: Hayav u-moto shel Rabi Ya'aqov Wazana* [Without Inhibitions: The Life and Death of Rabbi Jacob Wazana]. Jerusalem: Magnes, Hebrew University.

Binyamin-Gamliel, N. 1966. *Teiman u-mahane geula* [Yemen and Mahane Geula]. Tel Aviv: Hanun Series.

———. 1975. *Ahavat Teiman: Ha-shira ha-'amamit ha-Teimanit—shirat nashim* [Love of Yemen: Yemenite Folksong—Women's Song]. Tel Aviv: Afikim.

———. 1994. "*Shirat ha-nashim: Ha-shira ha-Teimanit ha-'amamit*" [Woman's Song: Yemenite Folksong]. In *Bat Teiman: 'Olama shel ha-isha ha-yehudit*

[Daughter of Yemen: The World of the Jewish Woman], edited by S. Serri, 145–54. Tel Aviv: A'aleh be-Tamar Association.

———. 2002. *Tahat kenafeha shel imam: Roman otobiografi me-hayav shel yeled yehudi be-teiman* [Under Mother's Wings: An Autobiographical Novel from the Life of a Jewish Child in Yemen]. Tel Aviv: Afikim.

Blackburn, S. H. 1986. "Performance Makers in an Indian Story-Type." In *Another Harmony: New Essays on Folklore in India,* edited by S. H. Blackburn and A. K. Ramanujan, 167–93. Los Angeles: University of California Press.

———. 1988. *Singing of Birth and Death: Texts in Performance.* Philadelphia: University of Pennsylvania Press.

Bloch, M. 1974. "Symbols, Song, Dance, and Features of Articulation." *European Journal of Sociology* 15: 55–81.

Bolen, J. S. 2002. *Goddesses in Older Women: Archetypes in Women over Fifty.* New York: HarperCollins.

Boorstin, D. 1987. *The Image: A Guide to Pseudo-Events in America.* New York: Atheneum.

Bourke, A. 1993. "More in Anger Than in Sorrow: Irish Women's Lament Poetry." In *Feminist Messages: Coding in Women's Folk Culture,* edited by J. N. Radner, 160–82. Urbana and Chicago: University of Illinois Press.

Bowlby, J. 1961. "Processes of Mourning." *International Journal of Psycho-Analysis* 42: 317–40.

———. 1981. *Attachment and Loss,* Vol. 3, *Loss: Sadness and Depression.* Harmondsworth, UK: Penguin.

Brauer, A. 1947. *Yehudei Kurdistan: Mehqar etnologi* [The Jews of Kurdistan: An Ethnological Study]. Jerusalem: National Institute for Folklore and Ethnology.

Brenneis, D. L. 1990. "Shared and Solitary Sentiments: The Discourse of Friendship, Play, and Anger in Bhatgaon." In *Language and the Politics of Emotion,* edited by C. Lutz and L. Abu-Lughod, 113–25. Cambridge: Cambridge University Press.

Breton, A. 1969. *Manifestoes of Surrealism.* Ann Arbor: University of Michigan Press.

Briggs, C. L. 1992. "'Since I Am a woman, I Will Chastise My Relatives': Gender, Reported Speech, and the (Re)production of Social Relations in

Warao Ritual Wailing." *American Ethnologist* 19, nos. 1–2: 337–61.

———. 1993. "Personal Sentiments and Polyphonic Voices in Warao Women's Ritual Wailing: Music and Poetics in a Critical Collective Discourse." *American Anthropologist* 95, no. 4: 929–57.

Brown, G. 2003. "Theorizing Ritual as Performance: Explorations of Ritual Indeterminancy." *Journal of Ritual Studies* 17, no. 1: 3–18.

Brown, N. O. 1985. *Life against Death: The Psychoanalytical Meaning of History.* Middletown, CT: Wesleyan University Press.

Browne, C. V. 1998. *Women, Feminism and Aging.* New York: Springer Series, Focus on Women.

Buber, M. 1959. *I and Thou.* New York: Scribner.

Burns, E. 1972. *Theatricality: A Study of Convention in the Theatre and in Social Life.* London: Longman.

Caraveli, A. 1986. "The Bitter Wounding: The Lament as a Social Protest in Rural Greece." In *Gender and Power in Rural Greece,* edited by J. Dubisch, 169–94. Princeton, NJ: Princeton University Press.

Caraveli-Chaves, A. 1980. "Bridge between Worlds: The Greek Women's Lament as Communicative Event." *Journal of American Folklore* 93: 129–57.

Carlson, M. 1996. *Performance: A Critical Introduction.* New York: Routledge.

Cassuto, M. D. 1967. *Hamesh megilot* [Five Scrolls]. Tel Aviv: Yavne.

Caton, S. C. 1990. *"Peaks of Yemen I Summon": Poetry as Cultural Practice in a North Yemeni Tribe.* Berkeley: University of California Press.

Chernela, J. M. 1993. *The Wanano Indians of the Brazilian Amazon: A Sense of Space.* Austin: University of Texas Press.

Chidester, D. 1990. *Patterns of Transcendence: Religion, Death and Dying.* Belmont, CA: Wadsworth.

Chodorow, N. 1974. "Family Structure and Feminine Personality." In *Women, Culture and Society,* edited by M. Z. Rosaldo and L. Lamphere, 43–66. Stanford, CA: Stanford University Press.

———. 1978. *The Reproduction of Mothering: Psychoanalysis and the Sociology of Gender.* Berkeley: University of California Press.

Clark, C. 1990. "Emotions and the Micropolitics of Everyday Life: Some Patterns and Paradoxes of Place." In *Research Agenda in the Sociology of Emotions,* edited by T. Kemper, 305–34. Albany: State University of New

York Press.

———. 1997. *Misery and Company: Sympathy in Everyday Life.* Chicago: University of Chicago Press.

Clifford, J. 1986. "Introduction: Partial Truths." In *Writing Culture: The Poetics and Politics of Ethnography,* edited by J. Clifford and G. E. Marcus, 1–26. Berkeley: University of California Press.

Cohen, A. 1991. "Shira-terapia: Tipul nafshi be-emtsa'ut shira" [Song-Therapy: Psychological Therapy and Aid by Means of Song]. *Ma'aglei qeriya* 20: 5–18.

Cohen, T. 1978. "Metaphor and Cultivation of Intimacy." *Critical Inquiry* 5, no. 1: 3–12.

Collins, R. 1979. *The Credential Society: An Historical Sociology of Education and Stratification.* New York: Academic Press.

Cooley, C. H. 1902. *Human Nature and the Social Order.* New York: Scribner.

Cooper, D. E. 1986. *Metaphor.* Oxford, UK: Basil Blackwell.

Corbin, J., and A. Strauss. 1990. "Grounded Theory Method: Procedures, Canons, and Evaluative Criteria." *Qualitative Sociology* 13: 3–21.

Covey, H. C. 1981. "Reconceptualization of Continuity Theory: Some Preliminary Thoughts." *Gerontologist* 21, no. 6: 628–33.

Csikszentmihalyi, M., and I. S. Csikszentmihalyi. 1988. *Optimal Experience: Psychological Studies of Flow in Consciousness.* Cambridge: Cambridge University Press.

Dahan-Kalev, H. 2002. "Menuhshalut: 'Ivron migdari be-te'oriyot politiyot u-sheqifutam shal nashim mizrahiyot" [Backwardness: Gender Blindness in Political Theories and the Transparency of Mizrahi Women]. *Sotsiologia Yisraelit* 4, no. 2: 265–87.

———. 2005. "Feminism Mizrahi ve-globalizatsiya" [Mizrahi Feminism and Globalization]. *Mifne: Bama le-'inyaneu hevra* [Mifne: Forum for Social Affairs] 46–47: 16–20.

Dahoah Halevi, Y. 1995. *Mabo'ei aviqim: Mehqarim be-moreshet yehadut Teiman ve-tarbuta* [Afikim Wellsprings: Studies on the Legacy and Culture of Yemenite Jewry]. Tel Aviv: Afikim.

Danforth, L. 1982. *The Death Rituals of Rural Greece.* Princeton, NJ: Princeton University Press.

Das, V. 1986. "The Work of Mourning: Death in a Panjabi Family." In *The*

Cultural Transition: Human Experience and Social Transformation in the Third World and Japan, edited by M. I. White and S. Pollak, 179–210. Boston: Routledge & Kegan Paul.

De Beauvoir, S. 2001. *The Second Sex.* Translated by Constance Borde and Sheila Malovany-Chevalier. New York: Knopf.

Deblitzky, D. 1979. *Qitsur shulhan 'arukh* [Abridged Code of Jewish Law]. Bnei Brak: Shabbetai Frankel.

Delanty, G. 2000. *Modernity and Postmodernity: Knowledge, Power and Self.* London: Sage.

Denzin, N. K. 1984. *On Understanding Emotion.* London: Jossey-Bass.

Deshen, S. 1970. "On Religious Change: The Situational Analysis of Symbolic Action." *Comparative Studies in Society and History* 12: 260–334.

Deutsch, H. 1961. *The Psychology of Women.* New York: Grune & Stratton.

Diderot, D. 1957. *The Paradox of Acting and Masks or Faces? A Dramabook.* New York: Hill and Wang.

Disney, R. 1996. *Can We Afford to Grow Older? Perspective on the Economics of Aging.* Cambridge, MA: MIT Press.

Dorsky, S. 1986. *Women of Amran: A Middle Eastern Ethnographic Study.* Salt Lake City: University of Utah Press.

Douglas, M. 1966. *Purity and Danger.* New York: Praeger.

Dunne, J. 1996. "Beyond Sovereignty and Deconstruction: The Storied Self." *Philosophy and Social Criticism* 21: 137–57.

Durkheim, E. 1952. *Suicide: A Study in Sociology.* London: Routledge & Kegan Paul.

———. 1964. *The Division of Labor in Society.* New York: Free Press.

———. 1965. *The Elementary Forms of Religious Life.* New York: Free Press.

Easty, D. E. 1994. *On Method Acting.* New York: Ivy Books.

El-Cheikh, N. M. 2003. "Mourning and the Role of the Na'iha." In *Identidades Marginales,* edited by C. de la Puente, 395–412. Madrid: Consejo Superior de Investigaciones Cientificas.

Elias, N. 1978. *The Civilizing Process: The History of Manners.* Translated by Edmund Jephcott. New York: Urizen Books.

Ellinson, A. G. 1997. *Ha-isha ve-ha-mitsvot: Meqorot hilkhati'im mevo'arim* [Woman and the Commandments: The Halakhic Sources Explained].

Jerusalem: World Zionist Organization, Department for Torah Education in the Diaspora.

Eraqi-Klorman, B. Z. 1993. *The Jews of Yemen in the Nineteenth Century.* New York: Brill.

———. 2004. *Yehudei Teiman: Historiya, hevra, tarbut* [The Jews of Yemen: History, Society, Culture], Vol. 2. Ra'anana: Open University Press.

———. 2006. "Ha-historiografiya shel yehudei Teiman ve-giyusa le-havnayat ha-zehut ha-leumit" [Yemeni Jewish Historiography and the Formation of National Identity]. In *Lehamtsi umma* [To Invent a Nation], edited by Henry Wasserman and Yosi Dahan, 299–330. Ra'anana: Open University Press.

———. 2011. "Muslim and Jewish Interactions in the Tribal Sphere." In *The Divergence of Judaism and Islam: Interdependence, Modernity, and Political Turmoil,* edited by M. Laskier and Y. Lev, 125–42. Gainesville: University Press of Florida.

Erickson, J. R. 1995. "The Importance of Authenticity for Self and Society." *Symbolic Interaction* 18, no. 2: 121–44.

Fegan, B. 1986. "'Tenants' Non-Violent Resistance to Landowner Claims in a Central Luzon Village." *Journal of Peasant Studies* 13: 87–106.

Feld, S. 1982. *Sound and Sentiment: Birds, Weeping, Poetics and Song in Kaluli Expression.* Philadelphia: University of Pennsylvania Press.

———. 1995. "Wept Thoughts: The Voicing of Kaluli Memories." In *South Pacific Oral Traditions,* edited by R. Finnegan and M. Orbell, 85–108. Bloomington and Indianapolis: Indiana University Press.

Feleppa, R. 1988. *Conversation, Translation, and Understanding: Philosophical Problems in the Comparative Study of Culture.* Albany: State University of New York Press.

Feral, J. 1982. "Performance and Theatricality: The Subject Demystified." *Modern Drama* 25: 170–81.

Ferrara, A. 1998. *Reflective Authenticity: Rethinking the Project of Modernity.* New York: Routledge.

Findlay, J. N. 1967. "The Perspicuous and the Poignant." *British Journal of Aesthetics* 7, no. 1: 3–19.

Finnegan, R. 2001. *Oral Traditions and the Verbal Arts.* New York: Routledge.

Fischer, A. H., and A. S. R. Manstead. 2000. "The Relation between Gender and Emotions in Different Cultures." In *Gender and Emotion: Social Psychological Perspectives,* edited by A. H. Fischer, 71–96. Cambridge: Cambridge University Press.

Fiumara, G. C. 1995. "Vicissitudes of Self-formation." In *The Metaphoric Process: Connections between Language and Life,* 125–42. New York: Routledge.

Fortier, M. 1997. *Theory/Theatre.* London: Routledge.

Frankel, S., and D. Smith. 1982. "Conjugal Bereavement among the Huli People of Papua, New Guinea." *British Journal of Psychology* 141: 302–5.

Fraser, N. 2000. "Rethinking Recognition." *New Left Review* 3: 107–20.

Frazer, J. G. 1923. *Folk-Lore in the Old Testament.* New York: Tudor Publishing.

Freud, S. 1918. *Reflections on War and Death.* New York: Moffet Yard.

———. 1952. *Totem and Taboo.* New York: Kegan Paul, Trench, Trubner.

———. 1953. "Mourning and Melancholy." In *The Standard Edition of the Complete Psychological Works of Sigmund Freud,* Vol. 14, *1914–1916,* edited and translated by J. Strachey, 237–58. London: Hogarth.

———. 1961. *The Standard Edition of the Complete Psychological Works of Sigmund Freud,* Vol. 21, *Civilization and Its Discontents.* Edited by J. Strachey. London: Hogarth.

Friedrich, D. D. 2001. *Successful Aging: Integrating Contemporary Ideas, Research Findings, and Intervention Strategies.* Springfield, IL: Charles C. Thomas.

Gamliel, T. 2001. "A Social Version of Gero-Transcendence: Case Study." *Journal of Aging and Identity* 6, no. 2: 105–14.

Gamliel, T., and Hazan, H. 2006. "The Meaning of Stigma: Identity Construction in Two Old-Age Institutions." *Ageing and Society* 26, no. 3: 355–71.

Ganzfried-Goldin. 1961. *Code of Jewish Law.* 4 vols. New York: Hebrew Publishing.

Geertz, C. 1975. *The Interpretation of Cultures: Selected Essays.* London: Hutchinson.

———. 1983. "The Way We Think Now: Toward an Ethnography of Modern Thought." In *Local Knowledge,* 147–66. New York: Basic Books.

Gergen, K. J. 1997. *Realities and Relationships: Sounding in Social Construction.* Cambridge, MA: Harvard University Press.

Giddens, A. 1990. *The Consequences of Modernity.* Cambridge, UK: Polity.

———. 1991. *Modernity and Self Identity in the Late Modern Age.* Stanford, CA: Stanford University Press.

Gilad, L. 1989. *Ginger and Salt: Yemeni Jewish Women in an Israeli Town.* London: Westview.

Gilligan, C. 1983. *In a Different Voice: Psychological Theory and Women's Development.* Cambridge, MA: Harvard University.

Glassgold, P. 1987. "Translation: Culture Deriving Wedge." In *Translation Theory,* edited by R. Schulte and D. Kratz, special issue of *Translation Review* 23, nos. 1–2: 18–21.

Gleitman, H. 1983. *Basic Psychology.* New York: Norton.

Goffman, E. 1959. *The Presentation of Self in Everyday Life.* Garden City, NY: Doubleday.

———. 1961. *Encounters: Two Studies in the Sociology of Interaction.* Indianapolis: Bobbs-Merrill.

———. 1963. *Stigma: Notes on the Management of the Spoiled Identity.* Englewood Cliffs, NJ: Prentice Hall.

———. 1976. "Performances." In *Ritual, Play and Performance: Readings in the Social Sciences/Theatre,* edited by R. Schechner and M. Schuman, 89–96. New York: Seabury.

Goldstein, K. S. 1964. *A Guide for Field Workers in Folklore.* London: Herbert Jenkins.

Gonzalez-Crussi, F. 1989. *On the Nature of Things Erotic.* New York: Vintage Books.

Goodenough, W. H. 1957. "Cultural Anthropology and Linguistics." In *Report of the Seventh Annual Round Table Meeting on Linguistics and Language Study,* edited by Paul L. Garvin, 167–73. Washington, DC: Georgetown University Monograph Series on Language and Linguistics, No. 9.

Goodwin, S. W., and E. Bronfen. 1993. *Death and Representation.* London: Johns Hopkins University Press.

Gorer, G. D. 1965a. *Death, Grief and Mourning.* New York: Doubleday.

———. 1965b. "Funeral and Bereavement Rituals of Kota Indians and Orthodox Jews." *Omega* 12: 117–28.

———. 1976. "The Pornography of Death." In *Death: Current Perspectives,* edited by E. S. Shneidmen, 49–52. Palo Alto, CA: Mayfield.

Granqvist, H. 1965. *Muslim Death and Ritual: Arab Customs and Traditions Studied in Village in Jordan.* Helsinki: Helsingfors.

Gubrium, J. F., and D. R. Buckholdt. 1977. *Towards Maturity.* Washington, DC: Jossey-Bass.

Guignon, C. 2004. *On Being Authentic.* New York: Routledge.

Gutmann, D. 1994. *Reclaimed Power: Men and Women in Later Life.* Evanston, IL: Northwestern University Press.

Halevi, L. 2004. "Wailing for the Dead: The Role of Women in Early Islamic Funerals." *Past and Present* 183: 3–40.

Handelman, D. 1990. *Models and Mirrors: Toward an Anthropology of Public Events.* Cambridge: Cambridge University Press.

Handler, R., and W. Saxton. 1988. "Dyssimulation: Reflexivity, Narrative, and the Quest for Authenticity in 'Living History.'" *Cultural Anthropology* 3: 242–60.

Hare, A. P., and H. H. Blumberg. 1988. *Dramaturgical Analysis of Social Interaction.* New York: Praeger.

Harries, K. 1978. "Metaphor and Transcendence." *Critical Inquiry* 5, no. 1: 73–90.

Hasan-Rokem, G. 1993. *Adam le-adam gesher: Pitgamim shel yehudei Georgia be-Yisrael* [Man Is a Bridge to Man: Sayings of the Georgian Jews in Israel]. Jerusalem: Ben-Zvi Institute.

———. 1996. *Riqmat Hayim: Ha-yetsira ha-'amamit be-sifrut hazal* [Texture of Life: Folk Art in the Literature of the Sages]. Tel Aviv: Am Oved.

Hasan-Rokem, G., V. Madar, and D. Sherira. 2006. "Mi-'mizrahim be-Yisrael' le-'qolot mizrahi'im': Mi-kibush ha-hegemoniya le-shinui radiqali—Ma'avaq hevrati, si'ah intelektualim ve-heqer h-folklore" [From "Mizrahim in Israel" to "Mizrahi Voices": From the Conquest of Hegemony to Radical Change—Social Struggle, Discourse of Intellectuals, and Study of Folklore]. *Theory and Criticism* 29: 247–54.

Hatfield, E. C., T. J. Cacioppo, and L. R. Rapson. 1994. *Emotional Contagion.* Cambridge: Cambridge University Press.

Heelas, P. 1996. "Introduction: Detraditionalization and Its Rivals." In *Detraditionalization,* edited by P. Heelas, S. Lash, and P. Morris, 1–20. Cambridge, UK: Blackwell.

Heidegger, M. 1962. *Being and Time.* New York: Harper and Row.

Hertz, R. 1960. *Death and the Right Hand.* Translated by R. C. Needham. London: Cohen and West.

Hewitt, J. P. 1989. *Dilemmas of the American Self.* Philadelphia: Temple University Press.

Hochschild, A. R. 1979. "Emotion Work, Feeling Rules, and Social Structure." *American Journal of Sociology* 85: 551–75.

———. 1983. *The Managed Heart: Commercialization of Human Feeling.* Berkeley: University of California Press.

———. 1990. "Ideology and Emotion Management: A Perspective and Path for Future Research." In *Research Agendas in the Sociology of Emotion,* edited by T. D. Kemper, 117–44. Albany: State University of New York Press.

Hollander, I. 2005. *Jews and Muslims in Lower Yemen: A Study of Protection and Restraint, 1918–1949.* Leiden and Boston: Brill.

Holst-Warhaft, G. 1995. *Dangerous Voices: Women's Laments and Greek Literature.* New York: Routledge.

Hozeh, S. 1973. *Sefer toledot ha-rav Shalom Shabazi u-minhagei yahadut shar'ab be-Teiman* [The History of R. Shalom Shabazi and Customs of the Jews of Shar-ab in Yemen]. Jerusalem: Aharon Hassid.

Huntington, R. 1973. "Death and the Social Order: Bara Funeral Customs (Madagascar)." *African Studies* 32: 65–84.

Hymes, D. 1975. "Breakthrough into Performance." In *Folklore: Performance and Communication,* edited by D. Ben-Amos and K. S. Goldstein, 11–74. The Hague: Mouton.

Irion, P. E. 1993. "Spiritual Issues in Death and Dying for Those Who Do Not Have Conventional Religious Belief." In *Death and Spirituality,* edited by K. J. Doka and J. D. Morgan, 93–112. New York: Baywood.

Jackall, R. 1988. *Moral Mazes: The World of Corporate Managers.* New York: Oxford University Press.

James, W., 1890. *The Principles of Psychology.* New York: Dover.

Jones, A. R. 1986. "Surprising Fame: Renaissance Gender Ideologies and Women's Lyric." In *The Poetics of Gender,* edited by N. K. Miller, 74–95. New York: Columbia University Press.

Jonte-Pace, D. 1987. "Object Relations Theory, Mothering, and Religion: Toward a Feminist Psychology of Religion." *Horizons* 14, no. 2: 310–27.

Jordan, J. V. 1991. "The Relational Self: A New Perspective for Understanding Women's Development." In *The Self: Interdisciplinary Approaches,* edited by J. Strauss and G. R. Goethals, 136–49. New York: Springer-Verlag.

Jung, C. G. 1959. "Conscious, Unconscious, and Individuation." In *The Collected Works of C. G. Jung,* Vol. 9, edited by H. Read, M. Fordham, and G. Adler, 275–89. Princeton, NJ: Princeton University Press.

———. 1960. "The Structure and Dynamics of the Psyche." In *The Collected Works of C. G. Jung,* Vol. 8, edited by H. Read, M. Fordham, and G. Adler, 281–97. London: Routledge & Kegan Paul.

———. 1984. *Dream Analysis: Notes of Seminar Given in 1928–1930.* Edited by William McGuire. Bollingen Series, Vol. 99. Princeton, NJ: Princeton University Press.

Kaeppler, A. L. 1993. "Poetics and Politics of Tongan Laments and Eulogies." *American Ethnologist* 20, no. 3: 474–501.

Kappah, Y. 2002. *Halikhot Teiman: Hayey ha-yehudim be-Sana'a uv-noteha* [The Ways of Yemen: Jewish Life in Sana'a and Its Satellite Towns]. Jerusalem: Yad Izhak Ben-Zvi and Hebrew University of Jerusalem.

Kashani, R. 1996. *Minhagei aveilut ba-masoret u-va-folklore* [Mourning Customs in Tradition and Folklore]. *Mahut* 18: 21–32.

Katz, Y. 1984. "Hevra masortit ve-hevra modernit" [Traditional Society and Modern Society]. In *Yehudei ha-mizrah: 'Iyyunim antropologi'im 'al he-'avar ve-ha-hoveh* [The Jews of the East: Anthropological Studies about the Past and the Present], edited by S. Deshen and M. Shokeid, 27–34. Tel Aviv: Schocken.

Katzir, Y. 1976. "The Effects of Resettlement on the Status and Role of Yemeni Jewish Women: The Case of Ramat Oranim." PhD dissertation, University of California.

Kielmann, K. 1998. "Barren Ground: Contesting Identities of Infertile Women in Pemba, Tanzania." In *Pragmatic Women and Body Politics,* edited by M. Lock and P. A. Kanfert, 127–63. Cambridge: Cambridge University Press.

Klass, D., P. R. Silverman, and S. L. Nickman. 1996. *Continuing Bonds: New Understandings of Grief.* Washington, DC: Taylor & Francis.

Koestenbaum, P. 1971. *The Vitality of Death: Essays in Existential Psychology and Philosophy.* Westport, CT: Greenwood.

Kristeva, J. 1982. *Powers of Horror.* Translated by L. S. Roudiez. New York: Columbia University Press.

Laird, J. D., and N. H. Apostoleris. 1996. "Emotional Self-Control and Self-Perception: Feelings Are the Solution, Not the Problem." *The Emotions: Social, Cultural and Biological Dimensions,* edited by R. Harre and W. G. Parrot, 285–301. London: Sage.

Lavie, S. 1990. *The Poetics of Military Occupation: Mzeina Allegories of Bedouin Identity under Israeli and Egyptian Rule.* Berkeley: University of California Press.

Leach, E. R. 1976. *Culture and Communication.* Cambridge: Cambridge University Press.

Levi, S., H. Levinson, and A. Katz. 2002. *Yehudim Yisraelim: Diyuqan* [Israeli Jews: A Portrait]. Jerusalem: Guttman Center, Israel Democracy Institute.

Lewis, H. S. 1989. *After the Eagles Landed: The Yemenites of Israel.* London: Westview.

Lifton, R. J. 1979. *The Broken Connection: On Death and the Continuity of Life.* New York: Simon & Schuster.

Lindemann, E. 1944. "Symptomatology and Management of Acute Grief." *American Journal of Psychiatry* 101: 141–48.

———. 1979. *Beyond Grief: Studies in Crisis Intervention.* New York: J. Aronson.

Lips, H. M. 1991. *Women, Men and Power.* Mountain View, CA: Mayfield.

Loeb, L. D. 1985. "Folk Models of Habbani Ethnic Identity." In *Studies in Israeli Society: After the Ingathering,* edited by A. Weingrod, 201–16. New York: Gordon and Breach.

———. 1999. "Jewish-Muslim Socio-Political Relations in Twentieth Century South Yemen." In *Judaeu-Yemenite Studies,* edited by E. Isaac and Y. Tobi, 71–99. Princeton, NJ, and Haifa, Israel: Institute of Semitic Studies, Princeton University.

Lofland, H. L. 1985. "The Social Shaping of Emotion: The Case of Grief." *Symbolic Interaction* 8, no. 2: 171–90.

Luke, T. W. 1996. "Identity, Meaning and Globalization: Detraditionalization in Postmodern Space-Time Compression." In *Detraditionalization,* edited by P. Heelas, S. Lash, and P. Morris, 109–33. Cambridge, MA: Blackwell.

Lutz, C. 1988. *Unnatural Emotions.* Chicago: University of Chicago Press.

Lutz, C., and G. M. White. 1986. "The Anthropology of Emotions." *Annual Review of Anthropology* 15: 405–36.

Madar, V. 2002. "Ish kal lakh almut khin ja: Ma amar lakh ha-mavet ke-she-ba? Qinot nashim mi-Teiman be-heqsheran ha-tarbuti" [What Did Death Tell You When It Came? Yemenite Women's Laments in Their Cultural Context]. Master's thesis, Hebrew University of Jerusalem.

———. 2005a. "Text bein qol li-t'nua: Qinot nashim mi-Teiman" [Text between Voice and Motion: Yemenite Women's Laments]. *Mehqarei yerushalayim be-folklore yehudi* [Jerusalem Studies in Jewish Folklore] 23: 89–118.

———. 2005b. "Ma amar lakh ha-mavet ke-she-ba? Qinot nashim mi-Eman be-heqsheran ha-tarbuti" [What Did Death Tell You When It Came? Yemenite Women's Laments in Their Cultural Context]. *Pe'amim* 103: 54–55.

———. 2005c. "Qinot nashim mi-Teiman: Shtei qinot u-meqonenet" [Yemenite Women's Laments: Two Laments and a Wailer—A Test Case]. In *Halikhot qedem be-mishkenot Teiman* [Ancient Practices in the Abodes of Yemen], edited by S. Serri and V. Kessar, 181–209. Tel Aviv: A'aleh be-Tamar Association.

———. 2006. "Ma Khabar and Qussat Hannah: A Gendered Reading of Two Stories in the Culture of Yemenite Jewish Women." *Nashim: A Journal of Jewish Women's Studies & Gender Issues* 11, no. 1: 84–104.

Marcel, G. 1965. *Being and Having.* New York: Harper & Row.

McCandless, N. J., and F. P. Conner. 1997. "Older Women and Grief: A New Direction for Research." *Journal of Women and Aging* 9, no. 3: 85–91.

Mead, G. H. 1934. *Mind, Self, and Society.* Chicago: University of Chicago Press.

———. 1964. "The Social Self." In *Selected Writings: George Herbert Mead,* edited by A. Reck, 142–49. Chicago: University of Chicago Press.

Meager, R. 1964. "The Sublime and the Obscene." *British Journal of Aesthetics* 4: 214–27.

Melucci, A. 1996. *The Playing Self: Person and Meaning in the Planetary Society.* Cambridge: Cambridge University Press.

Meneley, A. 1996. *Tournaments of Value: Sociability and Hierarchy in a Yemeni Town.* Toronto: University of Toronto Press.

Miller, J. B. 1976. *Toward a New Psychology of Women.* Boston: Beacon.

Miller, S. I., and L. Schoenfeld. 1973. "Grief in the Navajo: Psychodynamics and

Culture." *International Journal of Social Psychiatry* 19: 187–91.

Miller, W. F. 2002. "Public Words and Body Politics: Reflections on the Strategies of Women Poets in Rural Yemen." *Journal of Women's History* 14, no. 1: 94–122.

Millet, K. 1970. *Theory of Sexual Politics.* New York: Doubleday.

Mizrahi, H. 1959. *Yehudei Paras* [The Jews of Iran]. Tel Aviv: Dvir.

Moors, A. 1991. "Women and the Orient: A Note on Difference." In *Constructing Knowledge: Authority and Critique in Social Sciences,* edited by L. Nencel and P. Pels, 114–23. London: Sage.

Mor, T. 1998. *Ha-min ve-ha-neshama* [Sex and the Soul]. Tel Aviv: Opus.

Moshavi, B. 1974. "Customs and Folklore of Nineteen Century Bukharian Jews in Central Asia: Birth, Engagement, Marriage, Mourning and Others." PhD dissertation, Yeshiva University, New York.

Motzafi-Haller, P. 2001. "Scholarship, Identity, and Power: Mizrahi Women in Israel." *Signs* 26, no. 3: 697–734.

Muchawsky-Schnapper, E. 2000. *Two Thousands Years of Jewish Culture.* Jerusalem: Israel Museum.

Mundy, M. 1995. *Domestic Government: Kinship, Community and Polity in North Yemen.* New York: I. B. Tauris.

Myerhoff, B. 1976. "Balancing between Worlds: The Shaman's Calling." *Parabola* 1: 6–13.

———. 1990. "The Transformation of Consciousness in Ritual Performances: Some Thoughts and Questions." In *By Means of Performance: Intercultural Studies of Theatre and Ritual,* edited by R. Schechner and W. Appel, 245–49. Cambridge: Cambridge University Press.

Myers, G. D. 1988. "The Presence of Others Can Hurt Performance." In *Social Psychology,* 318–23. 2nd ed. New York: McGraw-Hill.

Neumann, E. 1974. *The Great Mother: An Analysis of the Archetype.* Translated by R. Manheim. Princeton, NJ: Princeton University Press.

Nicholson, R. A. 1942. *Toldot ha-sifrut ha-'ivrit* [History of Hebrew Literature]. Translated by Y. Y. Rivlin. Jerusalem: Hebrew University.

Nini, Y. 1988. *Yehudei Teiman* [The Jews of Yemen]. Tel Aviv: Ministry of Defence.

———. 1991. *The Jews of the Yemen, 1800–1914.* Philadelphia: Harwood Academic.

Nketia, J. H. 1969. *Funeral Dirges of the Akan People.* New York: Negro Universities Press.

Orvell, M. 1989. *The Real Thing: Imitation and Authenticity in American Culture.* Chapel Hill: University of North Carolina Press.

Padva, V. 1987–88. "Qol ha-met be-qina" [The Voice of the Dead in Elegy]. *Jerusalem Studies in Hebrew Literature* 10–11: 629–60.

Palgi, P. 1974. *Mavet, evel u-sh'khol be-hevra Yisraelit be-'itot milhama* [Death, Mourning, and Bereavement in Israeli Society in Times of War]. Jerusalem: Ministry of Health.

Palgi, P., and H. Avramovitch. 1984. "Death: A Cross-Cultural Perspective." *Annual Review of Anthropology* 13: 385–417.

Parkes, C. M. 1986. *Bereavement: Studies of Grief in Adult Life.* 2nd ed. London: Tavistock.

Parkes, C. M., and R. S. Weiss. 1983. *Recovery from Bereavement.* New York: Basic Books.

Parry, J. P. 1994. *Death in Banaras.* Cambridge: Cambridge University Press.

Piamente, M. 1984. "Mi-s'de ha-yofi ha-enoshi, ha-elohi ve-ha-meshihi be-shirat Teiman ha-'aravit" [From the Field of Human, Devine, and Messianic Beauty in Arabic Yemenite Song]. In *Orhot Teiman* [Ways of Yemen], edited by S. M. Gamliel, M. M. Caspi, and S. Avizemer, 36–66. Jerusalem: Shalom to the Tribes of Yeshurun Institute.

Pollock, G. 1972. "On Mourning and Anniversaries: The Relationship of Culturally Constituted Defense Systems to Intra-psychic Adaptive Processes." *Israel Annals of Psychiatry* 10: 9–40.

Radcliffe-Brown, A. R. 1964. *The Andaman Islanders.* New York: Free Press.

Raheja, G. G., and A. G. Gold. 1994. *Listen to the Heron's Words.* Berkeley: University of California Press.

Rank, O. 1958. *Beyond Psychology.* New York: Dover.

Raphael, B. 1984. *The Anatomy of Bereavement: A Handbook for the Caring Professions.* London: Hutchinson.

Rapp, A. 1973. *Sotsiologiya ve-teatron* [Sociology and Theater]. Tel Aviv: Sifriyat Poalim and Da'at Zemanenu.

Ratzhabi, Y. 1953. "Ha-isha be-mishlei Teiman" [Woman in the Proverbs of Yemen]. *Reshumot: Ma'asaf le-divrei zikhronot ke-antropologiya u-le-folklore be-Yisrael* [Reshumot: Collection for Memoirs, Ethnographies, and Folklore in Israel]. Tel Aviv: Dvir, 312–22.

———. 1968. "Tsura ve-lahan be-shirat yehudei Teiman le-sugeha" [Form and Melody in Yemenite Jewish Song]. *Tatslil* 8: 15–22.

———. 1975. "Love Songs about the Women of Sana'a." *Studies of the Center for Folklore Research* 4: 75–119.

———. 1987–88. "Motivim 'arvi'im ba-qina ha-'ivrit ha-sefardit" [Arab Motifs in the Sephardi Hebrew Lament]. *Mehqari yerushalayim be-sifrit 'ivrit* [Jerusalem Studies in Hebrew Literature] 10–11: 737–65.

———. 1988. *Shirat Teiman ha-'ivrit* [Hebrew Yemenite Song]. Tel Aviv: Am Oved.

Reed, G. S. 1984. "The Antithetical Meaning of the Term 'Empathy' in Psychoanalytic Discourse." In *Empathy,* edited by J. Lichtenberg, M. Bornstein, and D. Silver, 7–24. London: Lawrence Erlbaum.

Riesman, D., N. Glazer, and R. Denney. 1950. *The Lonely Crowd: A Study of the Changing American Character.* New Haven, CT: Yale University Press.

Rosaldo, M. 1974. "Women, Culture, and Society: A Theoretical Overview." In *Women, Culture and Society,* edited by M. Rosaldo and L. Lamphere, 17–42. Stanford, CA: Stanford University Press.

———. 1988. "Toward an Anthropology of Self and Feeling." In *Culture Theory: Essays on Mind, Self, and Emotion,* edited by R. A. Shweder and R. A. Levine, 137–57. Cambridge: Cambridge University Press.

Rosenblatt, P. C., R. P. Walsh, and D. A. Jackson. 1976. *Grief and Mourning in Cross-Cultural Perspective.* New Haven, CT: HRAF Press.

Rouse, S. 1998. "Feminist Representations: Interrogating Religious Difference." *Gender and History* 10, no. 3: 549–52.

Rubidge, S. 1996. "Does Authenticity Matter? The Case for and against Authenticity in the Performing Arts." In *Analyzing Performance: A Critical Reader,* edited by P. Campbell, 219–33. Manchester, UK: Manchester University Press.

Rubin, N. 1986. "Death Customs in Non-Religious Kibbutz: The Use of Sacred Symbols in a Secular Society." *Journal of the Scientific Study of Religion* 25: 292–303.

———. 1990. "Social Networks and Mourning: A Comparative Approach."

Omega 21, no. 2: 113–27.

———. 1997. *Qets ha-hayyim: Tiqsei qevura ve-evel bi-meqorot hazel* [The End of Life: Burial and Mourning Rituals in the Rabbinical Sources]. Tel Aviv: Hillel Ben-Haim Library, Hakibbutz Hameuchad.

Rubin, S. S., R. Malkinson, and E. Witztum. 1999. "The Pervasive Impact of War-Related Loss and Bereavement in Israel." *International Journal of Group Tensions* 28, nos. 1–2: 137–53.

Ruddick, S. 1989. *Maternal Thinking: Toward a Politics of Peace.* New York: Ballantine.

Russell, B. 1986. "The Forms of Power." In *Power,* edited by S. Lukes, 19–27. New York: New York University Press.

Ryle, G. 1949. *The Concept of Mind.* New York: Norton.

Sarris, M. 1995. "Death, Gender and Social Change in Greek Society." *Journal of Mediterranean Studies* 5, no. 1: 14–32.

Sartre, J. P. 1948. *The Emotions: Outline of a Theory.* Translated by B. Frechtman. New York: Philosophical Library.

———. 1956. *Being and Nothingness.* Translated by H. E. Barnes. New York: Philosophical Library.

———. 1962. *Sketch for a Theory of the Emotions.* Translated by P. Mariet. London: Methuen.

Schechner, R. 1976. "From Ritual to Theatre and Back." In *Ritual, Play and Performance: Readings in the Social Sciences/Theatre,* edited by R. Schechner and M. Schuman, 196–222. New York: Seabury.

———. 2002. *Performance Studies: An Introduction.* London: Routledge.

Scheff, T. J. 1977. "The Distancing of Emotion in Ritual." *Current Anthropology* 18, no. 3: 483–505.

Schieffelin, E. L. 1985. "Performance and the Cultural Construction of Reality." *American Ethnologist* 12, nos. 3–4: 707–24.

Scholem, G. G. 1961. *Major Trends in Jewish Mysticism.* New York: Schocken.

Schudson, M. 1989. "How Culture Works." *Theory and Society* 18: 153–80.

Schulte, R. 1987. "Translation Theory: A Challenge for the Future." In *Translation Theory,* edited by R. Schulte and D. Kratz, special issue of *Translation Review* 23: 1–2.

Schweid, E. 1984. *Sefer mahzor ha-zemanim* [Book of the Cycle of Times]. Tel

Aviv: Am Oved.

Scott, J. W. 1988. *Gender and the Politics of History.* New York: Columbia University Press.

Sered, S. 1988. "The Domestication of Religion: The Spiritual Guardianship of Elderly Oriental Jewish Women." *Man* 23: 506–21.

Sered, S. S. 1994. *Priestess, Mother, Sacred Sister: Religions Dominated by Women.* New York: Oxford University Press.

Seremetakis, C. N. 1990. "The Ethics of Antiphony: The Social Constraction of Pain, Gender, and Power in the Southern Peloponnese." *Ethos* 4: 481–511.

Seremetakis, C. N. 1991. *The Last World: Women, Death, and Divination in Inner Mani.* Chicago: University of Chicago Press.

Serri, S., ed. 1994. *Bat Teiman: 'Olama shel ha-isha ha-yehudit* [Daughter of Yemen: The World of the Jewish Woman]. Tel Aviv: A'aleh be-Tamar Association.

Sharaby, R. 2002. *Sinkretizm ve-histaglut: Ha-mifgash bein qehila masortit u-vein hevra sotsialistit* [Syncretism and Adjustment: The Encounter between a Traditional Community and a Socialist Society]. Tel Aviv: Cherikover.

Sheleg, Y. 2000. *Ha-dati'im ha-hadashim: Mabat 'akhshavi 'al ha-hevra ha-datit be-Yisrael* [The Newly Religious: A Current Look at Religious Society in Israel]. Jerusalem: Keter.

Shokeid, M. 1984. "Megamot hadashot be-datiyut shel yots'ei ha-mizrah" [New Trends in the Religiosity of the Mizrahi Jews]. In *Yehudei ha-mizrah: 'Iyyunim antropologi'im 'al he-'avar ve-he-'atid* [The Jews of the East: Anthropological Studies about the Past and the Present], edited by S. Deshen and M. Shokeid, 78–91. Tel Aviv: Schocken.

———. 1985. "Cultural Ethnicity in Israel: The Case of Middle Eastern Jews Religiosity." *American Journal of Sociology Review* 9: 247–71.

Siegman, A. W., and S. Boyle. 1993. "Voices of Fear and Anxiety and Sadness and Depression: The Effects of Speech Rate and Loudness on Fear and Anxiety and Sadness and Depression." *Journal of Abnormal Psychology* 102: 430–37.

Sills, D. L. 1968. *International Encyclopedia of the Social Sciences,* Vol. 15. New York: Mcmillan and Free Press.

Silverman, P. R., and S. L. Nickman. 1996. "Concluding Thoughts." In *Continuing Bonds: New Understandings of Grief,* edited by D. Klass, P. R.

Silverman, and S. L. Nickman, 349–55. Washington, DC: Taylor & Francis.

Simmel, G. 1950. *The Sociology of George Simmel.* New York: Free Press.

———. 1984. "Flirtation." In *On Women, Sexuality, and Love,* edited and translated by G. Oakes, 133–52. New Haven, CT: Yale University Press.

Simmons, L. W. 1970. *The Role of the Aged in Primitive Society.* Hamden, CT: Archon Books.

Stanislavsky, K. 1961. *Creating a Role.* New York: Theatre Arts.

Steele, R. L. 1977. "Dying, Death, and Bereavement among the Maya Indians of Mesoamerica: A Study of Anthropological Psychology." *American Psychologist* 32: 1060–68.

Stepper, S., and F. Strack. 1993. "Proprioceptive Determinants of Emotional and Nonemotional Feelings." *Journal of Personality and Social Psychology* 64: 211–20.

Stillman, N. 2002. "Me-heqer ha-mizrah u-me-hokhmat Yisrael le-rav-tehumiyut" [From Study of the East and Jewish Thought to Multidisciplinarism]. *Pe'amim* 92: 63–82.

Stroebe, M., M. Gergen, K. Gergen, and W. Stroebe. 1996. "Broken Hearts or Broken Bonds?" In *Continuing Bonds: New Understandings of Grief,* edited by D. Klass, P. R. Silverman, and S. Nickman, 31–44. Washington, DC: Taylor & Francis.

Stroebe, W., and M. S. Stroebe. 1987. *Bereavement and Health: The Psychological and Physical Consequences of Partner Loss.* Cambridge: Cambridge University Press.

Sulami, T. 1995. "Emuha ve-yahadut be-shirat ha-nashimi ha-yehudiyot be-Teiman" [Faith and Judaism in the Song of Jewish Women in Yemen]. *Afikim* 46–47: 16–20.

———. 2005. "Motivim shel meha'a be-shirat ha-nashim ha-teimanit" [Protest Motives in Yemenite Women's Song]. In *Halikhot qedem be-mishkenot Teiman* [Ancient Practices in the Abodes of Yemen]. Tel Aviv: A'aleh be-Tamar Association: 123–42.

Taylor, C. 1991. *The Ethics of Authenticity.* Cambridge, MA: Harvard University Press.

———. 1994. "The Politics of Recognition." In *Multiculturalism: Examining the Politics of Recognition,* edited by A. Gutmann, 25–74. Princeton, NJ:

Princeton University Press.

———. 1995. "Multiculturalism and the Politics of Recognition." *Auslegung: A Journal of Philosophy* 20, no. 1: 43–46.

Tilly, L. A., and J. W. Scott. 1989. *Women, Work and Family.* New York: Routledge.

Tiwary, K. M. 1978. "Tuneful Weeping: A Model of Communication." *Frontiers* 3, no. 3: 24–27.

Tobi, Y. 1999. *The Jews of Yemen: Studies in Their History and Culture.* Boston: Brill.

Tobi, Y., and S. Serri. 2000. *Yalqut Teiman: Leksiqon* [Yemen Glossary: Lexicon]. Tel Aviv: A'aleh be-Tamar Association.

Turnbull, C. 1990. "Liminality: A Synthesis of Subjective and Objective Experience." In *By Means of Performance: Intercultural Studies of Theatre and Ritual,* edited by R. Schechner and W. Apple, 50–81. Cambridge: Cambridge University Press.

Turner, R. H. 1990. "Role Change." *American Review of Sociology* 16: 87–110.

Turner, R. J., and W. R. Avison. 1989. "Gender and Depression: Assessing Exposure and Vulnerability to Life Events in a Chronically Strained Population." *Journal of Nervous and Mental Disease* 177: 443–55.

Turner, V. 1967. *The Forest of Symbols: Aspects of Ndembu Ritual.* New York: Cornell University Press.

———. 1969. *The Ritual Process.* Chicago: University of Chicago Press and Aldine.

———. 1974. *Dramas, Fields and Metaphors.* Ithaca, NY: Cornell University Press.

———. 1982. *From Ritual to Theatre: The Human Seriousness of Play.* New York: Performing Arts Journal Publications.

Tzadok, M. 1967. *Yehudei Teiman: Toldoteihem ve-orhot hayeihem* [The Jews of Yemen: Their History and Ways of Life]. Tel Aviv: Am Oved.

———. 1976. "Ha-yahasim bein ha-yehudim ve-ha-'aravim be-Teiman" [Relations between Jews and Arabs in Yemen]. In *Yahadut Teiman: Pirqei mehqar ve-'iyyun* [The Jews of Yemen: Chapters in Research and Study], edited by Y. Yeshayahu and Y. Tobi, 147–67. Jerusalem: Yad Izhak Ben-Zvi.

Ulrich, L. T. 1982. *Good Wives: A Study in Role Definition in Northern New*

England, 1650–1750. Ann Arbor, MI: University Microfilms International.

Urban, G. 1988. "Ritual Wailing in Amerindian Brazil." *American Anthropologist* 90: 385–400.

Van Gennep, A. 1960. *The Rites of Passage.* Chicago: University of Chicago Press.

Vineberg, S. 1991. *Method Actors: Three Generations of an American Acting Style.* New York: Schirmer Books.

Vingerhoets, A., and J. Scheirs. 2000. "Sex Differences in Crying: Empirical Findings and Possible Explanations." In *Gender and Emotion: Social Psychological Perspectives,* edited by A. H. Fisher, 143–65. Cambridge: Cambridge University Press.

Vitebsky, P. 1993. "Dialogues with the Self? Sora Bereavement and the Presuppositions of Contemporary Psychotherapy." In *Dialogues with the Dead,* 236–59. Cambridge: Cambridge University Press.

Walter, T. 1994. *The Revival of Death.* London and New York: Routledge.

———. 1996. "A New Model of Grief: Bereavement and Biography." *Mortality* 1, no. 1: 7–25.

———. 1999. *On Bereavement: The Culture of Grief.* Buckingham, UK: Open University Press.

Weber, M. 1958. *The Protestant Ethic and the Spirit of Capitalism.* Translated by T. Parsons. New York: Scribner.

Weich-Shahak, S. 1987. "Tiqsei ma'avar be-shira ha-sefaradit-yehudit mi-Maroko" [Transition Rituals in Sephardi Jewish Song from Morocco]. *Pe'amim* 30: 105–24.

Weir, S. 1985. *Qat in Yemen: Consumption and Social Change—The Trustees of the British Museum.* London: British Museum Publications.

Weiss, M. 1997. "Bereavement, Commemoration, and Collective Identity in Contemporary Israeli Society." *Anthropological Quarterly* 70, no. 2: 91–101.

Weizman, S. G., and P. Kamm. 1985. *About Mourning: Support and Guidance for the Bereaved.* New York: Human Science Press.

Wikan, U. 1982. *Behind the Veil in Arabia Women in Oman.* Baltimore and London: Johns Hopkins University Press.

———. 1986. "The Role of Emotions in Balinese Popular Health Care." Unpublished manuscript, Ethnographic Museum of the University of Oslo.

———. 1988. "Bereavement and Loss in Two Muslim Communities: Egypt and

Bali Compared." *Social Science and Medicine* 5: 451–60.

Wilce, J. M. 1998. "The Pragmatics of 'Madness': Performance Analysis of a Bangladeshi Woman's 'Aberrant' Lament." *Culture, Medicine, and Psychiatry* 22: 1–54.

———. 2009. *Crying Shame: Metaculture, Modernity, and the Exaggerated Death of Lament.* Oxford, UK: Blackwell.

Witztum, E. 2004. *Nefesh, evel u-sh'khol* [Mind, Loss and Bereavement]. Tel Aviv: Ministry of Defence.

Wouters, C. 2002. "The Quest for New Rituals in Dying and Mourning: Changes in the We-I Balance." *Body and Society* 8, no. 1: 1–27.

Wrong, D. H. 1988. *Power: Its Forms, Bases and Uses.* Chicago: University of Chicago Press.

Yeshayahu, Y., and V. Tobi. 1976. *Yehudei Teiman: Pirqei mehqar ve-'iyyun* [The Jews of Yemen: Chapters in Research and Study]. Jerusalem: Yad Izhak Ben-Zvi.

Zammuner, V. L. 2000. "Men's and Women's Lay Theories of Emotion." In *Gender and Emotion: Social Psychological Perspectives,* edited by A. H. Fischer, 24–47. Cambridge: Cambridge University Press.

Index

NOTE: Italicized page numbers indicate figures.

www.ingramcontent.com/pod-product-compliance
Lightning Source LLC
Chambersburg PA
CBHW071441260226
39925CB00043B/108/J

* 9 7 8 0 8 1 4 3 3 4 7 6 8 *